AF820916

Genre-Based Automated Writing Evaluation for L2 Research Writing

Genre-Based Automated Writing Evaluation for L2 Research Writing

From Design to Evaluation and Enhancement

Elena Cotos
Iowa State University, USA

palgrave
macmillan

© Elena Cotos 2014
Foreword © Carol A. Chapelle 2014

All rights reserved. No reproduction, copy or transmission of this publication may be made without written permission.

No portion of this publication may be reproduced, copied or transmitted save with written permission or in accordance with the provisions of the Copyright, Designs and Patents Act 1988, or under the terms of any licence permitting limited copying issued by the Copyright Licensing Agency, Saffron House, 6–10 Kirby Street, London EC1N 8TS.

Any person who does any unauthorized act in relation to this publication may be liable to criminal prosecution and civil claims for damages.

The author has asserted her right to be identified as the author of this work in accordance with the Copyright, Designs and Patents Act 1988.

First published 2014 by
PALGRAVE MACMILLAN

Palgrave Macmillan in the UK is an imprint of Macmillan Publishers Limited, registered in England, company number 785998, of Houndmills, Basingstoke, Hampshire RG21 6XS.

Palgrave Macmillan in the US is a division of St Martin's Press LLC, 175 Fifth Avenue, New York, NY 10010.

Palgrave Macmillan is the global academic imprint of the above companies and has companies and representatives throughout the world.

Palgrave® and Macmillan® are registered trademarks in the United States, the United Kingdom, Europe and other countries.

ISBN 978–1–137–33336–0

A catalogue record for this book is available from the British Library.

A catalog record for this book is available from the Library of Congress.

Typeset by MPS Limited, Chennai, India.

Transferred to Digital Printing in 2014

Contents

List of Figures and Tables

Figures

Tables

Foreword

Language educators are all too familiar with simplistic claims about how technology is revolutionizing teaching and learning, providing miraculous results, and dramatically expanding access to quality instruction. Professionals in language education are well aware that, despite such claims, substantial language improvement does not come easily. Professionals recognize the complexity of learners' language needs, particularly for students hoping to achieve a level of English language proficiency that allows them to compete in growing English-medium academic markets. The importance of such contexts is underscored by research and practice in applied linguistics that continues to develop a deeper understanding of academic language, its development, and the stakes associated with its effective use.

For educators wishing to fill the gap between the public discourse on learning technologies and their own experience of teaching and researching academic language, this book will be very welcome. It begins with a credible and detailed discussion of the challenges faced by a particular type of learner – the graduate student needing to learn how to write academic research articles. Cotos' discussion of the problem is anything but simple, taking into account the research investigating genres of academic writing and students' socialization into the genres in their respective disciplines.

With the problem described, Cotos walks readers through a careful examination of technologies intended to help address students' writing challenges. What follows is a revealing explication of theoretical and operational frameworks she finds are needed to do so. Each framework is selected as a basis for an aspect of the design and evaluation of the Intelligent Academic Discourse Evaluation (IADE) system, the pedagogical tool that Cotos invented. The frameworks, each familiar to some researchers in applied linguistics, will appear to create a clash of world views to ideologically motivated readers. However, Cotos' pragmatic goals demand an eclectic selection of theoretical perspectives and her demonstration of their use is one of the stimulating aspects of this book. The needs for the frameworks are evident in the following chapters where they are rallied in the service of pragmatic goals of software design and evaluation.

The design of the IADE system is described in terms of how it meets students' needs in an academic English writing course, where students from a variety of disciplines must learn how to construct texts that adhere to the appropriate genre and linguistic conventions of their own disciplines. The technology is essential in storing a corpus of texts from different disciplines, allowing students to edit and submit their own texts, producing feedback on their writing, and providing illustrations of writing in each student's field of study. The mixed-method research used to evaluate the system yields detailed data commensurate with the complexity of the problem. For example, readers gain considerable insight into writers' use of the system through qualitative data gathered from students' retrospective accounts of writing processes. The quantitative data summarize writers' performance and opinions about the system.

Because these data were gathered in classrooms where students were studying academic English, the findings attain a high level of credibility. The positive results help to demonstrate the utility of the theory-based pedagogical approach that guided the design. The presentation shows the value of an in-depth study of learning one aspect (research article introductions) of the overall syllabus. The final chapter describes how the findings from this study prompted development of a larger system for writing research articles, called Research Writing Tutor.

Overall, this book represents a classic example of applied linguistics research: it defines a language-related problem, devises a solution drawing on relevant theory, research and practice, and tests the solution in a manner that informs future action. More specifically, for technology studies in applied linguistics, it illustrates a pragmatically driven marshalling of relevant theory and research methods to design technologies precisely to meet defined language needs. In doing so, it demonstrates that despite the substantial challenge English language learners face in discipline-specific academic writing, technologies can be designed to play an important role in helping students to advance.

Carol A. Chapelle
Distinguished Professor
Iowa State University, USA

Acknowledgments

Part of the research with the genre-based AWE prototype presented in this monograph was funded by the Grant for Doctoral Research in Second/Foreign Language Assessment awarded by Educational Testing Service, USA. The research and development work on the Research Writing Tutor was funded by the Computation Advisory Committee, Graduate College, College of Engineering, and the English Department of the College of Liberal Arts and Sciences at Iowa State University of Science and Technology, USA.

In the long and challenging process of developing, implementing, and evaluating this innovative writing technology, I have been privileged to work with outstanding mentors, colleagues, and students at Iowa State University. First and foremost, I wish to acknowledge the central influence of Carol A. Chapelle, whose scholarship has profoundly impacted mine and whose personal guidance has given me long-term inspiration and encouragement to realize my ambitious ideas. I also owe a debt of thanks to Viviana Cortes who introduced me to genre pedagogy and showed me the great potential of corpora. Particular gratitude is due to Nick Pendar, to whom I am obliged for his expert computational linguistics contribution. I am profoundly grateful to Stephen Gilbert, without whom the Research Writing Tutor would not have come to fruition. During the development of the Research Writing Tutor, I have had the good fortune of working with a vibrant intellectual cross-disciplinary community of scholars and practitioners who have contributed in different ways at different times, as well as with a fleet of exceptional graduate and undergraduate students who have shown genuine passion and earnestness. I could not begin to list all their names, but I sincerely thank them all.

Most deeply I am indebted to all my family, especially my husband Aureliu, my daughter Delia, my father Vladimir, and my late mother Vera.

List of Abbreviations

AcLits	Academic Literacies
AES	Automated Essay Scoring
AI	Artificial Intelligence
ANOVA	Analysis of Variance
AWE	Automated Writing Evaluation
CAF	Conceptual Assessment Framework
CALL	Computer-Assisted Language Learning
CDO	Compare-Diagnose-Operate
DBR	Design-Based Research
EAP	English for Academic Purposes
ECD	Evidence-Centered Design
EPT	English Placement Test
e-rater	Electronic Essay Rater
ESP	English for Specific Purposes
GMAT	Graduate Management Admissions Test
IA	Interaction Approach
IADE	Intelligent Academic Discourse Evaluator
ICALL	Intelligent Computer-Assisted Language Learning
IEA	Intelligent Essay Assessor
IELTS	International English Language Testing System
IMRD	Introduction, Methods, Results, Discussion
ITS	Intelligent Tutoring Systems
LSA	Latent Semantic Analysis
NL	New Literacy
NLP	Natural Language Processing
NR	New Rhetoric
PEG	Project Essay Grade
RWT	Research Writing Tutor

SAT	Skill Acquisition Theory
SFL	Systemic Functional Linguistics
SLA	Second Language Acquisition
SVM	Support Vector Machine
TOEFL	Test of English as a Foreign Language

Introduction

Research writing is a craft central to the world of research and academia. It is the main means employed by scientific communities to disseminate and ratify knowledge, 'inject[ing] light on dusty areas' of academic enterprises (Barnett, 2005, p. 3). The journal articles, conference papers, grant proposals, theses, and dissertations, which are valued research-related genres, are viewed as major intellectual endeavors that earn their authors credentials and confer them academic status. For novice scholars such as graduate students, who are legitimate but peripheral participants in their scientific communities (Lave & Wenger, 1991), research writing is the first step towards accessing and actively engaging in the discourse of their discipline. The enculturation of these novice scholars in their disciplinary communities is high stakes, since dissemination of their research perceptibly impacts earning an advanced degree, professional growth, and academic recognition.

The expansion of the global economy worldwide has placed global demands to impose greater accountability on higher education in general and on graduate students in particular. An important accountability component is increased student publication output as a measure of institutional productivity and reputation (Eyres et al., 2001); thus, producing scholars who can communicate about research effectively has become a priority on the agenda of graduate education. With this strategic agenda, research writing has become a major point of tension (Aitchison & Lee, 2006, p. 265) as universities worldwide institute high quality evaluation standards for student academic productivity in addition to course and program requirements. In some doctoral programs, publications of both high quality and quantity are an explicit requirement for graduation; in others, publishing is an implicit, but consequential criterion in the assessment of graduate students (Caffarella & Barnett 2000; Lavelle & Bushrow 2007).

For graduate students as aspiring scholars, research writing is also the foundation of their academic career and of the credibility of their scholarly dossier. Continued academic success is largely determined by their ability to write research results as manuscripts for submission to prestigious refereed journals. Initially, publications give graduates a competitive entry into the job market, being the main indices of their potential. When a position is obtained (be that postdoctoral, academic, and even nonacademic professional), the research writing demands do not abate, but rather intensify and become even more challenging (Carter, 2012). Promotion, tenure, different reward systems, and recognition from professional groups are all largely dependent on a demonstrated ability to conduct and disseminate research (Blackburn, Behymer, & Hall, 1978; Boice, 1992). Young scholars are expected to produce a stream of publications in reputable venues that will be included in library databases and citation indexes (Flowerdew, 1999). This is true for early career researchers in all fields of study. For instance, growth on the academic ladder for scholars in the life sciences generally requires up to 15 publications in refereed journals as a benchmark measure of scientific potential. In the life sciences, as in most fields, dissemination of research findings is considered an 'irrevocable duty' that practicing scientists must complete (Gladon et al., pp. 5–6). Cuthbert and Spark (2008) concur that in the sciences 'publication culture is the norm' (p. 78). This is also the primary way to gain access to the engineering community (Kushner, 1997). Similarly, in computer science the so-called soft skill of writing is an asset that employers desire the most (Dansdill et al., 2008).

Publishing research outcomes means gaining membership of the disciplinary community. To accomplish that, novice scholars need to be able to demonstrate the worthiness of their scientific contributions. This implies engaging in a complicated process of review, refereeing, and feedback, which is in fact a process of negotiation with the disciplinary gatekeepers. Gatekeepers – from academic supervisors to journal reviewers and editors – are individuals who safeguard the scholarly discourse (van Dijk, 1996) and who position newcomers as knowing insiders or unknowing outsiders (Viete & Ha, 2007). They accept the validity of new claims, passing approval on the part of the research network, and confer membership to their community if they are persuaded of the originality, rigor, and significance of the reported work. Persuading these omniscient judges requires effective construction and negotiation of scientific knowledge through writing, which presents significant challenges for those who are relatively new to this task.

Unfortunately, very little is being done in higher education to equip graduate students, especially international graduate students for whom writing in English poses difficulties of its own, with the skills they need to become competent scholarly writers and to cogently communicate with their disciplinary community. There exists a myth of the always/already independent researcher (Johnson et al., 2000). When enrolling in graduate programs, students are expected to already possess advanced academic writing skills (Lillis & Turner, 2001) and to demonstrate the ability to effectively extrapolate their skills across the boundaries of different genres and rhetorical contexts. This covert expectation has cultivated some dangerous assumptions in higher education – that if students 'can think well, they can write well' (Turner, 2012, p. 18) – and, if not, they can relatively tenuously reach the expected writing standards (Whitehead, 2002).

The false assumption that research writing skills are sufficiently practiced or automatically acquired through the completion of disciplinary coursework and through apprenticeship go hand in hand with the opinion that graduate students, English speakers or not, have no need for explicit research writing instruction. Even though it has been convincingly argued that it should be formally included in graduate-level courses (Badley, 2009a; Kamler & Thomson, 2008), the focus on academic writing in disciplinary curricula is very weak. Cilliers (2012), for example, reports that in computer science writing is rarely endorsed as a foundational skill, and where it is the apportionment to such instruction is only 2 percent or less of the core study hours.

Turner (2012) problematizes the 'ready-made ease with which this broad assumption operates' (p. 18). Indeed, the research writing ability is too complex to be automatically acquired when learning about or doing research (Bjork et al., 2003). Graduate students openly admit that they need more guided practice, feeling 'all-too commonly isolated [as a] research writer' (Aitchison & Lee, 2006, p. 266). Fergie, Beeke, McKenna, and Creme (2011) quote a frustrated doctoral student, 'You're on your own, [...] and it's a lonely walk' (p. 236). Many second-language (L2) writers, in particular, are less than prepared for the demands of disciplinary writing, as their college-level assignments in English are generally non-scholastic in nature (Kushner, 1997). Even if L2 writers receive an undergraduate degree in an English-speaking country, the gap between their undergraduate writing courses and advanced-level research writing is too big. This often puts a major burden on the academic advisors. Some spend an enormous amount of hours correcting or even rewriting their disciples' theses or co-authored articles (Lax, 2002); others choose not to do that, expecting their advisees to seek this kind of help elsewhere. 'But where should this help come from, and what form should it take?' asks Cotterall (2011, p. 413) concerned with doctoral candidates' experience of writing.

Instituting a formal research writing curriculum in higher education has been an onerous task, and who is in a position to provide such a curriculum is still a difficult question. Should English departments, writing centers, or disciplinary departments take this call? Elton (2010) describes the situation as it currently is in most higher education institutions:

> Student writing in an academic discipline is, if taught at all, taught either in an academic writing unit, which rarely if ever can go beyond the generic, or within a disciplinary department, where there is rarely the appropriate expertise in academic writing. Seldom are the two functions of generic academic writing and writing in a discipline combined through being taught by an academic in the discipline who has additionally specialised in academic writing; as seldom is there a constructive collaboration between equals – discipline specialists and writing specialists. (Elton, 2010, p. 151)

Admittedly, teaching research writing is very demanding – both for writing specialists and discipline specialists. For writing teachers, the job is as complex as it can be, for while they can cover a gamut of things about the target research genres, they lack the insider knowledge needed to adequately address disciplinarity as well as socio-cultural contexts and embedded cultural values. The challenge is doubled by the traditionally heterogeneous composition of classes where the students come from a variety of majors and need to learn the discursive practices of their particular discipline. For discipline specialists, the task is also confounding. While they are familiar with the perspectives, debates, and assumptions about knowledge in their field and thus can judge the quality of the content and of the propositions in their students' writing, they often lack explicit knowledge of genre-specific communicative purposes, formal textual features, intertextual links that formulate and reference newly constructed knowledge, and so on.

Notwithstanding the fallacious assumptions about research writing as an unequivocal, easily generalizable skill and the undetermined institutional curricular aspirations, English-medium academic settings have witnessed a longstanding tradition of academic writing teaching practices. These practices, typically offered by departments of English, Linguistics, or English as a Second Language, spring from two major approaches to genre theory. One is the so-called linguistic approach, which includes English for Specific Purposes (ESP) and Systemic Functional Linguistics (SFL). The second is the New Rhetoric (NR) non-linguistic approach. The linguistic and non-linguistic perspectives to genre-based teaching may have gained the reputation of being adversative while, in fact, they should be adopted as mutually complementary. Each of these two dominant perspectives has its own epistemological strengths, which if conjoined can result in L2 writing pedagogy that builds upon second language acquisition (SLA) principles as well as upon cognitive and social constructivist tenets, inducing L2 writers into knowledge creation and facilitating meaning making for and with the scientific audience, which are crucial to the research writing activity.

The need to teach research writing, in general, and the need to teach it as a dynamic construction of knowledge artifacts that are socially oriented and that reflect the writer's constructionist dialog with a disciplinary community, in particular, has motivated me as a practitioner and as a researcher to seek solutions that could facilitate L2 writing pedagogy by promoting the learning of research genres. As an applied linguist, I envision L2 research writing pedagogy as being transformed, if not revolutionized, by corpus and genre-based automated writing evaluation (AWE) technologies designed to complement instruction with computerized affordances that are otherwise either unavailable or extremely time and labor-intensive.

This book illustrates my vision, building on a rich discussion that invites different domains, each directly or indirectly impacting the conceptualization, development, and implementation of a potent computer-assisted pedagogical solution to the research writing problem in higher education. In this discussion, I invite voices from the cognitivist educational psychology, which approach learning to write as acquiring knowledge that is tied to memory and cognitive processes. This allows me to subsequently summon intelligent tutoring systems and artificial intelligence that, I believe, have a lot to offer in terms of individualizing learning opportunities. I also bring in the perspective of social constructivism, where learning to write is viewed as acquiring knowledge that is constructed dynamically and negotiated socially. With this, I underscore the importance of feedback and justify a needed connection to scaffolded computer-assisted learning environments (see Harasim, 2012) such as automated writing evaluation (AWE) programs.

Further, more closely centering on writing as a language skill, I focus on theoretical tenets about language and skill acquisition that are informative for L2 writing pedagogy. Addressing pedagogy itself, I consider genre-based approaches as well as assessment practices, which, while of paramount importance, are constrained by practical limitations.

Drawing on this fertile landscape, I propose a model for designing corpus and genre-based AWE, develop and evaluate the effectiveness of a prototype, and expand the model to the design of a full-fledged program that I present as a compelling computer-assisted augmentation for L2 research writing pedagogy. This program – the Research Writing Tutor (RWT) – analyzes students' research articles and generates discipline-specific feedback based on the conventions of this genre. It is intended for use as a formative assessment tool during revision in order to facilitate this process with different forms of corpus-based scaffolding. A strong believer in principled design of computer-assisted language learning (CALL) applications, I adhere to Chapelle (2001), who construes CALL effectiveness in terms of an evaluation argument warranted by judgmental and empirical analyses of appropriateness 'on the basis of evidence and rationales pertaining to task use in a particular setting' (p. 53). Therefore, the AWE program I introduce here is justified with theoretical as well as empirical rationales supporting its use in a representative target context.

Part I
Designing Genre-Based AWE for L2 Research Writing

Introduction

Part I of this book lays the groundwork for the development of genre-based AWE for L2 research writing. The first chapter discusses the research writing construct and pedagogical aspirations, establishing a much needed dialogue that involves prominent views in cognitive psychology concerned with writing development, in rhetoric concerned with writing as social practice, and in the English for Academic Purposes (EAP) area of applied linguistics concerned with developing the language skills needed for effective academic communication. The second chapter provides a bird's eye view of the AWE state-of-the-art in order to then reinforce the theoretical and operational frameworks formulated in Chapter 3 and integrated in the conceptual design of the genre-based prototype introduced in Chapter 4.

1
Learning and Teaching Challenges of Research Writing

Research writing poses a great challenge for graduate students who are novice writers struggling with transitioning from peripheral to full participation in the discourse of their disciplinary community. At the same time, teaching research writing is often daunting for writing instructors due to the unfamiliar disciplinary conventions of research genres. Addressing these learning and pedagogical challenges necessitates an understanding of the individual-cognitive and socio-disciplinary dimensions underpinning research writing. In this first chapter, I elaborate on what these dimensions entail and how they intertwine in the construct of research writing competence. To further reason about how that applies to L2 research writing pedagogy, I discuss two epistemologically different genre teaching traditions – linguistic and rhetorical. I then put forth a rationale for enhancing L2 research writing instruction with genre and corpus-based AWE technology that can foster fundamental linguistic and rhetorical principles.

1.1 Research writing essentia

1.1.1 The cognitive dimension of research writing

L2 writers often think of writing as a language skill, and of research writing as a more advanced language skill, which can be perfected through brainstorming ideas, drafting, revising, and editing. While there is some truth to this perception, it is not entirely accurate. Research writing is arguably much more than such a linear sequence of steps. It is a process of knowledge transformation rather than transmission[1] (Bereiter & Scardamalia, 1987) and is thus definitely 'not just a mopping-up activity at the end of a research project' (Richardson, 1998, p. 345), or a write-up as it is often referred to. It is a process that involves intense cognitive activity to create comprehensive outcomes of various forms of academic inquiry. Badley (2009b) sees research writing as a constructive, creative, and transformative process of knowledge in the making. Assuming Dewey's (1991) view of learning from experience, he characterizes it as a dynamic and highly reflective process on the part of the writer, during which knowledge is constructed, deconstructed and reconstructed; concepts are connected, disconnected, and reconnected; and ideas are shaped, mis-shaped, and reshaped (Badley, 2009a, p. 209).

The complex cognitive paths and mechanisms triggered in the process of research writing can be described through the prism of cognitive models of writing that have evolved over the last 30 years. Flower and Hayes (1981), who proposed the most well-known cognitive process theory of writing of our contemporaneity, posited that writing as a process unfolds in a continuous series of reflective, generative, and inventive actions that activate the facets of individual cognition. Their theory explains writing as a set of distinctive thought processes that can be hierarchically organized and embedded in one another by the writer, for whom writing is goal-oriented. Their writing model contains three recursive processes – planning, translating, and reviewing. Planning entails creating an abstract internal representation of what the written prose would be. This representation is formed by generating ideas, giving those a meaningful structure, and by setting procedural and substantive goals (for example, how to begin and what content to present for what purpose). Translating is 'essentially the process of putting ideas into visible language' (p. 373). Reviewing is sub-divided into evaluative appraisal and actual modifications of the text. These two evaluation and revising sub-processes were expanded by Bereiter and Scardamalia (1983) who put forth the so-called compare-diagnose-operate (CDO) model, according to which when writers revise they first compare what they wrote with the mental representation of what they wanted to write. This comparison should result in diagnosing potential problems and then operating, or changing the text.

The importance of revision-oriented diagnostic operations was further substantiated in modified cognitive models with added processes and knowledge sub-stages (Flower et al., 1986; Hayes et al., 1987). The processes sub-stage includes evaluation in the form of reading to comprehend and identify problems, strategy selection, and modification of the writer's internal and/or external representation of the text. The knowledge sub-stage includes the goals, criteria, and constraints that define the writing task; detection of ill-defined and diagnosis of well-defined representations of the problem; and the revision procedures intended to improve the text. This modeling approach therefore encompasses a much more complex reviewing process, where the cognitive path for evaluation and revision clearly relies on reflective reading. Reading allows writers to evaluate whether the written text representation corresponds with the intended mental representation and, consequently, to detect or diagnose the cause of the mismatch and to identify a suitable correction strategy.

Revision is also contingent on well-developed metarhetorical, metastrategic, and metalinguistic awareness (Horning, 2002). These types of metacognitive awareness are ingrained in the internal processes activated when writers evaluate their text, detect a need for revision, and engage in strategy selection (Chenoweth & Hayes, 2001). Most novice writers lack this awareness, and their ability to detect and diagnose problems when revising, or, as Flower et al. (1986) put it, 'to see a problem in the text as a meaningful, familiar pattern' (p. 48), is weak. The same can be said about novice L2 research writers. Academic writing instruction needs to help them develop metacognitive awareness to improve this diagnostic ability, as it is often the most important cognitive factor in successfully revising texts, both on a surface and global level.

1.1.2 The socio-disciplinary dimension of research writing

Acknowledging the role of cognition, Viete and Ha (2007) compare creative knowledge construction in research writing to the making of a quilt because it requires investment of self, efforts, and time, but, most importantly, because its 'impact depends upon the expectations of the reader and the echoes of other texts in the mind of this reader as much as it does on the craft of the writer' (p. 39). This quote underscores the social dimension of research writing, which presupposes intricate interactions between the writer and the readers as the former engages with the latter to create texts (Hyland, 2002, 2004a). Li (2006) explains that in writing as social interaction, authors shape their texts in a way that meets the expectations of the target readership. This underlying conversation with the disciplinary audience makes texts a place where writers and readers intersect for meaning making (Hyland, 2002). More specifically, writers are not simply transmitting meaning, but rather co-creating it in view of someone else's reading and interpretation (Badley, 2009b). They are intertwining their ideas with the readers' anticipated critical stance so that challenging it is justified and accepted.

The socio-disciplinary interaction is well-enveloped by genres, which have evolved as a response to the social interactions within disciplines (Bazerman, 1988) and to the socio-disciplinary forces that institutionalize their conventions (Paltridge, 2002). Genres have traditionally been defined as text types with shared communicative purposes that are achieved by means of a set of discourse conventions including overall organization and lexico-grammatical choices (Swales, 1990). These text types are 'conventionalized forms of writing [...] by which knowledge and information get disseminated to a community of people with shared interests' (Ramanathan & Kaplan, 2000, p. 172). According to Berkenkotter and Huckin (1995), genres are also 'inherently dynamic rhetorical structures that strategically package content in ways that reflect the discipline's norms, values, and ideology (pp. 1–3). Research-related genres such as research articles, conference papers, theses, and grant proposals reflect the preferred discourse practices of the scientific community since they 'are grounded in disciplinary ways of knowing' (Paxton, 2011, p. 54). To engage in this particular type of social practice, writers draw on and conform to the representational resources of genres (Lillis & Scott, 2007) as vehicles that help create meaningful and intelligible communication with the members of the disciplinary community. Displaying such conformity is an important way of achieving consensus and making an impact on the discipline (Hyland, 2000).

I opened the discussion with the individual-cognitive and socio-disciplinary dimensions of research writing to contend that it should not be treated as a passive compilation of empirical outputs accrued and shared by individual authors or co-authors. On the contrary, research writing is a process that is contemplative, intellectual, and introspective, *and* communicative, interdiscursive, and communal. To successfully and productively engage in this process, L2 research writers need to be able to create texts that put forward credible and temporal scientific claims in ways that are acceptable by a social structure with an established system of practices called a discourse community (Giddens, 1979). This requires an advanced competency, which has yet to be explicitly defined as a construct. To arrive at a pedagogically informative description, I will further consider some insights from the socio-cognitive genre theory (Berkenkotter & Huckin, 1995; Bhatia, 1993).

1.1.3 Research writing competence

The ability to read and write academic texts has received the ostensible definition of academic literacy (Spack, 1997). Research writing can be considered an essential competency of a highly specialized academic literacy (Belcher, 1994). This competency involves reading that is no longer for comprehension but rather for reflective, critical evaluation. Badley (2009a) calls it 'de-constructing' scholarly texts, that is 'trying to tease out, for own critical appreciation and understanding, how a writer as maker or fabricator has gone about constructing and shaping that text' (p. 213). He suggests that deconstructive reading, through analysis, evaluation, and interpretation of literature, prepares authors to re-evaluate and re-interpret texts in a re-constructive synthesis, which is the writing itself.

The contours of this re-constructive synthesis are shaped by research genres, conceptualized by socio-cognitive genre theorists as a dynamic rhetorical 'form of situated cognition embedded in disciplinary activities' (Berkenkotter & Huckin, 1995, pp. 3–4) and used by writers in recurrent communicative situations to inculcate experience and meaning. Research genre writing thus can be viewed as applied metacognition (Hacker et al., 2009). As a process, it unfolds in a sequence of goal-oriented mental actions that involve monitoring and metacognitive awareness (Dunlosky & Metcalfe, 2009; Schraw & Dennison, 1994). Metacognitive awareness comprises knowledge of concepts relevant to the genre-related rhetorical task and knowledge of how to apply the concepts to complete the rhetorical task (Flower & Hayes, 1981). Research writing also involves metacognitive decisions with respect to genre-relevant features of content, organization, and style (Negretti & Kuteeva, 2011). Furthermore, it intertwines the metapragmatic ability to effectively convey scientific content and develop claims by routinely connecting rhetorical purposes with the symbolic resources of the target research genre (Berkenkotter et al., 1991; Hyland, 2000). These 'representational resources' (Kress, 1996, p. 18) are textual and linguistic features the use of which is necessary to realize intended communicative purposes.

It follows that research writing embodies the persuasive nature of knowledge created as a web of interrelated discipline-specific interactions in a rhetorically and linguistically explicit argument (Bazerman, 1988). It is 'essentially rhetorical behavior' (Jolliffe & Brier, 1988, p. 38) that seamlessly blends in the understanding of the rhetorical problem, awareness of the ways of knowledge construction established by the discourse community, and ability to use discipline-specific conventions and appropriate functional language. Tardy (2009) covers these aspects in her definition of genre knowledge, which contains four overlapping domains: rhetorical knowledge, formal knowledge, process knowledge, and subject-matter knowledge. Rhetorical knowledge 'captures an understanding of the genre's intended purposes and an awareness of the dynamics of the persuasion within a socio-rhetorical context', for example writer's positioning and readers' expectations and values. Formal knowledge refers to 'textual instantiation of the genre', that is the structure, discourse form, and lexico-grammatical conventions. Process knowledge comprises 'all of the procedural practices associated with the genre', such as the reading practices of the audience and the composing processes of the writer. And subject-matter knowledge includes knowledge of 'the relevant content' reflecting disciplinary expertise (p. 21). The description of formal knowledge can be extended to include the elements of discourse competence, which appears in different communicative competence models that integrate linguistic aspects with the pragmatics of creating conventionalized forms of communication (Bachman, 1990; Canale, 1983; Canale & Swain, 1980; Celce-Murcia et al., 1995). In general, genre knowledge is an abstract but systematic construct, and it is 'conventional in that form and style may be repeated' (Johns, 1997, p. 22).

On the grounds of this deliberation, a pedagogically informative definition of research writing competence as a component of advanced academic literacy should forefront the role of both individual cognition and socio-disciplinary factors. Ergo, I would describe research writing competence as the fusion of the writer's self-awareness and metacognitive knowledge of the rhetorical task, socio-disciplinary awareness about the discourse community, and metapragmatic ability to produce a research writing artifact as a communicative action realized with genre-specific language choices that are appropriate to the expectations of the disciplinary discourse community. Figure 1.1 illustrates the intersections among these elements, at the heart of which is genre knowledge. With the acquisition of genre knowledge, the overlap will increase, which means that the writer will advance from knowledge-telling to knowledge transforming, being able to create written artifacts, or texts representative of a given genre, that are congruent with the values of the target socio-disciplinary practice.

In view of this definition of research writing competence, L2 writing instruction should reinforce students' cognitive processes as well as the social and cultural practices surrounding research-related genres. Centering on the acquisition of the genre knowledge, it should provide abundant connections between scholarly reading and writing processes and '[m]ediat[e] the engagements of knowers with the knowledge represented by academic discourses [...] through the medium of language' (Hyland & Hamp-Lyons, 2002, p. 6). In Hyland's (2000) words, teachers must 'involve [students] in acquiring a metacognitive awareness of [genre] forms and contexts and a familiarity with the discoursal strategies they need to perform roles, engage in interactions, and accomplish goals in the target community' and help them 'gain an awareness of

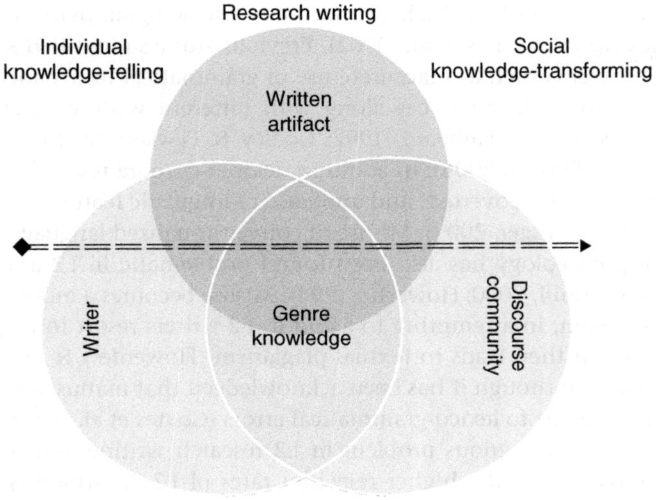

Figure 1.1 Research writing competence

the discipline's symbolic resources for getting things done by routinely connecting purposes with features of texts' (p. 145).

L2 research writing pedagogy should also be informed by the results of numerous studies that have examined academic writing produced by second language learners for more than four decades (see Belcher & Braine, 1995; Hamp-Lyons, 1991). Much of this research strand has not only confirmed the need to help students develop genre knowledge and become competent research writers, but also provided a baseline for instruction by revealing the nature of novice scholars' writing difficulties.

1.1.4 Research writing of L2 novice scholars

For L2 writers, who are under an increasing pressure to publish in English-dominant international journals (Flowerdew, 1999), writing about research in English is a very effortful and at times an agonistic challenge. It is not uncommon for them to ascribe their major difficulties to a lower level of language proficiency (Bitchener & Basturkmen, 2006; Mohan & Lo, 1985), and their manuscripts are indeed not without language issues. While the so-called non-standard English is generally tolerated by the gatekeepers (Flowerdew, 2001), it is often viewed as less than desirable (Li, 2006) or criticized for being almost unintelligible due to a high proportion of lexico-grammatical errors (Ammon, 2000; Coates et al., 2002). Previous studies identified a number of problems such as inaccurate use of grammatical forms and inappropriate vocabulary choices along with different writing mechanics issues (Casanave & Hubbard, 1992; Cooley & Lewkowicz, 1995, 1997; Dong, 1998; Surratt, 2006). In addition, learner corpora research reveals patterns of misuse, overuse, and underuse of linguistic features (Gilquin et al., 2007; Granger, 2009). Misuse of conventionalized language at the level of phraseology has also been found problematic in L2 academic writing (Gledhill, 2000; Howarth, 1996). Misuse becomes a more serious problem when, in attempting to avoid it, L2 writers resort to language re-use, which then leads to textual plagiarism (Flowerdew & Li, 2007). However, even though it has been acknowledged that manuscript rejections may be due to lexico-grammatical errors (Coates et al., 2002), they are not the most serious problem in L2 research writing and not the primary reason for the higher rejection rates of L2 contributors (Li & Flowerdew, 2007; Hewings, 2006). In fact, there is evidence that evaluators tend to be lenient to surface errors in the use of grammar and vocabulary (Jenkins et al., 1993).

L2 writers' inefficient uses of global and abstract features of writing appear to be more detrimental than their language errors (Flowerdew, 1999). Some studies document the difficulty of clearly expressing ideas in writing (Torrance & Thomas, 1994; Torrance et al., 1994), which is why it is not surprising that editors and reviewers make numerous requests for clarification of meaning (Li, 2006). Researchers also report on L2 writers' problems with the structural development of extended stretches of texts (Jenkins et al., 1993; Parry, 1998; Thompson, 1999) and coherence in presenting propositions (Cooleey & Lewkowicz, 1995, 1997; Dong, 1998). These global issues interfere with the comprehension of underlying ideas and have a negative impact on the overall communicative effectiveness of the produced texts. In a case study of an L2 doctoral student, for example, James (1984) found that sentence-level problems were distracting to the reader, while inappropriate weighing of propositions, ineffective organization, and lack of coherence considerably affected understanding of the intended meaning. Moreover, he argued that such discursive deficiencies as inadequate referencing and inappropriate signposting can cause a breakdown of meaning.

Related issues are lack of focus and the strength of arguments (Alter & Adkins, 2006; Knight, 1999; Ryan & Zuber-Skerritt, 1999). Some studies on thesis writing have revealed that a major concern is students' lack of ability to critically evaluate theories or methodologies and to develop and support counterarguments with relevant evidence (Cadman, 1997; Frost, 1999; Knight, 1999). In addition, L2 writers tend to weakly frame and position their work in relation to the existing knowledge territory (Blakeslee, 1997; Lim, 2012) and to over- or underestimate their own findings, especially when discussing their research results in comparison with published works (Cooley & Lewkowicz, 1995, 1997; Parry, 1998). Integrating and contextualizing sources is particularly difficult for L2 writers, as they are not able to monitor the degree of their critical evaluation of the cited material (Dudley-Evans, 1994; San Miguel & Nelson, 2007). They tend to suppress their opinion and fail to distinguish between their claims and the claims that are put forth in their sources (Borg, 2000; Groom, 2000). In San Miguel and Nelson's (2007) study, for instance, 'structuring the text so that the literature contextualizes and illuminates the problem' in order to justify the need for a new study was a considerable challenge faced by practice-based doctorates (p. 83). Given more thought, these research insights in fact indicate that L2 writers have great difficulty in appropriately expressing their stance; that is, to 'project themselves into their texts to communicate their relationship to subject matter and the readers' (Hyland, 1999, p. 101) as they are developing arguments and supporting counter-arguments.

Weak stance in L2 research writing is not surprising. On the one hand, L2 writers feel hindered by the very fact that they are non-native speakers of English (Canagarajah, 2003; Cho, 2004; Flowerdew, 2000; Torrance et al., 1992, 1994). As Wharton (2012) maintains, they may have insufficient linguistic means necessary to make stronger assertions and to express the degree of their commitment to their own propositions, especially considering their various language errors. On the other hand, given the demands of socio-disciplinary communication, their stance inhibition goes beyond language ability. The complex process of enculturation into a dynamic and continuously evolving discourse community involves an intense knowledge-construction dialog with the discipline's gatekeepers, which implies assuming roles that novice scholars are not comfortable with.

Research writing should involve much free but often combative, contestable, and polemical arguing and opining for making of new knowledge (Bradley 2009, p. 106). In this process of knowledge construction, novice L2 writers need to give their texts force and value; in other words, strongly position themselves in the targeted socio-disciplinary practice (Casanave, 2002). However, they encounter a personal predicament – the need for a critical shift in their scholar identity, which entails adopting a new sense of self by presenting a strong legitimate voice (Hirvela & Belcher, 2001; Mullen, 2001) and 'new ways to mean' as expected by the new community (Pavlenko & Lantolf, 2000, p. 172). Establishing such an identity, especially for graduate students, presents an additional, sociopolitical challenge since they are 'of lower status' (Soler-Monreal & Gil-Salom, 2011) and therefore 'less powerful' than their disciplinary gatekeepers, so the interaction with them is inherently power-unequal (Li, 2006, pp. 457–458).

Conscious about inequality in power-relations, novice writers in general fail to manifest the ability to write like an authoritative member of the discourse community (Boote & Beile, 2005) and to support their arguments with confidence and personal voice (Caffarella & Barnett, 2000; Kamler, 2008; Kiley, 2009). L2 writers, in particular, coming from non-English academic cultures, tend to even avoid projecting certainty and explicitly expressing their views (Koutsantoni, 2006; Li, 2006) and, thus, silence their way of developing knowledge (Ingleton & Cadman, 2002). As they struggle to present their propositions in ways that meet the expectations of their discourse community (Riazi, 1997), they unwillingly recreate their identities in an undesired negative way and are likely to yield to the fear of failure.

A significant part of the expectations of the discourse community is that authors adhere to the norms of writing in the discipline when new claims are presented and framed. Since novices have very little opportunity to contribute to shaping the largely privileged genre discourses (Eckstein et al., 2011), the gatekeepers demand conformity to disciplinary genre conventions. Hyland (2000) emphasizes that displaying such conformity is crucial for obtaining full membership in the community, which adds to the big challenge for L2 writers. Like L1 novice scholars (McNabb, 2001), L2 writers grapple with the research genres and the appropriateness of functional language needed to effectively communicate ideas (Cooley & Lewkowicz, 1995, 1997; Dong, 1998; Parry, 1998). In the new-to-them English-language educational system, students struggle with the new-to-them academic writing norms (Casanave, 2002; Casanave & Hubbard, 1992; Paltridge, 1997) and the various genre-specific language forms (McCune & Hounsell, 2005). Studies point out L2 writers' failure to follow organizational conventions of research genres (Cooley & Lewkowicz, 1995, 1997; Dong, 1998; Parry, 1998). In other words, L2 writers do not adhere to the structural and content patterns specific of individual parts of particular types of extended English discourse. Lacking familiarity with genre conventions, L2 writers are inadvertently likely to transfer their L1 culture-specific rhetorical organization as they write about research in English (Gentil, 2011; Mohan & Lo, 1985). The socio-rhetorical features of their texts inherit their native culture (Connor, 2004; Kaplan, 1968; Mauranen, 1993) and therefore deviate from the English-medium disciplinary genres.

This bird's eye view not only summarizes the wide range of challenges L2 writers face when writing for the purpose of disciplinary knowledge production and exchange. It also demonstrates that these challenges are multi-faceted and likely to erode L2 writers' confidence in their contributions and their ability to inspire scientific growth. Unfortunately, novice research writers are not prepared to face the challenges of knowledge production, text production, and self-formation – all 'complexly intertwined at the point of articulation' (Aitchison & Lee, 2006, p. 268), often because they haven't had appropriate learning opportunities or tools to do so. The task of a research writing course for L2 graduate students, then, is to help them develop metacognitive, metarhetorical, matapragmatic, and metalinguistic skills, and practice them as they create, translate, and revise research-related texts. Ferris and Hedgcock (2012) assert that to meet these objectives, L2 educators should provide socioliterate instruction where they can mediate students' apprenticeship into established target communities through work with such highly productive conceptual and pedagogical tools as genres (p. 110). For guidance, 'we have two rich disciplinary traditions to draw from: L1 rhetoric and composition studies, as well as applied linguistics and L2 writing' (Ferris & Hedgcock, 2012, p. 87), which have respectively established the so-called rhetorical and linguistic approaches to genre-based teaching.

1.2 Genre pedagogy

1.2.1 Anchors of genre-based teaching

Genre-oriented approaches to L2 writing pedagogy[2] had their genesis in different theoretical and ideological beliefs. It has been customary in the literature to characterize genre-based pedagogy as having a respective ternary epistemology that incorporates the linguistic perspectives of English for Specific Purposes (ESP) and Systemic Functional Linguistics (SFL), and the non-linguistic, rhetorical views of the North American New Rhetoric (NR) theorists. The rhetorical paradigm has also embraced the New Literacy (NL) and the affiliated Academic Literacies (AcLits) trends. These distinct approaches have their own definitions and interpretations of the genre construct, but they all include concepts related to social contexts, social practice, typified but flexible rhetorical acts, communicative purposes, texts, expected formal conventions, meaning, and functional linguistic features. Although the focal point and the degree to which the linguistic and rhetorical approaches emphasize these concepts varies, they all concur that genres represent responses to social interactions realized as recurring textual representations imbued with characteristics established and expected by parent discourse communities (Polio & Williams, 2011).

Genre ideologies are reflected in the models used to analyze genres. Genre analysis by linguists focuses on texts and may entail quantitative and qualitative explorations of language features indicative of lexicogrammatical and rhetorical patterns and descriptive of intertextual systems. Analyses of genre conducted in the rhetorical tradition seek to understand social contexts, ideological climates, audiences, writing purposes, and different conditions of genre use that may influence rhetorical structures and writers' choices. Ferris and Hedgcock (2012) maintain that genre analysis as a whole represents a 'fundamental source, inspiration, and tool for genre pedagogies', for it 'situates oral and written texts with respect to their textual and sociocultural contexts' (p. 116). Genre analysis and its theoretical, ideological, and methodological foundations guiding L2 writing instruction have been described at large (see Bawarshi & Reiff, 2010; Flowerdew, 2002; Hyon, 1996; Johns, 1997, 2002, 2008).[3] Here, I will briefly highlight the most essential tenets informative for socioliterate L2 research writing classroom practices.

1.2.2 Linguistic approaches

The ESP and SFL linguistic approaches have been the most influential trends in L2 writing classrooms worldwide (Hyland, 2003a). The broader field of ESP gave rise to English for Academic Purposes (EAP), which has had the greatest uptake in L2 writing pedagogy, particularly in terms of rhetorical consciousness raising. Drawing from a rich research base and an assortment of theoretically grounded techniques, EAP is concerned with the communicative needs and practices of language learners in academic contexts in view of the cognitive, social, and linguistic demands of their academic disciplines (Hyland & Hamp-Lyons, 2002, p. 2). Its roots spring from Swales' (1981, 1990) conceptualization of genres based on both linguistic concepts and social context dynamics. According to Swales (1998), genres 'structure the roles of individuals within wider frameworks and further assist those individuals with the actualization of their communicative plans and purposes' (p. 20). Genres are, then, theorized as actions that are situated in particular contexts and that are purposefully and routinely conducted by the members of a discourse community. EAP practitioners, especially those working with advanced L2 graduate writers, have widely adopted genre as a tool in teaching L2 discipline-specific writing (Johns, 2003), employing Swales' genre analysis framework of moves or 'bounded communicative act[s] [...] designed to achieve one main communicative objective' (Swales & Feak, 2000, p. 35). Students analyze discipline-specific texts compiled in specialized corpora. They examine how moves occur as well-regulated communicative events and observe how the structural and rhetorical organization of texts reflect ways in which discourse communities achieve specific social purposes. EAP pedagogy, overall, promulgates raising rhetorical awareness anchored in discipline-specific genres (Dudley-Evans, 2004) through a focus on texts as the starting point. Hyland (2003a) clarifies that the guiding principle is placing 'an explicit focus on the ways texts are organized and the language choices that users must make to achieve their purposes in particular contexts', and that beginning to learn about genre by doing text analysis allows learners to develop useful writing strategies (p. 75).

The Sydney School of genre analysis views texts as being determined by the social context (Martin, 1999) and genres as 'staged goal-oriented social processes' (Martin, 1993, p. 13). It motivated the adoption of SFL in higher education in Australia (Drury, 2004) as well as in the USA, Canada, UK, China, and other countries. SFL is not only a pedagogically but also a theoretically sophisticated approach, underpinned by functional linguistics (Halliday, 1994) and the sociocultural theory (Vygotsky, 1978). Similar to EAP, SFL focuses on texts and textual features (Halliday, 1978, 1985; Halliday & Hasan, 1989), but it also accounts for the purposeful and successive character of genres, for the textual patterns underlying socially recognized functions, and for the systematic relation between language and context. Pedagogically, it has been recognized as the 'most thoroughly articulated approach' addressing form as it relates to text function and the writer's purposes (Johns, 1995, p. 185). SFL teaching methods center on meaning as being inseparable from form, explicitly focusing on ideational, interpersonal, and textual resources necessary for meaning making. Classroom practice embodies a teaching-learning cycle (see Feez, 1998; Macken-Horarik, 2002), during which students are apprenticed into reading and writing texts through modeling how to explore these metafunctional resources. They are scaffolded into understanding how genres systematically connect social functions to linguistic actions.

In the widest sense, Bruce (2008a) generalizes the linguistic approaches and their advantages for L2 writing pedagogy as follows:

> [U]sing a sample text (an example of a particular genre), learners engage with tasks that focus on the organization and constituent features of the text in order to acquire the types of knowledge necessary for creating their own examples of the same genre. Often the outcome of the learning cycle will be tasks that require students to use the target genre knowledge (which they have been analyzing and practising) to create new examples of the same genre.
>
> For the teaching of the writing skill, it seems that genre-based courses have three major strengths: firstly, they make it possible to focus on larger units of language; secondly, they can provide a focus on the organizational and procedural elements of written discourse; and thirdly, they make it possible to retain linguistic components as functioning features of a larger unit of discourse, thereby avoiding atomistic approaches to language teaching. (p. 6)

Hyland (2007) provides a comprehensive description of the basic principles of teaching genres within SFL and in ESP/EAP, which share some tangencies and, therefore, some criticism. For instance, both approaches recognize the role of distinctive textual, rhetorical, and linguistic realizations in disciplinary genres and, in their own ways, centralize on text analysis to help learners understand and master the discourse conventions of their discipline. However, their focus on text and language features is regarded as biased by the proponents of the rhetorical approaches.

1.2.3 Rhetorical approaches

Unlike the linguistic approaches, NR emphasizes the link between rhetorical situation and text type, examining rhetorical contexts in which genres are used rather than the textual elements of genres. For NR scholars who prioritize evolving processes and contexts and look beyond structures, genres are not structurally fixed but rather process-based 'mediated interactions within a context' (Prior, 2007, p. 94). New Rhetoricians recommend that pedagogy embraces classroom inquiry and critical reflection about the values and beliefs perpetuated by the targeted genres, about their audience and respective communication constrains, and about the implied power relations – all leading to student critique and negotiation of genres for the purpose of aligning them with their immediate needs and purposes (Johns, 2011).

Associated with NR is the NL movement rooted in Bakhtinian post-structural philosophy of language and in anthropological studies. NL scholars see genres as means of social action shaded by 'power, authority, meaning making, and identity that are implicit in the use of literacy practices within specific institutional settings' (Lea & Street, 2006, p. 370). Exposure to genres, from their standpoint, should provide opportunities for understanding the multiple voices that populate, and even 'overpopulate', genres (Bakhtin, 1981, p. 294) in order to experience the multiple facets of the social encounter inherent to genre practice.

The AcLits movement, which draws on NL as well as on work in critical discourse (Fairclough, 1995) and sociology of knowledge (Latour & Woolgar, 1986), recognizes both disciplinary specifics and institutional and social dimensions, taking into consideration the issues of identity and power in writing as social practice (Lea & Street, 1998). AcLits conceptualizes the context of culture through the literacy practices of socially situated writers, deprecates the textual approaches to teaching academic writing for their lack of focus on practice, and, like NL, recommends that writing pedagogy encourages critique of disciplinary discourse (Johns, 1995). Lillis and Scott (2007), for example, call for a transformative agenda which is concerned with:

> a) locating [genre] conventions in relation to specific and contested traditions of knowledge making; b) eliciting the perspectives of writers (whether students or professionals) on the ways in which such conventions impinge on their meaning making; c) exploring alternative ways of meaning making in academia, not least by considering the resources that (student) writers bring to the academy as legitimate tools for meaning making. (p. 13)

1.2.4 Congruence between linguistic and rhetorical approaches

Genre theorists' views differ depending on their philosophical assumptions about the nature of texts and their role in literacy practices. Advocates of the linguistic approaches argue that teaching genres exposes students to various intricacies of the social dimension by revealing to them different ways in which the conventions that build texts 'produce the whys of social effect' (Cope & Kalantzis, 1993, p. 8). Opponents to the teaching of the structural and linguistic aspects of genre insist on focusing on the writer and on opportunities to challenge power relations existing in the disciplinary community discourse. Arguing for the value of enhancing students' metacognition by helping them learn abstract genre-related concepts, rhetoricians cast heavy doubts upon the linguistic approaches because of their confining inverse interpretations of the relationship between text and context and particularly because they infer recurring situations from textual features (Coe, 2002, p. 197). Another major objection is against the pragmatism of analyzing and emulating genres, which is viewed as imposing certain sociocultural norms on students and promoting their 'passive and dependent relationship toward the activities of [...] academic communities' (Canagarajah, 2002, p. 131).

As Ferris and Hedgcock (2012) argue, 'certain objections to genre pedagogies are overstated and consequently unfair' (p. 115), and many have put forth convincing arguments addressing the rhetoricians' criticism towards the linguistic genre approaches. A good example is Hyland's (2007) reasoning in response to some advocates of the NR school, who firmly believe that genres are evolving and variable and who therefore question the very feasibility of teaching genres as constant and regular (Freedman 1999; Freedman & Medway, 1994; Lankshear & Knoble, 2003; Lillis & Scott, 2007). Specifically referring to L2 writers, Hyland rationalizes that genre-based teaching is a time-saver in the lengthy process of situated acquisition rather than a curse for context authenticity, as the NR adherents fear (see Bishop & Ostrom, 1997). Hyland also counters opinions that blame linguistic approaches for limiting students to replicating the existing practices of the disciplinary dominant culture, clarifying that genre work in the classroom in fact enhances critical analysis and fosters student engagement with the textual practices of the discourse community. Admitting that genre conformity may hamper the writer's creativity, he argues that 'there is nothing inherently prescriptive' in the linguistic tradition (p. 152). On the contrary, it facilitates the expression of meaning by providing students with alternatives derived from the identification of certain patterns, which is particularly helpful and reassuring for novice L2 writers. Hyland summarizes the advantages of linguistic approaches to genre-based pedagogy as follows:

Explicit. Makes clear what is to be learnt to facilitate the acquisition of writing skills

Systematic. Provides a coherent framework for focusing on both language and contexts

Needs-based. Ensures that course objectives and content are derived from students' needs

Supportive. Gives teachers a central role in scaffolding students' learning and creativity
Empowering. Provides access to the patterns and possibilities of variation in valued texts
Critical. Provides the resources for students to understand and challenge valued discourses
Consciousness-raising. Increases teachers' awareness of texts to confidently advise students on writing. (Hyland, 2004b, pp. 10–11)

Another important consideration in the rhetorical versus linguistic controversy concerns the AcLits perspective. This arid critic is largely a research frame (Lillis & Scott, 2007), and although some instructional initiatives have explored opportunities for students to recognize power relations (Lea, 2004) and to challenge gate-kept literacy practices (Lillis, 2006), it is not yet a pedagogical design frame (Lea & Street, 2006) and does not articulate a theory of learning as it relates to genre writing literacy development. Wingate (2012), for instance, asserts that AcLits' criticism is subjective and unjust precisely because it hasn't been substantiated with a demonstrated alternative pedagogy. She presents a compelling argument for why contributions resulting from genre analysis should not be marginalized in pedagogical practice, reminding the AcLits promoters that linguistic approaches have long expanded from text-bound analyses and prescription to considering the contexts for which texts are produced (p. 28). In fact, the SFL and in ESP/EAP approaches recognize the dynamism of genres and the fact that genres evolve and change in view of new socio-cognitive needs of discourse communities (Ramanathan & Kaplan, 2000). Wingate also maintains that since 'the literacy practices of disciplines are manifested in texts, it seems that the analysis of texts must either precede the analysis of practices, or at least be the main focus of instruction' (p. 28), especially because analyzing texts systematically focusing on structural, rhetorical, and lexico-grammatical patterns promotes critical analysis (Hammond & Macken-Horarik, 1999). On a related note, scholars like Johns (1995) and Christie (1993) are convinced that the AcLits' transforming views are less suitable for teaching novice writers. Novices lack an objective and critical awareness of disciplinary expectations as well as discourse structure knowledge and linguistic precision, and are thus politically and linguistically not prepared to 'act as cultural critique surrogates' (Johns, 1995, p. 182).

Despite the debate between these seemingly mutually exclusive camps, which either advocate or reject text-focused instruction, it has been increasingly acknowledged that they essentially converge (Flowerdew, 2011; Johns et al., 2006). Acknowledging the strengths and the weaknesses of both and the focal point causing the dispute, Wingate agrees with a number of colleagues (Coffin & Donohue, 2012; Donohue, 2012; Gardner, 2012) who have highlighted an obvious affinity between the linguistic and rhetorical approaches – both interpret genre as the functional relationship between text and context. The linguistic approaches focus on texts in contexts, which are seen as determining language use; the rhetorical approaches focus on writers in context, emphasizing practice over the text dimension. Turner (2012) succinctly explains:

> [The] concern [should be] not so much with the dichotomy text v. practice, but rather with practices around the textual. In this way, by highlighting one of the poles but showing its relevance as a focus for the other, the dichotomy itself is disrupted. In other words, there need not be any oppositional dichotomy. There is scope for a kind of synergistic spiral whereby a focus on social practice feeds back in to an awareness of textual practice. At the same time, the vicissitudes of meeting the requirements of conventional textual practice, for example, point up the need to scrutinise and re-evaluate or critique those conventional expectations. They need not be treated as 'givens'. (p. 19)

Decades ago, Johns (1995) substantiated this train of thought with a practical model whereby teaching conceptualizes genres as 'repeated social action' (Miller, 1984, p. 151). In this model, students collect examples of the targeted genres, hypothesize about their sociocultural facets (context and discourse community, purposes of readers and writers, typification and variation, and so on), and then approach the task of writing based on what they learn about the genre. This approach to the analysis of other authors' texts introduces writing as practice that is based on the expectations of the readership. It also facilitates the identification of power roles as well as the awareness of discourse purposes as they are realized by language and form. Similarly, Devitt, Reiff, and Bawarshi (2004) outlined pedagogical guidelines for genre analysis suitable for both L1 and L2 writing. They propose to begin class instruction by having students collect genre samples themselves, with the underlying intent to give them opportunities to access and explore the context as well as the users of the assigned genre. The next task is to identify recurrent patterns in the student-compiled text collection and describe common features in terms of rhetorical appeals, structural development, style, syntactic complexity, and patterns of language use.

With this level of understanding about the genre, the students then proceed to analyze the meaning and significance of the rhetorical patterns as indicative of the beliefs, values, and ideologies of the social culture the genre operates in and even the ingrained power relations. At this stage, their analysis of the genre becomes critical, as they are asked to explain how certain language choices indicate relationships and connote boundaries between 'insiders and outsiders' (Reiff in Johns et al., 2006, p. 242). Another writing instruction design frame, which is explicitly rooted in the AcLits model, has made an implicit but distinguishable connection to the linguistic approaches. Specifically, Lea and Street (2006) intersect with John's and Devitt et al.'s models in that their students interact with genres in order to raise their awareness 'of the different language and semiotic practices [...] associated with the requirements of different genres in academic contexts' (p. 371).

The linguistic and rhetorical traditions are undoubtedly distinct, but they are not necessarily irreconcilable when it comes to L2 research writing pedagogy. Together, they can contribute to facilitating the development of research writing competence by unveiling the textual subtleties of socially situated discourse. In the next section, I elaborate on how this could be achieved, exploring the mutual endowment of these conceptually intersecting perspectives.

1.3 Genre-based L2 research writing pedagogy

1.3.1 Consonant linguistic and rhetorical fundamentals

With the goal of helping L2 students develop the aspects of genre knowledge essential to research writing competence, writing instruction has to center on the relationship between the text, the writer, and the targeted discourse community. To do that, it has to intertwine rhetorical and linguistic fundamentals, integrating the best from the two worlds.

The linguistic approaches can complement the non-linguistic focus on genre purposes in social practice by acquainting novices with genre conventions established by the discourse community, thus helping them recognize and assimilate ways in which rhetorical goals are achieved with the symbolic resources of the target research genre. This would facilitate the development of the formal and rhetorical domains of genre knowledge. Additionally, linguistic approaches can enhance the rhetorical focus on the writer by providing novices with the linguistic means necessary to critically evaluate and frame arguments as well as to position themselves as confident discussants. Knowledge of appropriate linguistic means may help them overcome or even avoid the pitfall of suppressive inferiority, since language is a prominent marker of writer's identity (Ricento, 2002; Giles & Johnson, 1987).

Genre analysis in the classroom can potentially enhance the process domain of genre knowledge. It can be a path for understanding the procedural practices associated with the genre. Through hands-on corpus exploration, the students can understand the reading practices of their discourse community and develop strategies for constructing genre-appropriate texts befitting socio-disciplinary communication. At the same time, the rhetorical approaches, with the help of ethnographic and emic analysis techniques, can amend the linguistic aspirations by not only enhancing the socio-disciplinary awareness but also accentuating genres as existing within intertextual networks that interlink to serve the needs of their receivers, enrooting the process domain of genre knowledge (Tardy, 2005, 2009).

Although neither linguistic nor rhetorical approaches are concerned with content knowledge, which is essential to the knowledge transformation task of research writing, the former's use of corpora, which I will discuss in the next section of this chapter, creates a contingency with the subject-matter domain of genre knowledge. By exploring discipline-specific corpora (especially specialized corpora compiled by the students themselves on topics relevant to their research), students unavoidably interact with scientific content that expands their scholarly erudition. Figure 1.2 depicts how the linguistic and rhetorical approaches to genre-based teaching address the elements of genre knowledge.

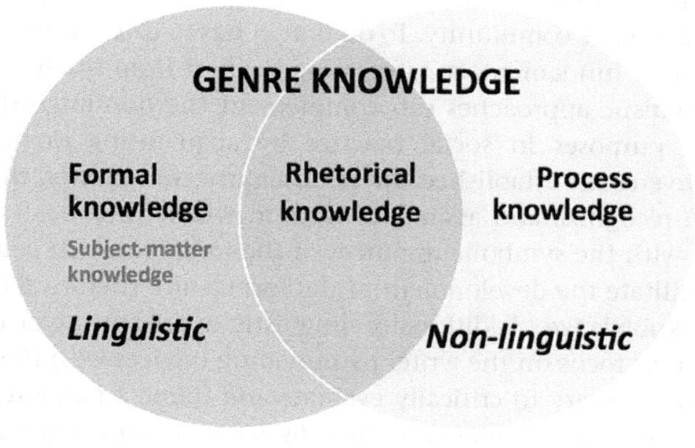

Figure 1.2 Genre knowledge

Finally, genre analysis in the linguistic tradition is also plausible for L2 writing because, while concentrating on creating academically compelling artifacts, it provides L2 writers with the opportunity to continue learning about the English use of lexico-grammar necessary to construct grammatically correct sentences and coherently developed stretches of text. It is of utmost importance to remember that acquiring writing proficiency in a second language is a demanding and lengthy process, and that the writing itself is more constrained and more difficult than in a native language (Silva, 1993). From the standpoint of language acquisition, focus on textual forms and linguistic realizations of communicative intent can facilitate learning by helping L2 writers notice and potentially address their own local and global language errors. Importantly, such a focus provides students with lexico-grammatical 'configurations of meaning that are recurrently phased together to enact social practices' (Martin, 2002, p. 269).

1.3.2 Connecting linguistic and rhetorical constructs through corpora

Corpora are defined as principled collections of electronic texts that are representative of a language or language variety to be used for linguistic description purposes (Sinclair, 2005). Since the 1980s, prominent L2 writing researchers have recognized and promoted corpus-based practice as very promising for L2 writing teaching and learning (Aijmer, 2009; Hyland, 2003b; Johns, 1988). Prolific work in the area of corpus linguistics that examined naturally occurring, authentic language use with various data-driven computational methods of analysis has motivated classroom implementations of corpora and generated a wealth of learning materials, including word frequency lists and profiles, keyword lists, lexical bundles, collocation and colligation patterns, and many more to guide EAP pedagogy (see Cheng, 2012). Writing teachers have been provided with fairly large general corpora containing a variety of text-types as well as with specialized corpora, which contain texts from a certain discipline and tend to be much smaller because they are compiled for specific purposes and for specific language users. Specialized corpora, in particular, are seen as an invaluable tool for genre analysis (Hyland, 2007). They are also recognized as a 'powerful methodology-technology' for 'determining how disciplines use language in their major genres' (Lee & Swales, 2006, p. 57) that can facilitate the identification of distinct lexico-grammatical features and rhetorical patterns (Aston, 2002; Bernardini, 2004; Cheng et al., 2003; Ghadessy et al., 2001; Hyland, 2000; Kettemann & Marko, 2002; Thompson & Tribble, 2001).

In L2 writing classrooms, students have been exposed to indirect and direct corpus applications (Römer, 2010), where corpora are used as reference tools and as research tools, respectively. Corpora are used as reference tools when the students are provided with corpus-informed materials either created by the teacher or available on the web as free access resources that they can consult, like a corpus-based dictionary. With such tools, students can learn from and about texts at any stage in the writing process when they encounter some difficulty, especially when they need to find alternative ways of expressing meaning. As research tools, corpora become tangible through concordancers, or search engines that allow queries of specific linguistic items and display a list of occurrences of the queried item. Concordancers provide students with hands-on opportunities for observation and discovery in the process of data-driven learning (Bernardini, 2004; Johns, 1991). In this case, the discovery is about how language works, and the students, encouraged by the teacher-coordinator, undertake the role of researchers who learn from conducting corpus analysis rather than from what is given to them in a textbook or prepared for them by another resource.

There are many advantages of discovery and reference uses of corpora. Most importantly, however, considering that both genre constraints (which are made salient by the linguistic approaches) and writer choice (which is propagated by the rhetorical approaches) are indispensable components of genre writing (Devitt, 2004), I believe that corpora can allow for a symbiosis of genre-based theoretical perspectives. In L2 research writing pedagogy, the use of specialized corpus-based materials and tasks can provide a seamless connection between the linguistic and rhetorical tenets, equipping students with the necessary means to learn about and apply the genre conventions established in disciplinary practice (Figure 1.3).

Specialized corpora can be particularly valuable, for they can provide students with opportunities to engage with the text-based social practices of their disciplinary community. Conducting multi-level analyses of representative texts from their field can introduce students to both the rhetorical and linguistic specifications of the genre. Corpus-based tasks, devised from ethnographic and textual perspectives (Bhatia, 2004), can help students develop heuristic processes to analyze and understand the epistemological motives of the disciplinary community, as 'the conventions of writing are embedded in deeper epistemological frameworks that are frequently discipline specific' (Hyland, 2000, p. 145). For instance, based on the texts in the corpus, the students can hypothesize about the purposes of the targeted readers and then be tasked to test their hypotheses by reaching out to their disciplinary professors,

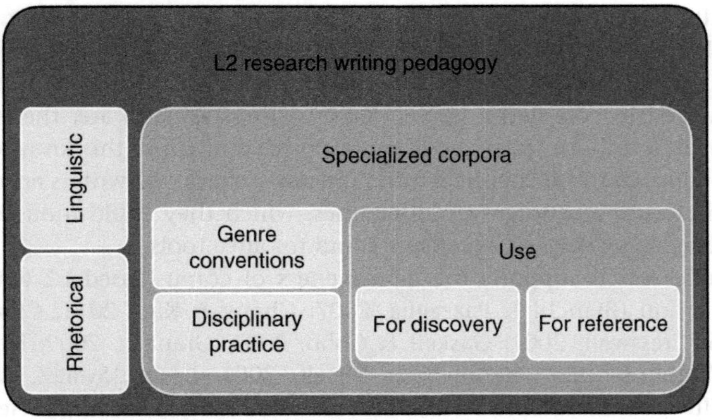

Figure 1.3 Corpora in L2 research writing pedagogy

who often act as discourse gatekeepers. A specialized corpus can also provide rich exposure to the culture of a particular discipline, raising students' awareness of its discourse flexibility and variation (described in numerous EAP studies including Anthony, 1999; Bhatia, 2002; Biber et al., 1999; Nwogu, 1997; Posteguillo, 1999; Samraj, 2002), especially when the corpus explorations focus on the rhetorical development of content in terms of communicative moves and functional steps. This particular type of exploration 'provides enriched input necessary for students to make the connection between general rhetorical purposes and specific lexico-grammatical choices' (Charles, 2007, p. 289), helping them discover underlying regularities, induce linguistic realizations of rhetorical shifts, and build specific associations between rhetorical functions and linguistic features commonly used to realize those functions (Gledhill, 2000). With that, L2 writers can develop the capability to evaluate the rhetorical and linguistic quality of their own discourse by comparing their writing with that of established writers in their field.

Concordance-based corpus investigations are especially useful for L2 research writers as language learners. Returned queries not only expose them to extensive input of authentic language use, but can also enhance the input in ways that draw their attention to salient features and help them notice genre-specific patterns and forms that are otherwise unnoticeable, thus providing a 'necessary [...] condition for the conversion of input to intake for learning' (Schmidt, 1994, p. 17). In addition to facilitating hypothesizing, verifying, and noticing, corpus-driven discovery can enhance motivation and learner autonomy

(Boulton, 2010). For that, the corpus-based activities should target genres that are relevant to students' needs, be inherent to their authentic writing processes, and be introduced to students at a time when they are vested in completing a real genre-writing task and are, therefore, motivated to both learn about genre norms and apply this knowledge first-hand. In the authentic writing process scenario, L2 writers encounter rhetorical and linguistic difficulties, which they could inductively solve by using corpora as reference and resource tools.

EAP research supports the effectiveness of corpus-based L2 writing instruction (Bianchi & Pazzaglia, 2007; Chang & Kuo, 2011; Charles, 2006; Cresswell, 2007; Gaskell & Cobb, 2004; Granath, 2009; Henry, 2007; Johns, 1988; Kennedy & Miceli, 2001; Lee & Swales, 2006; O'Sullivan & Chambers, 2006; Yoon & Hirvela, 2004). Having reviewed 12 studies investigating uses of concordancing in L2 writing, Yoon (2011) concluded that corpora can indeed be viable research/discovery and reference tools, provided there is appropriate learner training (both in how to use the technology and how to employ effective observation and logical reasoning strategies) and teacher help during corpus explorations, taking into account learners' different learning styles, language proficiency, and general computer literacy (p. 138). Learner training and teacher help are essential to effective corpus use, for without them students may experience a burnout, especially when concordance lines are used as the primary source and the only type of deduction (Thurstun & Candlin, 1998). Ädel (2010) also cautions against and provides specific recommendations for how to avoid the risk of learners drowning in decontextualized corpus data as well as other pitfalls like the possible lack of appropriate corpora and the difficulty for the uninitiated to interpret, evaluate, and generalize patterns identified during their explorations. Along the same lines, Lee and Swales (2006) recommend that pedagogues take into account the level of disciplinary acculturation of their students and do not fully commit to concordance-based activities when working with students who are only beginning to attempt the professional genres. In such cases, they should first focus on structural organization or audience analysis. If the students 'possess the appropriate genre knowledge, as is often the case with non-native speaker of English students completing their doctoral degrees, then what they may be mostly missing is fine-tuning of lexical and syntactic subtleties, particularly in terms of their strategic and rhetorical implications' (p. 57), and that's when corpus explorations are particularly appropriate. This last thought leads to another important consideration as to what is more appropriate at the beginning of L2 research writing instruction.

1.3.3 Opening the genre scene for L2 writing

L2 academic writing instruction often 'involves examining and deconstructing examples of genres' (Bruce, 2008a, p. 6). With this textual focus, writing courses are generally organized into units that reflect the IMRD (Introduction, Methods, Results, Discussion) structure of research-reporting genres and tend to rely on analytical models and frameworks rooted in genre analysis. Johns (2011) supports L2 writers' initiation to genres from this prism of linguistic practices, cogitating about directions for genre-based writing instruction:

> It appears from the comments by professionals in L2 contexts that responded to the 2009 SLWS survey and from the successes of ESP and SFL that curricula should, in fact, begin with texts and their structures, particularly among novice students; but then, using some of the suggestions made by the New Rhetoricians, a curriculum must move towards an integration of theories and practices that value analysis of context, complex writing processes, and intertextuality. Research into high road transfer suggests that students should view texts as both temporarily structured and evolving, that they should draw from prior knowledge of texts but be open to the demands of a new situation or assignment. [...] What is being suggested here, then, is to begin with text structures and then to move rapidly to viewing genres as socially mediated entities (p. 64)

Johns' recommendation relies on a key distinction – that linguistic approaches offer a great deal of explicitness, while the rhetorical approaches assume a more tacit knowledge acquisition approach through inductive discovery. According to multiple opinions that I will further summarize, novice L2 research writers need to gain a conscious understanding of genres and would benefit from explicit instruction and systematic explanations of how language functions in genre-specific disciplinary contexts. This would equip them with knowledge of the linguistic choices employed for certain purposes that they can use as tools to better understand and more effectively participate in socio-disciplinary discourse practices.

Halliday (1989a) explicates that familiarity with different genres is crucial for L2 writers, and that such familiarity does not develop automatically. He advises that learners need to be exposed to genres. For L2 writers, who in general face different language challenges, being initially exposed to genres from the linguistic perspective appears to be most plausible, for this approach has an integrative potential to inculcate the specific demands of the discourse community to novice research writers through a focus on language use in socially recognized ways. As peripheral participants to the genre practices of their discipline, they lack familiarity with the recurrent use of conventionalized forms that allow members of their disciplinary community to freely make rhetorical choices for their own meaning expression purposes. Quoted in Johns et al. (2006), Hyland argues that we need 'visible pedagogy, which makes what is to be learned and assessed clear to students, and methods which make such features explicit, such as investigating the texts and contexts of target situations in consciousness-raising tasks and "scaffolding" learners towards their potential level of performance through effective modeling and joint negotiation' (p. 238). This visibility can be enhanced with the help of a specialized corpus, which can give insights into unnoticed features of language use and can be an ideal approach for studying the features of written genres (Hyland, 2007). Moreover, specialized corpora can clarify genre specifics, reduce exceptions, define priorities, and even 'liberate the creative spirit' of the L2 writer (Sinclair, 1997, p. 38).

In terms of pedagogical soundness, Hyland (2007) argues that explicitness helps set clear learning objectives and avoid the 'hit or miss' of the inductive methods, 'shift[ing] writing instruction from the implicit and exploratory to a conscious manipulation of language and choice' (p. 151). Similarly, Johns (2011) maintains that, if the pedagogical goal is to help students acquire genre knowledge, direct teaching is needed, rather than the 'slippery' approach of examining relationships between texts and the possible contexts for which they may be created (p. 57), which would be more appropriate for raising genre awareness.

Hyland's call for an explicit pedagogy resonates with Elton's (2010) concern about the tacit knowledge which, if not explicitly expressed, can seriously affect good disciplinary writing. Elton believes that 'mak[ing] tacit knowledge overt is commonly associated with expressing it through words, the basic building blocks of any form of writing, but the complexity of which goes often unappreciated' (p. 152). In this context, Nightingale (1986) would add that the peculiarities of linguistic specifications in different subject areas need to be explicitly taught. The EAP and SFL approaches can help reduce genre complexity to a level of linguistic explicitness where L2 writers can acquire a conscious understanding of the target genre and can use concrete concepts to create their own meanings in context. Teaching textual features overtly does not necessarily mean constraining one's writing; it is only part of providing learners with declarative, or in Tardy's

(2009) terms, formal knowledge, necessary for the acquisition of the multi-faceted genre knowledge.

Continuing this standpoint, it is important to further mention that genre knowledge does not develop in a linear fashion from a beginning to a final domain, and that certain aspects of genre knowledge are learned better in certain environments, formal knowledge being best acquired in the writing classroom (Tardy, 2009). This is likely because L2 writers new to a given genre find it difficult to comprehend the complex socio-disciplinary interactions rendered through texts, especially given the multiple layers of requisite knowledge that they are lacking. In the context of classroom instruction, they tend to naturally focus on separate aspects of the discourse or lexico-grammatical features of formal knowledge; then, when they re-encounter and become familiar with these and other rhetorical and procedural aspects, they begin to integrate them all though a process that leads to increasing automaticity of genre knowledge. Tardy suggests that for some learners, perhaps especially those who are prematurely situated in the expert domain and for whom genre complexities are too abstract, it may be wise to compartmentalize and gradually introduce the domains of genre knowledge. She says, 'filtering out some genre dimensions at early stages – especially for learners who face greater cultural or linguistic challenges – can help students make initial observations about a genre without feeling overwhelmed', and proposes starting with the analysis of communicative moves (in Johns et al., 2006, p. 240), which is the cornerstone technique of EAP.

The idea of gradual initiation to genres intersects with views on how writers become expert. Acquisition of writer expertise begins with knowledge-telling (Bereiter & Scardamalia, 1987), when writers focus on texts perceiving them as 'isomorphic with the structure of the domain content' and entirely collapsing the rhetorical problem onto the domain content; in other words, 'texts are taken to be equivalent to what they say' (Geisler, 1994, pp. 41–42). At this stage, linguistic analysis can serve as a heuristics for invention since discovering the choices and constraints existing within genres would help writers see themselves in this symbolic world and textually inhabit it more meaningfully (Bawarshi, 2003). Gradually, novices tacitly acquire the abstract representations needed to write expertly, and only when their naïve representation of rhetorical knowledge evolves as distinct from the domain content concept are they able to transform knowledge. This is when writers perceive texts as acts performed by authors for certain audiences and when texts are written 'not simply to say things, but to do things: to persuade, to argue, to excuse' (Geisler, 1994, p. 43). Without scaffolding, acquiring writer expertise can be a lengthy and inefficient process because tacit learning of genre has a very steep curve. Even 'professional writers who move between disciplines or who become students again can find writing conventions mysterious and difficult to embrace or own' (McKenna, 2003). The linguistic approaches can help bridge knowledge with the rhetorical dimension, making the rhetorical tacit explicit through linguistic realizations and thus facilitating knowledge transformation in writing. SFL pedagogical techniques, for example, employ explicit pedagogy in a teaching/learning cycle where the teacher has a 'visible and interventionist role' (Martin, 1999, p. 124), first modeling texts types with a focus on linguistic features in relation to their social functions and then constructing texts jointly with the students in order to scaffold their independent text construction.

Beginning to develop genre knowledge through an explicit focus on conventionalized forms and on the way social meanings are linguistically constructed can also provide a foundation for developing L2 writers' metacognitive awareness of social practices within their discourse communities. Exploring expressive means of disciplinary discourse can shape learners' genre schemas as they begin to better understand the implicit relationship between socio-communicative goals and textual features, which materialize genres as repeated yet evolving social actions. Becoming aware of how meaning is made by a writer for a readership in a particular context and for particular purposes allows for '*writerly* engagement with texts' (Cheng, 2008, p. 66, author's emphasis) and for gaining better insights about the abstruse interaction of various rhetorical dimensions. This assumption is supported by empirical evidence obtained in a range of studies reporting on the potential of explicit linguistic analysis to increase L2 writers' rhetorical awareness and to better contextualize the genre they are producing (Hanauer, 1998; Henry & Roseberry, 1998; Pang, 2002; Yasuda, 2011). These studies substantiate Tardy's recommendation to begin teaching genre with move analysis by showing that L2 novice writers not only became cognizant of communicative functions but also continued to use them and significantly improve their writing.

Another reason for opening the genre scene with move analysis is that EAP research has provided teachers and students with tools that make genre pedagogy explicit and visible, in Hyland's words. John Swales' (1981, 1990, 2004) seminal work has generated a wealth of research, which provides analytic frameworks of move and step-level functional discourse elements that describe the rhetorical development of research article (henceforth RA) sections (Brett, 1994; Bruce, 2008b; Cortes, 2013; Cotos et al., 2013a,b, 2014; del Saz Rubio, 2011; Dudley-Evans, 1994; Holmes, 1997; Kanoksilapatham, 2007; Lim, 2006, 2010; Loi, 2010; Ozturk, 2007; Parkinson, 2011; Peacock, 2002; Samraj, 2002; Williams, 1999). Swales' Create a Research Space (CARS) model for Introduction sections, in particular, has been validated through analyses of corpora in a range of academic fields and is therefore very popular in L2 writing instruction (Chang & Kuo, 2011; Cortes, 2007; Swales & Feak, 2004). The Swalesian framework has also been adopted at my institution, Iowa State University. In the next section I describe how L2 graduate writing instruction here has come to employ genre-based pedagogy and how it still needs some form of enhancement, advisably technological, to better address discipline-specificity and individualization of instruction.

1.3.4 Instructional challenges

Similar to many other universities in English-speaking countries, Iowa State University offers several academic writing courses. The writing course for international graduate students brings together young scholars from various disciplinary programs, and such heterogeneity makes the instruction very challenging. It would certainly be ideal to have field-specific writing classes (Cargill et al., 2001; Hyland, 2002), which would be designed for graduate students in certain disciplines, or to have instructors who would be members of students' discourse communities and who would also be trained in language matters (Levis & Muller-Levis, 2003). Since Iowa State University, as well as many other English-medium universities, operates in less than ideal conditions in this respect, L2 writing instructors have experimented with different teaching methods in their efforts to bridge the gap between genre writing and disciplinary conventions.

Early on, this course included a wide range of genres, such as memos, literature reviews, research reports, and critiques. The number of genres has gradually decreased, the major focus being placed on the research report. Vann and Myers (2001) exercised an inductive approach to the analysis of individual texts, in which students examined the format, content, and grammatical and rhetorical conventions of each section of the research report. Supplements to this approach were tasks that required students to write journal entries about the rhetorical conventions of prominent journals in their disciplines and tasks that placed the writing research experience 'in the framework of an interactive, cooperative effort with cross-cultural interaction' (Vann & Myers, 2001, p. 82).

Later, after having followed a primarily skill-based approach, whereby the students wrote field-specific literature reviews, summaries, data commentaries, and other discipline-specific texts, Levis and Muller-Levis (2003) reported on transforming the course into a project-based one. The project consisted of carrying out original research, the topic of which was the same for all students and was determined by the instructor. From the start, the students were provided with a limited set of articles on, for instance, cross-cultural adjustment, with which they worked to identify potential research questions for further investigation and to write the literature review. This approach placed a heavy emphasis on collaboration as students worked in small groups on developing data-collection instruments and on analyzing data. Oral presentations about the group-research project wrapped up the course.

Although no empirical evaluations were carried out, experience showed that there were both advantages and disadvantages to these practices. Advantageous were tasks, collaborative and individual, that helped students become acquainted with academic genres through analyses of sample texts and that geared them towards the production of writing samples similar to those studied in class. What appeared to be a major drawback was the fact that the problem of disciplinarity was not addressed. Students in different disciplines worked with a limited number of texts, typically on general topics, examining generic features of a given genre, but not being able to discover the peculiarities of writing in their particular fields. For that, students needed to be exposed to a large amount of authentic texts that would exhibit the features of the genre as established by their discourse communities. That is why the search for an appropriate pedagogical approach to genre teaching has focused on the use of corpora.

Cortes (2007) revamped the course, implementing a corpus-based methodology to emphasize the connection between research writing and disciplinarity. In this version of the course, each student worked with a corpus of research articles published in top journals of his/her discipline. The tasks focused on corpus explorations of the research article sections one at a time. Students analyzed the texts in their corpus guided by move frameworks. The course was largely learner-oriented in that the students conducted corpus analyses in order to discover discourse tendencies and linguistic patterns characteristic of research articles published in their particular discipline. They reported on their observations and then applied the insights gained from the corpus in writing a research article for the final project of the course. Although justifiable and sound, this model, just like its predecessors, did not provide L2 writers with more writing practice and individualized guidance. Move frameworks adopted only as guidelines did not seem to be sufficient for learning, for they fell short of confirming the accuracy of students' corpus observations and of revealing the variation inherent to the disciplines. In other words, students were not receiving any kind of feedback on their corpus observations, so their understanding of the discourse norms and identification of rhetorical patterns remained unscaffolded by the instructor and unconfirmed by the members of the disciplinary community.

Arguably, L2 research writing pedagogy would need to provide sufficient opportunities for students to practice conveying genre-specific messages and to actively engage with the discourse in their discipline. In this book, I propose that this considerable pedagogical challenge is alleviated by genre-based automated writing evaluation (AWE) technology developed to enhance students' encounters with specialized corpora and to facilitate their learning of a research genre by providing individual and discipline-specific feedback on the strengths and weaknesses of their own discourse. To demonstrate proof-of-concept, Chapter 2 introduces a prototype program responsive to practical needs, the Intelligent Academic Discourse Evaluator (IADE). Before that, however, I will provide the background necessary to better understand the potential of AWE, which is not without controversy.

2
Automated Writing Evaluation

The global dominance of academic English and the increasing importance of developing an ability to effectively communicate in writing have put a strain on second language education programs worldwide. Faced with time-consuming and copious commenting on student drafts and inspired by the promise of computerized writing assessment, many 'educational technology enthusiasts are looking to AWE as a silver bullet for language and literacy development' (Warschauer & Ware, 2006, p. 175). This chapter examines the state of the art of AWE, discussing its current affordances and demonstrating that, as is, it is not a silver bullet for meeting the writing needs of learners and teachers. Nevertheless, if carefully conceptualized at the earliest design stage, AWE can realize its full potential in writing classrooms in general and in L2 research writing in particular.

2.1 Evolution of AWE

Automated evaluation of writing, defined as 'the ability of computer technology to evaluate and score written prose' (Shermis & Burstein, 2003, p. xiii), is informed by educational measurement, computer science, and linguistics, as well as cognitive science and pedagogy. In other words, psychometric evaluations of reliability and validity, considerations of intelligent operational systems and their functionality, and models that reflect thought processes and factors considered to be most beneficial for learners – all have contributed to the development of technologies for writing evaluation. AWE technologies originated from automated essay scoring (AES) and were initially referred to as computerized essay scoring, computer essay grading, computer-assisted writing assessment, machine scoring of essays, and more recently automated essay evaluation (Shermis et al., 2013). They employ a suite of techniques that underpin automated analysis of writing, generally combining statistics, natural language processing (NLP), artificial intelligence (AI), and machine learning to assess constructed written responses based on grammar, syntactic complexity, mechanics, style, topical content, content development, deviance, and so on.

Most notable in terms of performance and efficiency and, therefore, most frequently cited are Project Essay Grade (PEG), Intelligent Essay Assessor™ (IEA), Electronic Essay Rater (e-rater®), and IntelliMetric. PEG, a pioneer in the area of automated scoring (Page, 1994), was developed in 1966 'to predict the scores that a number of competent human raters would assign to a group of similar essays' (Page, 2003, p. 47). It mainly relies on an analysis of surface linguistic features of the text and is designed based on the concepts of *trins* and *proxes*. Trins represent intrinsic variables such as grammar (parts of speech, sentence structure), fluency (essay length), and diction (variation in word length), while proxes are the approximations or correlations of those variables, referring to actual counts in student texts. Focusing on writing quality and stemming from the assumption that quality is displayed by the proxes, PEG applied multiple regression analysis to generate a score. PEG has gone through significant modifications and currently yields scores based on 300 measures that reflect the intrinsic characteristics of writing. Dictionaries, parsers, and special collections and classification schemes have also been added.[1]

In the late 1990s, the Pearson Knowledge Analysis Technologies group produced the IEA – a set of software tools developed primarily for scoring content related features of expository essays. IEA is presented as being suitable for analysis and rating of essays on topics related to science, social studies, history, business, and so on. It also provides quick customized tutorial feedback on the form-related aspects of grammar, style, and mechanics (Landauer et al., 2003). Additionally, it has the ability to detect plagiarism and deviance in essays. IEA is based on a text analysis method, Latent Semantic Analysis (LSA), and, to a lesser extent, on a number of other NLP techniques. This allows the system to score both the quality of conceptual content of traditional essays and of creative narratives (Landauer et al., 2003) as well as the quality of writing. In order to measure overall essay quality, IEA is trained on a collection of domain-representative texts.

The e-rater® is an evolution of the Educational Testing Service in 1997, which was deployed for operational scoring of the Graduate Management Admissions Test (GMAT) Analytical Writing Assessment in 1999. e-rater® analyzes the organization, sentence structure, style, and content of essays and produces a holistic score, accomplishing this with the help of a combination of statistical and NLP techniques (Burstein, 2003). For its model building, e-rater® uses a corpus-based approach,[2] the corpora containing unedited first-draft essay writing. Outputs for model building and scoring are provided by several independent modules. The syntactic module is based on a parser that captures syntactic complexity; the discourse module detects discourse-based relationship and organization with the help of cue words, terms, and syntactic structures; and the topical analysis module has the role of identifying the vocabulary use and topical content.

A product of Vantage Learning, IntelliMetric, was initially used for placement purposes and is now implemented for the rating of the Analytical Writing Assessment section of GMAT. IntelliMetric is an automated scoring system developed on the basis of AI blended with NLP and statistical technologies. It is 'a learning engine that internalizes the characteristics of the score scale [derived from a trained set of scored responses] through an iterative learning process,' creating a 'unique solution for each stimulus or prompt' (Elliot, 2003, p. 71). To attain a final score, more than 300 semantic, syntactic, and discourse level features are analyzed by this system. They are categorized into five groups: focus and unity (cohesiveness and consistency in purpose and main idea), development and elaboration (content through vocabulary use and conceptual support), organization and structure (logical development, transitional flow, relationship among parts of the response), sentence structure (syntactic complexity and variety), and mechanics and conventions (punctuation, sentence completeness, spelling, capitalization). Apart from the scoring ability, IntelliMetric modes allow for student revision and editing as well as for diagnostic feedback on rhetorical, analytical, and sentence-level dimensions. A special attribute of IntelliMetric is its ability to score constructed responses in multiple languages.

AES emerged to meet a critical need in testing contexts, and, before long, was reconfigured to generate feedback on a wide range of aspects of the writing construct. Such feedback-generating systems became known as automated writing evaluation (AWE) programs. Both AES and AWE programs and their performance abilities have been comprehensively reviewed in the literature (Chapelle & Chung, 2010; Dikli, 2006; Valenti et al., 2003). I will expand these previous reviews by introducing a wider range of examples of this technology, many of which were not commercialized and are therefore not widely applied in practice. In Figure 2.1, I place them all on a timeline that shows the increasing scope of developments in the automated evaluation of writing. I should

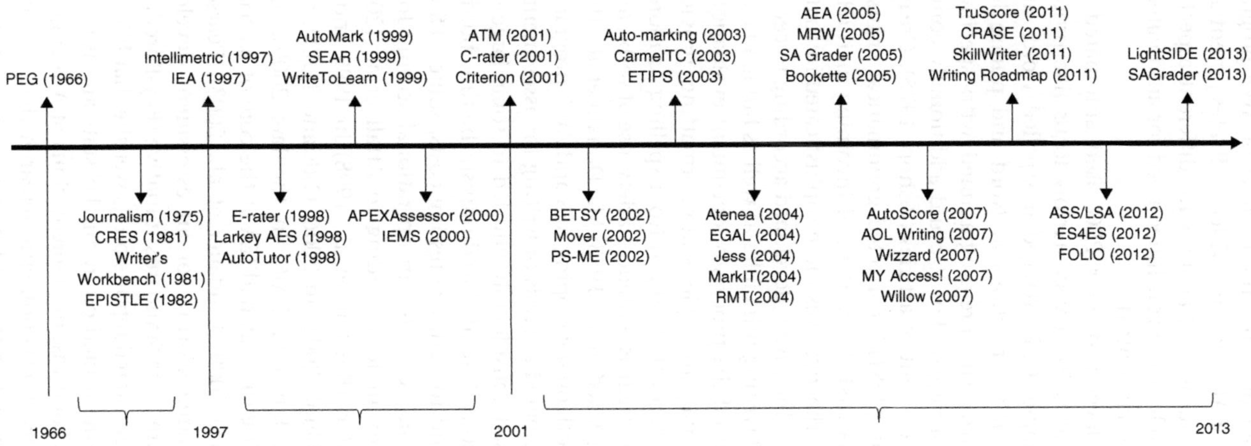

Figure 2.1 Historical development of AES and AWE systems

hasten to point out here that the number of AWE programs is higher than the number of AES systems, which indicates potential adaptability and suitability of automated analysis for different aspects of the writing construct as well as the continued need for automated feedback in different instructional contexts.

Early systems developed after PEG used automated text analysis mainly for feedback with a very narrow focus like proofreading and spelling; for example, CRES flagged misspelled words and long sentences and suggested corrections at word and phrase level (Kmcaid et al., 1981). Journalism, pre-programmed with specific knowledge, was also able to proofread, but it could additionally comment on the organization and content of articles (Bishop, 1975). Created as a business office system, EPISTLE corrected grammatical errors in outgoing letters and summarized the content of incoming mail (Heidorn et al., 1982). Writer's Workbench was more sophisticated in that it contained a set of programs, which were developed according to certain rhetorical and psychological writing principles as well as human factor principles. This software assisted the process of document evaluation and editing by proofreading, analyzing style, and reformatting, providing different types of error messages that ranged from spelling to more specific linguistic information such as sentence variety, use of verbs, and readability (Frase et al., 1981; Macdonald, 1983; MacDonald et al., 1982).

In the 1990s, work on developing AES and AWE programs continued. The focus on automated analysis of writing for assessment purposes, in particular, increased considerably and led to some large-scale present-day implementations. Intended to diminish the time burden of scoring student writing and to optimize testing costs, some AES engines have been successfully implemented in operational scoring for high-stakes assessments. For example, according to Attali et al. (2013), GMAT® began to use e-rater® (Burstein et al., 1998) in 1999 and transitioned to Intellimetric (Elliot, 2003) in 2006. GRE and TOEFL also deployed e-rater® (Attali & Burstein, 2006) in the late 2000s. Similarly, PTE (Pearson Test of English) has had IEA at the core of its scoring of written responses since 2009 (Landauer et al., 2003). Pearson has been promoting automated scoring for an assessment developed for the new Common Core State Standards Initiative (Bay-Borelli et al., 2010). Measurement Incorporated reports on its website that PEG is used as the sole writing assessment method in one US state and is being piloted in three other states. Such vast implementations of AES engines are taking place due to extensive psychometric research that demonstrates close alignment between automated and human rating, suggesting that the measurement techniques can produce reliable scores compared to those given by humans (Attali & Burstein, 2006; Burstein, 2003; Rudner et al., 2006; Shermis et al., 2010; Valenti et al., 2003).

Given their impressive technical abilities, leading AES systems have been integrated in AWE applications: IEA underpins WriteToLearn, e-rater® – Criterion℠, IntelliMetric – MyAccess!, and PEG has recently been revived and deployed in a feedback program called Folio. These commercially viable products are being increasingly used in writing classrooms, shifting the role of AWE from summative assessment to formative assessment, or assessment for learning (Chen & Cheng, 2008; Grimes & Warschauer, 2010). They offer opportunities for students to submit their writing for quick evaluation, receive individualized feedback, and interact with complementary resource features when needed (Burstein et al., 2004; Pearson Education, 2007; Vantage Learning, 2007). I will briefly review these AWE programs in terms of what they can offer to students and teachers in order to further argue that, before their functionality can be extrapolated to L2 research writing pedagogy, AWE design needs to be reconceptualized to both address existing validity concerns and to meet the demands of discipline-specific genre writing.

2.2 AWE for teaching and learning

2.2.1 The 'almighty' AWE

Automated evaluation of writing is deemed to have immense advantages both for summative and formative assessment. Formative assessment is distinguished from summative assessment, the definitions of the two revolving around differences in function and timing. Summative assessment measures students' performance at the end of a course or a program with the purpose of grading, certification, or accountability, while formative assessment is conducted during the teaching process for the purpose of identifying students' difficulties and monitoring the instructional process (Brown & Knight, 1994; Ebel & Frisbie, 1991; Torrance & Pryor, 1998). Automated analysis systems can assess student writing as well as humans do, only in a much more time and cost-effective way. The efficiency of AES has a strong appeal for higher education institutions and has become a real and viable complement to human evaluation of writing. Under the weight of policy changes and the push to common standards, institutions welcome immediate and reliable computer-based scoring, which reduces personnel, training, and facilities expenses.

Similarly, AWE applications are believed to bring change in instructional dynamics. The vendors of these programs promote them as effective supplements to process writing instruction and as vehicles of consistent writing and evaluation across the curriculum. AWE integration into the curriculum is said also to be accordant with the drive toward individualized assessment and instruction and to support process writing approaches that emphasize the value of multiple drafting (Burstein, 2012). It has been likewise suggested that AWE programs can motivate and guide student revision, foster learner autonomy, and serve as potent cognitive tools due to automated feedback (Attali & Powers, 2008), which is arguably the principal feature aimed at helping students improve their writing.

The feedback can be quite complex and can be provided with a great level of detail and explanation. Most AWE programs return the student draft with comments highlighting issues that require attention, which can be related to language errors, usage and mechanics, syntactic complexity, variation in sentence type, style, organization, idea development, conceptual content, and other writing traits (Table 2.1). This qualitative feedback is often embedded in the draft that is submitted for analysis by the student. Some programs can indicate potential errors and suggest corrections based on its training approach and/or on the student's error correction history (TechWriter); others are able to generate multilingual feedback for L2 writers (Criterion℠ and MY Access!). Students can also view numeric feedback presented as a performance summary, which usually includes a holistic score, the number of errors, and links to detailed qualitative feedback on each error category. A few programs provide the option of interactive teacher feedback; for instance, in Criterion℠ the students can solicit and receive feedback from their instructor in addition to the automated feedback. This helps them focus not only on automatically detectable errors, but also on other, more subtle aspects of writing pointed out by the teacher.

Criterion℠ is also notable for another feature – it can provide feedback even in response to new essay prompts, which is not possible in other programs since their scoring capabilities are predetermined by training methods that use collections of essays scored by human raters. Keeping in mind the focus of this book on disciplinary writing, I want to mention that the domains represented in AWE technology also vary, and include journalism (Journalism), navy (CRES), biology (SAGrader), business (EPISTLE; SAGrader), sociology (APEX Assessor), education (ETIPS), history (SAGrader), information technology (AntMover), and psychology (SAGrader, RMT) in addition to English (all others).

Table 2.1 AWE programs

AWE program	***Developer***	***Feedback***
Journalism	Bishop (1975) University of Michigan (USA)	Proofreading, organization, content
CRES	Kmcaid et al. (1981)	Spelling, words, phrases
Writer's Workbench	Frase et al. (1981) Bell Laboratories (USA)	Spelling, mechanics, diction, organization, style, prose
EPISTLE	Heidorn et al. (1982)	Grammar, content, abstract
WriteToLearn	Pearson Education (USA)	Ideas, organization, conventions, sentence fluency, word choice, writer's voice, spelling, copying, redundancy, irrelevancy
APEX Assessor	Dessus et al. (2000) Laboratorie des Sciences de L'Éducation, Université Pierre-Mendés (France)	Outline, coherence
IEMS	Ming et al. (2000) NGEE ANN Polytechnic (Singapore)	Content, style
AOL Writing Wizzard	AOL LLC	Organization, grammar, spelling
Criterion[SM]	Educational Testing Service (USA)	Syntax, discourse, topical content, lexical complexity, grammar, usage, mechanics, style
Mover	Anthony and Lashika (2003)	Move structure of RA Abstracts
PS-ME	Mason and Grove-Stephenson (2002) Birmingham University (UK)	Subject area performance
ETIPS	Riedel et al. (2003)	Content, style
MarkIT	Williams and Dreher (2004) Curtin University of Technology (Australia)	Content/concepts
RMT (from AutoTutor)	Wiemer-Hastings et al. (2004) DePaul University (USA)	Subject area performance
MY Access!	Vantage Learning (USA)	Focus and meaning, organization, content and development, language use and style, mechanics
Willow	Pérez Marín (2007)	Content/concepts
TechWriter	Napolitano and Stent (2009) Stony Brook University (USA)	Language errors
Bookette	CTB McGraw-Hill (USA)	Grammar, spelling, conventions at the sentence level
SkillWriter	Bookette Software Company (USA)	Voice, word choice, organization, ideas and content, fluency and conventions

(*continued*)

Table 2.1 Continued

AWE program	*Developer*	*Feedback*
TruScore and CRASE	Pacific Metrics (USA)	Ideas, organization, voice, word choice, sentence fluency, conventions
Writing Roadmap	CTB/McGraw-Hill (USA)	Organization, development, sentence structure, word choice, grammar, mechanics
Folio	Measurement Incorporated (USA)	Organization, support, sentence structure, word choice, mechanics
ES4ES	Ade-Ibijola et al. (2012)	Subject area performance
SAGrader	The Idea Works, Inc.	Content and ideas

AWE programs are also appealing because they include a myriad of complementary instructional tools that are intended to assist both students and teachers. Criterion^{SM} has a context-sensitive Writer's Handbook that provides additional definitions and examples of correct and incorrect use accessible to the students during revision. It also offers a Make a Plan tool with a choice of eight templates for planning strategies to assist students in their planning process. MY Access!, in turn, has an online writing coach, which evaluates student writing and provides revision goals and remediation activities for each of the writing traits, as well as an editor, which highlights errors and provides editing suggestions. It also offers a writer's checklist for guidance, scoring rubrics for self-assessment, word banks for appropriate vocabulary use, and graphical pre-writing tools for better formulation and organization of ideas. WriteToLearn has similar options; plus, it allows students to hear the text in reading passages through text-to-speech technologies and to see the translation of words and their dictionary definitions through pop-up windows on demand. Its feedback is based on an inference of semantic similarity of words and passages based on analyses of large bodies of relevant text. The WritingRoadmap has a suite of tutorials on grammar and syntax, tips for essay improvement, visualizations in the form of sentence diagrams, a thesaurus, and a spell checker. Folio also contains engaging tutorials, which are animated and grade-level appropriate, along with interactive writing activities, grammar exercises, and practice passages for revision.

A number of different options are designed for teachers as well. Teachers can set certain parameters for their assignments and select topics from the system's library representing persuasive, informative, narrative, expository, issue, and argumentative essays. In WritingRoadmap and in Criterion℠, teachers can choose from more than a hundred topics that can be used for writing practice in the classroom as well as for placement, benchmark, and exit testing. Alternatively, educators can create their own prompts on topics tailored to specific needs. In MY Access!, teachers can choose from a large pool of over 700 prompts for narrative, persuasive, informative, literary, and expository essay topics. WriteToLearn has a comprehensive database of more than 300 reading passages in science, history, language arts, social studies, and fiction, targeted at students in grades 4 through 12. Some topics are intended to prepare for high-stakes assessments: Criterion℠ offers topics that can be used for GRE® and TOEFL®, and WritingRoadmap helps prepare students for state writing assessments as well as the GED® Test, SAT®, and ACT®.

Additionally, AWE programs have powerful data-analysis and reporting features concerning student performance at the student, class, school, and in some cases even district level. Criterion℠ is in fact referred to as 'a comprehensive electronic portfolio administration system' (Shermis et al., 2010). Other programs also allow for organizing essays into individual student portfolios, storing them for quick retrieval, and generating error and score reports. The reports can also be at the level of class performance summary, group comparison, and student history, helping teachers to monitor student progress individually and as a class. Structured online training modules are available to ensure that teachers have a positive experience and that the prompts they create follow criteria that will result in effective feedback and scoring. Depending on the purpose of use and the stage in the writing process, teachers have the flexibility to impose a time limit or allow unlimited writing time (Criterion℠), turn on or off access to specific help options (WritingRoadmap), and customize trait scores or pre-set combinations of traits (CRASE). CRASE is also highly customizable in terms of building the machine scoring models and in terms of building hybrid models where the system can blend human scoring and machine scoring (Shermis & Hamner, 2012).

All these advanced functional features built into AWE, along with the vendors' claims about their numerous advantages, render this technology as almost almighty, and the applications of automated analysis of writing as potentially boundless. One of the most sensible links is between AWE and intelligent tutoring systems, and work in this direction has been under way. Willow, for instance, not only processes and scores free-text responses, but also keeps track of students' use of terms and the relationships between them, and generates conceptual models from their input, adapting its behavior to individual students

(Pérez Marín, 2007). LightSIDE (Mayfield & Penstein Rosé, 2013) is another example of future groundbreaking technologies, which will help address very specific needs without much technical training. It is an open-source, machine learning-based software package for users with no programming experience, whether educators or researchers. The package offers users a wide range of text analysis choices, including Naïve Bayes classification, support vector machines, logistic regression, and decision trees, which they can use for research as well as for practical purposes like writing assessment. Following detailed tutorials, these techniques can be employed to run multiple algorithms and extract specific writing features that are indicative of a variety of writing traits in order to model trait level and holistic scores and to generate feedback.

Finally, NLP and statistical modeling-based AWE holds great promise for applications targeting genres other than the essay, which is the text type analyzed by the programs listed in Table 2.1, except one – the Mover. Mover deviates from this even tradition in that it analyzes abstracts of journal manuscripts. Motivated by instructional needs, Anthony and Lashika (2003) developed it to be used by English language learners for academic reading and writing purposes. The name of their software reflects Swales' move terminology, and the output it generates presents learners with the move structure of abstracts (Anthony & Lashika, 2003). To develop the Mover, the authors conceptualized their approach based on Mitchell's (1997) task-experience-performance sequence, where the task was to automatically identify the rhetorical structure of abstracts, the experience was a supervised learning approach, and the performance was the evaluation of accuracy. After experimentation with various algorithms, including Decision Tree and Neural Network, the Naïve Bayes classifier was chosen as the supervised learning approach; it performed better than others, yielding an average first-order accuracy of 68 percent. The authors estimated that this could be improved to over 86 percent. Although the feedback the Mover provides is a simple display of the text split into sentences categorized as rhetorical classes, it demonstrates that it is possible to automatically detect the communicative conventions of research-related genres in the EAP tradition. This step forward motivated the development of the AWE prototype that I will introduce in Chapter 4.

2.2.2 Implementations of AWE – how does it work?

Due to the increasing demand for educational technology worldwide and the publicity of vendors, AWE programs are being implemented or at least considered for use in a growing number of institutions: elementary, middle, and high schools; community colleges; universities; national job training programs; and military establishments (Burstein et al., 2004). This ample user coverage and broad access to commercialized AWE has created some tension, where AWE is perceived as a perfect solution by some and as a threat by others. At the same time, it has motivated the emergence of a vibrant area of inquiry within the field of computer-assisted language learning (CALL) that focuses on evaluating the 'almightiness' of AWE.

Numerous studies have investigated whether AWE can facilitate improvement in L1 writing. Having conducted four studies on the use of MYAccess! by 5–11-graders over a period of 6 weeks to a full academic year, Elliot and Mikulas (2004) reported that student writing skills, as measured by performance on statewide writing assessments, significantly improved after they submitted on average 4 essays and revised them 2–5 times. Their survey results indicated that the students were highly satisfied with the automated feedback and judged it as both helpful and accurate. In Foltz et al. (1999), students used WriteToLearn to revise their essays in an undergraduate course, and their improvement in scores ranged from 0 to 33 points over an average of 3 revisions. Attali (2004) investigated how Criterion^SM^ was used nationwide by 6th–12th-graders throughout a school year and found an increase in scores for essays submitted more than once and a significant decrease in error rates, although the revisions were made mainly at the level of spelling and grammar and not so much in structure. Similarly, in Leah Rock's (2007) study, 9th graders who used Criterion^SM^ for four weeks received higher analytic scores on their essays written at the end of the study period and improved the mechanical aspects of their writing. Criterion^SM^ also reportedly facilitated the writing improvement of criminal justice students in Schroeder et al. (2008) and helped them understand their errors. Here, the final grades of two out of three experimental groups were significantly higher than those of the comparison group. The results of a regression analysis suggested that the participants' grades improved by one-third of a point with each submission to Criterion^SM^.

The state of West Virginia in the US has adopted automated evaluation of writing in three ways: to score large-scale state tests, to connect formative assessment to summative assessment, and to extend teachers' professional development by means of using this technology and validating automated scores (Rich et al., 2013). For formative assessment purposes, the Writing Roadmap™ was adapted into a customized AWE version called West Virginia Writes™2.0. Rich et al. (2013) cite three studies that found positive effects of West Virginia Writes™2.0 on writing performance. One study focused on the relationship between summative assessment and the use of this tool in instruction, revealing that students were able to improve their writing due to regular AWE-enhanced practice and immediate feedback (Rich et al., 2008). The second study involving West Virginia Writes™ 2.0 found a positive association between the use of the tool and student achievement as measured by the summative online writing test deployed in the state (White et al., 2010). A subsequent study conducted by the same group of researchers developed a linear regression model to examine the impact of AWE classroom implementation, which indicated that the relationship between using AWE and students' online writing test scores was statistically significant, though moderate (White et al., 2011). In addition, Writing Roadmap™ appears to increase motivation and autonomous learning (Tang & Rich, 2011). Based on these research results, this program was recommended for continued integration as a formative assessment application.

However, there are also works that raise questions with regards to the impact of AWE. Warschauer and Grimes (2008) present evidence that is not so supportive of the effectiveness of Criterion℠ and MY Access! Although both these programs left a positive imprint on students by motivating them to write and revise, no significant improvement was found, and the revisions focused mainly on spelling, punctuation, and grammatical errors, similar to Attali's (2004) findings. When Shermis et al. (2004) compared the performance of high school students who were randomly assigned to either a treatment group or a control group, they also found no significant differences between the two groups.

Research on the use of AWE with L2 learners can be considered in its infancy. Existing studies are relatively narrow in focus and less sound in the quality of their research methodology, targeting small samples of participants and concentrating mostly on perceptions. For instance, Fang (2010) reported somewhat ambiguous findings regarding the attitudes of 45 low-proficiency EFL learners towards MY Access!'s feedback. While the participants perceived automated feedback as having a positive effect on their writing skill development, most of them indicated that they would still prefer teachers' feedback. Along the same lines, Yang (2004) reported that while most of her 300 participants valued the instant feedback of this program, they complained about it being fixed, repetitive, and unspecific compared to teacher feedback. Repetitiveness and complexity of various functions of MY Access! was noted as an issue by Lai (2010) as well.

Some studies attempted to evaluate AWE effectiveness though comparisons with other computer software. For instance, Tsou (2008) examined MY Access! in contrast with Microsoft Word, analyzing post-test scores, a student questionnaire, and teacher interviews. In a similar manner, Yeh et al. (2007) used a questionnaire and self-reported checklists to compare improvement in student writing completed with MY Access! and with a bilingual concordancer. Given that these writing tools are intended for different purposes – MY Access! for the use of automated feedback, the concordancer for queries of word usage, and Microsoft Word for word processing – claims of helpfulness of AWE feedback in these studies are difficult to justify and hardly yield to generalization. Another comparative study is that of Lai (2010). Although the data was limited to 22 questionnaires and interviews, this study is more insightful in that it compared the effectiveness of automated feedback by MY Access! with peer feedback, alternating them over a period of 16 weeks. Lai found that Taiwanese college learners of English made more revisions in their descriptive and narrative essays on the basis of peer feedback, especially paying attention to the focus and meaning category. Overall, peer feedback was preferred over automated feedback and led to greater improvement. Interestingly, the participants indicated that they would have been more motivated had the peer feedback been scored. Perhaps that is why they used the automated feedback more frequently to improve content and rhetorical development. Chen and Cheng (2008), who also examined the use of MY Access! with Taiwanese college learners of English, presented similar findings. Their research employed a more complex methodology, using questionnaires, focus group interviews with the students, individual interviews with the instructors, students' writing samples, and MY Access!'s scores and feedback data. Their findings highlight major differences in students' perceptions of AWE usefulness and in instructors' implementation choices. Most importantly, though, Chen and Cheng reveal the role of the context and of the human factor, showing how pedagogical practices can affect students' attitudes towards AWE and, consequently, impact its effectiveness.

An ongoing longitudinal mixed-methods study of Criterion^{SM} by Hegelheimer et al. (2011) reports positive preliminary findings about both students' and teachers' perspectives. Their student participants expressed confidence in using this program and satisfaction with its feedback, explaining that it helped them better understand their weaknesses in writing. They also self-reported that they were better able to find and correct language errors after having used Criterion^{SM}.

At the same time, the students made negative comments regarding fixed feedback or unclear suggestions, which is a drawback that has also been noted for MY Access! (Lai, 2010; Yang, 2004). The teacher participants' use of Criterion^{SM} varied in scope and approach. Some used it more extensively for a variety of activities such as pre-writing strategy training, peer review, grammar lecturing, and grading. Others used it mainly for the purpose of error correction. Classroom and teacher observations indicate that Criterion^{SM} may influence instructors' teaching approach.

So far, AWE evaluation research has been ambivalent and has not lent clear support as to whether AWE is effective or not. But why is the picture not so encouraging? To answer this question, I will further consider some views on writing teaching and assessment, which can help explain a few issues that have surfaced through research. If not accounted for, those issues are likely to re-occur when this technology is put to action in different contexts.

2.3 Understanding AWE issues

2.3.1 Apprehension toward AWE

Despite the practical benefits and the plethora of additional features, major reservations and continuous skepticism have been leveled at AWE. The claims about AWE 'almightiness' made by the promoters of commercial products are questioned by many in the writing pedagogy community (Ericsson & Haswell, 2006; Jones, 2006; McGee, 2006; Perelman, 2012a). First, the very fact that the computer is allowed to score is excoriated. For instance, Neal (2011) doubts the computer's ability to assess writing ability because it is not capable of replicating the cognitive processes activated in the brain when humans make evaluative judgments about the quality of writing. 'A human rater and a computer may record a similar number, but their scores mean very different things' because 'humans score writing quality, while computers can only identify aspects of surface text quality,' comments Condon (2013, pp. 101, 102). Second, it is contended that the social and communicative dimensions of writing are not supported in scoring systems since they are grounded in a cognitive information-processing model (Ericsson, 2006). Student texts are evaluated automatically against generic writing traits, eliminating the value of human audiences in real-world contexts. These systems cannot read for meaning, identify communicative intent, evaluate the quality of argumentation, or verify factual correctness. 'While they may promise consistency, they distort the very nature of writing as a complex and context-rich interaction between people' (CCCC, 2006), which means that using them as an audience for a writer is at the very least unwise (Herrington & Moran, 2001; Perelman, 2012b). Third, it is presumed that, although it is unlikely that students will trick the software, they may consciously or unconsciously adjust their writing to meet the assessment criteria of the software. Fourth, teachers may feel pressured to support such adjustment in an attempt to raise test scores (CCCC, 2006). This might consequently undermine teachers' theoretical and practical knowledge.

Cheville (2004) has voiced a very critical stance towards automated essay evaluation. She is concerned that 'early acculturation to such a program might undermine the language and learning of students' (p. 48) and that the machine analyzer is calibrated to static compositional features and formulaic expression, heavily subordinating meaning. Therefore, Cheville suspects, automated scoring may encourage students to pay more attention to the surface features that are more easily detected by the scoring engine than to the construction of meaning for communicative purposes. She even fears that 'automated scoring technologies make it possible to eliminate the evaluative influence of teachers altogether' and that 'what we know and what we do in the classroom is in jeopardy' (p. 49). Her prognosis is that 'assessments produced by private corporations will dictate how and what our students know' (p. 51). Even more drastic are Herrington and Moran (2012) who compellingly argue that such programs should be expelled from writing classrooms.

Many such claims lack substantiation, however, being either hypothetical or weakly supported. Herrington and Moran (2012), for instance, who found that Criterion℠ may point to errors that are not in fact errors, base their pungent remarks on findings that cannot be generalized for a simple and obvious reason – only one essay was submitted for analysis to Criterion℠, and it is not even clear who authored the essay and how representative that student was of the targeted learners. Furthermore, Criterion℠, MY Access! and WriteToLearn were reviewed as exemplars of writing assessment technologies in terms of their strengths and weaknesses to promote writing as a socially situated activity, which can be functionally and formally diverse (Vojak et al., 2011). This review is a rather limited analysis because it relies solely on observations from trying out programs or, if not available, their demos. Vojak et al. (2011) lack strength of evidence as they followed a methodological path similar to Herrington and Moran's (2012) – 'our research team submitted a short essay in response to a prompt [...]. We received a score of 4.3 out of 6. We then tacked onto our initial essay several unrelated paragraphs and received a score of 5.4 out of 6. [...] In another instance, our research team wrote and submitted a nonsense essay' (p. 103).

Chapman (2013), having reviewed an edited volume with 27 essays on writing assessment, explains that criticisms of automated assessment spring from discordances between college composition practitioners and educational measurement researchers who approach the writing construct differently. The latter view writing as a construct that contains quantifiable features, or 'aspects of writing that, in the aggregate, embody the meaning of writing for the assessment' (Williamson, 2013, p. 166). The measurement of the features in AES can help make relatively accurate predictions of holistic evaluation by human raters.[3] The former, however, contend against such metrics, arguing that the writing construct can by no means be broken down into formulas and evaluated computationally because writing is a deeply human and creative activity. From this perspective, the writing construct includes 'the rhetorical ability to integrate an understanding of audience, context, and purpose when both writing and reading texts; the ability to think and obtain information critically; the ability to effectively employ multiple writing strategies; the ability to learn and use the conventions appropriate to a specific genre of writing; and the ability to write in various and evolving media,' but '[t]here is no construct of AES that comes close to assessing these skills' (Perelman, 2012a, p. 129). Yet, for a machine to measure the same construct that humans do, it is important to have a clear understanding of how they evaluate writing. This is still a challenge in both practice and research, which show that human raters are often idiosyncratic in their interpretations of the evaluation criteria (see Bridgeman, 2013).

The problem is that what composition practitioners and educational measurement researchers 'have in common is a clear view of their own fields but an understanding of the other' (Chapman, 2013, p. 183).[4] Concerned with this lack of shared conceptions, which discourages AWE as an innovative classroom practice, Elliot and Klobucar (2013) accentuate that 'understanding [automated essay evaluation] is a complex endeavor that can best be understood in the context of research traditions: Applied Linguistics; Business Administration and Management; Cognitive Psychology and Psycholinguistics; Computer and Information Sciences; Educational Assessment, Testing, and Measurement; Psychometrics and Quantitative Psychology, and Rhetoric and Composition/Writing studies' (p. 17).

The intersection of all these fields needs to become more transparent indeed, and perhaps the first bridge that needs to be built is that between instruction and assessment. Note that the negative reactions from the rhetoric and composition community refer largely to the constraints of automated scoring engines used for testing. Condon (2013), an expert in computer-enhanced writing pedagogies, hastens to explain his own and others' criticisms of AWE by highlighting that the real problem is related to construct representation in tests, which is different from the way the writing construct is understood by the writing community, rather than the nature of the scoring.

> Whether a 25-minute essay written on an unfamiliar topic is scored by a human or a computer – or by a human and a computer – it is still a poor representation of writing and can provide only severely limited information about the writer. [...] Ultimately, the focus of large-scale, nationally normed tests to judge a sample of writing is itself too constraining to be useful within an educational context, where the focus is on improving the competencies of a writer. Thus, the type of test AES can score is in conflict with the needs of a student to learn how to improve as a writer and of a teacher, who needs to know how to facilitate that improvement.
>
> The controversy over AES may hide the real issue, but it is nevertheless a significant part of the conversation between the goals involved in teaching writing as a full, rich construct and the goals involved in designing large-scale tests of writing. (Condon, 2013, p. 101)

If the adversaries of automated evaluation delve into the essence of this technology, they may refrain from drawing radical conclusions about completely abolishing it. It is not the technology that should be condemned but 'the vision of writing and assessment [...] in an era of testing and accountability' (Vojak et al., 2011, p. 108) and 'the practices that have led to the development and use of AES as we know it today' (Condon, 2013, p. 105). The 'discourse of rejection' (Whithaus, 2006, p. 167) does not offer a tenable path. In support of this thought, Deane (2013a) argues:

> [I]t would be a mistake to focus only on polar positions. Writing is a complex skill, assessed for various audiences and purposes. AES is one instantiation of a larger universe of methods for automatic writing analysis. A more nuanced view may be necessary to assess accurately how automated essay scoring – and other forms of automated writing evaluation – fit into education and assessment. (p. 8)
>
> [T]here is room to expand the range of features that enter into AES to make it more responsive to a richer understanding of the

> construct. But it is also important to recognize that AES can be deployed in innovative ways that might provide better support for writer cognition and integrate more fruitfully with the social practices that encourage quality writing. In other words, much of the promise of the technology arises in a different range of applications in which there might be less perceived conflict between AES and the teaching of writing as a humanistic practice. (p. 20)

A new outlook and a great deal of theoretical and research efforts are needed to reconcile the AWE dispute and, most importantly, to ensure that this technology realizes not only its technological potential, but also its full learning potential. As Ramineni and Williamson (2013) see it, a 'healthy tension' will continue, and it 'will be successfully navigated only if the legitimate goals and concerns of multiple perspectives are represented and clear expectations for what constitutes satisfactory performance of AES systems for assessment are made clear and explicit' (p. 37). AWE is the kind of technology that is capable to mediate writing instruction and assessment to the benefit of developing writers and, from the 'many roads to literacy, [it] can and arguably should be viewed as but one tool to help students and their instructors along the way' (Elliot & Klobucar, 2013, p. 30).

2.3.2 Unfounded transfer of automated scoring to AWE

Overall, the opponents of implementing AWE programs in writing instruction express significant concerns that are related to washback, defined as the influence of assessment on teaching and learning (Shohamy et al., 1996) and as 'the extent to which the introduction and use of a test influences language teachers and learners to do things they would not otherwise do that promote or inhibit language learning' (Messick, 1996, p. 241). Negative washback concerns are not unreasonable since AWE programs function on the basis of scoring engines initially developed for summative assessment purposes. This means that AES technology has been transferred to learning contexts with the assumption that it is suitable for high quality formative assessment. It is also relatively simple to transform the analysis of writing features into feedback comments. The feedback, then, is nothing but a direct output of the scoring system, which is why it does not necessarily suit all pedagogical purposes (Warschauer & Ware, 2006, p. 166). Grimes and Warschauer (2010) argue that it is absolutely imperative to distinguish between AWE and 'its scoring technology [...] because they serve different purposes' (p. 5). Weigle (2013a) also insists on making a clear distinction between automated 'scoring – that is, using automated tools to produce a score that is intended to be equivalent to a human score on the same essay for the purpose of some decision, such as admission or placement – and feedback: the use of automated tools to provide information that will help students improve their writing' (p. 41). Unfortunately, the scoring engines in programs like Criterion[SM], MY Access!, and WriteToLearn were extrapolated based on functionality without special regard to these significant differences in purpose and without explicit guidance for instructional use.

Furthermore, because assessment (be it summative or formative) is never context-free, washback is inter-related with ecology, a concept used to describe 'phenomena in their context and to understand both the context and the interactions that create that context' (Garner & Borg, 2005, p. 121). The concept of ecology of writing where assessments are context-sensitive (see Huot, 1996; Wardle & Roozen, 2012) is a strong belief among writing pedagogues, but not explicitly tackled. In the dispute between AWE supporters and opponents, little consideration is given to contextual factors that may cause one or another kind of washback. Because of the transfer of automated scoring across purposes, disregarding the ecology of implementation in target contexts, AWE programs are often misused, as has been tangentially documented in much of the research discussed in the previous section. For instance, Warschauer and Grimes (2008) noted that some teachers used AWE as an explicit form of test preparation. Others simply adapted these programs for their scoring, not feedback capabilities, being convinced that 'it doesn't matter if [students] get a lot of feedback' (p. 32), thus obviating the need for much revision. There were also some paradoxes. First, teachers participating in their study valued revision, but scheduled little time for it. Therefore, it is not surprising that students focused on grammar and mechanics; to revise at more complex levels, students need to become more deeply cognitively engaged, and for that they would need sufficient time revising with the AWE tool. Warschauer and Grimes explain that providing limited revision time is consistent with more general school practices, where revision 'invariably focuses on a quick correction pointed by the teacher or peer' (p. 29). Second, although teachers expressed very positive views about AWE, they rarely used it in the classroom often because much of the curriculum was in reading and language arts and not in composition. Another reason was that some writing tasks (newspaper articles, brochures, letters) were representative of genres outside the AWE program's analytical capabilities.

Warschauer and Ware (2006) argue that 'any classroom innovation, and especially those using technology, will likely have its best effect if it is fully integrated into instruction' (p. 169). 'No matter how much teachers claim that they like a type of software [...], if they find various reasons not to use the software, it cannot be expected to have much impact' (Warschauer & Grimes, 2008, p. 28). Decades ago Pufahl (1984) surmised that computers would not be of use for writing improvement if teachers failed to effectively embed them into instruction. Indeed, Shermis et al. (2004) speculated that their discouraging results were partly due to poor implementation and high attrition, with only 112 of the 537 treatment students completing all the essays. The researchers estimated that if students had written five more writing assignments each, their performance would have significantly improved. This may also have been the case in Attali (2004) and Warschauer and Grimes (2008), where the students did not exploit the revision capabilities of the AWE programs; 71 and 72 percent of the students, respectively, submitted their essay to the system only once, without revising it. In Rich et al. (2008), half of the students did not use the Writing Roadmap™ in class at all.

In contexts where AWE implementation is more rigorous, the technology appears to benefit both students and teachers. Chen and Cheng (2008) suggest that when MY Access! is used at earlier stages of drafting and revision, with teacher and peer feedback provided at a later point of the writing process, the students perceive it more favorably. Hegelheimer et al. (2011) find that when teachers adopt Criterion℠ for formative assessment, they see it as a suitable tool despite differences in the way they integrate it. Moreover, some teachers explain that Criterion℠'s detailed and more or less accurate feedback on grammar and mechanics saves them class time and allows them to focus on more complex issues like content development.

Some concerns raised regarding AWE use in writing classes may be alleviated if future programs are context-sensitive and initially conceptualized with the needs of the targeted students and teachers in mind. Shermis et al. (2013) recommend that prior to developing such systems, those involved should exercise such considerations as ecological settings (state-level assessment or in-class writing), tasks (timed content-area essay or expository writing), audience (unknown test rater or classroom teacher), and measurable skills (use of appropriate writing conventions or content-area knowledge) (p. 4). In such a way, developers will foreground principled implementation and will make it possible to substantiate the potential of AWE with appropriate evidence of validity, which is major factor feeding the AWE debate.

2.3.3 AWE validity

In the context of assessment, validity is defined as 'an overall evaluative judgment of the degree to which empirical evidence and theoretical rationales support the adequacy and appropriateness of interpretations and actions based on test scores or other modes of assessment' (Messick, 1989, p. 13). Bachman (1990) explains that 'such evidence can include but is not limited to various forms of reliabilities' (p. 96). However, evidence accumulated to support AWE validity is still weak, and this problem is related to the issue of unfounded transfer from AES to AWE (Cotos, 2012).

In the case of AES, the same measure is generally used to evaluate both reliability and validity. This measure is agreement between human-computer scores and scores assigned by different human raters. Correlations and agreement rates between the scoring engine and human raters are relatively high, cross-validated correlations between the scoring engines generally ranging from .70 to .90 and often being in the .80–.85 range (Dikli, 2006; Elliot, 2003; Landauer et al., 2003; Page & Petersen, 1995; Shermis & Hamner, 2012). Automated scores also behave relatively well when compared with external measures such as standardized tests and some non-test measures (Keith, 2003; Weigle, 2010, 2013b). Construct validity and its association with writing instructional activities (Attali & Burstein, 2006; Page et al., 1995) have also been within the scope of automated scoring research.

When it comes to AWE, validity has largely been judged based on the same evidence of reliability that is derived from psychometrically-driven and de-contextualized research comparing automated and human scores (Keith, 2003; Warschauer & Ware, 2006). Such evidence of system efficiency and accuracy is necessary, especially for evaluation inference assumptions (Xi, 2010), but it is not the only prerequisite attribute for valid interpretations of AWE use for non-summative assessment purposes. Plus, much system-centric research has been conducted primarily by commercial or non-for-profit companies, which are vested in marketing their products. This is why Warschauer and Ware (2006) rightfully warn that 'research conducted to date should be considered with a highly critical eye' (p. 7).

While automated scoring reliability research satisfies the validity requirement whereby developers of these systems must furnish relevant evidence in support of scoring for summative assessment, it does not satisfy the same requirement for formative assessment. Shermis et al. (2013) expect that future research will contribute to evaluation of writing in learning contexts in contrast to only the evaluation of writing in assessment contexts as interest in automated evaluation 'shifts from that of summative evaluation to a more formative role' (p. 10). Since validity is a complex judgment grounded in multifaceted evidence, relevant empirical backing for AWE formative assessment use is certainly needed. Such backing could be obtained by gathering appropriate evidence integrated in a manifold validity argument (Chapelle et al., Enright, & Jamieson, 2010; Kane, 2006, 2013; Williamson et al., 2012), which has to be developed by answering specific questions about different aspects of validity. Elliot (2013) and Xi (2010) exemplify topics and questions for this type of inquiry, some of which are beginning to be addressed. For example, Chapelle et al. (2013), who also argue that validation of AWE requires a comprehensive argument-based approach, formulate interpretive arguments for two different AWE programs and present empirical backing for assumptions related to ramification, explanation, and utilization inferences. The findings from some of the research reviewed in the previous section, although not interpreted as validity argument evidence, also shed light on the latter inference by presenting evidence related to usefulness of AWE for improvement in writing performance, language learning gains, and impact on teaching and learning.[5]

AWE argument-based validation research is only at its outset, but the conceptual tools of a validity argument are especially well-suited to evaluating AWE-based assessment not only because they provide a framework for formulating inferences about use, but also because the evidence generated as backing to support interpretations and uses can inform more grounded conceptual AWE design. This way, it will be a matter of endorsing a warranted and principled extrapolation as opposed to simple transfer of scoring to feedback. To ensure that AWE programs are beneficial for learning, their design should, first and foremost, integrate relevant theoretical tenets and targeted learner needs. For L2 writing, it is arguably a problem that AWE programs, and their scoring systems in particular, were initially designed for native speakers and then used with language learners without substantial grounding in second language acquisition theory. Second, it is of concern that the machine analyzers are calibrated to static compositional features and formulaic expressions, potentially subordinating meaning (Cheville, 2004), and that the form-focused feedback is not meant to direct learners' attention to meaning. AWE programs need to extend their analysis and feedback capabilities to include a substantial emphasis on the contextual richness and functional meanings of discourse. Third, the analysis and feedback generated by AWE systems have been limited to one genre – the prototypical five-paragraph essay, which is not always the writing goal. In different educational contexts, especially in higher education, L2 writers are expected to produce different academic genres; and to master those, they would benefit from genre-specific feedback pointing to rhetorical shifts that are more sophisticated and subtle than thesis and topic sentences.

All these issues have had their share in the existing resistance towards AWE, but the scarcity of validity evidence reinforces the AWE debate since many arguments, although sound and reasonable, have yet to be adequately rebutted or supported. Scholars have called for understanding how AWE can facilitate learning and teaching goals through contextualized studies of *how* it works rather than *if* it works (c.f., Chen & Cheng, 2008; Grimes & Warschauer, 2008; Warschauer & Ware, 2006). This means that the evaluation of AWE programs should involve more complex analyses to include not only validation of the scoring system independent of the context of application, but also validation of the scoring system used in the application context (Chung & Baker, 2003, p. 27). Construing automated evaluation as a complement to assessment, summative and formative, can facilitate mutual knowledge and a productive discussion about the potential merits of this technology (Attali, 2013).

Weigle (2013a) affirms that AWE 'is here to stay, and the focus should be on continuing to improve both the human and technological sides of the equation' (p. 50). At present, practitioners should set realistic and consistent expectations of AWE performance and inspect the criteria used for scores and feedback generation before deciding whether it is useful in instructional contexts (Burstein, 2012). Looking into the future, it seems inevitable that AWE will undergo continuous transformations. Given the need for validity evidence that would reflect the construct definition valued by teachers as being true to the meaning of humanistic writing as well as the need for technologies that would be decidedly useful for developing writers, forthcoming AWE applications will need to be designed in view of a conceptual framework which integrates pedagogical needs identified in target instructional contexts with relevant theoretical premises.

One major step forward would be redefining the construct currently used in computational modeling to account for writing as a complex activity 'where reasoning skills, writing processes, genre practices, and the cultural and social contexts in which genres develop take center stage' (Deane, 2013a, p. 9). Deane (2013b) recommends that modeling aspects of the writing construct should be informed by a socio-cognitive approach and that the construct-based feature sets for machine processing should be genre-specific (p. 308). I adhere to this position, and later in this volume I will canvass a design space for a new genre-based AWE, where concepts from different theoretical and operational perspectives synergistically merge together in a conceptual framework that is responsive to the challenges of L2 research writing pedagogy as well as to some broader concerns articulated in this chapter.

3
Conceptualizing Genre-Based AWE for L2 Research Writing

This chapter presents a conceptual model for the design of genre-based AWE for L2 research writing. The model is needs-based and combines theoretical and operational frameworks. The theoretical framework underscores desired learning phenomena, drawing from Systemic Functional Linguistics (SFL), the Interactionist Approach to Second Language Acquisition (SLA), and Skill Acquisition Theory (SAT). I discuss these theories here in terms of their main tenets as well as in terms of their relevance to L2 writing, indicating areas that could be strengthened by genre-based AWE.

The operational framework contributes with operative solutions to enhance the theoretical constructs that are generally underrepresented in instruction. It integrates three perspectives: formative assessment, Intelligent Computer-Assisted Language Learning (ICALL), and Evidence-Centered Design (ECD). Formative assessment establishes the roles automated feedback has to fulfil, the conditions it has to satisfy, and the qualities it has to possess in order to be effective. ICALL applications and research inform about the different types of intelligent feedback that can help better address individual learner needs. Finally, the ECD framework offers conceptual clarity for the design of new AWE and constitutes a valid approach to operational efficiency based on evidence obtained from learners' performance on a given writing task.

3.1 Theoretical framework

3.1.1 Systemic-Functional Linguistics

Systemic-Functional Linguistics (SFL) has already been introduced in Chapter 1, where it was presented as a pedagogical approach to teaching genre writing. Here, I consider its value as a theory that treats language as social semiotics central to communicative activity. Concerned with how language serves communication rather than how its grammatical structure elements and their combinations abide by certain rules, SFL forefronts the role of language functions to explain how people exchange meanings through the use of language. Language is thus a systematic semantic resource for expressing meanings, called meaning potential (Halliday, 1971). People encode meanings in their oral and written discourse through the use of functional language, where functional means 'language that is doing some job in some context, as opposed to isolated words or sentences' (Halliday & Hasan, 1989, p. 10). Contexts are interactive events of social exchange of meanings encapsulated in texts 'through a systematic relationship between the social environment on the one hand, and the functional organization of language on the other' (Halliday & Hasan, 1989, p. 11). They define how meaning potential is realized in texts, determining the language choices made to express particular meanings.

The semantic system of language is organized into functional components identified as ideational, interpersonal, and textual (Halliday, 2007). The ideational component includes experiential meaning, which reflects a representation of reality as apprehended in one's experience, and logical meaning, which refers to the expression of fundamental logical relations among ideational elements. In its interpersonal function, language is a way of acting, in that it is a piece of action between interlocutors. The textual component comprises features that make the text a text: semantic and grammatical balance, thematic structure, information focus, and so on. Halliday (1989b) explains that these 'strands of meaning are all interwoven in the fabric of discourse' and asserts that 'every sentence in a text is multifunctional' (p. 23). The functional meanings characterize the relation of texts to their contexts and are systematically related to the abstract components of field (what is going on), tenor (who is involved), and mode (role assigned to language). The field is expressed through the experiential function, the tenor – through the interpersonal function, and the mode – through the textual function in the semantic system.

Another important notion in SFL is that of register, considered to be a semantic concept referring to the meanings that are associated with the field, mode, and tenor of a particular context. Register is 'a variety according to use [...] determined by the nature of activity in which language is functioning' (Halliday, 1989a, p. 43). The semantics of registers can differ, and so can their lexico-grammatical features that realize certain meanings. Registers may have indexical features in the form of particular lexical or grammatical signals. For example, *once upon a time* is an index that denotes a tale. The functions of a research article introduction can be indexed by such expressions as *increasing interest in*, *no work has been reported on*, and *the purpose of this study was*. Furthermore, in some registers, the number of possible functional meanings and their linguistic realizations may be limited, while in others they are not really constrained. All texts are different from one another because every instance of language use is in some sense unique. At the same time, as Halliday theorizes, any text is in some way similar to other texts.

Martin (1992) extends the notion of register, defining it as a 'metafunctionally organized connotative semiotic between language and genre' (p. 502). Viewed as constraining the possible combinations of field, mode, and tenor variables, genre is considered by systemic functionalists a semiotic system underlying register. At an abstract level, it 'represents the verbal strategies used to accomplish social purposes of many kinds. These strategies can be thought of in terms of stages through which one moves in order to realize a genre' (Martin, 1985, p. 251). They are known as schematic, generalized structures (Hasan, 1978; Martin, 1985; Ventola, 1982) representing ways in which texts perform the functions of given genres in given contexts. For example, according to Ventola (1982), the schematic structure of service encounters consists of:

Greeting (exchange of *hello, good morning*)
Attendance allocation (addressing the next customer: *Next please*)
Service bid (offer of service: *How can I help you?*)
Service (statement of needs: *Yes, I'm looking for*)
Resolution (decision to or not to buy: *Yes, I'll have the*)
Pay (exchange of payment)
Goods handover (exchange of goods)
Closing (exchange of *Thanks*)
Good-bye (exchange of *Bye*)

The sequence of these schematic structure elements may vary. Some elements may be obligatory and some optional. Hasan (1989) argues that 'the obligatory elements define the genre to which a text belongs' (p. 62). The optional elements, however, are not random. They can occur as predicted by some attribute of the contextual configuration, that is, by some values that realize field, tenor, and mode. In other words, the schematic structures are generated by the register. Martin (1985) inverts this formulation to say that the elements of schematic structure determine particular values of field, mode, and tenor and that 'the elements themselves are generated by genre networks' (p. 252). Whatever the theoretical interpretation, what is important to acknowledge is the direct relationship between the values of register and schematic structure.

3.1.2 Interaction approach to second language acquisition

The Interaction Hypothesis emphasizes the role of the linguistic environment and of learners' internal processes in the acquisition of L2 (Long, 1983, 1996, 2007). It draws from the Input Hypothesis (Krashen, 1985) and the Output Hypothesis (Swain, 1985, 1995) and has evolved from a hypothesis, that is 'an idea about a single phenomenon' (VanPatten & Williams, 2007, p. 5), to a model (Block, 2003; Ramirez, 2005) or paradigm (Byrnes, 2005). Carroll (1999) even calls it the Interaction Theory. Gass and Mackey (2007) refer to it as the Interaction Approach (IA), explaining that it 'is a model in the sense that it describes the processes involved when the learners encounter input, are involved in interaction, and receive feedback and produce output. However, it is moving towards the status of a theory in the sense that it also attempts to explain why interaction and learning can be linked, using cognitive concepts [...] such as noticing, working memory, and attention' (p. 176).

The major concepts of IA are input, interaction, feedback, and output. Input, or the target language to which learners are exposed, assumes a central role in any SLA theory and 'is perhaps the single most important concept of second language acquisition' (Gass, 1997, p. 1). An underlying tenet of the IA is that 'the input to the learner coupled with the learner's manipulation of the input through interaction forms a basis for language development' (Gass, 1997, p. 87). Long (1996) argues that the input has to provide both positive evidence in the form of 'target-like models' (Mackey, 2006, p. 406) and negative evidence in the form of 'direct or indirect information about what is ungrammatical and/or unacceptable' (Gor & Long, 2009, p. 445). Such evidence becomes available through interaction.

During interaction, which is in itself a language use context, learners' attention is drawn to problematic aspects of their language production. They notice a gap (Schmidt & Frota, 1986), or a 'mismatch between the input and their own organization of the target language' (Gass & Mackey, 2007, p. 184), and that 'provok[es] adjustments to linguistic form, conversational structure, message content [...] until an acceptable level of understanding is achieved' (Long, 1996, p. 418). In other terms, learners engage in negotiation of meaning. They adjust their L2 use based on feedback from the interlocutor, which either confirms that the meaning was successfully conveyed or points to communication failure.

Feedback is an essential aspect of interaction, and it is generally viewed as a form of negative evidence that can help learners notice the mismatch between the target language and their own interlanguage form (Mackey, 2006, p. 408). Interactional feedback can be explicitly provided in the form of corrections and metalinguistic explanations. It can also be implicit, taking the form of confirmation checks, clarification requests, comprehension checks, or recasts (see Gass et al., 2005; Mackey et al., 2000; Oliver & Mackey, 2003). Such feedback is valuable in that it can stimulate learners to generate hypotheses concerning the nature of their problematic L2 use.

Output 'serves as a means of hypothesis testing' (Gass, 1997, p. 7). It gives learners the opportunity to produce language and make meaning. After having used a language form unsuccessfully and after having created a certain hypothesis based on the received feedback, learners are pushed to modify their linguistic form and produce more precise and appropriate output – that is, comprehensible output (Swain, 1985). Modified output is useful provided that learners see the connection between their erroneous form, the feedback, and the revised output (Carroll, 2001; Gass & Mackey, 2006). Continued production of output is important because, in the long run, it is expected to lead to automaticity.

Traditionally, interaction referred to learners' engagement in conversations with interlocutors. Ellis (1999) expanded the idea of interaction from interpersonal to that of intrapersonal interaction, that is 'interaction that can occur in our minds, [...] and, more covertly, when different modules of the mind interact to construct an understanding of or a response to some phenomena' (p. 1). Chapelle (1998, 2001, 2007) connected these concepts to learner-computer interaction, showing how IA constructs can be enhanced to facilitate language learning with the help of computers. Specifically, the linguistic features in the input can be made salient through highlighting, glosses, hyperlinks, and pictorial or video representations. The input itself can be automatically adapted or modified through restatements, repetitions, non-verbal prompts, change of presentation modes, and the like. Interaction can also be enhanced through mouse clicks and hypertext links that provide learners with opportunities to request help on demand, which offers them immediate assistance during the learning process with explanations, examples, definitions, concordancing lines, and so on.

3.1.3 Skill Acquisition Theory

The acquisition of a skill is in essence a form of learning that elicits cognitive activity. Skill Acquisition Theory (SAT) is concerned with how learning progresses from the first intentional exposure to a particular behavior to proficient performance of that behavior. Behaviors can include any non-innate responses ranging from overt physical actions like driving a car to covert mental processes like solving a mathematical problem (Newell & Rosenbloom, 1981).[1] Consequently, SAT has found application in various research directions in psychology (behaviorism, cognitivism, connectionism) as well as in practical applications that involve explicit instruction (sports, industry, teaching).

SAT is a theory of cognitive representation, which is believed to be constructed by firsthand experience with a task. The theoretical premise is that 'learning a wide variety of skills shows remarkable similarity in development from initial representation of knowledge through initial changes in behavior to eventual fluent, spontaneous, largely effortless, and highly skilled behavior' (DeKeyser, 2007a, p. 97). Cognitive scientists view skill acquisition as a function of automaticity of operating processes (Anderson, 1995) and attribute the similarity in the acquisition of different skills to a cognitive architecture that they construe as a production system model, which underlies the cognitive processes activated when learning to perform a task. This cognitive architecture embodies three consecutive stages of development, all different in the nature of knowledge and use. They are interchangeably referred to with different terms: cognitive, associative, and autonomous (Fitts & Posner, 1967); declarative, procedural, and automatic (Anderson, 1983); or presentation, practice, and production (Byrne, 1986).

To elucidate how a cognitive representation is translated into action, SAT proponents make a clear distinction between two types of knowledge – declarative, which is the representation of factual information, and procedural, which is the representation of how to do things in particular situations. Masson (1990) defines these terms as follows:

> Declarative knowledge consists of information that can be described verbally, retained and manipulated in working memory, and is represented in the form of propositions or mental images. [...] Procedural knowledge is embodied as production systems with condition-action pairs represented in long-term memory. Unlike declarative knowledge, procedural knowledge is not verbalizable or open to conscious introspection. (pp. 223–224)

The first, presentation, stage in the sequence of events leading to skill acquisition presumes that knowledge relevant to the performance of a skill begins in declarative form. Declarative knowledge, characterized by verbal mediation, is acquired consciously through attending to explicit demonstration or explanation of aspects of the task as well as through perceptive observation, analysis, and reasoning. It can be 'encodings of examples of instructions, encodings of general properties of objects, and so on' (Anderson, 1987, p. 197) – anything relevant to developing an in-depth understanding of the skill to be learned. The declarative representation of task components is maintained in the working memory, and the cognitive processing is deliberate. The learner memorizes the factual pieces relevant to the skill. For example, dancing tango requires knowing that in this dance walking movements dominate, that walks normally curve to the left, and that at times the movements are sharp and staccato. To help their students remember the basic movements, instructors often use vocal cues like *Slow, Slow, Quick Quick Slow* or *Walk, Walk, Tan–Go–Close*. The working memory resources are stretched at this stage, which is why processing is more error-prone compared to the subsequent stage (Ackerman, 1988; Woltz, 1988).

'If a certain type of situation is encoded in working memory, then a certain action should take place' (Anderson, 1987, p. 193). This assumption predicts the proceduralization of knowledge (Anderson, 1983), which is the second, practice, stage. During practice, declarative knowledge relevant to the performance of a skill is acted upon and transformed into productions, or task-specific procedures. Transition from declarative to procedural knowledge occurs when the learner engages in the target behavior while still depending on the props of the declarative knowledge. In the tango example, the novice dancer relies on the declarative knowledge about the movements and other tango related facts, but at the same time that knowledge is restructured due to actual practice as the dancer alternates predominantly smooth steps with a quick foot flick or a sharp head snap. DeKeyser (2007a) explicates this process as 'turning "knowledge that" into "knowledge how"' (p. 98); in other words, proceduralization encodes declarative knowledge into behavior. Repeated practice is key here because it creates conditions for knowledge composition into a larger schema. Extensive and deliberate practice allows for refining task-performing procedures and, thus, leads to performance improvement and considerable cognitive speedup because repeatedly practiced actions are performed better and faster. This also means that practice, during which one can monitor or get feedback on the outcomes of produced actions, leads to determining and selecting the most efficient procedures for performing the task. This proceduralization stage is associated with the dropout of verbal rehearsal and therefore with the reduction of working memory load since the need to refer to the declarative knowledge decreases. Performance at this stage begins to resemble expert performance, but it may still be slower and errors still occur.

During the last production phase, the ability to automatically execute the skill is developed as performance becomes increasingly fine-tuned and 'component processes become increasingly autonomous' (Fitts & Posner, 1967, p. 14). Proceduralization enables gradual automatization of knowledge and somewhat effortless elicitation of certain actions. DeKeyser (2007a) points out that it 'is not an all-or-nothing affair' (p. 99). An experienced Argentinian style tango dancer may no longer need to think about the *Walk, Walk, Tan–Go–Close* routine, but may still stumble or accidentally step on their partner's toes when dancing to European-style music. Although procedural knowledge is presumably acquired, practice is still needed for qualitative change in cognitive mechanisms before skillful behavior becomes fluent and consistent. Nevertheless, at this last stage, skillful behavior is characterized by an advanced level of performance with a greatly reduced error rate as well as by decreased cognitive demand, reaction time, and external interference.

The production system model of knowledge is an important SAT notion. It implies that the productions entail condition-action pairs, that they have a hierarchical structure, that they must occur in a sequence, and that they are driven by the same overall goal. Productions, which can be generic and domain-specific, occur under conditions that can be generalized as IF-THEN statements. A simple example of a production system knowledge model, where the completion of the specified action is contingent upon instantiation of the specified condition, is provided by Masson (1990). He demonstrates how the knowledge about shifting a manual transmission into reverse is proceduralized (p. 225):

(a) Declarative knowledge
Shifting into reverse, disengaging the clutch, moving gear to upper left

(b) Generic production

IF	the goal is to achieve state X
	and M is a method for achieving X
THEN	set as subgoal to apply M

(c) Domain-specific production

IF the goal is to go into reverse

THEN set as subgoals

(1) to disengage the clutch
(2) then to move the gear to upper left
(3) then to engage the clutch
(4) then to push down on the gas

SAT researchers made similar analogies with respect to language acquisition. For instance, Anderson (1987) illustrated generic production rules such as 'IF the goal is to generate the present tense of "verb," THEN say "verb" + s' and domain-specific production rules such as 'IF the goal is to generate the present tense of "hug," THEN say "hug" + s' (p. 205). Indeed, the SAT mechanisms offer a rich source of alternative ways of thinking about language acquisition phenomena.

Although research on the contribution of SAT to L2 acquisition is scant, partially due to methodological sophistication expected in this area, the connection between SAT and SLA has been explored and justified (de Jong, 2005; DeKeyser, 1997, 2007a; DeKeyser & Sokalski, 2001; Robinson, 1997), as it is accordant with major SLA research findings which are often interpreted in terms of SAT cognitive processes (de Bot, 1996; Macaro, 2003; Ranta & Lyster, 2006; Towell et al., 1996). There is no need for sophisticated explanation to see that the concept of input intersects with the declarative phase of skill acquisition and that feedback and output are indispensable components of practice during proceduralization. The theoretical implications rest with the significance of both declarative and procedural knowledge. Explicit declarative knowledge of language rules and examples is quintessential because it creates the springboard conditions for proceduralization and automatization of language skills. For instance, talking about past experiences in English requires knowing that English uses regular *–ed* verb forms and irregular verb forms in the past tense. The connection is even more apparent in second language instruction, where pedagogical strategies commonly rely on the presentation-practice-production sequence. Another particularly helpful link has been made to adult L2 learning (Lightbown & Spada, 1997). DeKeyser & Sokalski (2001) hypothesize, 'If adult SLA is an explicit learning process, then one would expect to find the same patterns of learning as for other cognitive skills: Knowledge acquired in declarative (explicit) form is then transformed and automatized through analogical reasoning and specific kinds of practice' (p. 83). In DeKeyser's (2007b) opinion, SAT is most applicable in L2 instructional contexts where high aptitude adult learners are at fairly early stages of learning and where the structures to be learned are clear and understandable.

3.1.4 Reinforcing theoretical grounding with AWE

In the last section of Chapter 1, I introduced a research writing course at Iowa State University as an example of genre-based instruction. A major challenge in this course was providing the students with genre writing practice opportunities that would situate them within a disciplinary discoursal context and would reinforce learning with individual discipline-specific feedback. I will continue to use this example to ponder the extent to which the theoretical tenets overviewed above are generally accounted for by corpus and genre-based pedagogy and also to consider how genre-based AWE may further reify the theoretical grounding.

Halliday reasons that the only way to learn how to make texts is by making texts, just like the only way to learn a language is by using it. According to him, 'a theory of language [is] essentially consumer-oriented' and 'the value of a theory lies in the use that can be made of it' (Halliday, 1985, p. 7). He explains that 'systemic theory is designed not so much to prove things as to do things' (p. 11). This is precisely the concept that should underpin genre-based pedagogy – *using* SFL as part of a theoretical framework that guides instruction as opposed to *doing* SFL, which means studying the language in order to understand how it works and what people do with it.

SFL is clearly applicable to genre-based pedagogy. The graduate academic writing course at ISU familiarizes students with the research article genre through exposure to specialized corpora, which exhibit genre artifacts written in ways that meet the expectations of the target discourse community. Students' focus on corpus texts is plausible from the SFL perspective, where texts are viewed as the most appropriate units for analysis (Halliday & Hasan, 1976, p. 1). SFL also posits that texts are products of choices made from the meaning potential available in particular contexts and of meaning exchanges between the participants (here, writers and readers). This interactive nature of texts as linguistically unfolding social events (Hasan, 1978, p. 229) is an aspect that the corpus-based approach exercised in the course has yet to develop. Advantageous is the fact that the students analyze professional texts in their own disciplines in order to learn how to engage in socio-disciplinary interaction by producing texts that model on those in their specialized corpus. The disadvantage is that the analysis is mostly oriented towards observing the structural components of texts, or, in systemic-functionalist terminology, the schematic structures of the genre. While the students become acquainted with these structures, their attention to functional meaning is minimal. Since '[e]very structural feature has its origin in the semantics, that is, it has some function in the expression of meaning' (Halliday & Webster, 2003, p. 193), genre pedagogy needs to include a focus on language as a systematic resource that the students should learn to use taking into account rhetorical development, multifunctionality, and the higher-level semiotics that build the discourse.

Further, in SFL genres are viewed as 'staged goal-oriented social purposes' (Halliday & Martin, 1993, p. 36). Genre artifacts are analyzed by being divided into stages, which contribute to specific communicative goals indicative of socio-disciplinary values. The corpus tasks iterated in the course for Abstract, Introduction, Methods, Results, Discussion, and Conclusion sections help students discern cultural values by examining text organization as well as by comparing and contrasting texts to glean a generic structure potential. For example, based on Swales' CARS model, the students analyze Introduction texts in terms of three moves (establishing a territory, establishing a niche, and occupying the niche) with the metaphorical coloring 'of ecological competition for research space in a tightly contested territory' (Swales, 2004, p. 226). Each move contains a number of strategic steps, and these steps fulfill particular functional meanings, which may be obligatory or optional depending on the norms adopted by field-specific discourse communities. Additionally, certain lexico-grammatical features can indicate certain moves (Swales, 2004). For instance, the present continuous tense can invoke recency in statements of topic centrality, lexical units with negative connotations can indicate a gap or a problem, and deictics and personal pronouns can signal the introduction of new research. In other cases, the placement of a discourse piece can help interpret its function. Although the moves and their possible steps seem quite clear-cut in Swales' framework, for students move identification is not as easy as it may seem. Nwogu (1990) claims that it is more of a bottom-up process, which is influenced by one's schemata about the structuring of text-type and genres. Because the students are only beginning to develop the necessary schemata, they need to be scaffolded when conducting move analysis of their corpus. They would likely benefit from exposure to annotated texts, where the moves are easily distinguishable and the functional language clearly tied to communicative intent. Obviously, teachers cannot be expected to analyze a corpus and present this kind of input, but a genre-based AWE platform could.

SFL is congruent with the IA perspective in that they are both concerned with mappings between form and meaning (Norris & Ortega,

2003). The course in question does well by exposing students to corpora, which present a large amount of input, a key IA construct. However, while conducting move analysis is expected to help the students notice the characteristics of discourse form, noticing may not be sufficiently triggered because the input texts are not enhanced in any way. Moreover, meaning-making is weak since interaction and feedback are largely in deficit. Interaction is limited to in-class teacher-student group explanatory exchanges, and occasional feedback is not sufficient for the students to notice and address infelicities in their texts, which they try to model on the conventions observed in the input corpora. Learners need to have a way of knowing whether their hypotheses regarding discourse form and meaning are plausible. AWE can be designed to offer better opportunities for input enhancement, noticing, and interaction, as well as facilitate output production through automated feedback.

Finally, SAT can serve as not only an appropriate but also a binding link in the theoretical framework at hand, as it can supply a production system model for the formal domain of genre knowledge. For instance, Masson's (1990) proceduralization formula can be adapted to research article Introduction writing as follows:

(a) Declarative knowledge
Three types of communicative moves (establishing a territory, establishing a niche, occupying the niche)
(b) Generic production
IF the goal is to achieve the communicative intent of moves and using steps is a method for achieving the communicative intent of moves
THEN set as subgoal to apply steps
(c) Domain-specific production (also specific to a particular discipline)
IF the goal is to achieve the communicative intent of move 2, establishing a niche
THEN set as subgoals
(1) to highlight a problem
(2) to indicate a gap
(3) to propose a general hypothesis
(4) to present a justification

The domain-specific production can further be thought of as rules like *IF the goal is to indicate a gap, THEN use linguistic means that express this functional meaning (however; there is a lack of evidence for; remain unknown; previous work has not examined; etc.).*

Looking back at my corpus-based course example, the students are familiarized with the research article genre conventions through the presentation of the communicative goals and corresponding rhetorical strategies, which equips them with appropriate declarative knowledge. The declarative knowledge is acquired through teacher explanation as well as guided observation and analysis of the moves in the corpora. The problem is that the students are expected to draw on their declarative knowledge and produce a research article, abiding by the norms in their disciplines, without being provided with sufficient opportunities for targeted writing practice. This means that the students are expected to bypass the second stage of skill development, but still perform well. To address this problem, the instructional approach in question needs to exercise the powerful role of procedural knowledge in governing expert performance by adding a core element – that of practice. Iterative revision with AWE can facilitate proceduralization and help set the learners on the right path toward automatizing the research writing skill.

SAT is also informative with respect to feedback, which can make practice more helpful and meaningful. SAT theorists posit that knowledge of results, or feedback, plays a significant role in performance improvement. Welford (1968), for instance, reported that delaying feedback slows learning; that performance deteriorates if feedback is provided during training (or declarative stage) and then subsequently removed; and that increasing the precision of feedback also increases the quality of performance. AWE has all the attributes necessary for creating unrestrained practice opportunities with immediate feedback during the writing and revision process. If trained on a specialized corpus, it can also generate reliable genre and discipline-specific feedback based on learned knowledge of authentic texts.

Overall, SFL, SLA, and SAT are informative theoretical components for the design of genre-based AWE. These complementary perspectives all accentuate explicitness – particularly necessary at the initial stage in genre pedagogy; practice – so coveted and so difficult to sustain; and cognition – contemplated as part of the writing construct for AWE.

3.2 Operational framework

3.2.1 Formative assessment

Chapter 2 introduces formative assessment for the purpose of discussing automated evaluation of writing and the issues that arise when the difference between summative assessment and assessment for learning is taken for granted. In this chapter, I take a related but distinct angle.

I focus on the cornerstone of the formative assessment practice – the formative feedback and its essential characteristics needed to enhance the teaching-learning process.

The major goal of formative assessment, or assessment for learning (Sutton, 1995), is to improve student learning and motivation with the help of directive and facilitative feedback. The definition of formative assessment has evolved with the accumulation of supporting evidence about its role in teaching and learning. It emphasizes the importance of such instructional actions as conducting activities that can generate feedback (Black & Wiliam, 1998), generating feedback that includes 'some degree of prescription about what must be done' (Wiliam & Black, 1996, p. 543), supplying feedback during learning (Cowie & Bell, 1999; Shepard, 2008), and providing feedback frequently and interactively (Looney, 2005). Effective formative assessment therefore entails continuously informing learners about their progress in order to actively involve them in their own learning by creating opportunities for self-assessment and understanding how to improve. Feedback functions formatively when it fulfills the following set of roles (Sales, 1993):

- evaluate (acknowledge the accuracy of learners' production)
- direct (provide information about what and how to improve)
- advise (inform learners of the status of their efforts in relation to expected performance)
- instruct (provide additional information to improve students' understanding of what is being learned)
- motivate (provide a motive for continuing effort)
- stimulate (encourage students to continue)
- summarize (offer a cumulative report of individual performance)

To modify thinking and behavior for more successful learning and improved performance, formative feedback should also possess five essential qualities – goal orientation, cognitive involvement, complexity, specificity, and timing.

3.2.1.1 Goal orientation

Feedback on learner performance can be a powerful motivator, especially if it is provided based on the progress toward a desired goal, because the degree of motivation depends on learners' orientation toward certain goals and their expectations for achieving those goals (Ford et al., 1998). In psychology, goal orientation refers to individuals' motivation to achieve goals and is distinguished between performance orientation and learning orientation (Dweck, 1986). Learners with a learning orientation believe that intelligence is ductile and are therefore willing to improve their competence by developing new skills. Learners with a performance orientation, on the other hand, believe that intelligence is innate and thus wish to demonstrate their competence to others and to be positively evaluated by others (Farr et al., 1993). The two goal orientations may influence learners' possible reactions to feedback. Let's consider two scenarios examined by Wiliam (2011) – in one the feedback indicates that performance exceeds a given goal, and in another the feedback indicates that performance falls short of a given goal. In the first scenario, students with a learning orientation are likely to change the goal for a more demanding one with an increased aspiration, while those with a performance orientation are likely to decide that the goal is too easy and exert less effort. In the second scenario, the former are likely to increase effort, while the latter are likely to decide that the goal is beyond their ability and simply abandon it.

Fisher and Ford (1998) adduce that the learning orientation is more desirable, for it leads to more positive outcomes. It has also been suggested that learners with such goal orientation direct their attention to the task, learn for the sake of learning, and thus devote greater effort to learning (Button et al., 1996; Dweck, 1986) by employing complex learning strategies, pursuing challenging tasks, and not giving up in case of failure (Dweck & Leggett, 1988). To influence learners' goal orientation, shifting it from a focus on performance to a focus on learning, the formative feedback should allow learners to verify their expectations and to know how close they are to meeting their goals (Shute, 2008).

3.2.1.2 Cognitive involvement

'If we are to harness the power of feedback to increase student learning, then we need to ensure that feedback causes a cognitive rather than an emotional reaction – in other words, feedback should cause thinking,' asserts Wiliam (2011, p. 132). Thinking is a powerful trigger of learners' active engagement, so the feedback should activate their metacognitive mechanisms by pointing to 'a gap between actual and desired levels of performance' (Wiliam & Black, 1996, p. 543). Engaging in metacognition occurs when learners notice that they have more difficulty with A than B; when it strikes them that they should verify C before accepting it as a fact; when they recognize that they had better make a note of D because they may forget it; and when they realize that they need to clarify E to see if they have it right (Flavell, 1976, p. 232). This kind of cognitive involvement helps learners monitor the quality of what they produce as they work towards minimizing the gap highlighted by the feedback (Sadler, 1989). Effective formative feedback should thus act as a cognitive support mechanism that provides explicit facilitative scaffolding during the learning process. Scaffolded feedback is not only indicative of the differences between learners' production and desired outcomes, but also makes the task more manageable and achievable (Bransford et al., 2000).

3.2.1.3 Complexity

The complexity of formative feedback can be interpreted in terms of verification and elaboration (Kulhavy & Stock, 1989). Verification feedback assesses the correctness of learners' performance in a number of possible ways: knowledge-of-response, which tells learners whether their answers are correct or incorrect; try again, which informs learners about an incorrect response and allows them more attempts; and knowledge-of-correct-response, which provides the correction (Dempsey et al., 1993; Mason & Bruning, 2001). Elaboration feedback is more complex in that it elaborates on learners' input by providing relevant hints to direct them towards the expected performance. It can also take different forms. It can be response-contingent, focusing on the learner's specific response and describing why something is wrong and why the correction is right; it can consist of hints/cues/prompts on how to proceed without providing an explicit correction; or it can be bug-related indicating what is wrong and why based on a formal error analysis. Informative tutoring feedback is the most complex in that it combines different verifying and elaborating information (Narciss & Huth, 2004). Verification and elaboration were both found to enhance learning efficiency and student achievement (Mason & Bruning, 2001; Mory, 2004) and should therefore be combined so that feedback fulfills its formative roles.

3.2.1.4 Specificity

Research has attested that formative feedback leads to improvement and is more effective when it is specific (Berkenkotter et al., 1991; Pridemore & Klein, 1995). Wiliam (2011) contends that feedback is formative only if it can be used by the learner to improve performance, and to be effective it must provide a recipe for future action. For example, if a comedian is told that his performance was not entertaining enough, this would be accurate feedback, but hardly of any help. In other words, if the feedback indicates only deficiencies and does not advise on what to do to improve, then it is 'like the scene in the rearview mirror rather than through the windshield' (p. 120). The specifics of the feedback may vary depending on the learning goal and the learner's current state vis-à-vis the goal. In any case, it should suggest a forthright path toward progression. Provided with specific feedback, students are less likely to have negative learning experiences or to be confused as to how to react to the feedback, as was the student in Wiliam's (2011) example who, having received the 'You need to be more systematic in planning your scientific inquiries' feedback, responded – 'If I knew how to be more systematic, I would have been more systematic the first time' (p. 120).

3.2.1.5 Timing

Formative feedback can be delivered at different points in time during the writing process. Immediate feedback is returned instantly when learners finish a given task, and the feedback is called delayed if it takes a certain amount of time before the learners receive it (this may vary from minutes, to hours, to days). In general, there are benefits to either timing. Immediate feedback is believed to prevent errors from being encoded in the memory, and delayed feedback is thought to reduce the interference factor, allowing the errors to be forgotten. However, immediate feedback has been found superior for the acquisition of verbal materials and for procedural skills (Corbett & Anderson, 2001). Writing can be viewed as a procedural skill in that it entails a mental procedure that involves the execution of a sequence of operations (explicable by cognitive writing models as well as in SAT terms discussed earlier). Therefore, it is reasonable to assume that immediate feedback may be more beneficial for the development of academic writing skills.

3.2.2 Intelligent Computer-Assisted Language Learning

With the emergence of computer assisted language learning, the impetus of feedback has been materialized in multiple modes and forms. Garrett (1987) identifies four types of computer-based feedback: (1) only the correct answer is presented; (2) the location of errors on the basis of a letter-by-letter comparison of the learner's input with the machine-stored correct version is indicated; (3) based on an analysis of the anticipated incorrect answers, error messages associated with possible errors are stored in the computer and are presented if the learner's response matches those possible errors; and (4) based on a linguistic analysis of the learner's response compared to an analysis derived from relevant grammar rules and lexicon of the target language, problematic or missing items are pinpointed (Garrett, 1987). The last type of feedback, known as intelligent feedback, is the most sophisticated and is superior to the so-called pattern markup and error-anticipation techniques used in other conventional types of feedback. It is superior because it is capable of diagnosing errors, providing detailed explanations about the nature of those errors, and responding to multiple problematic aspects of language use that may occur in learner production. Intelligent feedback is intelligent per se because it can be adapted to the level and needs of individual learners, as it is done in the area of Intelligent Computer-Assisted Language Learning (ICALL), which has gained great popularity in language instruction.

ICALL has its roots in the intelligent tutoring systems (ITS) of the late 1950s (Sleeman & Brown, 1982). Koschmann (1996) explains the motivation by which artificial intelligence (AI) was translated to ITS and migrated into the educational community as follows:

> Research in AI is founded upon the conjecture that cognition is, in some sense, a computational process than can be studied through the construction of 'intelligent' systems that serve as functional models of the otherwise inaccessible processes of the human mind. (Pylyshyn, 1989)
>
> If machines can be programmed to display intelligent behavior, there is no reason, at least in principle, that systems could not be designed to assume the role of a skilled teacher. Since one-on-one tutoring is commonly considered the gold standard against which other methods of instruction are measured (Bloom, 1984), the paradigm is founded on the proposition that education could be globally improved by providing every student with a personal (albeit machine-based) tutor (Lepper et al., 1993). (p. 7)

Like ITS, ICALL programs act on the principle of one-on-one tutoring, engaging learners in pre-programmed activities. Unlike ITS, which are designed to help learners complete well-defined tasks that involve a number of anticipated steps, as it is in mathematics for instance, ICALL is much less directive. Because language learning is not predictable like mathematical problem solving, ICALL generates informative tutoring feedback that is response-contingent rather than task-contingent.

The early 1990s witnessed the piloting of numerous ICALL systems. Capitalizing on the ability of NLP techniques and tools, most of them started with a focus on the grammatical analysis of short written output. For example, Grammar-Debugger (Si-Quing & Luomai, 1990) was a parser designed to analyze grammatical as well as ungrammatical sentences produced by Chinese learners of English. Another parser, Syncheck (Juozulynas, 1994; Sanders, 1991) analyzed syntax to help learners write German compositions. GPARS (Loritz, 1992) included parsers for several languages such as English, Russian, Japanese, and Chinese. LINGER (Yazdani, 1991) relied on a combination of tools such as a language-independent parsing mechanism, a language-specific dictionary, and a language-specific grammar, which allowed the system to cope with various aspects of Romance and Germanic languages. Levin et al. (1991) developed ALICE, a multi-media workbench that offered a set of tools for designing different types of intelligent programs in any language. ALICE included tools and resources for syntactic parsing, morphological analysis, error detection, online dictionaries, and other reference materials, as well as for indexing and retrieval of video/audio/text corpora examples. They were applied to grammar and vocabulary tasks, games and simulations, reading and writing assistants, and open-ended learning environments.

A number of ICALL programs used the analysis of learner output for error feedback generation and interaction. Miniprof (Labrie & Singh, 1991) was an early intelligent tutor for elementary topics in French built to provide grammar exercises. This system generated tutorial messages based on the decisions of three components – parsing, diagnosis, and tutoring. The function of the parser was to assign a grammatical structure both to the question and to the student's response, and if the response was an incorrect sentence, it parsed as much of the sentence as possible to identify the errors. Errors that could not be identified by the parser, typically context errors, were detected by the diagnostic component. Then, modeling the way in which a teacher would respond when tutoring a student, the tutoring component asked the student questions about identified errors. Consequently, the program engaged the student in a Socratic dialogue, leading her/him to identify and correct each error.

A parser-based program aimed at checking the grammar in EFL students' compositions was described by Liou (1991). To build the grammar-checker, errors from a collection of student writing samples were first found and classified into an error taxonomy. Then, a small electronic dictionary with word stems and necessary features was compiled, a suffix processor to accommodate morpho-syntactic variants of each word stem was designed, after which a parser equipped with phrase structure rules and error patterns was constructed. Once a grammatical error was detected, the program output a message to the learner, in which a flag attached to each processing rule was matched with a message file. The feedback message was created from a template and consisted of the erroneous sentence, an explanation, and possibly examples.

BRIDGE was another program that functioned based on a parser (Holland et al., 1993). This German tutor analyzed learners' free sentence-level responses. It was developed for the use of military linguists in the US Army. Upon the reception of the response, the program passed the sentence to the parser, and the tutor informed the learner of a primary error offering a chance for correction. Secondary errors were not automatically displayed. The learner was alerted of a secondary error but had the choice to look it up or not. If the revised response was grammatical, the tutor returned a message to that effect. Holland et al. (1993) claim that their system's 'feedback can be couched in pragmatically relevant terms. For example, besides saying "verb and subject don't agree", as in BRIDGE, we could add "This might confuse the reader/hearer as to whether you mean singular or plural" or "This kind of mistake will lead people to doubt your competence in the language". In this way, the feedback could "call attention to the public consequences of grammatical acts"' (p. 41). The program's interface also included a given text, graphical aids, learner aids, and lesson exercises that consisted of oral or written questions to which the learner responded with a written sentence.

NIHONGO-CALI (Nagata, 1993), a Japanese language computer-assisted instruction program, provided exercises for passive structures, which learners could complete by inputting full sentences. It employed NLP to facilitate error analysis and feedback in the light of morphological and syntactical rules of the Japanese language. At the core of the program was an analyzer that consisted of a morphological parser, a syntactic parser, and a knowledge base with three components: a core lexicon, a set of morphological rules, and a set of grammar rules. Capable of parsing both grammatical and ungrammatical input, NIHONGO-CALI generated error messages, which were then sent to the pattern matching program to verify whether the learner's response was appropriate for the question in the given exercise. Depending on the pattern matching result, the learner received feedback in terms of the grammatical functions and thematic roles of each sentence constituent. Several error types could be detected by the analyzer and the pattern matching program – vocabulary, particle, verbal predicate, and nominal modifier. The system was also teacher-friendly in that it allowed instructors to create feedback messages themselves, depending on their instructional focus.

Yang and Akahori (1998) developed a web-based system which, similar to NIHONGO-CALI, accepted free response sentences in Japanese. The difference between these two tutors was that the former worked with the Latin alphabet, while the latter analyzed Japanese characters. Major components of the system included a sentence analysis system with a morpheme analyzer, a syntax analyzer, and an error analyzer. It also contained grammar rules, a dictionary, a feedback system with a message generator, a knowledge database, and a list of students' learning histories. Learners' typed-in sentences were processed by the morpheme analyzer, and the sentence was checked by a case grammar. If an error was found, the grammar rules were applied to identify the type of error and the order of priority so that a relevant feedback message was created. The sentence analysis component sent an error ID to the feedback component, which determined the feedback message to be displayed to the learner. This message indicated the type of error and pointed to its location rather than correcting the error, therefore directing the learner to attempt self-correction. The learner could choose to correct her/his sentence immediately, or to access grammatical explanations first and correct the sentence later. An advantage of this program is the fact that the feedback was displayed not only depending on the type of error identified, but also depending on the learner who submits the sentence, taking an adaptive individualized approach to feedback generation.

Azalea, an interactive intelligent language tutoring system, was developed for an ESL composition course (Chen & Tokuda, 2003; Chen et al., 2002; Tokuda & Chen, 2001, 2004). It consisted of a template automaton structure for knowledge representation, a diagnostic engine based on a matching algorithm, a part-of-speech tagged parser for syntactic analysis, a parser-based learner model, and a visual interface authoring tool. The error messages provided through template matching resulted from a total of 164 errors that the system could diagnose, these errors being classified as grammatical errors, word and usage errors, and non-preclassified errors. Feedback messages were returned depending on whether the learner's response found an exact match with the model translations or with the finite states of the template, whether the response did not exactly match the finite states of the templates, or whether the response matched less than half of the template path. The error contingent feedback was provided in the form of suggested corrections like 'This noun should be plural' or 'When referring to general classes of things, do not use "the" before plural countable nouns (boats, motors, meetings, countries). This part is not needed' (Tokuda & Chen, 2004, p. 196).

Reuer (2003) reported on an ICALL system that invited learners to use language interactively in order to enhance the development of communicative competence. It provided small question-answer dialogs with the computer during which learners were required to produce complete written sentences. The parser relied on lexical functional grammar and used an unrestricted grammar and lexicon. It contained some linguistic knowledge obtained from a learner corpus of German to constrain the search space, but it did not include any mal-rules for describing erroneous sentences. Although Reuer did not directly tackle the issue of individualized feedback, he argued that parser-generated structures were suitable for constructing error messages.

Arabic ICALL was designed by Shaalan (2005). It had two main types of items for interaction with the learner: selection questions (matching, true/false, identify, or multiple-choice) and supply questions (short-answer/fill-in-the-blank). Like other intelligent systems, it encouraged free production of sentence-length input and guided learners towards the recognition of erroneous or inappropriate language use. The analysis module contained an error analyzer that parsed ill-formed input, compared the student answer with the correct answer generated by the system, and issued feedback driven by commands (for example, a command to issue a message describing that the unrestricted object should be the infinitive of a verb). In addition to the sentence analysis and feedback module containing a lexicon, a morphological analyzer, a syntax parser, and grammatical and buggy rules, this application included teaching units, an item bank, a test generator, and an acquisition tool.

E-Tutor (originally German Tutor) is a program that has become an integral part of the German curriculum at Simon Fraser University in Canada. It is similar to other ICALL programs described above in that it analyzes sentence-level input and detects language errors (Heift, 2002, 2003, 2005; Heift & Nicholson, 2001). As a tutor, this program incorporates exercises that elicit the use of vocabulary, building of sentences, translation, and dictation-based writing. E-Tutor contains a domain knowledge that represents the knowledge of language encoded in the grammar, an analysis module that yields possible responses to the learner's input, and a filtering module that makes decisions regarding the order of feedback. Superior to the functionality of other programs, it has an adaptive student model, which maintains a record of individual learners' performance. Heift (2002) explains that 'performance over time is monitored across different grammatical constructs; the information is used to tailor feedback messages suited to learner expertise within a framework of guided discovery learning' (p. 298). The output of the grammar parser is used to select error-specific feedback messages, which differ depending on the level of language competence. Beginners receive explicit explanations of their errors, intermediate learners are provided with a hint at the error type expressed in more metalinguistic terms, and advanced learners only see errors highlighted (Heift, 2005). In the case of multiple errors, E-Tutor follows the principle of error prioritization, presenting feedback on errors one at a time. The tutor also provides recommendations for remediation by suggesting follow-up exercises depending on the number and type of errors that have been detected. Similar intelligent tutoring systems with the same feedback features have been developed for English (Toole & Heift, 2002) and Greek (Heift et al., 2000). The student model in these systems keeps track of various error types such as grammar, vocabulary, and punctuation, and at the end of every exercise set the learners receive a detailed summary of the errors they made.

Robo-Sensei (Nagata, 2009) has also been fully integrated in language instruction, cross-referencing textbooks commonly used by teachers of Japanese. This interactive program contains 24 grammar modules ranging from beginner to advanced levels, which offer learners a series of communicative practice exercises. The sentences composed by learners in response to a given situation are analyzed by the program's NLP system that includes a morphological parser, a syntactic parser, a word segmentor, a lexicon, and a morphological generator. Robo-Sensei also has an error detector and a feedback generator. The former classifies errors into categories like unknown word, missing word, unexpected word, predicate form error, modifier error, and word order error (p. 569). The feedback generator uses error-specific feedback templates to produce error messages, creates possible correct answers, and provides feedback on the nature of identified errors. Robo-Sensei does not account for individual learner proficiency level or knowledge of language items and is, therefore, not as learner-adaptive as E-Tutor when providing feedback.

Maintaining that intelligent feedback can be more effective than traditional non-computerized feedback, Nagata (1995) argues that '[i]f we use an intelligent system, we should examine carefully what kind of error messages should be provided [...] and how effective they are' (p. 49). Research on written corrective feedback conducted with L2 writers in instructional contexts has supported the error-directed practice with evidence of overall positive influence on L2 writing development, although corrective feedback has been a long-debated issue (Ferris, 2006).

The pro and con arguments range from providing feedback that corrects all errors (Lalande, 1982), to selective feedback (Bates et al.,

1993; Ferris, 1995), and even to calls for the elimination of any degree of corrective feedback (Cook, 1991; Krashen, 1984). These views have generated extensive research into the effectiveness of feedback guided by various theories, including behaviorist approaches, activity theory, and Vygotsky's socio-cultural theory. Empirical investigations have addressed feedback efficacy from two major angles. One is in the composition tradition and focuses on impact on revising drafts. The other is SLA-focused and examines the impact on writing new texts. A comprehensive review of written corrective feedback studies can be found in Bitchener and Ferris (2012), who present these lines of inquiry as complementary. Many works speak in favor of different types of traditional feedback such as: explicit (Carroll & Swain, 1993; Lyster, 1998), individual-specific (Hyland, 1998), metalinguistic (Rosa & Leow, 2004), negative cognitive (Mitchell & Myles, 1998), detailed iterative (Hyland & Hyland, 2006), and precise, one at a time (Van der Linden, 1993).

Though not as extensive, research on intelligent feedback corroborates some traditional feedback findings. For example, Yang and Akahori (1999) indicate that feedback corresponding to the input created by the learner is superior to feedback displaying the correct answer because it enhances self-correction. In terms of correction, van der Linden (1993), while examining the strategies learners employed when interacting with different levels of feedback, observed that learners felt motivated to self-correct when they received feedback about specific types of errors. Other studies showed that the more detailed the feedback is, the better the learning outcomes can be (Heift, 2001, 2002, 2004, 2005); therefore, the feedback should not only display the error, but also explain why the response is inappropriate. Heift (2008) explored the effects of two types of feedback (metalinguistic explanation and metalinguistic clue) on beginner, advanced beginner, and low intermediate learners of German, looking into the longitudinal effects of these types of feedback and into their impact on grammar and spelling error classes. Overall, she concluded that learners show significantly more learner uptake over time with the more error-specific/explicit feedback type. In another study, Heift and Rimrott (2008) considered three distinct feedback types for spelling errors: meta-linguistic with emphasis (feedback includes suggestions for the misspelled word in addition to displaying the incorrect sentence and highlighting the error), metalinguistic (feedback indicates that a spelling error has occurred and provides a list of suggestions), and repetition (feedback does not contain any suggestions for correction). Here, too, learners had the most correct responses and the greatest uptake with the most explicit feedback type (meta-linguistic with emphasis), repetition being the least effective. Finally, Kulik and Kulik (1988) suggest that error feedback needs to be immediate to be effective.

3.2.3 Evidence-Centered Design

Evidence-Centered Design (ECD) is a general framework created to guide the design and delivery of new assessments. It facilitates the adjustment of delivery, scoring, and feedback assessment components to multiple purposes and supports a broad range of assessment types, including high-stakes standardized tests, low-stakes placement and diagnostic tests, classroom quizzes, portfolios, and systems for coached practice such as ICALL and AWE. This may seem overly ambitious for an assessment design framework not only because the requirements for different tests are completely different, but also because test delivery formats and authoring systems vary a lot. However, what allows ECD to assume this level of generality is the fact that it 'describes a process that begins by defining the decisions to be made based upon the results of an assessment and then works backwards to develop tasks, delivery mechanisms, scoring procedures, and feedback mechanisms that provide evidence that informs the pre-defined purposes' (Almond et al., 2002, p. 4). Strictly speaking, ECD relies on evidentiary reasoning whereby the assessment provides an opportunity to obtain observable evidence about learners' knowledge or skill to be measured, which would be elicited with relevance to the purpose of the assessment and the intended inferences (Mislevy et al., 2003). Evidentiary reasoning is thus cognate with validity since obtaining the evidence is construct-centered, and the decisions are based on performance features that indicate what a learner can or cannot do construct-wise.

ECD presents designing, implementing, and delivering an educational assessment as having multiple layers, which suggests a sequential design process with cycles of iteration and refinement (Mislevy & Haertel, 2006). One of these layers, the Conceptual Assessment Framework (CAF), serves as a blueprint for the operational elements of the assessment. This blueprint contains six different models that determine materials, commands, rules, and lots of other information about the design specifications for a particular assessment. Mislevy et al. (2003) describe the CAF models as follows. The Student Model defines the knowledge, skills, and abilities to be measured and about which inferences are to be made. The Task Model delineates the tasks that can elicit the kinds of evidence needed for the Evidence Model. The Evidence Model supplies instructions on how to interpret learners' work products, or their performance on given tasks. The Assembly Model controls the selection of tasks for the creation of an assessment. The Presentation Model specifies how a particular task is to be presented in a given delivery environment. The Delivery System Model describes how student, evidence, task, assembly, and presentation models work together.

Each of these CAF models is connected with another important layer – the Four Process Delivery Architecture. The processes it contains are: Activity Selection, Presentation, Response Processing, and Summary Scoring. They all interact and produce an assessment cycle with the participation of the test administrator who initiates the process and configures options, and the learner who engages in completing the tasks set by the administrator. The four processes are mandatory for any assessment system in order to make appropriate observations and inferences that form a given assessment argument (Almond et al., 2002). It is these processes that give the ECD framework the flexibility for accommodating a range of different assessment delivery formats and platforms (paper and pencil, oral, computer-based).

The Activity Selection Process carries out the selection and sequencing of tasks, which can be assigned for any test purpose or instructional goal and are therefore generally specified by the assessment administrator. It can also create template-based tasks depending on what is known about the student performance or assessment context. The Presentation Process is responsible for displaying the task (and supporting material if needed) to the learners as well as for regulating interaction and collecting learners' work products in the form of responses to the task. For example, for a multiple-choice paper-based test this process would involve providing learners with test booklets and collecting their answer sheets, while for a computer-based test it would be concerned with presenting a sequence of items one at a time, each time recording the response for instant evaluation and subsequent selection of the following item. Response Processing collects observable evidence from the outcomes of the task by evaluating specific features of the work products. Evidence from a paper-based test can be gathered by comparing the responses with an answer key, and from a computer-based test by recording the correspondence of clicks to the correct answers pre-programmed in the system. Depending on the assessment purpose, the Response Processing Process can unfold in more than one phase, especially in the case of computer-based assessment that relies on automated scoring. Also depending on the purpose, the evidence can be forwarded for scoring or returned to the learner for task-level feedback. When the response is ready for final evaluation, the Summary

Scoring Process, which accumulates all the evidence from all the tasks, is responsible for producing section and assessment-level scores. This process can take the simple form of counting correct answers on paper sheets or much more complex forms like measurement models with scoring weights or conditional probabilities used in computer-based scoring. In adaptive testing, this process can also feed information to the Activity Selection Process when it is necessary to choose the task for follow-up presentation.

The Response Processing and the Summary Scoring processes both involve scoring, the differences being in scope, nature, and stage. The former yields evidence about the learner's knowledge and abilities at the time of assessment and is an initial step in the evaluation process (there may be more than one such processing steps). The latter represents the tester's beliefs and interpretations about the learner's knowledge and abilities at the time of assessment and is the final step that summarizes the evidence and produces score reports. Also, these two processes require different scoring models and imply different levels of detail for two distinct types of feedback. Response Processing performs task-based scoring and therefore can facilitate the generation of a piece of feedback on a single task; such feedback is not related to performance on other tasks and can be provided formatively during assessment as well as when the assessment is complete. The Summary Scoring Process performs test-level scoring, and the feedback is based on evidence compiled from performances across multiple tasks and can only be reported upon the completion of all assessment tasks. It is important to make clear distinctions between these two evaluation processes and to separate them from Response Processing because these distinctions are essential to evidentiary reasoning. Almond et al. (2002) explain that the 'ability to separate scoring from presentation and decision-making allows us to reuse tasks in different contexts and to meet the requirements of different assessment purposes. [...] For example, tasks retired from a high-stakes exam could be used in a diagnostic exam, or a practice test, or a tutoring system' (p. 4).

The four ECD delivery system processes are connected to the Task/Evidence Composite Library, which plays a central role in the assessment cycle. This library is a database that contains all the data needed for each process to function effectively. Specifically, it contains: (1) information describing the properties of tasks summoned by the Activity Selection Process; (2) task materials to be displayed by the Presentation Process; (3) evidence rule data such as answer keys, rubrics and algorithms used by Response Processing to evaluate work products; and (4) scoring weights, conditional probabilities, or psychometric parameters used by the Summary Scoring Process to combine all observable evidence and to produce score reports from statistics describing the final state of the learner's scoring record.

3.2.4 Reinforcing operational grounding with AWE

Formative assessment, ICALL, and ECD together can level the limited focus on meaningful feedback in academic writing instruction. The operative solutions to pedagogical issues they offer can be strengthened if AWE builds on and adds to these practices.

AWE can bring several important advantages to L2 writing instruction in general, and to genre pedagogy in particular once the requisite programming is in place. As summarized in Table 3.1, AWE can substantially enhance formative feedback qualities compared to the more traditional sources of feedback given in writing classes. Conventional CALL feedback is the least advantageous since non-intelligent computer-based applications do not analyze written constructed responses. Teacher feedback, on the other hand, is undoubtedly very valuable, but there are certain limitations to human ability as well. It is a well-known fact that teachers rarely have time to provide feedback, while a custom-designed AWE program could inexhaustibly respond to student writing. Automated feedback is reliable, specific, and nonjudgmental, unlike teacher feedback, which may sometimes take the form of cryptic and vague comments like 'Why? Relevance? Explain!' (Ferris, 2003, p. 26) leading to frustration and resentfulness (Ferris, 1995; Straub, 1997). Immediacy is another affordance that AWE has demonstrated and that can be easily implemented. Interaction with AWE could also potentially increase the students' role in the learning process, stimulating their cognitive engagement and goal orientation, especially if timely feedback is complex enough to provide genre-specific details.

ICALL exercises different types of intelligent feedback, which meet the expectations of good formative assessment practices in a number of ways (Figure 3.1). The complexity quality is realized as informative tutoring feedback, supplementing verification of correctness with various response-contingent elaboration hints and prompts. Also, intelligent feedback tends to explicitly point to specific errors, that way orienting learners toward a specific goal for improvement. Some ICALL programs provide direct feedback by suggesting corrections, while others provide indirect feedback by pointing to the error and encouraging the learner to self-correct. Indirect feedback, as well as explanations, examples, and dialoguing, create conditions for cognitive involvement

Table 3.1 Formative feedback qualities in teacher and AWE feedback

Formative feedback quality	Teacher feedback	AWE feedback
Cognitive involvement	– Points to gaps, but possibly inconsistently or subjectively – Not available for scaffolding during writing	– Points to gaps objectively and reliably – Available for scaffolding during writing – Allows monitoring the quality during writing
Goal orientation	– Not available at any point during writing – Hardly goal-oriented	– Available at any point during writing – Offers opportunities to self-assess progress – Goal-oriented
Complexity	– Tends to be more verifying and less elaborating	– Informative-tutoring, combining verification and elaboration
Specificity	– Tends to be of selective specificity – Not always individualized	– Very specific – Individualized
Timing	– Mostly delayed	– Immediate – Possibly considering student level and task difficulty – On demand, if needed

since such scaffolding can help learners notice erroneous language use, understand how to modify their output, and make more appropriate use of language. Because intelligent feedback is immediate, and because learners have the opportunity to act upon the feedback iteratively, this process of cognitive involvement is likely to be continuously active. Moreover, intelligent feedback possesses the specificity quality of formative feedback – some programs prioritize error messages highlighting primary versus secondary errors, while others provide comprehensive feedback highlighting all the identified errors according to specific categories in their error taxonomies. In some cases, the feedback is tied to the learner's language proficiency level and is generated adaptively. Finally, although ICALL has mostly focused on short linguistic output and not on extended written discourse, the different ways in which it approaches the generation of intelligent feedback are illustrative in terms of how to best tailor formative AWE feedback to the needs of individual learners. In a genre-based course, it is important that the

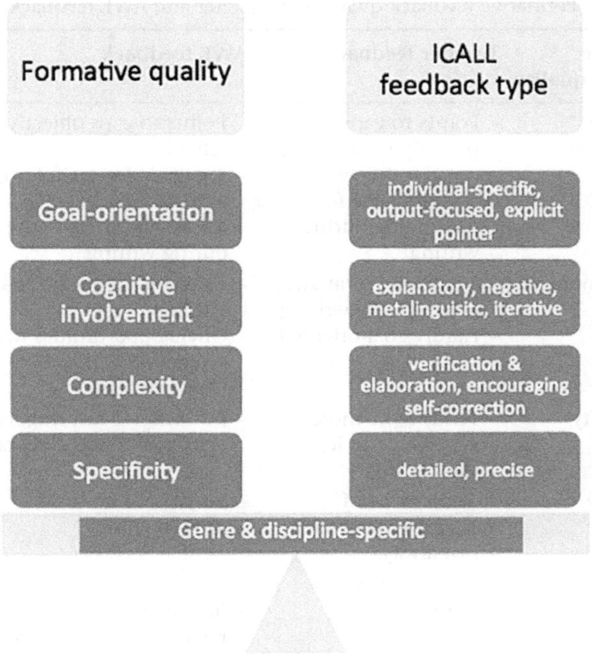

Figure 3.1 Feedback qualities and types for new genre-based AWE

feedback directs L2 writers towards the specifics of disciplinary writing. A new AWE program could be designed to expand on the NLP techniques exploited in ICALL and link the feedback to the results of intelligent analyses of genre and disciplinary writing norms. In this way, AWE would connect learner output to writing conventions exhibited by specialized corpora, thus enhancing goal-orientation and specificity, and also ensuring that the feedback is a meaningful response that provides a learning opportunity for students.

ICALL approaches to the individualization of feedback can be substantiated by the ECD framework, which can be directly applied to the design of genre-based AWE. ECD has already found a wide range of application including task-based language assessment (Mislevy et al., 2002) and intelligent tutoring systems (Mislevy & Gitomer, 1996) largely because it 'provides language, concepts, and knowledge representations for designing and delivering [any] educational assessments' (Mislevy & Haertel, 2006, p. 6). Adopting ECD for the development of new AWE can establish a comprehensive formative assessment cycle with an underlying structural and procedural architecture, where models and delivery processes interact appropriately and effectively in view of the purpose and context of L2 genre-based writing pedagogy. Evidentiary reasoning based on observable evidence obtained from the automated analysis of individual learner writing can reinforce the validity of AWE use as a construct-centered implementation with conceptual, substantive, and empirical support for intended inferences and attendant consequences. Underscoring observable evidence can fulfill evidentiary requirements for writing performance diagnosis and formative feedback and thus allow for developing a compelling interpretive argument with relevant backing for anticipated assumptions and claims. Furthermore, designing Response Processing as separate from Summary Scoring would generate feedback in principled ways, thus averting the problem of obtaining evidence for one purpose and using it for another (as in the case of automated essay scoring). Overall, ECD principles can help not only evoke and capture evidence of the construct in complex written performances, but also create an AWE environment capable of stimulating learning with the help of automated feedback that is driven by leaner responses and fully integrated in the writing and revision processes. ECD offers feedback delivery mechanisms that can also realize the theoretical tenets underrepresented in pedagogical practice – input enhancement, output, and interaction (SLA) and practice through iterative revision (SAT). To support learning even further, various help options can be provided as part of the task performance environment based on corpus materials that can be accumulated in the unified Task/Evidence Composite Library database.

The various theories and practice-focused perspectives overviewed in this chapter will be assembled in a symbiotic conceptual design of a prototype of new genre-based AWE. I will show how these markedly different theoretical and operational landscapes can construct a synergetic complementarity and steer the process of automated feedback generation for L2 research writing, placing a significant emphasis on individual written production and the targeted genre.

4 Prototyping Genre-Based AWE for L2 Research Writing: The Intelligent Academic Discourse Evaluator

This chapter introduces a conceptual design model and demonstrates how this model was applied to a prototype genre-based AWE program – the Intelligent Academic Discourse Evaluator (IADE). I explain how the intended purpose of IADE dictated by the needs of targeted learners and teachers can be realized through a synthesis of the theoretical and operational principles covered in Chapter 3. This complex rationale is a judgmental analysis, which is an important segment of the evaluation argument (Chapelle, 2001) about IADE. The judgmental analysis will further be warranted by empirical analyses in Part II of this volume. I also include here a brief description of two empirical prerequisites – the preparation of training data from a specialized corpus and the development of the analysis engine for feedback generation.

4.1 Conceptual design

The previous chapter culminated with my considerations of how new AWE technology can reinforce theoretical and operational tenets applicable to L2 genre pedagogy. IADE is a web-based proof-of-concept prototype of such technology, which was developed for the research writing course referred to several times in my earlier discussions. As a prototype, it assumes a relatively narrow scope on the research article genre by focusing only on the Introduction section. IADE analyzes students' Introduction drafts, generates feedback at the level of rhetorical moves, and offers a number of other features – all with a bearing on the objectives of L2 research writing pedagogy. It also addresses disciplinary variation, which is an inevitable challenge in graduate-level writing courses, by providing students in 50 different fields with discipline-specific feedback. Figure 4.1 lists the learning and teaching needs along

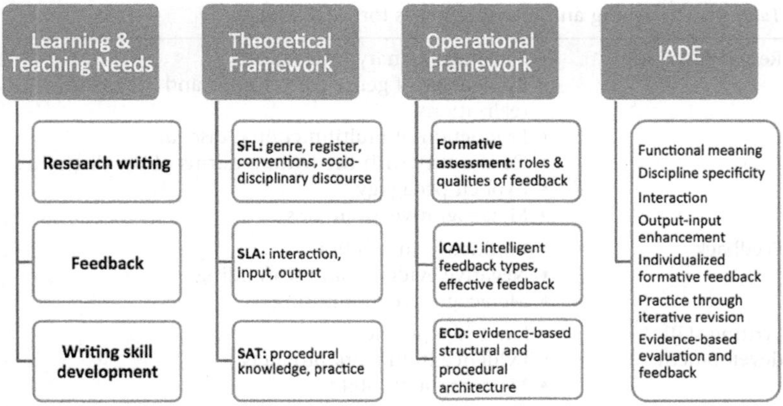

Figure 4.1 IADE conceptual design

with relevant theoretical concepts and operational factors, and highlights how those are realized in the design of IADE.

4.1.1 Learning and teaching needs

IADE was conceived to meet the learning and teaching needs of a specific context – graduate-level L2 writing course at Iowa State University introduced in Chapter 1. These narrowly targeted needs, however, are reflective of the demands of genre-based L2 research writing pedagogy in general. Both teachers and students wrestle with major challenges pertaining to the research writing task, feedback, and writing skill development specified in Table 4.1.

As discussed in Chapter 1, writing about research is not the mere production of a written artifact by an individual. Rather, it entails the development of research writing competence, which encompasses the socio-cultural dimension in that the writing has to meet the expectations of its readers and their experience with analogous texts. To successfully engage in social interaction with their disciplinary community, novice L2 writers need to be able to effectively intertwine strands of functional meaning in multifunctional discourse. For that, they have to be well acquainted with the conventions of the targeted genre since those are representative of accepted socio-disciplinary norms of interaction within their discipline. Teachers, in turn, need to employ an explicit pedagogy with an initial focus on deconstructive analysis, evaluation, and interpretation of textual artifacts geared towards the discovery of discipline-specific rhetorical and linguistic resources

Table 4.1 Learning and teaching needs for IADE design

Research writing	• Socio-disciplinary interaction • Knowledge of genre conventions and linguistic realizations • Production of multifunctional discourse • Conformity with the writing norms of the discipline • Explicit pedagogy • Metacognitive awareness
Feedback	• Productive interaction • Negative evidence and scaffolding • Metacognitive monitoring
Writing skill development	• Extensive practice • Evidence from work products • Metapragmatic ability

in order to help their students advance from knowledge-telling to knowledge-transformation. Equally important is for teachers to have the means to foster their students' metacognitive awareness as they use different discoursal strategies to complete research writing tasks.

Of the issues associated with the shortcomings of genre pedagogy incrementally considered in Chapter 3, feedback presents a particularly difficult challenge and a need that is emphasized by theory as much as by praxis. Feedback is invaluable for learning and language development. It is *the* expedient of productive interaction, which should connect any genre-related input that L2 writers are exposed to with every piece of writing they produce so that their attention is directed to identified inaccuracies or deviations and so that they can engage in metacognitive monitoring to be able to self-evaluate and modify their written output accordingly. In this role, feedback is a cognitive trigger.

Feedback is also needed to scaffold L2 writers' attempts to communicate specific functional meaning to their audience. Students need different types of feedback in order to know where they are on their path to the writing goal and how to better to get there. They also need some guiding information to make sure that they are abiding by the norms established by their disciplinary community. Writing teachers, being only human, need alternative techniques that can compensate for their inability to be a perpetual source of such formative feedback and an absolute source of knowledge about disciplinary conventions.

Feedback and practice are inseparable when it comes to acquiring skills; therefore, developing research writing as a skill requires a considerable amount of practice. But what are good ways to practice? Students, even if they are in an advanced writing course, cannot be told 'You need to practice writing an Introduction section for your homework'. They need to be provided with adequate opportunities for practice, which would take into account the cognitive processes involved in skill acquisition as well as the level of individual students' ability at different stages in the writing and revision process. Moreover, they need to acquire the metapragmatic ability to apply the aspects of genre knowledge to the process of writing as knowledge-making. Teachers, respectively, need to be able to create and sequence practice opportunities based on concrete evidence about what their students can and cannot do in writing so that those opportunities are more beneficial.

4.1.2 Theoretical underpinnings

IADE design is underpinned by theoretical insights vis-à-vis the identified learning and teaching needs. SFL is informative both as a theory and as a pedagogical approach. Underscoring the function of texts as products of social environments, it grounds IADE's focus on texts as the unit of analysis in order to help students grasp the connection between academic texts and the professional practice they realize, and to help them discern how the linguistic system is used to create meaningful socio-disciplinary interaction through the research article genre. IADE also endorses SFL in defining the construct of formal genre knowledge (see Chapter 1), which is targeted for automated formative assessment in the given instructional context. Its analysis engine is not trained on static compositional features; on the contrary, it examines functional meaning and is based on the communicative dimensions of disciplinary writing. IADE uses the move framework as a model for the overall approach to text analysis. Specifically, it uses Swales' move schema for Introductions in the following ways: to train the analysis engine (more about this in the next section), to identify the rhetorical structure of a student's text, and to generate two types of feedback. The first type is color-coded feedback on the rhetorical structure of the Introduction draft, indicating whether the student has fulfilled the communicative purposes of the moves (Figure 4.2a). The second type is feedback on the distribution of moves, indicating how it compares with move distribution in the student's particular discipline (Figure 4.2b). This discipline-specific feedback is numerical in nature and is based on a comparison of the student's draft with a corpus of Introduction sections in the respective discipline, annotated for rhetorical moves. In this way, IADE intends to help students follow the writing norms of their discipline, at the same time establishing a relation between their texts and socio-disciplinary practice. Lastly, by employing the move schema representative of a

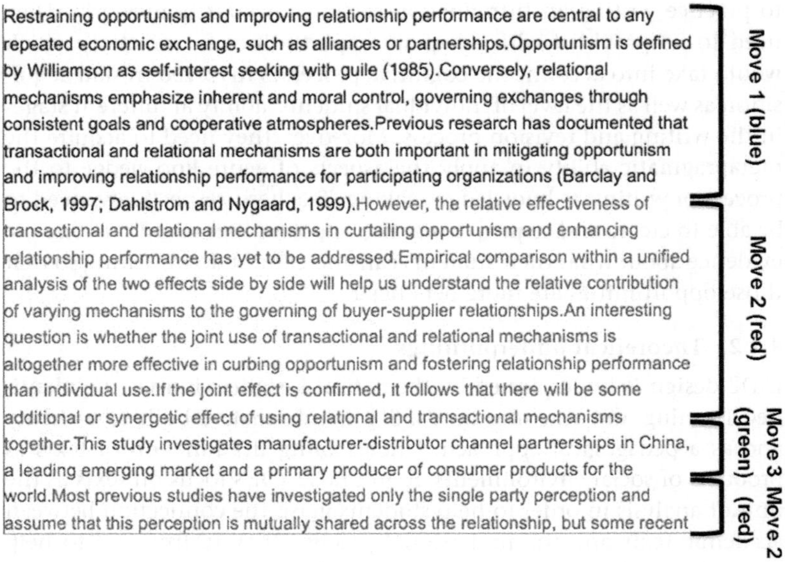
Restraining opportunism and improving relationship performance are central to any repeated economic exchange, such as alliances or partnerships.Opportunism is defined by Williamson as self-interest seeking with guile (1985).Conversely, relational mechanisms emphasize inherent and moral control, governing exchanges through consistent goals and cooperative atmospheres.Previous research has documented that transactional and relational mechanisms are both important in mitigating opportunism and improving relationship performance for participating organizations (Barclay and Brock, 1997; Dahlstrom and Nygaard, 1999).However, the relative effectiveness of transactional and relational mechanisms in curtailing opportunism and enhancing relationship performance has yet to be addressed.Empirical comparison within a unified analysis of the two effects side by side will help us understand the relative contribution of varying mechanisms to the governing of buyer-supplier relationships.An interesting question is whether the joint use of transactional and relational mechanisms is altogether more effective in curbing opportunism and fostering relationship performance than individual use.If the joint effect is confirmed, it follows that there will be some additional or synergetic effect of using relational and transactional mechanisms together.This study investigates manufacturer-distributor channel partnerships in China, a leading emerging market and a primary producer of consumer products for the world.Most previous studies have investigated only the single party perception and assume that this perception is mutually shared across the relationship, but some recent

Figure 4.2a IADE color-coded feedback on moves

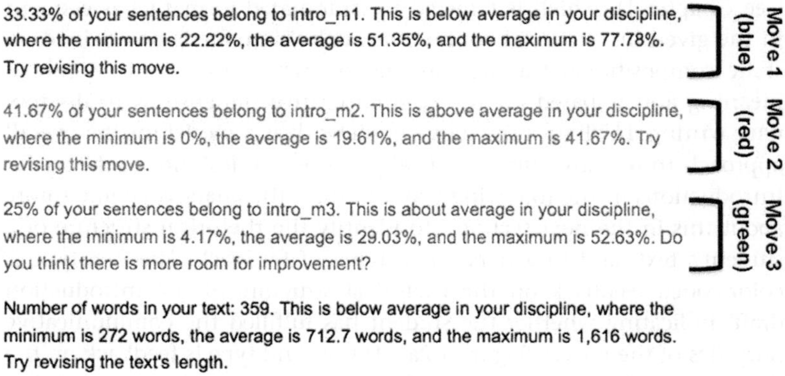
33.33% of your sentences belong to intro_m1. This is below average in your discipline, where the minimum is 22.22%, the average is 51.35%, and the maximum is 77.78%. Try revising this move.

41.67% of your sentences belong to intro_m2. This is above average in your discipline, where the minimum is 0%, the average is 19.61%, and the maximum is 41.67%. Try revising this move.

25% of your sentences belong to intro_m3. This is about average in your discipline, where the minimum is 4.17%, the average is 29.03%, and the maximum is 52.63%. Do you think there is more room for improvement?

Number of words in your text: 359. This is below average in your discipline, where the minimum is 272 words, the average is 712.7 words, and the maximum is 1,616 words. Try revising the text's length.

Figure 4.2b IADE discipline-specific numerical feedback

variety of functional meanings and meaning potential techniques, it provides the explicitness of SFL pedagogies that novice academic writers need in order to develop their metacognitive awareness.

Designed for L2 writers, IADE centers on the concepts of input, interaction, output, and salience. The process of feedback generation is conceptualized with a focus on these interactionist tenets. IADE analyzes student texts, or written output, and then uses it to generate feedback on the use of communicative moves, which is returned as modified input. The feedback is color-coded; that is, each move is marked with a particular color – move 1 is blue, move 2 is red, and move 3 is green. The color codes serve as input enhancement designed to encourage noticing of and focus on discourse form and to facilitate metacognitive monitoring. Intended to stimulate interaction during the writing process, IADE feedback either confirms the student's communicative success or points to shortcomings in production. This is meant to trigger testing of linguistic hypotheses with respect to functional meaning that the students may generate with regards to the nature of their rhetorical problem. To scaffold the students' actions upon noticing negative evidence, IADE offers four different help options: revision tips on how to revise a draft with the program more effectively, definitions of Introduction moves and steps, discipline-specific statistics on the distribution of steps in the student's discipline (similar to the numerical feedback generated for move distribution), and an annotated corpus of research article Introductions in the discipline. The annotated corpus is displayed with the same color-coding for moves, but it has the additional feature of sentence-level glosses. These glosses appear as pop-up messages showing the move and the step and are available upon clicking on individual sentences (Figure 4.3). The glosses show more than one move and step

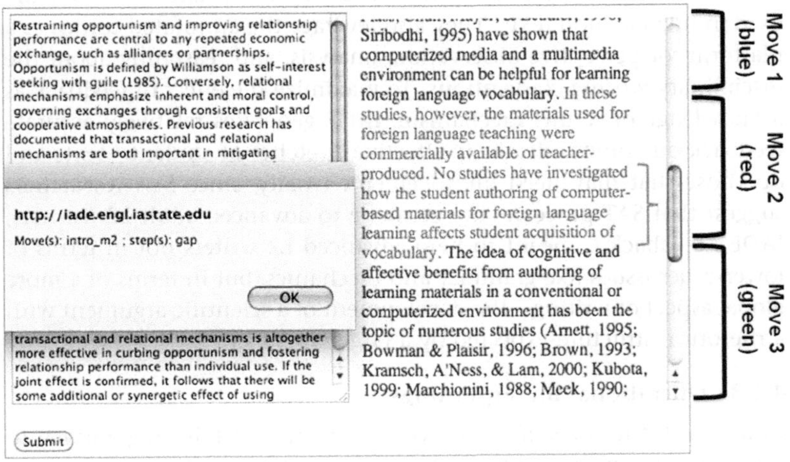

Figure 4.3 Example of a color-coded and glossed text

in cases when sentences are multifunctional. This help option is meant to allow the students to deconstruct model published texts, observe how expert writers intertwine different functional meanings, and use published texts as scaffolding as they shape their own written communication with the disciplinary community.

The screenshot in Figure 4.3 shows a Submit button located under the text-editing box. This is the practical embodiment of the SAT stipulation that repeatedly acting on new knowledge is essential for gradual automatization of that knowledge. In other words, by providing students with the opportunity to submit their work for immediate formative evaluation, IADE encourages an iterative revision process that entails extensive and deliberate practice through which students can repeatedly apply certain aspects of their declarative knowledge about the rhetorical conventions of the genre. This is deemed beneficial because, on the one hand students could develop their metapragmatic ability and, on the other hand transition to procedural knowledge. Considering that proceduralization depends on engaging declarative knowledge when attempting a task, IADE intends to reinforce the translation of students' cognitive representations into action by propping up their revision process with access to the help options as mediation sources. The help options are meant to facilitate encoding of the declarative representation of the Introduction writing task components in the students' working memory and to gradually reduce the cognitive load. The content of the help options includes explicit explanation and demonstration of what each move and step mean and how they are used in Introduction texts. They also leverage the annotated corpus as a platform for perceptive observation, analysis, and reasoning about the disciplinary writing conventions. To maximize the effect of feedback as a knowledge of results mechanism, IADE generates relatively accurate feedback on communicatively effective stretches of students' texts and on those that may need improvement. Finally, since SLA researchers suggest that SAT processes are germane to advanced adult L2 learners, IADE's feedback is meant to help advanced L2 writers not in terms of lower-order issues like grammar and mechanics, but in terms of a more global aspect of writing – the development of a scientific argument with a rhetorical structure expected by a target audience.

4.1.3 Operational underpinnings

In line with the goals of formative assessment, IADE is programmed to continuously inform students about their progress as they are working on improving their Introduction drafts. During students' interaction with IADE, this tool is presumed to assume roles necessary to boost the teaching-learning process. First, being custom-made for specific formative goals, IADE evaluates the rhetorical development of students' drafts, acknowledging with its feedback how student writing may approximate the distribution of moves in their discipline. If the writing diverges from disciplinary norms, the program directs the students with feedback that encourages the revision of unsatisfactory moves – *Try revising this move* – in order to motivate ongoing effort. Even if some moves seem to be close to the distribution in the discipline, the feedback still prompts – *Do you think there is more room for improvement?* – in order to encourage students to continue perfecting their writing. The numerical feedback indicates the status of the draft in relation to expected written performance – *[percent] of your sentences belong to move 1. This is [way below|below|about|above|way above] average in your discipline, where the minimum is [percent], the average is [percent], and the maximum is [percent].* In this advisory role, IADE also summarizes individual performance in a cumulative report.

Informed by ICALL techniques for processing natural language, IADE feedback is not a simple response automatically generated based on matching with an answer key or anticipated errors; rather, it is based on a linguistic analysis of students' texts compared to authentic language use. This intelligent feedback is designed considering the qualities that formative feedback should possess. The program's analysis engine evaluates student performance reliably every time a draft is submitted, and it is consistent in the generation of individual-specific feedback that points to move-level gaps during the revision process. The color-coded and numerical feedback is expected to ignite cognitive involvement and to promote students' monitoring of the rhetorical quality of their texts. It is also anticipated that the feedback can help students self-assess their performance and orient them towards achievable goals by informing them about minimum, average, and maximum move distribution ranges. Although rather simply presented, the feedback is complex and specific enough in that it verifies the communicative effectiveness of individualized performance against disciplinary standards and also elaborates on the results of that verification with numerical details in accompanying comments. Table 4.2 summarizes the qualities and types of feedback realized in IADE as conceptualized in the previous chapter.

The operationalization of the process of feedback generation is guided by ECD principles. The main component of the ECD blueprint informing IADE is the Evidence Model concept of observable evidence. It is

Table 4.2 IADE feedback description

Formative quality	*Feedback type*	*Description*
Goal orientation	Individual-specific	Provided to the student based on his/her input and on its comparison to the respective discipline
	Output-focused	Is based on student's written production
	Explicit	Is clearly stated and color-enhanced
Cognitive involvement	Metalinguisitc	Provided in definitional terms
	Iterative	Provided as often as requested
	Negative	Points to drawbacks in discourse development
Complexity	Verification	Identifies the presence of rhetorical moves
	Elaboration	Directs towards expected performance
	Encouraging self-correction	Contains performance-contingent prompts
Specificity	Detailed	Provides details about move distribution in targeted discipline
	Precise	Represents precise representation of discipline-specific discourse based on knowledge learned from authentic corpora
Timing	Immediate	Provided almost instantly, less than 60 seconds from the time of submission

operationalized through the program's ability to identify the discourse moves in students' drafts, which constitute evidence, and to evaluate this evidence by comparing it to respective knowledge learned from disciplinary corpora. Considering that IADE is meant for formative assessment during the revision task, only the Presentation and the Response Processing Processes from the delivery framework appear pertinent and are thus implemented in IADE. In addition, based on the Evidence Composite Library contained in the ECD framework, a database storing all the data is built into the program as well. The ECD influence is reflected in the system overview shown in Figure 4.4 and in the description below.

The Presentation Process is operationalized through a web-interface where the students can access a sign-up page, a log-in page, and a sign-out option as well as a drafting page with instructions, a resubmit button, and help options. After the first submission, the drafting page displays both the system's feedback (color-coded and numerical) and the revision textbox in which the students can make the necessary changes to be submitted for further evaluation.

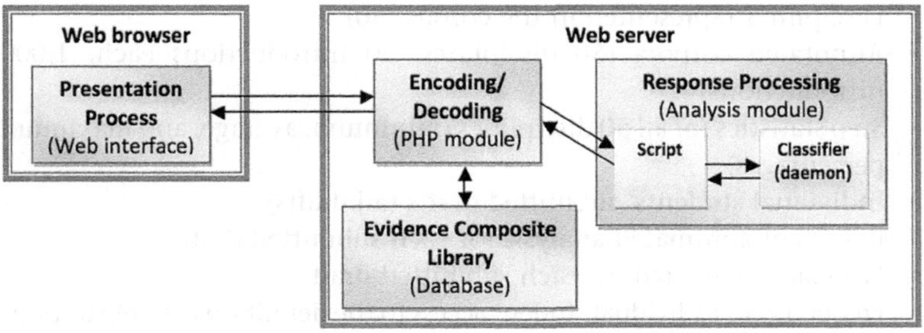

Figure 4.4 IADE system overview based on ECD

IADE's Response Processing is an analysis module, which incorporates two components: a Python script and a Support Vector Machine (SVM) classifier. The Python script executes pre-programmed commands such as breaking the text into sentences and sending each sentence to the classifier for automated analysis. The classifier analyzes and classifies each sentence as belonging to a particular move. The classification is done by means of identifying the lexical features that are indicative of a certain move (the classification process is explained in the next section of this chapter). Then, percentages for the move distribution in the student's draft are automatically calculated and compared with the distribution of moves in the annotated corpus of the respective discipline. The classification into moves and the numerical information about the distribution of moves both in the student draft and in the annotated corpus are included in the feedback. On a side note, SVM models are generally very big, and that presents a technical problem for development. First, loading and unloading the model for every draft submission is not practical, and second, loading more than one model at the same time when multiple users submit their drafts for processing is not feasible. Nevertheless, it is imperative that the system allows concurrent access by multiple users and concurrent analyses by the same model. To address this challenge, the SVM classifier is integrated as part of a module continuously running as a background process on the server, which in the Unix world is known as a daemon.

The Evidence Composite Library is a database containing the following information that is necessary to make IADE functional both as a revision tool and as an evidence gathering platform:

- Student information (first and last name, login name, e-mail address)
- Student classification (master's or doctoral)

- Disciplines represented in the corpus (50)
- Annotated corpora (50 disciplines, 20 Introductions each, 1,000 Introductions)
- Step statistics for all 50 disciplines (minimum, average, and maximum percentages)
- Individual students' submitted drafts (all drafts)
- Results of automated analysis for each submitted draft
- Feedback generated for each submitted draft
- Frequency of individual student access to the definitions in help options
- Frequency of individual student access to the annotated corpora in help options
- Frequency of individual student access to the step statistics in help options
- Frequency of individual student access to the revision tips in help options
- Date and time of each draft submission and of individual student access to help options

The Encoding/Decoding module, which is a hypertext preprocessor (PHP) module with a number of extensions, is an intermediary functional link that connects the three ECD-based system components. It handles queries with the help of the database. It also takes in the texts submitted by students and transforms them into a format recognizable for processing. Then, it receives the analyzed texts and the feedback from the analysis module, transforms the texts in color-coded readable hypertext markup language (HTML) format, and makes all that available on the user interface.

4.2 Empirical prerequisites

4.2.1 Corpus data

Equally important to the development of IADE is the specialized corpus data needed for the program's automated analysis and feedback. The data were prepared through a thorough move analysis of a corpus of 1,000 published research article Introductions. The articles for the corpus were obtained from reputable online academic journals in 50 disciplines, each discipline being represented by 20 texts. All articles in the corpus reported on empirical research and were published between 2003 and 2009. The Introduction sections from the corpus were converted to plain text files and were manually annotated using a schema of 3 moves and 17 steps based on the Swalesian framework (Table 4.3).

Table 4.3 Annotation schema

Move	***Step***
Move 1: Establishing a territory	Step 1: Claiming centrality
	Step 2: Making topic generalizations
	Step 3: Reviewing previous research
Move 2: Identifying a niche	Step 4: Indicating a gap
	Step 5: Highlighting a problem
	Step 6: Raising general questions
	Step 7: Proposing general hypotheses
	Step 8: Presenting a justification
Move 3: Addressing the niche	Step 9: Introducing present research descriptively
	Step 10: Introducing present research purposefully
	Step 11: Presenting research questions
	Step 12: Presenting research hypotheses
	Step 13: Clarifying definitions
	Step 14: Summarizing methods
	Step 15: Announcing principal outcomes
	Step 16: Stating the value of the present research
	Step 17: Outlining the structure of the paper

Text annotation was done in Callisto, open source software for linguistic annotation by the MITRE Corporation, which allows annotators to create unique tag-set definitions depending on text analysis needs – in this case, the move and step tags. The texts were annotated at sentence level, each sentence being labeled with a move and a step within that move. Consider the following example from a Chemical Engineering text:

> <intro_m1 'Metal complexes containing porphyrin, salen, and phthalocyanin ligands are frequently used in oxidation and hydroxylation reactions as chemical models to mimic enzymes [1], [2], [3] and [4].' step = review>
>
> <intro_m1 'A recent trend of research in biomimetic study is to immobilize these organometallic complexes onto a solid support.' step = centrality>
>
> <intro_m2 'It is anticipated that this immobilization process will make the catalyst easier to handle especially during separation from the liquid medium.' step = hypothesis>
>
> <intro_m2 'Besides, the support might also play certain roles in stabilizing the catalytic activity and/or modifying the chemoselectivity, regioselectivity, and shape selectivity of the catalyst.' step = hypothesis>

<intro_m3 'Our long-term research interest is to mimic enzymes, especially hemocyanin which acts as an O2 carrier in mollusk and arthropod.' step = purpose>

The notation <intro_m1> refers to Move 1, Establishing a territory; <intro_m2> refers to Move 2, Establishing a niche; and <intro_m3> refers to Move 3, Occupying the niche. As shown in the examples above, the move notation precedes each sentence. Following the sentence is the notation for the step within the identified move. The notations for steps are labeled with a key word from the name of each step, for example <step = review> stands for Reviewing previous research; <step = centrality> stands for Claiming centrality; <step = hypothesis> stands for Proposing general hypotheses; and <step = purpose> stands for Announcing present research purposefully.

Annotations were frequently multi-layered for cases when the same sentence signified more than one move or more than one step. This made it possible to capture an array of semantic shades rendered by a given sentence. For example, the sentence *'This paper presents an application of simulation, multivariate statistics, and simulation metamodels to analyze throughput of multiproduct batch chemical plants.'* combines several steps of Move 3 and is annotated accordingly: *This paper presents an application of* introduces the present research descriptively, *simulation, multivariate statistics, and simulation metamodels* are indicative of the methodology employed in the study, and *to analyze throughput of multiproduct batch chemical plants* states the research purpose.

<intro_m3 'This paper presents an application of step = description>

<intro_m3 'simulation, multivariate statistics, and simulation metamodels step = method>

<intro_m3 'to analyze throughput of multiproduct batch chemical plants' step = purpose>

The corpus was annotated by two well-trained coders. The inter-coder agreement was calculated for a random sample of 487 sentences using the Kappa (*k*) metric, which is the probability of agreement minus chance agreement calculated as follows:

$$\kappa = \frac{P(A) - P(E)}{1 - P(E)}$$

where *P(A)* represents observed probability of agreement, and *P(E)* is the expected probability of agreement (that is chance agreement). Given three moves and uniform distribution among them,

$$P(E) = \left(\frac{1}{3}\right)^2$$

The two annotators had an average *k* of .94 over the three moves and high agreements for each move (.93 for move 1; .92 for move 2; and .98 for move 3).

Corpus annotation was not only a prerequisite for training and developing the analysis module of IADE, but also a source for the feedback. The content of the numerical feedback draws from analyses of the distribution of moves in each discipline. Similar statistics were included in IADE's help options for the purpose of providing the students with a more detailed description of the discourse development of Introductions at the level of steps. The annotated corpus was also integrated as one of the help options.

4.2.2 Automated analysis approach

A sub-corpus of 401 randomly selected Introductions was used to train IADE's analysis engine to classify Introduction sections. This was a stratified sample of 267,029 words; each file was on average 665.91 words long. It contained 11,149 sentences as data instances. The training task was approached as a classification problem. In other words, given a sentence and a finite set of moves and steps, what move/step does the sentence signify? (This task is very similar to the identification of the discourse structure of short argumentative essays discussed in Burstein et al. (2003), the difference being in the genre and the type of the discourse functions.) In order to classify sentences correctly, features that can reliably indicate a move needed to be identified first. A text-categorization approach was chosen for this purpose (Pendar & Cotos, 2008), where each sentence is treated as a data item to be classified, and is represented as an n-dimensional vector in the R^n Euclidean space. More formally, a sentence *Si* is represented as the vector $\bar{s}_i = <f_1, f_2, \ldots, f_n>$ where each component f_j of the vector $\bar{s}_i$ represents a measure of feature *j* in the sentence s_i. The task of the learning algorithm is to find a function $F{:}S \rightarrow C$ that would map the sentences in the corpus (*S*) to classes (*C*) in *M* = {m1, m2, m3} (where m1, m2, and m3 stand for move 1, move 2, and move 3, respectively).

An important problem was choosing features that would allow for proper classification of the data instances into the classes in question. For this purpose, word unigrams, bigrams, and trigrams (single words, two word sequences, and three word sequences) were extracted from the annotated corpus. Not all the *n*-grams were used. The low frequency *n*-grams at a cut-off point of five were removed from the data pool. The total number of each remaining set of *n*-grams used was 3,951 unigrams, 8,916 bigrams, and 3,605 trigrams. To identify which *n*-grams were better indicators of moves, odds ratios were calculated using the formula

$$OR(t_i, m_j) = \frac{p(t_i|m_j)\cdot(1-p(t_i|\bar{m}_j))}{(1-p(t_i|m_j))\cdot p(t_i|\bar{m}_j)}$$

where $OR(t_i, m_j)$ is the odds ratio of the term (*n*-gram) t_i occurring in move m_j; $p(t_i|m_j)$ is the probability of seeing the term t_i given the move m_j; and $p(t_i|\bar{m}_j)$ is the probability of seeing the term t_i given any move other than m_j. The above conditional probabilities were calculated as maximum likelihood estimates.

$$p(t_i|m_j) = \frac{\text{count }(t_i \text{ in } m_j)}{\sum_{k=1}^{N} \text{count }(t_k \text{ in } m_j)}$$

where N is the total number of *n*-grams in the corpus of sentences S. The terms with maximum odds ratios were selected as features and were used to build IADE's classifier. More details can be found in Pendar and Cotos (2008), but it is worth mentioning here that the classifier's performance was tested by means of five-fold cross validation on 14 different feature sets. The evaluation measures employed were accuracy (proportion of classifications that agree with human assigned labels), precision (proportion of classifications assigned to a category that actually belong to it), and recall (proportion of classifications belonging to a category that are labeled correctly). The accuracies for the unigram, bigram, and trigram models ranged between 60 and 75 percent. The trigram models resulted in the best precision (87 percent), and the unigram models in the best recall (64 percent). With respect to the bigrams, increasing the size of the bigram feature set caused a decline in model precision and a rise in model recall. Therefore, only the unigrams and trigrams were used to develop the prototype analysis engine.

4.2.3 Reliability

In addition to the system-centric evaluation of the analysis engine, its performance was assessed by comparison with human judgment. Two raters evaluated the quality of the rhetorical development of the first and last drafts produced by 16 students who took the targeted L2 research writing course. Before rating, the raters attended 18 hours of training, where they were acquainted with Swales' move schema and the class materials. The training covered not only explanatory and example materials, but also practice, which consisted of annotating research article Introductions as well as rating student Introduction drafts (other than the ones to be rated for analyzer evaluation purposes). The raters were first trained to annotate texts in order to gain a better understanding of the genre and of the variation among disciplines. Aspects of the training included demonstration and explanation, individual scoring, and debriefing. The raters practiced scoring student texts according to a move-based rubric developed to mirror IADE's approach to text analysis. The texts were provided to the raters without any identification signs or information that would disclose whether the drafts were first or last. To make better judgments about the drafts, the raters were also given the statistics for all the steps in each student's discipline. The statistics were helpful in that they informed the raters of the presence or absence of certain steps in the students' discipline as well as of the length of the steps. With this information, the raters were able to evaluate the students' use of moves more objectively.

Given that the raters each had to score 32 drafts (16 first drafts and 16 last drafts) and to judge the quality of three moves in these texts, there were 96 overall cases for possible agreement, of which they agreed on 77 cases. In other words, the raters agreed about 8 out of 10 times. A more robust measure of inter-rater reliability, Cohen's kappa was also calculated as it was done to estimate inter-coder reliability between the two corpus annotators. Cohen's kappa was chosen because this measure operates under the assumption that the same raters evaluate the same set of items, which was precisely the case here. All the coefficients indicate a satisfactory level of agreement between the raters (k .63 for move 1; k .72 for move 2; and k .76 for move 3).

Final human scores on moves and the scores assigned based on IADE's automated analysis were then used to measure IADE-human reliability. IADE and human raters agreed on 70 out of 96 cases, the agreement being 73 percent. IADE-human rater reliability was also estimated through calculations of Cohen's kappa, which showed that the agreement was moderate for each move (*k* .58 for move 1; *k* .53 for move 2; and *k* .61 for move 3). It is worth noting that, unlike disagreement among human raters, who almost equally disagreed on both first and last drafts, the disagreement between IADE and humans occurred mostly on first drafts (17 of 27 percent of disagreement cases). The disagreement rate between automated and human scores decreased for last drafts.

Part II
Implementing and Evaluating Genre-Based AWE for L2 Research Writing

Introduction

The second part of this volume shapes an empirical evaluation argument about the potential effectiveness of genre-based AWE for L2 research writing based on a comprehensive investigation of the IADE prototype. After a description in Chapter 5 of the implementation context and of the methodological approach employed to investigate the effectiveness of IADE, I focus on an in-depth account of empirical evidence in Chapter 6. I exhibit multifaceted evidence that elucidates the nature of the Language Learning Potential, Meaning Focus, Learner Fit, and Impact qualities (Chapelle, 2001) of IADE, and then discuss the implications of the empirical findings and of the utilized conceptual framework for genre-based AWE design. Building on an interpretation of the results vis-à-vis cognitive and socio-disciplinary dimensions of research writing, I illustrate in Chapter 7 the transformation of the prototype into a full-fledged genre-based AWE program that presents a viable augmentation to L2 genre pedagogy.

5
Exploring the IADE Genre-Based Prototype

Chapter 5 places the IADE prototype in the instructional context for which it was developed. The chapter begins with a description of the context, first explaining the procedure by which graduate students are generally placed in the targeted writing course. Then, I elaborate on the pedagogical approach of this course, providing examples of tasks and technologies employed to help the students acquire declarative knowledge about the writing conventions in their particular disciplines. The second part of the chapter introduces the setting-up of a large study carried out to evaluate the potential of IADE to meet learning and teaching needs.

5.1 L2 writing context

5.1.1 Placement

Iowa State University is home to more than 3,700 international students from more than 100 foreign countries. These students are admitted to the university if they meet both academic and English language requirements. To meet the language requirement, graduate students need to have Internet-Based TOEFL (IBT) scores of 71 with minimum scores of 17 in the speaking and writing sections; a Paper-Based TOEFL (PBT) score of 530; or an International English Language Testing System (IELTS) overall band score of 6.0 with no sub score below 5.5. Upon arriving on campus, international graduate students are required to take the institutional English Placement Test (EPT), which contains three components – reading comprehension, listening comprehension, and writing. The task for the writing component of EPT requires students to respond to a prompt, which includes an excerpt from empirically obtained data and elicits data analysis leading to interpretations of results and drawing conclusions. Students' responses to the writing prompt are scored by human raters who assign them a score with one of three potential uses – pass, which means that a student passes the test and is not required to take English writing courses; placement in an advanced academic writing course, which focuses on academic genres; and placement in an intermediate level writing course, which focuses on lexico-grammatical aspects of English writing. IADE was implemented in the advanced academic writing course.

5.1.2 Course description

The advanced academic writing course for international graduate students at Iowa State University is a semester-long course. The teaching approach is briefly described in my discussion of practical challenges of genre-based pedagogy in Chapter 1 (also see Cortes, 2007). Here, I will describe some major aspects of the course at the time of IADE implementation. For coursework, the students were encouraged to collect a small corpus of 20 to 30 research articles published in their discipline. Alternatively, they could choose a relevant sub-corpus from a specialized corpus of research articles in 50 disciplines provided by the instructor. Since the course units focused on individual sections of the research article, the corpora for each discipline were separated into Abstract, Introduction, Methods, Results, and Discussion/Conclusion components.

The instructional activities combined top-down and bottom-up approaches to corpus analysis. In other words, the students analyzed text structure, at the same time examining the use of lexico-grammatical features at the level of discourse and observing typical patterns of their occurrence. The top-down approach was realized through deductive activities, which were based on the reading materials compiled from genre analysis works, where researchers examined disciplinary writing and provided pedagogical recommendations. The readings served as reference materials for students, guiding their corpus analyses and completion of so-called *Exploration for structure* tasks. An example of such a task for Introduction analysis is presented in Figure 5.1.

The bottom-up approach relied on inductive activities called *Exploration for language use*, which required the students to observe the linguistic means typically used in the research article genre. The students were first asked to select words and expressions that were representative of a particular rhetorical element of a given RA section and that would help them effectively build it. For example, expressions such as *we first determined, was calculated as, the proposed approach is mainly demonstrated through* indicate the research procedure; *the expression of … resulted in, the data indicated that, differences were found in* report the

In this corpus exploration task, you will explore the communicative functions of **Move 2, Identifying a Niche**. This move can be realized by the following steps:

- Indicating a gap
- Highlighting a problem
- Raising general questions
- Proposing general hypotheses
- Presenting justification

Using Callisto, open and read annotated Introduction sections in your discipline. Observe whether Move 2 (the parts of text colored in red) is at the beginning, middle, end, or throughout the Introduction. While reading, take detailed notes on the peculiarities of Move 2 in your field of study. Pay close attention to the steps within this move and try to identify the characteristic features of each step. The following questions will guide your observations and conclusions:

1. How is Move 2 distributed in the Introduction?
2. Do all the steps appear in Move 2? Why or why not?
3. Is there any particular order in the distribution of the steps? Do you think the order matters? Why or why not?
4. Which step is the most extensive? Why?
5. Is there any overlap in Move 2? That is, are there sentences that represent more than one step? Why do you think authors may combine the functions of several steps?

Figure 5.1 Corpus-based top-down analysis task example

findings; *this suggests that, it seems noteworthy that, could be ascribed to* are used in commenting on the results. For the purpose of clarity, the students were advised to organize their findings into lists of words or expressions with move and step subheadings. They also used a concordancing program to observe the linguistic environment in which the selected language items occurred.

5.1.3 Computer tools

The course was taught in computer labs. The disciplinary corpora, the reading materials, and the class tasks were all provided to students through the Moodle course management system. The forums in Moodle added a supplementary source of reference – peers. By uploading their responses to the corpus-based tasks, the students were able not only to document the writing patterns that they identified in their corpora, but also to access each other's postings and compare their corpus observations with the observations and interpretations of their classmates. The students often included specific examples in their forum posts, which were particularly helpful for those who were not entirely sure whether they understood what characterizes a particular move or step. Moodle was also used as a submission portal for students' RA sections drafts, on which they received peer and teacher feedback, as well as for the research article final assignment.

To complete the Introduction exploration activities, the students accessed the annotated corpus by opening the annotated texts in

Callisto one by one. Callisto was chosen for this purpose because it displays the texts in a visually clear way. Figure 5.2 shows an annotated text in Callisto. The move-level annotation is reflected by three colors for each move. By scrolling over or by clicking on a sentence, one can see the step that the sentence represents and the multiple layers of steps when there are such. This information is organized by move and step below the text window.

WordSearch was another computer tool used by students in this course (Cortes, 2007). This concordancer facilitated searches of up to four consecutive words, displaying concordance lines resulting from the query, the number of matches, and the processed corpus files. The query output contained stretches of text with 30 words before and 30 words after the searched linguistic item; this provided the students with the immediate context in which the item was used. The searched items could be words or word combinations that the students identified as indicative of certain rhetorical functions when completing the *Exploration for language use* corpus tasks. For instance, the students could identify clusters like *remains to be, have not yet been, lack of* characteristic of indicating a gap in Move 2 and then query Wordsearch to further observe the linguistic environment in which they occurred. Queries could also include the * wildcard, which, when accompanying lemmas, yielded instances of both base forms and derivatives. For example, if the * wildcard was used with *importan**, the search returned *important, importance, importantly*. The students saved the output of each search in a separate automatically created Word or text document.

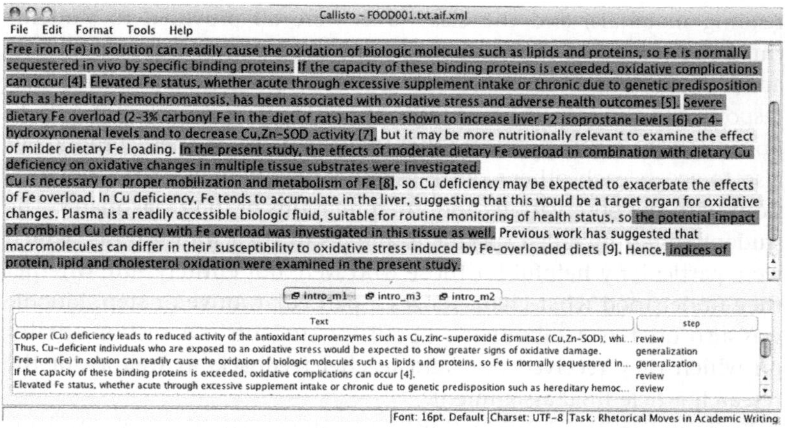

Figure 5.2 Example of annotated text in Callisto

5.1.4 Classroom implementation

IADE was implemented as part of classroom instruction during two semesters in six sections of the course. The first instructional unit focused on the writing conventions of Introductions based on Swales' move schema. In class, the students completed corpus exploration tasks as described above and collected observations that they could use for writing an Introduction for their own paper. To provide the students with an opportunity for practice guided by formative discipline-specific feedback, the instructor introduced IADE before they had to submit their draft for peer and teacher feedback. She explained the way it functioned, demonstrated how to work with it, and then assigned the revision task. Students' interaction with the program consisted of submitting the draft for automated evaluation, receiving immediate individualized feedback, making revisions, and resubmitting the revised draft to the system. This process began in class, but the students were encouraged to spend as much time as they needed with IADE outside of class. The implementation of IADE unfolded in parallel with an empirical study aimed at evaluating the effectiveness of this AWE prototype for L2 genre writing pedagogy.

5.2 Methodological approach

5.2.1 Research design

On the level of evaluating technology for language learning in general, Chapelle (2007) specifies three targets for evaluation: 'what is taught in a complete course,' 'what is taught through technology in a complete course,' and 'what is taught through technology' (p. 30). In the first case, an entire technology-based course is evaluated; in the second case, CALL materials used for learning a subset of course objectives; and in the third case, the use of technology as support and enhancement of a face-to-face course. In the study of IADE, 'what is taught through technology in a complete course' was the target for evaluation since this program represents a CALL tool used for the learning of rhetorical moves in research article Introductions, which is one subset of the course objectives.

The evaluation of innovative technologies, such as IADE, is 'perhaps the most significant challenge teachers and curriculum developers face when attempting to introduce innovation into language education' (Chapelle, 2007, p. 30). A great challenge is that the technology cannot be isolated to investigate its effects. Evaluation requires an approach that conjoins techniques for studying both how the software is used and what results from using the software. Therefore, this study pursued the process-product approach to CALL research (Warschauer & Ware, 2006) to investigate the interaction between IADE use and learning processes and outcomes.

Given this complex focus, I employed a mixed methods research design, 'in which the researcher tends to base knowledge claims on pragmatic grounds' and in which data collection 'involves gathering both numeric information [...] as well as text information [...] so that the final database represents both quantitative and qualitative information' (Creswell, 2003, pp. 19–20). To maintain a strong theoretical grounding for the empirical evaluation of IADE, I chose the concurrent transformative strategy, which requires that research is conducted under the umbrella of a theory-guided framework (Creswell, 2003). Here, the guiding theory is instructed SLA represented in Chapelle's (2001) conceptual framework. Drawing on SLA, this framework places an emphasis on identifying evidence in learners' observable behaviour during the completion of language learning tasks, bringing together the CALL materials and the ways in which learners interact with them. The framework contains six qualities that CALL materials should possess and that are, therefore, put forth as criteria for evaluation: Language Learning Potential, Learner Fit, Meaning Focus, Impact, Authenticity, and Practicality. The first four criteria are particularly relevant for the empirical evaluation of IADE, as they allow for the formulation of specific hypothetical claims steering the accumulation of necessary evidence (summarized in Figure 5.3).

5.2.1.1 Language Learning Potential claims

- IADE feedback can stimulate focus on and noticing of discourse form;
- Focus on discourse form triggered by IADE feedback can facilitate learning gains;
- Focus on discourse form triggered by IADE feedback can facilitate improvement in rhetorical quality;
- Practice and modified interaction with IADE may contribute to improvement.

5.2.1.2 Meaning Focus claims

- IADE feedback can stimulate learners' focus on the functional meaning of their discourse;
- Interaction with IADE can facilitate more effective construction of functional meaning.

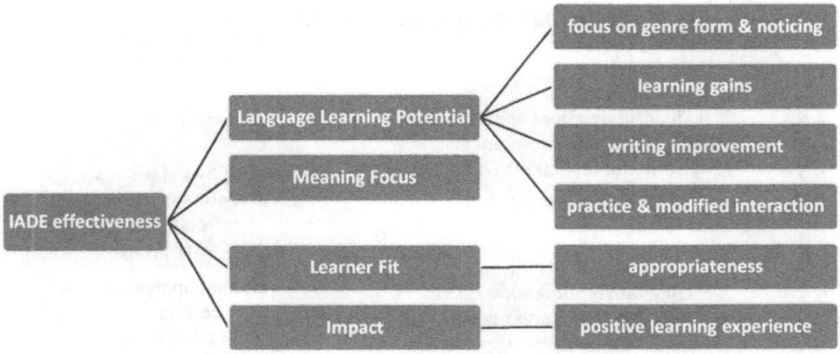

Figure 5.3 IADE effectiveness evaluated in view of claims about CALL qualities

5.2.1.3 Learner Fit claim

- IADE feedback on targeted rhetorical forms is appropriate for students with the characteristics of intended learners.

5.2.1.4 Impact claim

- Revising with IADE can be a positive learning experience.

To fully understand the nature of factors that can potentially shed light on the formative effectiveness of IADE and its feedback, evidence was elicited from a variety of data sources. The quantitative data consisted of Likert-scale and yes/no survey responses, scores that measured learning gains based on pre-/post-tests, scores that measured discourse improvement based on automated and human ratings, and frequencies of submission and access to IADE's help options. The qualitative data consisted of open-ended survey responses, participants' first and last drafts, and screen captures, as well as recordings of think-aloud protocols, observations, and interviews. These data were collected during the implementation of IADE over the course of two semesters.

Figure 5.4 shows how Chapelle's (2001) CALL evaluation framework overarches the chosen methodological approach. Under this framework, the quantitative and qualitative data, listed in the first two oval shapes, were collected concurrently and integrated during the analysis and interpretation phase, shown in the circle on the right. In this phase, the main focus was on quantitative evidence, which was collected from

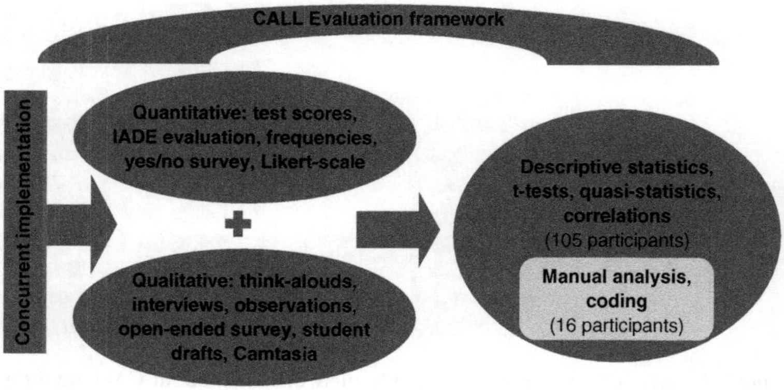

Figure 5.4 Mixed-methods approach

105 participants. Qualitative data, consisting of 83 participants' open-ended survey responses as well as audio and screen recordings of 16 participants, were examined to obtain a deeper understanding of the investigated phenomena and to support the generalization claims to be made based on numerical results.

5.2.2 Participants

The 105 students (59 male and 46 female) participating in this study were international students who were registered in six sections of the course. They were all enrolled in graduate programs: 37 were Master's degree students and 68 were doctoral students specializing in one of the following disciplines:

1. Accounting
2. Aerospace Engineering
3. Agronomy
4. Analytical Chemistry
5. Animal Science
6. Biochemistry
7. Bioinformatics
8. Biology
9. Biomedical Science
10. Bionanotechnology
11. Chemical Engineering

12. Computer Engineering
13. Computer Science
14. Curriculum and Instruction
15. Economics
16. Electrical Engineering and Power Systems
17. Environmental Engineering
18. Ergonomics
19. Food and Lodging Management
20. Genetics
21. Human Health and Public Performance
22. Industrial Engineering
23. Journalism
24. Materials Science and Engineering
25. Mathematics
26. Mechanical Engineering
27. Physics and Astronomy
28. Plant Breeding
29. Public Administration
30. Sociology
31. Statistics
32. Textiles and Clothing
33. Urban and Regional Planning
34. Veterinary Medicine

The students, aged between 22 and 44, had different language backgrounds. English was a second language for 79 participants, 24 spoke two languages other than their native and English, and 2 spoke three other languages. Their English language proficiency levels also varied, ranging between 80 and 104 on TOEFL IBT, between 243 and 255 on TOEFL CBT, and between 520 and 667 on TOEFL PBT. When asked to self-evaluate their writing skill, none of the students believed it was excellent; most thought it was somewhere between good and fair. Their period of study at a US university ranged from a few months to two years. Given that the course targeted the research article genre, of interest was the students' research writing experience. Most students were in the first year of their graduate program and had not written a research article in English before enrolling in this course. Of the 19 students who had written research articles in English, 14 had produced them as part of their course work and did not pursue publishing (Table 5.1).

Table 5.1 Participants' characteristics

L1 (# stud)	Other lang-s (# stud)	Semesters at US univ. (# stud)	TOEFL scores (test type)	RA in L1		RA in English	
				Yes	No	Yes	No
Chinese (72)	1 (79)	1 (67)	80–104 (IBT)	43	62	19	86
Thai (1)	2 (24)	2 (19)	243–255 (CBT)	(22 no/pub)		(14 no/pub)	
Italian (1)	3 (2)	3 (10)	520–667 (PBT)				
Spanish (7)		4 (4)					
Korean (11)		5 (5)					
Portuguese (2)							
Arabic (3)							
Turkish (4)							
Telugu (2)							
Filipino (1)							
Greek (1)							

5.2.3 Procedure

Figure 5.5 outlines the procedural steps and the types of data collected during the implementation of IADE in the classroom. Data collection began after the teacher's explicit instruction on Introduction writing. The students were given a pre-test on the Introduction moves and steps. The pre-test was delivered at this time as opposed to prior to instruction because its purpose was to measure not the learning gains after instruction, but rather after having revised with IADE. After the pre-test, the students were assigned to write a draft of their own Introduction section as homework and then began revising it with IADE in class. Introspective data were collected during students' revision with IADE, different pieces of interaction evidence being recorded in the program's database. When the final Introduction draft was due for submission, a post-test and a survey were delivered. Interviews were also conducted at that point in time. The consent form approved by the university Institutional Review Board was handed out prior to data collection.

5.2.4 Data collection instruments

5.2.4.1 Pre- and post-tests

The pre-test and post-test were designed to measure the students' knowledge of Introduction moves and steps before and after their interaction with IADE. Both tests consisted of two tasks: the first task required the students to label the moves and the steps in decontextualized examples, and the second task required them to do the same with the sentences of a sample Introduction. In the second task, being given

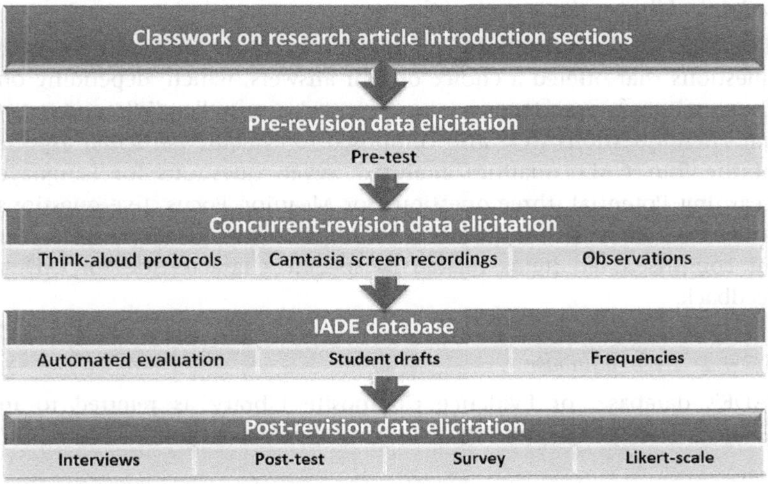

Figure 5.5 Study procedure

the entire text, the students could make their judgments about the function of each sentence based on the context. The texts were carefully selected to exhibit the same moves and steps and to be comprehensible enough, not burdened by discipline-specific terminology. Both texts included in the tests were in Economics and proved to satisfy these requirements after being piloted with a group of 17 students who had taken the course one semester prior to this study.

5.2.4.2 Yes/no and open-ended survey questions

The survey contained 25 yes/no questions about the four CALL qualities under investigation. The first 12 elicited information related to the Language Learning Potential of IADE by inquiring about students' focus on moves as well as their perceptions of learning and self-improvement. The Learner Fit quality was addressed by five questions, through which the students were asked to evaluate the appropriateness and helpfulness of different features of IADE. Three other questions aimed to obtain evidence of Meaning Focus, or whether and how the students paid attention to the meaning of their discourse while revising with IADE. Evidence of the fourth quality, Impact, was elicited through five questions about the students' experiences during their interaction with the program. All the questions in the survey were accompanied by open-ended follow-up questions such as *Why?* or *How?*

5.2.4.3 Likert-scale survey questions

The Likert-scale instrument complemented other data sources with questions that offered a choice of four answers, which, depending on the question, were: *a lot* or *very well, somewhat* or *well, a little,* and *not at all.* These questions were also composed to evaluate particular aspects of the four CALL qualities analyzed: seven questions for Language Learning Potential, three questions for Meaning Focus, five questions for Learner Fit, and four questions for Impact. One question for Learner Fit comprised ten items related to specific characteristics of IADE's feedback.

5.2.4.4 IADE database

IADE's database, or Evidence Composite Library as referred to in Chapter 4, helped capture the following types of data:

- Individual students' submitted drafts (all drafts)
- Results of automated analysis for each submitted draft
- Frequency of individual student access to the definitions in help options
- Frequency of individual student access to the annotated corpora in help options
- Frequency of individual student access to the step statistics in help options
- Frequency of individual student access to the revision tips in help options
- Date and time of each draft submission and of individual student access to help options

5.2.4.5 Think-aloud protocols

Sixteen students volunteered to interact with IADE in a controlled experimental setting outside of class for the purpose of introspective data collection through think-aloud protocols (Ericsson & Simon, 1987). To ensure that the students understood this task – which was unusual for them – they were given written instructions asking them to say whatever they were thinking about, whatever they were looking at, whatever they were feeling, and whatever they were doing to go about the task. Additionally, they watched a short live demonstration of a think-aloud protocol before they began revising with the program. The think-aloud time ranged from 25 to 37 minutes. Whenever it was necessary, the students were prompted to verbalize their thoughts.

Camtasia Studio 5 by TechSmith was used to unobtrusively record the protocols.

5.2.4.6 *Screen capture*

The screen recording function in Camtasia Studio 5 was used to record these 16 students' interaction with IADE visible on the computer screen.

5.2.4.7 *Observations*

The same 16 students were observed as they were revising with IADE. Observation notes about each student's behavior were made on paper, and question marks were put next to the entries that required further clarification. For example, a question mark accompanied this observation note: *'Then he thinks more about what he wrote and how it sounds (he keeps reading and re-reading those pieces of text), and decides that there is indeed a reason for why the program shows what it shows.'*

5.2.4.8 *Interviews*

Immediately after the revision sessions with IADE, retrospective interviews of 10–15 minutes were conducted. The interviews were semi-structured because the questions originated from the notes marked with a question mark during the observation. The potential point of interest in the note exemplified above was followed up in the interview with the question *'At that point, after having thought a little bit about that sentence, you said that the program was right. What made you say that?'* Audacity, a free open source digital audio editor and recording application was used to record the interview data.

5.2.4.9 *Transcription and coding*

The think-aloud, screen recording, observation, and interview data were transcribed and coded in Transana, open source qualitative data analysis software developed at the Wisconsin Center for Education Research at the University of Wisconsin-Madison. In Transana, these data were organized into so-called 'series' with the video, audio, and transcript files for each participant. The think-aloud protocols and screen captures recorded with Camtasia were combined into one transcript containing both the participants' utterances and the specific modifications they made while thinking aloud. For example, the insertion in square brackets in this excerpt represents the modification a student made as he was speaking, *'I'm still looking at the last sentence ... and to see if I can make some changes and the program can respond to these changes. Maybe I can try to be specific and say that "the results of this paper". Yeah, let's try to do that. [makes the change: The results show that... → The results of this study show that .... and submits].'*

The qualitative data analysis in Transana was done according to a coding taxonomy developed based on the results of a pilot study. The taxonomy consisted of several coding categories, which will be presented further as part of the data analysis for each of the four CALL qualities investigated. To ensure the reliability of coding, the think-aloud protocols, interviews, and observations from the pilot study data were coded twice with an interval of eight months. The comparison of coded data helped increase intra-coder reliability (Cohen's kappa .88) and refine the coding categories.

5.2.5 Data analysis

5.2.5.1 Language Learning Potential

Following from the theoretical assumptions in the conceptual design of IADE, for Language Learning Potential the data were examined to support four hypothetical claims about the effects of the program with respect to: (1) noticing of and focus on discourse form; (2) learning gains; (3) improvement; and (4) role of practice and modified interaction. Table 5.2 presents each claim along with respective data sources and analyses.

The analysis of survey data was the same for all four CALL qualities investigated. To quantitatively examine the points of interest, percentages for yes/no and Likert-scale responses were calculated and compared. For the ultimate purpose of overall evaluation of a given CALL quality, the four choices were equaled to a certain degree of evidence strength. In other words, *a lot* or *very well* was considered as excellent evidence, *somewhat* or *well* as good evidence, *a little* as weak evidence, and *not at all* as lack of evidence. The responses to the open-ended survey questions were analyzed by identifying emerging themes, which were then quantified in terms of percentages of students who mentioned them.

To measure the degree of learning gains, the pre- and post-tests were scored for every sentence in each of the two tasks. The decontextulized sentences in task one had unambiguous and clearly expressed functions realized through vocabulary that signaled a certain move and step. Similarly, the texts chosen for the second task had a clear rhetorical development signposted by functional lexical items. Only one correct answer was possible for each sentence in both test tasks. A score of 2 was assigned for a correct move and a correct step; 1 – for

Table 5.2 Data analysis summary for Language Learning Potential

Claims	**Data and analysis**	
(1) Automated feedback can stimulate focus on and noticing of discourse form	Quantitative: yes/no responses; Likert-scale responses	comparison of response percentages
	Qualitative: open-ended survey responses; think-aloud protocols; observations; semi-structured interviews	manual analysis of responses; coding; quasi-statistics for themes
(2) Focus on discourse form triggered by automated feedback can facilitate learning gains	Quantitative: yes/no responses; Likert-scale responses; pre- and post-test scores	comparison of response percentages; descriptive statistics; *t*-tests for pre- and post-test scores
	Qualitative: open-ended survey responses	manual analysis of responses; quasi-statistics for themes
(3) Focus on discourse form triggered by automated feedback can facilitate improvement in rhetorical quality	Quantitative: yes/no responses; Likert-scale responses; automated evaluation of all first and last drafts converted to scores; human rater evaluation of 16 first and last drafts	comparison of response percentages; descriptive statistics of first and last draft scores for moves and length; *t*-tests for first and last draft scores
	Qualitative: open-ended survey responses; think-aloud/ Camtasia transcripts; student first and last drafts	manual analysis of responses; coding; manual analysis of output modifications in 16 first and 16 last drafts; quasi-statistics for themes
(4) Practice and modified interaction with IADE may contribute to improvement	Quantitative: frequency tallies in IADE database	One-Way ANOVA; Pearson product-moment correlation

an incorrect move, but a correct step, or for a correct move, but an incorrect step; and 0 – for an incorrect move and an incorrect step. Descriptive statistics and *t*-tests were calculated for each task as well as for overall test scores.

Furthermore, to establish the degree of improvement in the rhetorical quality of student writing, the comments generated by IADE to present the numerical feedback were provisionally converted to scores as follows:

IADE comment: about average → score: 3
IADE comment: below average or above average → score: 2
IADE comment: way below average or way above average → score: 1

The score of 1 was the lowest score, and 3 was the highest score since it represented a range closest to the discipline average. Then, descriptive statistics were calculated, and the mean scores for move 1, move 2, move 3, and draft length were compared through *t*-tests. The scores were also used to classify improvement into four categories as shown in Table 5.3.

Table 5.3 Categories of improvement in rhetorical moves and draft length

First draft scores	Last draft scores		Improvement category
1	3	→	Considerable improvement
1, 2	2, 3 (respectively)	→	Noticeable improvement
1, 2 or 3, 2	1, 2 or 2,1 (respectively)	→	No improvement
3	3	→	No need for improvement

To find whether improvement also occurred in rhetorical quality, the first and last drafts of the 16 volunteering students were scored by two specially trained raters. The Cohen's kappa coefficient indicates a good level of agreement between the raters (*k* .71). In cases of disagreement, a third rater was involved. Consistent with the improvement analysis based on IADE's evaluation, *t*-tests comparing the scores assigned by human raters to the moves in first and last drafts were also calculated. Then, the scores were classified into the improvement categories shown in Table 5.4.

Table 5.4 Score difference as the improvement variable

First draft scores	Last draft scores	Score difference	Improvement
1	3	2	highest
1, 2	2, 3 (respectively)	1	moderate
1, 2, 3	1, 2, 3 (respectively)	0	no improvement
3, 2	2, 1 (respectively)	–1	N/A

Deeper introspective insights were gained from the think-aloud protocols, semi-structured interviews, and observations. The latter three data sources were analyzed in Transana according to the four coding classes exemplified below. For coding, data were segmented into idea units, defined as 'a chunk of information which is viewed by the speaker/writer cohesively as it is given a surface form [...] related [...] to psychological reality for the encoder' (Kroll, 1977, p. 85). Quasi-statistics were also calculated for each coding category.

- Focus on discourse form: *I find many colors mixing around; it's not very clear structure. (Student 54, think-aloud)*
- Noticing of negative evidence: *So, I paid attention to that only because the program showed me that move 2 is missing. (Student 28, interview)*
- Output modification: *Let me try this sentence... [goes to the revision box. reads a sentence from there] maybe I can say like this – 'we chose the wavelength from 532 nanometers' [makes this change] ok. [submits] (Student 40, think-aloud/screen capture)*
- Enhanced understanding: *At this point he realizes that maybe he doesn't understand the 'justification' properly. Therefore he checks the class materials again trying to understand the 'justification' from the examples provided there. (Student 61, observation)*

Since one of the purposes of implementing IADE was to provide students with sufficient writing practice through multiple draft revisions and iterative resubmissions, determining whether such practice had an effect on rhetorical improvement was expected to yield additional evidence of learning potential. Submission frequency data extracted from IADE's database was used as an indicator of practice. Improvement was reflected in the score difference between first and last drafts. The effect of practice on the improvement of move 1, move 2, move 3, and length was explored through One-Way Analysis of Variance (ANOVA). The number of draft submissions was considered as the independent variable, and the score differences for each move and length between first and last drafts were considered to be the dependent variables. Given that the assigned scores were 1, 2, and 3, the score difference fell into one of the four groups shown in Table 5.4 above. The last group (improvement = −1) had only one observation for move 1 and was thus excluded from the analysis. ANOVA was used to compare the means of the remaining three groups in order to see if the number of submissions was different for improvement at different levels (Move 1, Move 2, Move 3, and length).

The effect of practice on the overall draft improvement was examined with the help of the Pearson product-moment correlation metric. The same number of draft submissions used in the ANOVA analyses was correlated with the sum of score differences for each move and length, which was used as an indicator of overall draft improvement. For example, if the score difference for a student's move 1 was 2, for move 2 was 1, for move 3 was 2, and for length was 0, then the overall draft improvement was the sum of these figures, amounting to 5. This number was then correlated with the number of submissions this particular student made.

Modified interaction operationalized through help options was another aspect of IADE's Language Learning Potential quality. It was analyzed with the help of automatically tracked students' clicks on the four available options: definitions of moves and steps, step statistics, annotated corpus, and revision tips. To establish whether modified interaction had an effect on writing improvement, the same kinds of statistical analyses as for the effect of practice on improvement were done. The variables used in this analysis were the frequency of participants' access to each of the four available help options and the difference between the first and last draft scores for the three moves.

5.2.5.2 Meaning Focus

To evaluate the Meaning Focus quality, two aspects were examined: focus on functional meaning and construction of functional meaning. The quantitative and qualitative data enumerated in Table 5.5 were analyzed to find whether feedback could enhance focus on discourse meaning and whether this could lead to more successful construction of meaning.

Table 5.5 Data analysis summary for Meaning Focus

Claims	**Data and analysis**	
Automated feedback can stimulate focus on functional meaning of discourse	Quantitative: yes/no responses; Likert-scale responses Qualitative: open-ended survey responses; think-aloud protocols; observations; semi-structured interviews	comparison of response percentages manual analysis of responses; coding; quasi-statistics for themes
Automated feedback can facilitate more effective construction of functional meaning	Qualitative: think-aloud protocols; Camtasia screen recordings; observations; semi-structured interviews; open-ended survey responses	manual analysis of responses; coding; quasi-statistics for themes

For Meaning Focus, the think-aloud protocols, observations, and semi-structured interviews were coded as follows:

- Reflection on functional meaning: *Seems to think that what he really wants to express is the advantage of his method.* (*Student 43, observation*)
- Noticing of mismatch between feedback and intended meaning: *The second sentence, I think it should be blue. That means it should be move 1, but it turned out to be move 2. Maybe the sentence is not clearly or correctly written.* (*Student 41, think-aloud*)
- Identifying a connection between meaning and lexical choice: *I tried to see some examples and expressions, and sometimes I could find some word that fit very well with what I want to say in that move. So if I see such expressions, it is easier for me to tell my meaning more effectively.* (*Student 63, interview*)
- Construction of new functional meaning: *[changes: 'A large number of scenarios can be gained to test forecasting tools with the scenario generation method.' (which is move 1) TO 'It is possible that if scenario generation method were adopted, a large number of scenarios could be gained to test forecasting tools.' (which is move 2)]* (*Student 29, think-aloud/screen capture*)

5.2.5.3 *Learner Fit*

Learner Fit represents the level of linguistic difficulty for learners with specific characteristics or, in other words, the 'extent to which a CALL task engages learners in language at a useful level of difficulty in a way that is appropriate to their individual characteristics' (Chapelle, 2001, p. 80). Therefore, the hypothetical claim was that IADE with its feedback would be appropriate for targeted L2 writers as they engaged with the Introduction writing task. Table 5.6 summarizes how the data were analyzed to support this claim.

Table 5.6 Data analysis summary for Learner Fit

Claim	**Data and analysis**	
IADE feedback is appropriate for students with targeted characteristics	Quantitative: yes/no responses; Likert-scale responses	comparison of response percentages
	Qualitative: open-ended survey responses; think-aloud protocols; observations; semi-structured interviews	manual analysis of responses; coding; quasi-statistics for themes

In the coding scheme applied to the analysis of the transcripts, Learner Fit was represented by the following categories:

- Fit for individual learner characteristics: *I like that the feedback is not just something in general; it's meant for me personally and it reflect only my writing advantages and disadvantages. Plus, it tells me about the introductions in my discipline. (Student 58, interview)*
- Facilitating problem-solving: *Reads, thinks, checks the definitions, says that it was helpful and that it's clear now. (Student 32, observation)*
- Learner control: *I know I'm right here. First, I introduce our research, then I talk about what we did, and then about our result. So, it can't be move 1. Maybe it looks like move 1? Why? Hm... maybe because sometimes author can talk about previous research and what other people did. Like, if I review a study from before, I can tell what they did and what they find. Yeah, I think so. But not here. I think my reader is smart enough to understand that I'm not talking about other study from somebody else here. I already said 'Herein, we report our first study...', so it is clear enough. (Student 65, think-aloud)*
- Appropriateness of feedback for task completion: *The feedback helps me to avoid overemphasizing some move and to improve. (Student 30, interview)*
- Appropriateness of evaluation method: *I like that the program doesn't give a grade or a score, because, if it's wrong for some sentences, the grade will be wrong, and then I will be upset. But now it allows me to practice, but doesn't dictate what I should to do, or doesn't criticize me. It doesn't say – this is the last time and you get A, B, or C and so on [laughs]. It just gives me the picture compared to other introductions in my field. (Student 30, interview)*

5.2.5.4 Impact

The same data sources were analyzed to gain an understanding of whether and how IADE may positively influence L2 writers' learning experience (Table 5.7).

Table 5.7 Data analysis summary for Impact

Claim	Data and analysis	
Revising with IADE can be a positive learning experience	Quantitative: yes/no responses; Likert-scale responses	comparison of response percentages
	Qualitative: open-ended survey responses; think-aloud protocols; observations; semi-structured interviews	manual analysis of responses; coding; quasi-statistics for themes

The following are the Impact categories used in the coding taxonomy:

- Positive learning experience: *He looks very satisfied when he sees the feedback because he sees improvement in both m1 and m2, which were problematic in the first draft.* (Student 32, observation)
- Negative learning experience: *I don't know what to do now. I tried so much, but nothing changed in the colors.* (Student 40, think-aloud)
- Motivation: *Although the program's feedback shows improvement in move 2, I still decided to do more revision of that part because it is not as close to the average in my field as I would like.* (Student 33, interview)
- Cognitive involvement: *Hmmm, ok... Hmm, yeah, let me think about it... Ok.* (Participant 41, think-aloud)
- Affective involvement: *She gets very excited every time the program analysis showed improvement both in the colored text and the numerical feedback. She even claps her hands!* (Student 28, observation)
- Strategy development: *I think this program help me with every sentence. I can write a sentence and give it to the program to check if it is right move. If it is not right move, I can revise it. If it is correct move, I will write a new sentence and check with the program. So I check every sentence and make sure that I make my structure and ideas clear.* (Student 43, interview)
- Influence on the revision process: *Usually, I revise my paper one time and that's it. It's because I don't know what else to revise. I make some changes and I think it's good. But this program helped me organize how to revise.* (Student 54, interview)

6

Evaluating the IADE Genre-Based Prototype

This chapter recounts empirical evidence supporting theory-driven claims about four CALL qualities investigated to evaluate IADE: Language Learning Potential, Meaning Focus, Learner Fit, and Impact. In reporting the findings, I first introduce the students' perspective and then present the insights derived from introspective and inferential interpretations. Throughout the chapter, I diligently infiltrate students' voices and writing excerpts to illustrate phenomena that help construe the effects of this corpus-based AWE prototype.

6.1 Language Learning Potential

6.1.1 Focus on discourse form and noticing

The claim that automated feedback can stimulate focus on discourse form and noticing of negative evidence found support in multiple data sources (Table 6.1). For survey questions, percentages stand for participants in whose responses respective evidence was found. For introspective data, the presence of evidence is represented by idea units (460 idea units in total).

6.1.1.1 L2 writers' perceptions

The survey responses yielded a rich representation of learner perceptions, as the students repeatedly mentioned having focused on the rhetorical moves in their Introduction discourse. Likert-scale choices, as detailed in Table 6.2, show that excellent evidence of such focus averaged 44.3 percent; good, 47.7 percent; and weak, 6.8 percent. Students' noticing of negative evidence about their use of moves is also indicated by high percentages. Similarly, they positively self-evaluated the degree to which they noticed vocabulary indicative of a particular move.

Table 6.1 Overall evidence of focus on discourse form and noticing

Data source	N	Evidence	No evidence
Likert-scale	88		
Q-n 1 [focus on moves]		92.05%	7.95%
Q-n 2 [noticing move language]		100%	0%
Q-n 3 [noticing weaknesses]		90.91%	9.09%
Yes/No and open-ended	83		
Q-n 1 [focus on moves]		100%	0%
Q-n 2 [noticing foci]		89.16%	10.84%
Think-aloud protocols/Camtasia	16		
(total 1,227 idea units)		484 idea units	
Semi-structured interviews	16		
(total 233 idea units)		63 idea units	
Observations	16	118 idea units	

Table 6.2 Evidence of noticing and focus on discourse form (Likert-scale)

	Not at all (lacking)	*A little (weak)*	*Much (good)*	*Very much (excellent)*
Focused on discourse form	1.1%	6.8%	47.7%	44.3%
Noticed negative evidence	1.1%	7.9%	50.0%	40.9%
Noticed move-specific vocabulary	0.0%	9.1%	52.3%	38.6%

All 83 respondents to the yes/no and open-ended questions indicated that working with IADE helped them pay attention to rhetorical form, and provided a number of reasons for this. The majority of the respondents (95.2 percent) explained that it was the feedback that made them focus on the moves (Table 6.3). Many clarified that the color codes made them pay attention to the shape of their moves (*The color is very striking for finding different moves* (*Student 33*); *Its colorful highlights brought my attention to my moves* (*Student 54*); *different colors make me think about the structure of moves* (*Student 27*); *This program helped me focus on the moves a lot because with colors I can tell which one is move 1, 2, 3 very easily* (*Student 24*)). Some thought that the numerical feedback was valuable (*Percentages of moves made me focus on them* (*Student 22*); *It focused me on the moves and how they are usually distributed in my discipline* (*Student 8*); *It could determine whether I am focusing in one move or another depending on the percentages* (*Student 30*)). Others appreciated both color-coded and numerical feedback (*I always looked at the colors and the percent that I need to follow* (*Student 47*); *it was very helpful to concentrate, when we can look at*

Table 6.3 Evidence of noticing and focus on discourse form (survey)

Triggers of focus on discourse form	
Color-coded feedback	59.0%
Numerical feedback	12.1%
Color-coded and numerical feedback	24.1%
Noticing foci	
Lexical realizations of discourse form	71.1%
Negative evidence	93.2%
Effects of form focus and noticing	
Enhanced understanding	61.3%
Output modification	89.6%

the moves and percent and analyze its distribution (*Student 39*); *The feedback is all about the moves by colors and percent so that it makes me look on moves which I was not concerned a lot* (*Student 7*)).

Table 6.3 also shows that IADE helped the students notice a few peculiarities of the moves that they had not paid attention to during their corpus explorations in class and when writing their first draft out of class. Specifically, they noticed that certain phraseology typically signals the function of a step within a move very clearly and that step functions can be fulfilled in a number of different ways with different vocabulary choices. For instance, *I saw that there are specific words or expressions researchers use for specific moves or steps. I actually notice that many researchers say the same function with different key words* (*Student 41*); *The pop messages in* IADE *show me that I can use different ways for my centrality, but in fact say the same thing* (*Student 5*). Of 71.1 percent of students who mentioned noticing and possibly learning new words or expressions that signal particular moves/steps, more than half attributed that to accessing the annotated corpus in IADE (*The corpus which is provided by this program did help me to grasp the words and expressions, which are very useful in my own paper writing* (*Student 86*); *Using the program with several different articles showed that there are certain words for each move* (*Student 27*)); 27.1 percent did so to the explanations of moves provided in the help options (*From the examples in definition and corpus, I learn some new words/expressions in Move Three* (*Student 44*); *I could see new words for moves from the definition part and examples part* (*Student 11*)); and 13.5 percent to the multiple modifications they made upon repeated re-submissions (*When I changed the words to express my meaning, sometime the move changed* (*Student 67*); *If I change certain words, the move of the sentence can possibly be changed. Especially for move 3, when I wrote a certain sentence of methodology, it cannot recognize it. Only when I use the word 'we', or 'in this paper', it can indicate that this paragraph belong to move 3. But I think it is awkward to use these words in each sentence, so I need to collect more such expressions* (*Student 72*)).

Most respondents (93.2 percent) noted that they were greatly influenced by the negative evidence in the feedback, such as missing or underrepresented moves and a mismatch between the intended function and its actual verbal realization (*The colors make me notice what move are written and what are not* (*Student 65*); *It visualizes in color what I need to add on or reinforce* (*Student 34*); *It gives me idea on what is the average length of the move, so I pay more attention to what is not enough* (*Student 74*)). Awareness of certain rhetorical inaccuracies in their discourse appeared to engage them cognitively (*It makes me analyze my own sentences and see what are the problems of each sentence* (*Student 38*)) and consequently lead to enhanced understanding (*I realize now the construction of introduction using this program. Before that, I mainly wrote the present condition, problems, and purpose as memory serves. I could see that there are many types and steps in moves to logically write research through inherent characteristics of this program* (*Student 74*)). Given these effects of focus on form and noticing, modifying output seemed to be a natural progression for 89.6 percent (*When the program tells me that certain move in my article is below the average in my discipline, I start to focus on that move* (*Student 59*); *When I didn't know what's wrong with my move 2, I looked at many examples and then I changed things in my move 2* (*Student 31*)).

6.1.1.2 *Introspections*

The think-aloud/Camtasia, observation, and interview data recorded for 16 students provided evidence that all of them referred to rhetorical form in one way or another. Of the idea units coded as indicative of Language Learning Potential in the think-aloud and interview transcripts, roughly half were coded for focus on discourse form. The idea units are rendered as percentages in Table 6.4.

Table 6.4 Evidence of focus on discourse form (transcripts)

	Think-aloud/ Camtasia	***Observations***	***Interviews***
Focus on discourse form	53.7%	27.2%	43.1%
Noticing of negative evidence	24.2%	42.1%	31.1%
Output modification	14.0%	27.2%	15.8%
Enhanced understanding	8.1%	10.5%	10.0%

The transcript data confirmed the students' perception that the feedback generated by IADE was the driving factor of focus on discourse form. Consider some examples from different data sources:

I see it's, m1 and m2 it's basically in the front, and most of m3 is in the end of the introduction. And m1 and m2 are... they are intertwined, and m3 are basically at the end (*Student 29, think-aloud*).

[Looks at his colored text, then opens a text in the annotated corpus, scrolls up and down to see the overall distribution of moves/colors.] (*Student 44, Camtasia*)

Looks carefully at the color-coded text returned by IADE and keeps it highlighted. Frowns (*Student 65, observation*).

Researcher (*following up on the observation note [keeps highlighting sentences colored differently]*): *Why were you highlighting different colors?* Participant: *Because the colors helped me see how I structure my moves* (*Student 64, interview*).

The other three themes that surfaced in these introspective data also found a match in the students' responses to the survey, supporting their perceptions about the positive consequences of focusing on discourse form. As a result of such focus, the students noticed negative evidence in their drafts and consequently modified their written output. Since their modifications were not always successful upon first attempt, the students consulted IADE's help options and compared the help materials with their own draft. This helped them better understand the moves and the steps, prompting repeated attempts at improvement. For example:

- Noticing of negative evidence: *stating the value of present research. I think I missed that part. And this sentence is duplicating the previous one.* (*Student 43, think-aloud*)
- Output modification: *[Highlights the previously modified sentence. Adds 'it means' to 'the absorption mechanism is different from activated carbon.' Pauses. Reads this sentence again, cursor over. Changes: 'It means that, compared to activated carbon, the absorption mechanism is different from activated carbon.']*. (*Student 65, Camtasia*)
- Enhanced understanding: *Realizes that move 3 generally does not contain descriptions of previous research.* (*Student 27, observation*)

A closer analysis of the students' thoughts and actions suggests that IADE's feedback seemed to have stimulated a cycle that they appeared to follow during revision once they received automated feedback

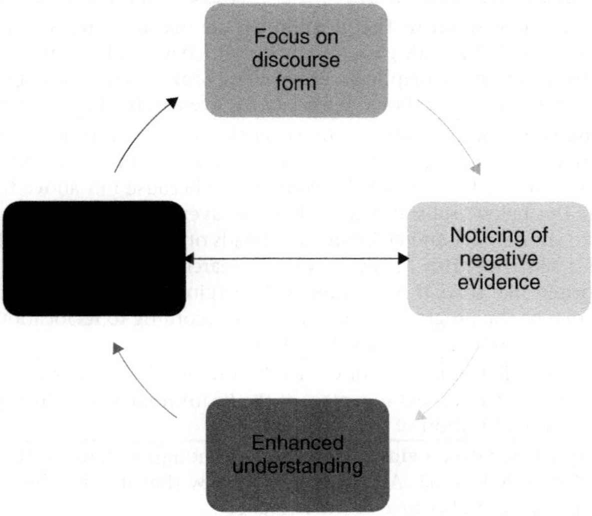

Figure 6.1 Revision cycle stimulated by IADE's feedback

(Figure 6.1). The head of the cycle was the focus on discourse form; one cycle ended with successful output modification of a certain discourse element reflected in the feedback, and a new one began with learners' focus on another part of their text. Inside this cycle, there appeared to be an integrated mini-cycle, during which the learners noticed negative evidence in their drafts, sought to understand its nature, and attempted corrective changes.

Let's observe the elements of this cycle through the lens of different data sources. Figure 6.2 presents an excerpt from a combined think-aloud and Camptasia transcript that demonstrates how Student 27 went through the stages of this cycle. First, the feedback, both color-coded and numerical, prompted his focus on the distribution of the three moves in his Introduction draft. Then, the student noticed negative evidence pointed to by the numerical feedback. While reading the color-coded text, he realized that a function of his Introduction was identified by IADE differently than what he had intended. Having noticed this negative evidence, the student made a change in his text based on a personal hypothesis, and, upon re-submission, saw that his hypothesis was faulty. This motivated him to think more and consult IADE's help options, which led to an enhanced understanding of the genre norms in his particular discipline. Equipped with a better understanding, the

Focus on discourse form: The program tell me that the blue is m1, red is m2, and green is m3. First, it's good to know that I have all three moves. Let's see what's in each move. Discipline... 66% belong to m1... above average. Yeah, so, that means in m1 I have about 20% above the average, but below the maximum.
Noticing of negative evidence: [looks at the numerical feedback] So there is more room for improvement. [reads the feedback prompt – try to revise this move] OK, now I know what I'm going to do because I'm above the average for m1, I'm below, substantially below the average for m3. So, maybe now I need to shorten m1 and elaborate m3. [reads one of his sentences. highlights part of a sentence] Hm ... my previous research was identified as m3. Why it happened like this? If it appears at the beginning of this paragraph ... so I guess maybe the program just sees it as m1 according to its location. Let's see if I change the position, what will happen.
Output modification: [goes down to the revision box. reads his text again. Copy-pastes a piece of text to a place at the beginning]. OK, I already changed it, changed the location of it.
Noticing of negative evidence: Hmm... Although I changed the location, it is still regarded as m3. All right, now I know that it is not because of the location. Maybe it's because of the language ...
Enhanced understanding: Let's see some examples. [goes to the help options, Annotated Corpus (AC), and looks at one annotated introduction] [whistles quietly] M3 in this example does not have the previous research review, so I will look at other examples. [opens other annotated texts trying to find review in green] I realized that all the examples, in the m3, there's no previous research. So, I guess, that's a problem ... I can just keep the previous research in m1 and try to add something in m3, like ... let's see ... methods ... add some parts like the structure or the summary of the outcomes.
Output modification: Now I'm focused on the last paragraph of my introduction. I'm trying to add something. [reads the last part of his text. Goes to IADE's colored text. Goes back to the revision box and adds: 'For its methodology, this study used content analysis to find out the historical flow of Chicago downtown. The paper is structured in accordance with the five stages of Florida's creative economy. The results show that, indeed, the Chicago downtown, although has a relatively short history, matches Florida's theory.'] Just now I just added some sentences in m3. First of all, I added a summary of my paper. Secondly, I added a brief review of my structure, and then, finally, I added something about the results. Now let's see how the program will do my next draft.
Focus on discourse form: Now the program told me that it indeed detected some additional m3, and yeah!.. I'll try to revise more, I think. [reads on. highlights a sentence and reads carefully. Highlights it again].
Noticing of negative evidence: And here I find another misunderstanding. [reads the sentence] My intent is to ... I guess it could be m2 or m3, but not m1, so I'm thinking, if it is m2 or m3. [reads the sentence aloud again and takes time to think] It is hypothesis.

Figure 6.2 Example of the revision cycle (think-aloud/Camtasia)

Output modification: I'm trying to use the word 'assume' as an indicator of m2 hypothesis. [Changes: 'So it is possible to set downtown Chicago into Florida's five economic transitions' → 'So this paper assumes that it is possible' Let me see if it works and if the program can recognize this change.
Noticing of negative evidence: Hmm... no? it is still recognized as m1. Let's see some examples. I'll find out what kind of indicators words the previous papers. The annotated corpus...
Enhanced understanding: This example text does not have this part [meaning step], so I'll look at another. [clicks on red sentences, most of which are 'problem'. Since he doesn't find hypothesis, he opens another annotated text] I'm looking for some indicator words for hypothesis in m2. I already went through two example texts, but both of them m2 just have justification and statement of problems. I didn't find indicator words for hypothesis, so I'll just keep looking for it. No. gap, gap, justification, problem, gap ... I went through several other examples, but still I didn't get indicator words for hypothesis in m2. So, I'm wondering why the previous research papers do not have that. Maybe they just don't include hypothesis in my field? [opens the stats in Help Options and confirms his idea] I guess so ... because only 0.14% for hypothesis. So, according to my observation, maybe it's true that the other authors in my field don't have hypothesis included in m2. Then I will do more what they do. Let me look at my results.
Output modification: I'm looking at the last sentence ... and to see if I can make some changes and the program can respond to these changes. Maybe I can try to be specific and say that 'the results of this paper'. Yeah, let's try to do that. [makes the change' 'The results show that...' → 'The results of this study show that...' and submits]
Focus on discourse form: Yep! All right! Now it changed to m3, it's what I mean. So that's good! Ok, so now what I'll do ... I'll analyze sentence by sentence and ... and then I can change when things wrong.

Figure 6.2 Continued

student modified his output again – this time successfully, as he was able to see by focusing on form again. His revision process continued with another iteration of the cycle.

The same phenomenon is depicted in Figures 6.3 and 6.4, which present excerpts from observation and interview transcripts for Student 28 and Student 43, respectively.

In the interview data, which was very much like the example in Figure 6.4, it was especially interesting to note that the students' answers to questions about a particular element of the revision cycle tended to be an explanation in retrospect. In other words, their responses about their actions during one stage of the cycle were related to the effect of the

Focus on discourse form: Looks carefully at the color-coded text returned by IADE. Frowns.
Noticing of negative evidence: The first thing she says upon receiving IADE's feedback is 'Wow! No move 2 and lots of m1!' She immediately says that it's not what she means.
Output modification: Decides that she definitely needs to revise. Moves closer to the computer and takes a position for focused work. Makes changes to her text in the revision box.
Noticing of negative evidence: Goes back to the color-coded feedback. Highlights parts of the color-coded text. Notices that she actually meant m2.
Enhanced understanding: Thinks. Begins reading and thinking about the first sentence. Accesses the AC (annotated corpus) for examples of m2 Problem. After seeing examples, thinks that she may need to elaborate on the Problem. But also thinks that it may be better not to start with m2 because she didn't see it at the beginning of any annotated introductions. The second sentence is also meant as m2, but appears as m1. She thinks that because it's too long it doesn't reflect the problem clearly.
Output modification: Decides to split the sentence into 2 → one as Generalization and the second as Problem. Makes changes in the two sentences. Submits.
Focus on discourse form: Is happy to see a successful change. Now m2 appears as she wants it. Reads and thinks.
Noticing of negative evidence and **Output modification:** Says that some information is not very essential, so she may want to delete it. Then, wants to combine the rest of the sentence, part of which she has just deleted, with the next sentence because, as she explains, that one shows the advantage and is therefore more important.
Enhanced understanding: Classifies her next sentence as move/step; then checks with the definition of m3 and reads the examples there. She now has plenty of ideas on how to manipulate with her information and content (many times she says 'maybe I can do this; maybe I can do that…').
Output modification: Decides to combine sentences. Then deletes the detailed sentences about the reference. Modifies the placement of sentences for more coherence of ideas. Also deletes something that seems redundant to her.
Focus on discourse form: Looks carefully at colors, then at numbers …

Figure 6.3 Example of the revision cycle (observation)

Focus on discourse form and **Noticing of negative evidence:** *Researcher* (following up on the observation note [doesn't like the distribution of her moves]): What did you mean when you said that your introduction is 'not that centralized'? *Student 43*: I mean not coherent, not logical, not as should be. *Researcher*: How do you know? *Student 43*: Because I saw how colors are all over the place.
Output modification: *Researcher* (following up on the observation note [decides to try combining a green and a blue sentence]): Why did you decide to combine those two blue and green sentences at the beginning? *Student 43*: Oh, because it wasn't right. They should both be move 1, but I didn't write like that. I thought if I combine it helps, but it doesn't. *Researcher* (following up on the answer and on the observation note [combining doesn't work, so he checks examples in the AC and makes a number of changes at lexical level]): So that's why you changed that part several times?
Enhanced understanding: *Student 43*: Yes. I look at the corpus and I didn't see 'we'; in move 1, but I saw 'we' in move 3. So I finally understood the problem there. *Researcher* (following up on the answer and on the observation note [repeatedly looks at examples of moves/steps in HO and then highlights/reads his own sentences]): Yes, I noticed that you used the Help Options to see examples and then you went back to your own sentences. Why were you doing that? *Student 43*: I just compare corpus with my sentence. Because I can see that they are different, and then I think why it's different and I find out why. I like also definitions because if I go to definitions and examples, then I understand little things ... like why I can't use 'we' in move 1. I understand that 'we' tells about this research, not research in general, right? I didn't pay attention before. *Researcher*: So that helps?
Output modification: *Student 43*: Yeah, sure. Then I know finally what to change, and it works.
Focus on discourse form: *Researcher*: How do you know? *Student 43*: Because I see the colors and I know what to do next to make it good.

Figure 6.4 Example of the revision cycle (interview)

preceding stage. This inference is captured in the following synthesized and simplified questions and answers:

How did you know that there were imperfections in your introduction? (Noticing of negative evidence) → *Because I saw the distribution of my moves in color and in percentages.* (Focus on discourse form)
Why do you think you better understood how to build each move more effectively? (Enhanced understanding) → *Because I saw what and where my problems were and tried to clarify them.* (Noticing of negative evidence)
Why did you make changes to particular parts of your introduction? (Output modification) → *Because I could see my problems and because I could better understand the purpose, function, and realization of each move.* (Noticing of negative evidence + Enhanced understanding)
Why did you pay attention to your moves after resubmission? (Focus on discourse form) → *Because I wanted to see how good they were.* (Output modification)

In short, the students noticed negative evidence because of focus on discourse form; acquired a better understanding of rhetorical conventions

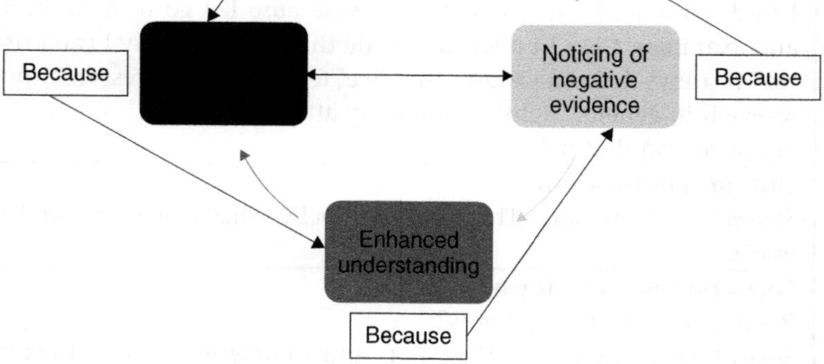

Figure 6.5 Sequential and causative relation between the elements of the revision cycle

because of noticing of negative evidence; modified their output because of noticing of negative evidence and acquiring a better understanding of discourse conventions; and focused on discourse form because of wanting to verify the quality of the modified output and to continue revision of other parts of the text. Considering these insights, it can be inferred that the relation between the four elements of the identified cycle is sequential and causative; Figure 6.5 depicts this generalized causation.

6.1.2 Learning gains

The second claim about IADE's Language Learning Potential hypothetically made at the outset of the study was that focus on discourse form could contribute to learning gains. The evidence summarized in Table 6.5 sustains this claim.

Table 6.5 Overall evidence of learning gains

Data source	*N*	Evidence	No evidence
Likert-scale	88		
Q-n 1 [learning of moves]		98.9%	1.1%
Yes/No and open-ended	83		
Q-n 1 [learning of moves]		94.0%	6.0%
Q-n 2 [what helped learn]		92.8%	7.2%
Q-n 3 [focus on moves and learning]		94.0%	6.0%
Q-n 4 [transfer of knowledge]		77.1%	22.9%
Q-n 5 [learning of move language]		71.1%	28.9%
Pre-/post-tests	104		
Tasks 1 and 2		*t*-tests $p < .001$	

6.1.2.1 L2 writers' perceptions

In general, most participants expressed confidence in their newly acquired knowledge of Introduction moves. Of the positive Likert-scale responses, 79.5 percent thought that they learned the moves *well*; 6.8 percent, *very well*; and 12.5 percent, *a little*. Only 1 student chose *not at all* when self-evaluating his learning gains. In response to a yes/no question, 94 percent agreed that they learned the moves after having revised their drafts with IADE (*I didn't know these moves well before I actually revised my draft with the program. Now, I know* (*Student 52*); *The program helps me see things I usually don't really think about, and that made me learn the complicated moves very well* (*Student 6*)).

Considering the theoretical importance of focus on form and its hypothesized role in this study, the students were asked whether they thought they had learned the moves, whether their learning of moves was a result of having focused on them, and why they thought so (Table 6.5). Most of the respondents (94 percent) said *yes*; 2.4 percent were *not sure*, and 3.6 percent said *no*. The themes that emerged in the open-ended answers present justifiable interest because they are supportive of the elements of the revision cycle uncovered in the introspective data. For example, responses like *Yes, if I haven't focused on moves, I can't even recognize them and see where my structure is not so good* (*Student 27*) and *It made me see my weakness part of my writing* (*Student 31*) are indicative of focus on form and noticing of negative evidence. Such responses as *Yes, first, I have to focus on them then I can learn them* (*Student 11*) and *Yes, because focus on my moves helped me not only to recognize the moves but to understand them* (*Student 43*) suggest enhanced understanding. And explanations like *Yes, if I focus on my moves I know how I can put a certain bad sentence in a way that I want others to know which moves I'm in* (*Student 53*) and *Yes, more focus on them make me change and write the article clearly* (*Student 41*) hint at output modification.

Related to revising with IADE, the students mentioned ideas that could be grouped into causes of learning (why students thought they learned the moves) and observed outcomes (outcomes that students could actually see and make a judgment about). As shown in Figure 6.6, focus on discourse form and enhanced understanding surfaced again as causes of learning (*because the program already highlighted the moves* (*Student 54*); *Now it made me distinguish which sentence belongs to which move and learn the structure of the introductions in my discipline* (*Student 50*)). In addition, the students thought that they learned the moves during revision with IADE because of its feedback (*I learned because I had a plan to think which sentence belongs to which move because the feedback gave*

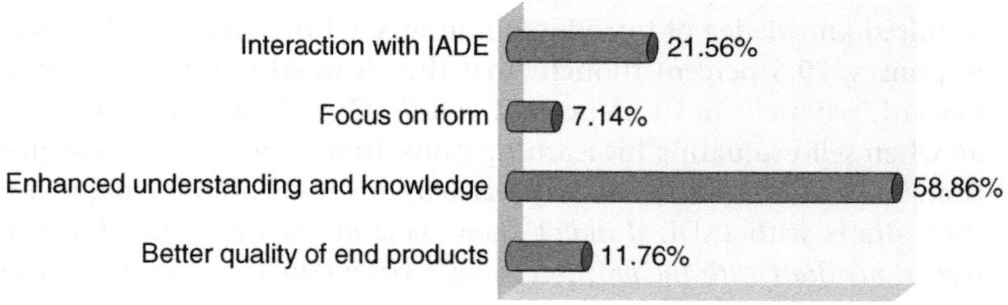

Figure 6.6 Student perceptions of causes of learning

me different answer (*Student 44*)) and of its help options (*I learned because of the examples in the software of my discipline* (*Student 10*)). The observed outcome in their view was better quality final drafts (*I learnt the moves because my introduction is more organized* (*Student 67*); *I learnt the moves because I could write what I intended to write and the decision of IADE was good* (*Student 31*)), which touches upon their positive perceptions of writing improvement discussed in the next sub-section.

A survey question asked what helped the students learn the moves. The responses summarized in Figure 6.7 can be aligned with the above-mentioned themes. More precisely, the help options (definitions and accompanying examples of moves and steps as well as the annotated corpus) were mentioned most often. A number of students believed that the color-coded feedback helped them learn the most because it drew their attention to segments of their text that needed improvement. The process of interaction with IADE in general was noted as helpful; some students referred to such effects as the focus on discourse form and noticing of certain problems in their discourse. A few students noticed vocabulary indicative of a particular function of a move. One of them even mentioned learning about lexical variation (*When I worked with the corpus, I learned many expressions. For example, I can replace describe with examine, assert, dispute, or claim* (*Student 35*)). Additionally, classroom instruction and the opportunity to practice by resubmitting modified drafts for automated analysis were perceived by some as factors that led to the learning of moves.

Table 6.5 also shows that 77.1 percent of students thought they could transfer the new knowledge of rhetorical conventions to their actual writing; 16.9 percent were not so confident, saying *I don't know, I am not sure, I will try, possibly, maybe, I hope so,* or *kind of,* and

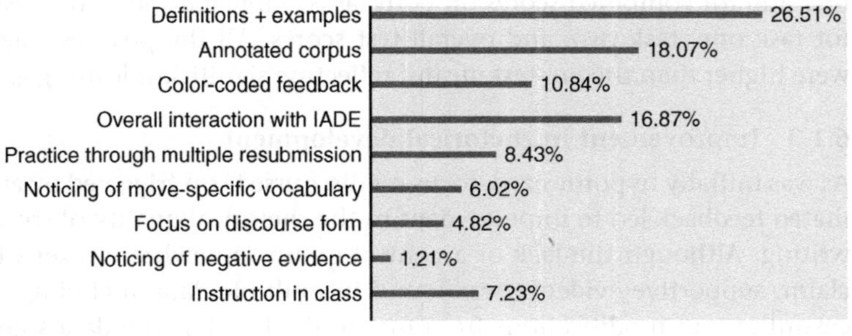

Figure 6.7 Student perceptions of most helpful learning factors

6 percent did not think they were ready to apply the new knowledge and produce well-rounded introductions. These students could have used more practice (*It's too time consuming and too complex, so I need to use the software more and maybe write introduction not for only one paper* (*Student 15*); *My knowledge is too fresh. It take time and writing before I transfer it* (*Student 38*); *Not yet, I still try to figure it out and write some more, then I can say I can transfer my knowledge* (*Student 4*)). Those who were more optimistic thought they could apply the new move/step knowledge by taking some actions: 64.1 percent mentioned paying attention to and analyzing their moves (*I know that there exists a better way to write a scientific article, and I will pay attention to that. I will pay a lot of attention to every move I write* (*Student 82*); *I didn't know there're moves before, but now I will focus on them as much as I can, I mean I'll try to identify them in my paper and do what I did for this paper to make it better* (*Student 68*)); 14.1 percent, comparing their draft with published texts (*I know I will look for sure at my corpus for good models to make sure my is good too* (*Student 22*); *Because it is very useful if I look at how other papers are written, I think I'll compare with corpus again and again* (*Student 34*)); and 21.8 percent, verifying whether the communicative purpose of their moves was successfully expressed through vocabulary (*I know keywords in sentence are very important to make my paper understood. I used them and I will use them* (*Student 61*); *I will pay attention to the words and the meaning I want to present in the sentences* (*Student 57*)).

6.1.2.2 Statistical discernment

Students' pre- and post-test scores were analyzed to measure their learning gains after revising with IADE. Since the tests contained two tasks requiring the identification of moves and steps (the first task consisting of de-contextualized sentences and the second of an entire Introduction text), descriptive statistics and *t*-tests were calculated for scores on each task and for combined scores on both tasks. Table 6.6 shows the results for task one, task two, and overall test scores. All the post-test means were higher than the pre-test means, reflecting significant leaning gains.

6.1.3 Improvement in rhetorical development

As was initially hypothesized, focus on discourse form triggered by automated feedback led to improvement in the rhetorical quality of student writing. Although the lack of a control group somewhat weakens this claim, supportive evidence was found in multiple data, including successful output modifications from first to final drafts. The data sources and respective evidence are listed in Table 6.7.

Table 6.6 Pre-/post-test scores

	M	*SD*	*T*	*DF*	*Effect size*
Pretest task 1	20.50	4.942	18.26*	103	.77
Posttest task 1	29.65	1.909			
Pretest task 2	21.05	6.750	13.75*	103	.68
Posttest task 2	30.16	1.596			
Pretest overall	41.55	10.161	17.99*	103	.77
Posttest overall	59.82	2.988			

*$p < .001$.
All references to effect size statistics in the tables denote a moderate to large effect based on Cohen's *d* values.

Table 6.7 Overall evidence of rhetorical improvement

Data source	***N***	**Evidence**	**No evidence**
Likert-scale	88		
Q-n 1 [draft improvement]		100%	0%
Yes/No and open-ended	83		
Q-n 1 [draft improvement]		92.8%	7.2%
IADE evaluation of 210 first and last drafts	105	*t*-tests $p < .001$	
Moves and length	16	*t*-tests	
Human rating of 32 first and last drafts		$p < .001$	
Moves	16		
Manual analysis		285 output modifications	
32 first and last drafts	16		
Camtasia		77 output modifications	

6.1.3.1 *L2 writers' perceptions*

All the participants believed that they improved their writing of a research article Introduction to a certain degree: 26 percent thought they improved *a lot*; 55 percent, *somewhat*; and 19 percent, *a little*. In response to a similar yes/no question, only 7.2 percent were not certain (*I don't know, I have never written such paper before* (*Student 38*); *Not quite sure how much for now* (*Student 5*)). The explanations of the 92.8 percent who believed their Introduction writing skill improved formed two major themes. The students appeared to judge improvement on the basis of what they thought caused it (focus on form, practice, enhanced understanding) and of observed outcomes (better quality final product), which resonates with the themes that emerged in the survey data on

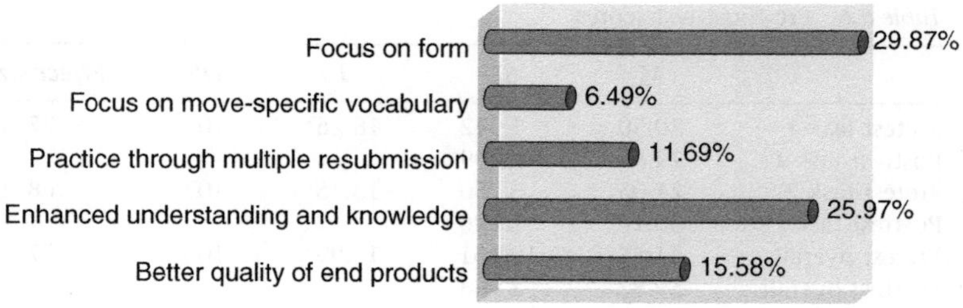

Figure 6.8 Student perceptions of causes of improvement

learning gains. The occurrence of these themes is quantified in Figure 6.8 and also exemplified by quotes from the survey data.

- IADE's ability to direct attention to the discourse form of the draft: *I improved my writhing skill by using the program and focusing the moves. (Student 57)*
- Opportunity for practice through multiple resubmissions: *I wrote and submitted my introduction many times and for several days until now, so I guess my skill got improved.* (*Student 34*)
- Enhanced understanding and knowledge of rhetorical conventions: *I know I improved because I have a better idea about how to organize the introduction now. And also I have now a different look and I can know what is good and what is not good even when I read others papers.* (*Student 77*)
- Better quality of end products: *I think so, because my major professor said my introduction is really good.* (*Student 31*).

These ideas substantiate the focus on form and enhanced understanding stages of the revision cycle stimulated by IADE. Additionally, practice through multiple resubmissions implies output modification that is likely to result in better quality of end products.

6.1.3.2 Introspections and statistical discernment

IADE's database recorded the feedback comments for each move generated based on percentages comparing students' texts to the corpus in their discipline. The comment that reflected desired performance suggested an *about average* compared to the targeted rhetorical norms of a particular discipline. The other comments indicated how far or how close the students' drafts were relative to those norms. Automated evaluation of moves and length of all students' drafts is given in Table 6.8. Overall, the level of desired performance increased from first to last draft.

Table 6.8 IADE evaluation of moves and length of first and final drafts

IADE evaluation	***First draft***	***Last draft***
Move 1		
Far below average	9 (8.6%)	0 (0%)
Below average	7 (6.6%)	0 (0%)
About average	**43 (41%)**	**99 (94.3%)**
Above average	35 (33.3%)	6 (5.7%)
Far above average	11 (10.5%)	11 (10.5%)
Move 2		
Far below average	20 (19.1%)	0 (0%)
Below average	23 (21.9%)	3 (2.9%)
About average	**36 (34.3%)**	**95 (90.5%)**
Above average	13 (13.3%)	7 (6.6%)
Far above average	12 (11.4%)	0 (0%)
Move 3		
Far below average	25 (23.8%)	0 (0%)
Below average	48 (45.7%)	10 (9.5%)
About average	**16 (15.2%)**	**91 (86.7%)**
Above average	7 (6.6%)	4 (3.8%)
Far above average	9 (8.6%)	0 (0%)
Length		
Far below average	5 (4.8%)	0 (0%)
Below average	33 (31.4%)	14 (13.3%)
About average	**60 (57.1%)**	**85 (81%)**
Above average	4 (3.8%)	2 (1.9%)
Far above average	3 (2.9%)	4 (3.8%)

As was described in Chapter 5, IADE's evaluative comments were converted into scores. Specifically, the comment containing *about average* was considered equal to a score of 3; *below average* or *above average,* to a score of 2; and *way below average* or *way above average,* to a score of 1. The distribution of the scores assigned to each move and the length was better in the last drafts compared to the first drafts. As shown in Table 6.9, considerably more last drafts were assigned the highest score of 3 (move 1 – 97.1 percent, move 2 – 92.4 percent, move 3 – 87.6 percent, length – 83.8 percent). The highest score of 3 was assigned 159 times to first drafts and 379 times to last drafts. Conversely, considerably fewer scores of 1 and 2 were assigned to last drafts compared to first drafts.

These numbers suggest that the students' work products improved at move level. *t*-tests comparing the mean scores for each move and length indicate that improvement from first to final draft was statistically

Table 6.9 Scores for first and final drafts based on IADE evaluation

Element	**Score 1**		**Score 2**		**Score 3**	
	First draft	**Last draft**	**First draft**	**Last draft**	**First draft**	**Last draft**
Move 1	16 (15.2%)	0 (0%)	43 (41%)	3 (2.9%)	46 (43.8%)	102 (97.1%)
Move 2	31 (29.5%)	0 (0%)	36 (34.3%)	8 (7.6%)	38 (36.2%)	97 (92.4%)
Move 3	35 (33.3%)	0 (0%)	55 (52.4%)	13 (12.4%)	15 (14.3%)	92 (87.6%)
Length	8 (7.6%)	1 (0.9%)	37 (35.2%)	16 (15.2%)	60 (57.1%)	88 (83.8%)
Total	90 (21.4%)	1 (0.2%)	171 (40.7%)	40 (9.5%)	159 (37.9%)	379 (90.2%)

significant (Table 6.10). It is worth mentioning that the standard deviations in each case decreased for the last drafts compared to the first drafts, which means that some students who did not do so well on their first draft performed better after revising with IADE.

Table 6.10 Moves 1, 2, 3, and length scores in first and final drafts based on IADE analysis

	M	*SD*	*T*	*DF*	*Effect size*
Move 1 first draft	2.29	0.717	9.88*	104	.54
Move 1 final draft	2.97	0.167			
Move 2 first draft	2.04	0.808	11.34*	104	.59
Move 2 final draft	2.92	0.267			
Move 3 first draft	1.81	0.666	14.57*	104	.71
Move 3 final draft	2.88	0.331			
Length first draft	2.46	0.665	6.25	104	.31
Length final draft	2.83	0.403			

*$p < .001$.

To analyze the degree of rhetorical improvement, the scores assigned to the moves and draft length were used to classify improvement into four categories:

- *Considerable improvement* (improvement from first to last draft from a score of 1 to a score of 3)
- *Noticeable improvement* (improvement from first to last draft from scores 1,2 to scores 2,3 respectively)
- *No improvement* (no change of lower to higher scores from first to last draft)
- *No need for improvement* (score of 3 for both first and last drafts)

Figure 6.9 details the degree of improvement from first to last draft expressed as percentages for each move and length. The *noticeable*

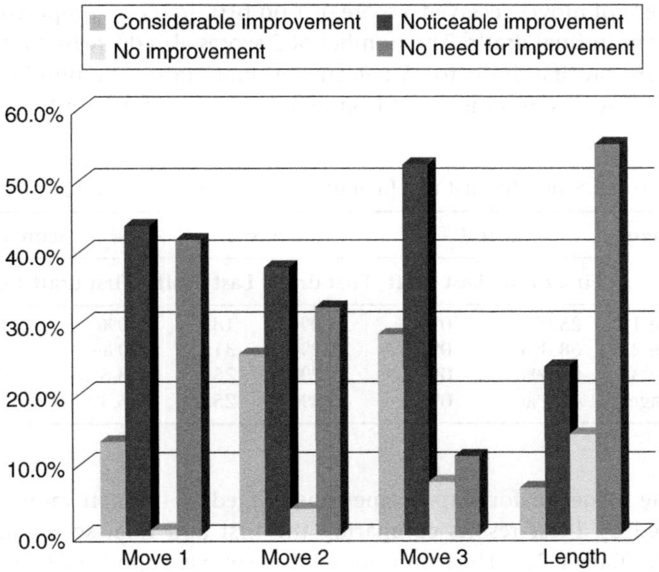

Figure 6.9 Degrees of improvement in moves and length based on IADE evaluation

improvement and *no need for improvement* categories are the most prominent. On average, 39.5 percent of students improved their drafts noticeably, and 18.5 percent did so considerably. Most *noticeable* and *considerable* improvements were made at the level of Move 3 (52.4 and 28.6 percent). Move 3 may have been easier for students to develop since, to accomplish the functions of this move, they had to briefly describe their own work, which is something they knew very well. Length was the aspect that was improved the least; however, 55.2 percent appeared to need *no improvement*. The percentages of students whose first draft saw no improvement were the lowest (0.9, 3.8, 7.6, and 14.3 percent). The *no need for improvement* category had a relatively high percentage, perhaps because the analysis engine detected move indicators and perhaps because some students' first drafts were relatively good.

In addition to the automated analysis of all students' drafts, a sample of 32 first and last drafts written by 16 students was analyzed by human raters. The human scores assigned to this sample revealed that the first drafts were weaker in rhetorical quality and that they became stronger after revision with IADE. As shown in Table 6.11, an average of 47.9

percent of moves received a score of 1 on first drafts as compared with 0 percent in final drafts. The number of 2 scores also decreased from 45.8 percent on first drafts to 25 percent on final drafts. The number of the highest scores of 3 increased from 6.3 percent to 75 percent.

Table 6.11 Scores for first and final drafts based on human ratings

Element	**Score 1**		**Score 2**		**Score 3**	
	First draft	**Last draft**	**First draft**	**Last draft**	**First draft**	**Last draft**
Move 1	25.0%	0%	75.0%	18.7%	0%	81.3%
Move 2	68.8%	0%	31.2%	31.2%	0%	68.8%
Move 3	50.0%	0%	31.2%	25.0%	18.8%	75.0%
Average	47.9%	0%	45.8%	25.0%	6.3%	75.0%

The evidence for improvement as judged by human raters is supported by *t*-test results comparing the first and final scores for each move (Table 6.12). The means for all three moves significantly increased in final drafts, similar to the results obtained on comparisons between the scores based on IADE's automated analysis.

Figure 6.10 further shows that in this 32-draft sample the highest average percentage belongs to *noticeable improvement* (54.4 percent) and the lowest to *no need for improvement* (6.6 percent), a finding which is similar to the degrees of improvement that resulted from the automated evaluation. *Considerable improvement* and *no improvement* (31.2 and 8.1 percent, respectively) are somewhat opposite to the numbers for the same improvement categories based on automated evaluation. These results may be accounted for by the environment in which the participants interacted with the program. More specifically, improvement

Table 6.12 Moves 1, 2, 3 scores for first and final drafts based on human ratings

	M	*SD*	*T*	*DF*	*Effect size*
Move 1 first draft	1.75	0.447	7.41*	15	.77
Move 1 final draft	2.81	0.403			
Move 2 first draft	1.31	0.479	8.88*	15	.82
Move 2 final draft	2.69	0.479			
Move 3 first draft	1.69	0.793	5.51*	15	.63
Move 3 final draft	2.75	0.447			

*$p < .001$.

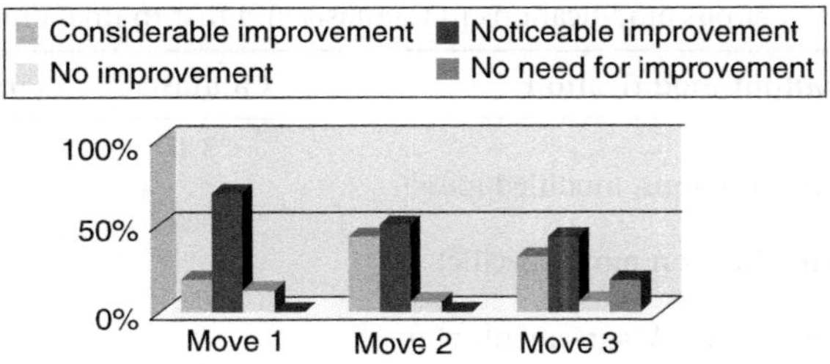

Figure 6.10 Degrees of improvement in moves based on human rating

categories based on human scores reflect the performance of the same 16 students who were observed and recorded, which may have influenced them to invest more efforts in the revision process. Automated evaluation, on the other hand, captured the work of all the students, who may not have addressed everything they otherwise would have.

Improvement in the same 16 students' writing was also reflected in the modifications they made during revision, which were traced in Camtasia screen recordings and also identified by manual comparison of their first and final drafts. The Camtasia transcripts contained 77 output modifications. Manual analysis identified 285 output modifications in 200 sentences revised from first to final draft; 31 sentences remained unchanged. The participants modified their output at different levels (Table 6.13). More changes were made to content, vocabulary, and structure and fewer to grammar and mechanics. This is not surprising given the nature of the feedback, which made the moves in students' texts salient and triggered thinking about intended functional meaning and more appropriate language use.

Output modifications were considered to be at the level of content when new material was added or when old material was either deleted or replaced with more accurate information. Additions were the most frequent type of content modifications identified, and deletions were rare. The remaining content changes were typically modifications of ideas that were imprecise or not sufficiently tackled. For example, Student 28 modified the content by expanding the initial idea and by providing more specific information about old and new approaches:

[Not like old approaches which treat user cognitive process as predictable, UCD makes user the center during the entire design process. → There are several methodologies to implement different systems. Early ones tend to treat users' cognitive processes as predictable and quantifiable (references). New ones like User-Centered Design focus on constant conversations with users

Table 6.13 Output modifications in Camtasia and first to final drafts

Level of output modification	Camtasia	First-last drafts
Content (additions, deletions, modified ideas)	23%	28%
Lexical (move-specific, non-move-specific)	49%	42%
Grammar (verb tense/form, SV agreement, plurals)	7%	5%
Structure (sentence, paragraph)	13%	21%
Mechanics (citation format, punctuation)	8%	4%

(reference). Users are made the center of designing process – this ensures that what is designed is what users need.] (first to last drafts)

Here is another example of additions and deletions selected from the Camtasia transcript of Student 29:

[I'm adding m1 step 2. [Adds: 'With easier' Deletes. Adds 'The design of HCI interface is normally' Deletes 'is normally' Adds 'is normally focused on how to make computers understand human orders better. With easy' Replaces 'orders' with 'instructions'. Thinks. Continues: 'With easy operating systems or graphical interface, users will find it' replaces 'easy' with 'user-friendly.' Continues: 'users will find it easy to give orders. So the computers can' Adds 'precise orders.' Continues: 'can react to the users better.' OK, I added some sentences here.]. (Camtasia)

The content modifications appeared to often be move-specific, as demonstrated by the following examples. Student 54 changed the content of the sentence so that it reflects a function of Move 1 – the centrality of the topic – through emphasizing its importance (the importance of cement fitness) as opposed to what it leaves unaffected.

[Deletes It is important to note that the total heat released during hydration is unaffected by the cement fineness. and adds The cement fineness is very important to control the heat of hydration.] (Camtasia)

Student 63 claimed the interest of the research community in the topic (Move 1, claiming centrality) and the need for a better understanding of the topic (Move 2, justification).

[Added → 'The demand for statistical information about the Brazilian population has become an issue of considerable interest. The society and politicians need to understand the effects of policies on certain groups of the population.']. (first to last draft)

Student 62 added Move 2 content in order to highlight an existing problem that will be addressed in his study.
[Added → 'However, the integration of that stream of population has not shown the results expected for the agricultural development's projects. Latino farmers are not well connected to USDA and other agricultural organizations.']. (*first to last draft*)

Student 27 added new content which carries the functions of move 3 – stating the purpose of current research, indicating the methodology used, summarizing the findings obtained, and outlining the structure of the paper.
[Adds: 'Within the process of analysis, this study used content analysis to find out the historical flow of Chicago downtown. And the paper is structured in accordance with the five stages of Florida's creative economy. The results show that, indeed, the Chicago downtown, although has a relatively short history, match Florida's theory.'] (*Camtasia*).

Many output modifications were lexical. Some lexical changes were directly related to certain rhetorical moves, while others were more general; therefore, they were divided into move-specific and non-move-specific. The move-specific lexical modifications were changes that consisted of vocabulary signaling a particular function of a move. For instance:

- Move 1 lexical modification: *[Changed: 'The separation of enantiomers has been focused because of the impurities of chiral drug [1]. → <u>Numerous efforts have been invested in</u> the separation of enantiomers because of the impurities of chiral drug* (1)*.'*]. (*Student 32, first to last draft*)
- Move 2 lexical modification: *[Changed: 'This is a batch solution (needs all measurements first) and also the resulting joint optimization is computationally complex. → <u>However, there is one major limitation</u> in that this batch solution needs all measurements first. <u>Another problem is</u> that the resulting joint optimization is computationally complex.'].* (*Student 30, first to last draft*)
- Move 3 lexical modification: *[Changes: 'So it is possible to set downtown Chicago into Florida's five economic transitions' → '<u>This paper assumes that</u> it is possible ...'].* (*Student 27, Camtasia*)

Non-move-specific lexical changes were fewer and more generic in nature. They were made to repair inappropriate expression, informality, and lack of cohesion as well as to improve the clarity of ideas through paraphrasing.

- Expression: *[Changes: '[reference] also introduced a variance estimator for ordered frames in order <u>to attend demands</u> of Statistics Sweden.'*

→ *'[reference] also introduced a variance estimator for ordered frames in order <u>to address the needs of</u> users of official data.']*. (*Student 30, Camtasia*)

- Formality: *[Changed: '[reference] <u>talked about</u> a spin self-assembly method as an alternative for making well-organized multilayer films in a very short process time. → [reference] <u>reported on</u> a spin self-assembly method as an alternative for making well-organized multilayer films in a very short process time.']*. (*Student 29, first to last draft*)
- Cohesion: *[Changed: 'The work will focus on the identification and optimizationof key parameters for producing desired core-shell polymer nanoparticles morphologies by RAFT microemulsion polymerizations with surf-CTAs. → <u>Overall</u>, this work focuses on the identification and optimizationof key parameters for producing desired core-shell polymer nanoparticles morphologies by RAFT microemulsion polymerizations with surf-CTAs.']*. (*Student 58, first to last draft*)
- Paraphrasing: *[Changes: 'In order to get better insight into these massive data, many visualization tools have been invented specifically to view biological data.' → 'Many visualization tools have been invented specifically to view biological data inside these massive dataset.']*. (*Student 43, Camtasia*)

Grammar corrections were less frequent than other types of output modifications (Table 6.13). Grammatical changes were mostly related to verb tenses and forms, and a few were related to subject-verb agreement and plural noun forms:

- Verb tense: *[Changes 'is' to 'was' in 'The objective of this study <u>is</u> to monitor the formation of lipids in the mesocarp and its change in terms of composition of TG, vitamin E and carotenes in the oil palm fruits of E. guineensis from week 12 to 24 after anthesis in Tenera materials planted in the central area of Colombia.']*. (*Student 44, Camtasia*)
- Subject-verb agreement and verb form: *[Changes: 'Currently, activated carbon <u>adsorption are utilized</u> and <u>research</u> mostly [10] [11]. → Currently, activated carbon <u>adsorption is utilized</u> and most commonly <u>researched</u> [10] [11].']*. (*Student 65, first to last draft*)
- Plural: *[Changes: 'In this model, tungsten cones with different <u>size</u> are used to enhance the optical field. → In our model, tungsten cones with different <u>sizes</u> were used to enhance the optical field.']*. (*Student 40, first to last draft*)

Structure changes were made at sentence level and at paragraph level. When clauses were altered, split, or combined, they were classified as sentence-level changes. The modifications were considered paragraph-level when sentences were moved to a different paragraph.

- Sentence-level modifications: *This sentence should be changed. Maybe it should be added in the former sentence. [Goes to the revision box. reads aloud changes: 'However, the estimated value is much larger than the experimental results [4–7,4–11]. This probably because in their experiments the tips used were larger than the laser wavelength, hence they could not be treated simply as small dipoles.' → 'However, the estimated value is much larger than the experimental results [4–7,4–11], which is probably because in their experiments the tips used larger than the laser wavelength, hence they could not be treated simply as small dipoles.] I just put a single sentence into a complex one.'* (Student 40, think-aloud/Camtasia)
- Paragraph-level modifications: *I can move it right before the last sentence. [Cuts the sentence and places it later in the text.].* (Student 61, think-aloud/Camtasia)

In addition, the students made edits at the level of mechanics. Specifically, they modified the format of the in-text citations and changed the punctuation in a few of instances.

- In-text citations: *[first and last name; year] made an experimental analysis around the topic of FDI and its effect as a double-edged sword to developing countries. → [last name, year] made an experimental analysis around the topic of FDI and its effect as a double-edged sword to developing countries.* (Student 53, first to last draft).
- Punctuation: *In this work we use [1] to develop a KF-CS algorithm to causally reconstruct image sequences using MR data. → In this study, we use this technique to develop a KF-CS algorithm to causally reconstruct image sequences using MR data.* (Student 30, first to last draft)

The output modifications were not always made at a single level. Some combined changes in content, vocabulary, grammar, structure, or mechanics.

[Goes to the revision box] I just delete the 'but', so... And then I add 'however', and it becomes a separate sentence. [Changes: 'Traditional design of anti-infection surface includes mechanical mixture of antibacterial drugs and grafting of antibacterial drugs by chemical methods, but these methods are difficult to process and to control the concentration of antibacterial drugs on the surface (references).' → 'Traditional design of anti-infection surfaces, which has attracted the attention of many researchers, includes mechanical

mixture of antibacterial drugs and grafting of antibacterial drugs by chemical methods (references). However, these methods are difficult to process and to control the concentration of antibacterial drugs on the surface.'] (*Student 28, Camtasia*)

6.1.4 Practice and modified interaction

Like other claims regarding IADE's Language Learning Potential, the claim that practice via multiple resubmissions and modified interaction with IADE may contribute to learning and improvement was supported by the outcomes of the survey data analysis, although it found less strong statistical support (Table 6.14).

Table 6.14 Overall evidence of effects of practice and modified interaction

Data source	N	Evidence	No evidence
Likert-scale	88		
Q-n 1 [practice opportunity]		100%	0%
Q-n 2 [use of help options]		92.1%	7.9%
Yes/No and open-ended	83		
Q-n 1 [practice and improvement]		92.8%	7.2%
Q-n 2 [helpfulness of help options]		83.1%	16.9%
Q-n 3 [use of help options]		91.6%	8.4%
Q-n 4 [use of annotated corpus]		65.1%	34.9%
IADE database and IADE evaluation	105		
of 210 first and last drafts		93.3% 1173 submissions $r = .286, p < .01$ 1312 help option clicks	6.7%; $r = -.177, p > .01$ $F = 2.712, p = .07$

6.1.4.1 L2 writers' perceptions

All the students felt that they had sufficient opportunities for writing practice: 21.6 percent indicated that they had *a lot* of practice; 56.8 percent, *sufficient*; and 21.6 percent, *a little*. Only four respondents to the open-ended question did not think of practice per se as a helpful factor, and two were not sure whether it was helpful or not, explaining their uncertainty as follows: *I don't know if I improved because of revising and resubmitting but I do know that I tried to pay more attention when I wrote* (*Student 23*) and *Not sure, no one except the program gave me the feedback of my draft* (*Student 34*). The remaining 92.8 percent considered practice exercised through multiple revisions and resubmissions as being helpful for improvement. Roughly 30 percent of these students explained that the opportunity for practice actually helped them consolidate the knowledge about the moves that they were acquiring (*Practice is always helpful. For me writing is like something else I learn to do. You do it many times and you finally do very well. Like experiments.* (*Student 43*); *Revising with this software helping me to learn new things. Like the bicycle, I fall and stand up many times and I finally learn to ride the bicycle. So it's the same with my introduction, I revise and revise until I have no problem.* (*Student 86*)). Here, a connection may be made between students' perceptions of consolidated knowledge and their confidence that they would be able to transfer the newly acquired knowledge to their further academic writing practice (mentioned in their survey responses about learning gains). Also, although not very strong, this perception of knowledge consolidation may serve as indirect evidence speaking in support of the role of practice for transforming declarative knowledge (which the participants were exposed to in class instruction) into automated skill, as sustained by the Skill Acquisition Theory.

A new theme mentioned by 16.9 percent was focus on meaning, which in fact presents great interest for the claim regarding the Meaning Focus quality discussed in the next section of this chapter. In this regard, the students made it clear that, because they had the chance to repeatedly resubmit their work for automated analysis and feedback, they found themselves thinking more and more about the meaning they were trying to convey (*This revising practicing made me go back and think what I wrote is really what I meant or not before I submit every time.* (*Student 41*); *I know with this practice I start to think a lot about if my moves sound with the right meaning and how I want every time I revised.* (*Student 6*)).

Among other reasons why the students perceived revising and resubmitting as helpful were the elements of the revision cycle discussed in the first section of this chapter. A few students (6.5 percent) indicated that resubmitting helped them focus on their discourse form (*Because every time I submit I can look to see if my moves are logical and follow the order in my field. I revise and submit and check again* (*Student 82*); *Of course this process helps the learning procedure because you see how your moves get better organized* (*Student 28*)). More students (24.7 percent) believed that the more they revised and resubmitted, the more negative evidence they could identify (*Revising my drafts with this program helped me to find a lot of problems in my draft and know the shortage of my writing* (*Student 59*); *because every time it analyzes I can see what's wrong again and again* (*Student 36*)). Some (18.2 percent) claimed to have been able to make more output modifications that were eventually successful (*Resubmitting was really helpful as through it I changed and improved each move* (*Student 29*); *The statistics in IADE after every submission really helped me to revise with good changes and improve my introduction* (*Student 70*)). There were also a few explanations (5.2 percent) suggesting that this type of practice led to enhanced understanding of the rhetorical moves (*Revising and resubmitting helped me understand the expression of each move and how it affect or helps what I want to do in my introduction* (*Student 57*); *I understand much better how writing works because revision makes the writer to look from others point of view to his writing* (*Student 31*)).

The role of modified interaction through IADE's help options was an additional point of interest elicited by the survey. In their Likert-scale responses, 23.9 percent of students indicated that they made use of IADE's help options *a lot*; 26.1 percent, *somewhat*; 42.1 percent, *a little*; and 7.9 percent did not use them at all (Table 6.14). Very similar results were obtained from another survey question, where 91.6 percent indicated that they accessed different help options. Of these participants, 83.2 percent thought the availability of such a feature in a program like IADE was helpful; 3.6 percent thought it was not; 4.8 percent were not sure; and 8.4 percent did not have an opinion because they did not access IADE's help options. The students who were not sure whether such options would help or not did not provide any explanations for their uncertainty, while those who were confident of their positive answers provided reasoning that formed three themes: knowledge consolidation, revision strategy development, and practicality. The knowledge consolidation category contained 48.3 percent of the positive answers, which indicated that the help options can remind students of what they learn in class and can help them consolidate their new knowledge (*sometimes I cannot remember the moves so I can turn to the help option* (*Student 65*); *I can get help when I'm not so sure about the individual move* (*Student 85*)). The revision strategy development theme appeared in 15.6 percent of answers, which made reference to the revision tips that guided students through the revision process (*It gives me guiding when I am lost* (*Student 63*); *This gave some hints to go on and I know what to do first and next to improve the writing* (*Student 31*)). The third theme, practicality, or the convenience that the help options would ensure, surfaced in the answers of 36.1 percent of students (*Without the help options, the program would become much less convenience* (*Participant 59*); *It could help you to better use the program. Otherwise I may get confused of the recommendation of the software* (*Student 72*); *It makes it simple to understand the IADE better* (*Student 55*)).

The themes of knowledge consolidation and revision strategy development also appeared in another open-ended survey question, which asked students why they accessed IADE's help options. Of the 76 students who indicated that they had used IADE's help, 53.9 percent said they needed it because they did not have solid knowledge of the moves and steps (*I used the definition and examples in the Help Options. Sometimes, I forgot the meaning of the moves and steps. So, the Help Options can help me to understand them* (*Student 28*); *Because sometimes I am confused about different steps and their function and help options can tell me about what I need* (*Student 13*)). Other students (14.5 percent) wanted some guidance in their revision process (*When I start, I didn't know how to revise except mistakes in my grammar, but the Revision Tips help me make a plan of steps* (*Student 7*); *Sometimes I don't know how to revise my drafts, and I will access Help Options* (*Student 57*)). Students who needed assistance in order to address negative feedback (26.3 percent) also consulted the help options (*When I revised my drafts, I confused some sentences that I suppose it is move 3; however, IADE appeared it is move 2. Thus, I use Help Options* (*Student 40*); *I needed to know reason for the negative evaluation by the IADE* (*Student 66*)). A few students (5.3 percent) accessed help options to search for some move-specific vocabulary (*I was trying to find synonym for steps in order to avoid repetition* (*Student 16*); *I used examples and annotated corpus because I am not very sure about the steps, and I want to find some expression to write my own draft* (*Student 44*)).

Given that class instruction followed a corpus-based approach and included work with annotated corpora, a survey question referred to the students' use of the annotated corpus in IADE. Answering this question, 65.1 percent said that they did make use of this help option (Table 6.14). The 34.9 percent who did not access the annotated corpus mentioned reasons such as simply not having noticed the availability of the annotated corpus in IADE or not seeing the relevance of the corpus because it was either not in their discipline or because the texts were on topics too different from their research area. The positive answers were accompanied by explanations that coincide with some themes identified elsewhere in the survey – knowledge consolidation (19.4 percent) and vocabulary search (27.8 percent). Another prominent theme mentioned by 30.6 percent of students was accessing the annotated corpus to read examples of moves and steps (*It's really good for examples. You can click on sentence and see the step* (*Student 24*); *I used many times during the work session to read examples of steps when I'm not sure* (*Student 49*)). In addition, 22.2 percent looked up the corpus to compare their drafts with published texts in their discipline (*I accessed to check other articles moves and see if my introduction is like them* (*Student 79*); *it helps me to compare my draft with classical papers' method to organize their introduction and their expression methods* (*Student 86*)).

6.1.4.2 Introspections and statistical discernment

The practice aspect was also explored in terms of submission frequency. As recorded in IADE's database, 105 students submitted their drafts a total of 1,173 times over a period of six days. Table 6.15 summarizes the frequencies and the number of submissions, divided into frequency bands for a more compact presentation. The lowest submission frequency band was 3–5 times. More students revised and resubmitted their drafts 6–10 times and 11–20 times. A few students submitted their work more than 30 times.

Most submissions were done within three days, with an average of 43 submissions per student; 12.4 percent finished their work within one day, submitting their drafts for automated analysis on average 10 times; 20.8 percent continued working for three days with 10 submissions on average; and a few other participants took up to 6 days to revise, although they did not make many submissions (Table 6.16).

To examine the relationship between practice and overall draft improvement, the score differences for each move and length were summed up and used to calculate the Pearson product-moment correlation. A statistically significant correlation was found at the 95 percent

Table 6.15 Submission frequency

Frequency band	**Students**
3–5	17.1%
6–10	44.8%
11–20	27.6%
21–30	7.6%
35	1.0%
43	1.0%
65	0.9%

Table 6.16 Number of submissions by time period

Days	***Students***	***# submissions***	***Avg # submissions/student***
1	12.4%	137	10
2	57.3%	722	43
3	20.8%	221	10
4	5.7%	66	11
5	1.9%	22	11
6	1.9%	5	2

level of confidence with a correlation coefficient $r = .286$ ($N = 105$), which suggests that practice through multiple resubmission of revised drafts was positively related to overall improvement of students' writing.

In order to find whether the frequency of submission, or the practice variable, had an impact on the improvement of individual aspects of students' drafts, One-Way ANOVA tests on three score difference groups (score difference = 2, score difference = 1, and score difference = 0) were conducted for Move 1, Move 2, Move 3, and draft length, respectively. Variances for these groups satisfied the constant variance assumption (except length), and ANOVA tests at .05 significance level were performed to compare the group means for each aspect at a time (descriptive statistics in Table 6.17). The ANOVA results showed that there were no significant differences in the number of submissions across the three score difference groups for Move 1 ($F = .975$, $p = .381$), Move 2 ($F = 1.480$, $p = .233$), and draft length ($F = .602$, $p = .549$). Move 3 was the only aspect for which more encouraging evidence was found. For this move, the number of submissions was highest for the group with the highest score difference and therefore with the highest improvement. Although the results showed no significant difference among the

Table 6.17 Relationship between practice and improvement

Draft aspect	*Score difference group*	*N*	*M*	*ST*
Move 1				
	0	45	9.93	8.971
	1	45	11.76	10.377
	2	14	13.85	9.929
	Total	104	11.25	9.727
Move 2				
	0	38	9.03	5.838
	1	40	12.23	12.050
	2	27	12.63	10.024
	Total	105	11.17	9.714
Move 3				
	0	20	11.10	8.522
	1	55	9.38	6.940
	2	30	14.50	13.549
	Total	105	11.17	9.714
Length				
	0	73	10.59	8.244
	1	25	11.96	8.502
	2	7	14.43	22.619
	Total	105	11.17	9.714

groups (F = 2.788, p = .066) at 95 percent confidence level, it was statistically significant at 90 percent confidence level. This result corroborates a finding introduced earlier, according to which most noticeable and considerable improvement was made for Move 3. It is reasonable to assume, then, that better progress on Move 3 could be related to practice through more frequent resubmissions.

The fact that no statistical significance was found for the relationship between individual moves and draft length and the submission frequency may be due to the small sample (N ranged between 7 and 73), which resulted in low power of ANOVA. However, the fact that a strong relation was found between the submission frequency and overall improvement may be explained in view of the nature of resubmitted revisions. As the qualitative analysis of improvement revealed, the students acted upon the negative evidence they noticed, which was not only related to discourse form, but also to discourse meaning. Consequently, they made revisions which improved the rhetorical quality of the entire text, not only its form.

Data on students' access to IADE's help options was recorded in the program's database and was used to examine modified interaction. Of the 105 students, 6.7 percent did not access any help options (as they admitted in the survey), while the remaining 93.3 percent actively interacted with IADE in this way. Apparently, most of the students' modified interaction activity fell into one of three bands for frequency of clicks: 1–5 (24.8 percent), 6–10 (28.6 percent), or 11–20 (23.8 percent). A few students elicited help more than 20 times, one of them doing it 87 times. The frequency bands on all four options per student are given in Table 6.18.

A total of 1,312 clicks were recorded, the overall average per student being approximately 12 clicks. The explanations of moves and steps

Table 6.18 Frequency of clicks on all help options

Frequency band	**# students**
0	6.7%
1–5	24.8%
6–10	28.6%
11–20	23.8%
21–30	8.5%
31–40	5.6%
51–60	1.0%
81–90	1.0%

were consulted most frequently (742 times), followed by the examples in the annotated corpus (243 times). Disciplinary statistics and revision tips were accessed less frequently (178 and 149 times, respectively). This frequency distribution is similar to what was revealed by the survey. With more details, Figure 6.11 presents the frequency bands for students' access to each help option. Judging by the most prominent frequency band for all help options, most of the participants engaged in modified interaction using IADE's help at least 1 to 5 times.

The high frequency of clicks on definitions, where students could see explanations of the rhetorical functions of moves and steps, is clearly related to the knowledge consolidation theme identified in the survey data. This link was also supported by the data from think-aloud/ Camtasia, observations, and interview transcripts. It can be inferred that modified interaction through IADE's help with definitions was a factor that played an important role in the enhanced understanding element of the revision cycle (shown in Figure 6.1). Similarly, the students' search for examples and move-specific vocabulary as well as their need to compare

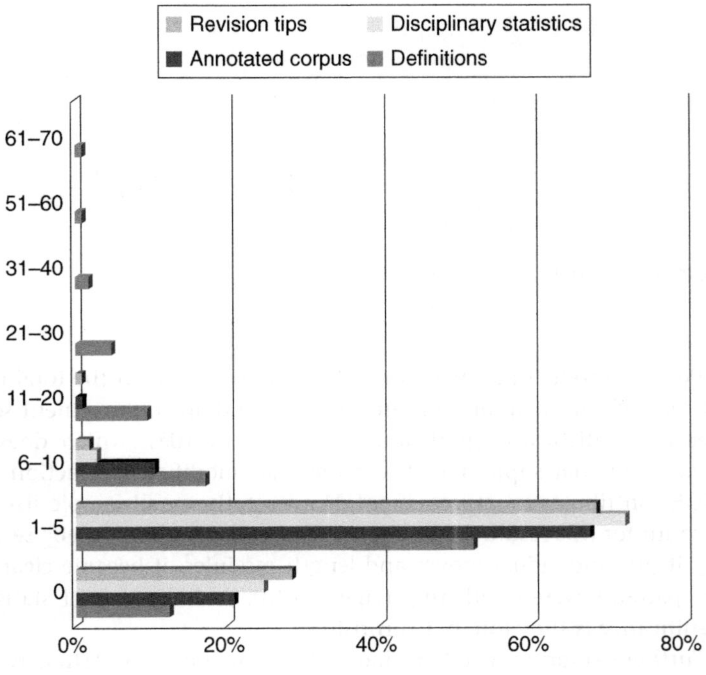

Figure 6.11 Frequency of clicks on each help option

their writing with that of professionals in their field may be connected to their access to the annotated texts, which had the second highest frequency. Although rarely mentioned in responses to open-ended questions, the disciplinary statistics given as a help option may have also been consulted for the purpose of comparison since this type of help was the next in frequency after the annotated corpus. Finally, students' access to the revision tips may have contributed to their development of new revision strategies and, in particular, actions taken to follow-up on the negative feedback. These connections are represented in Figure 6.12.

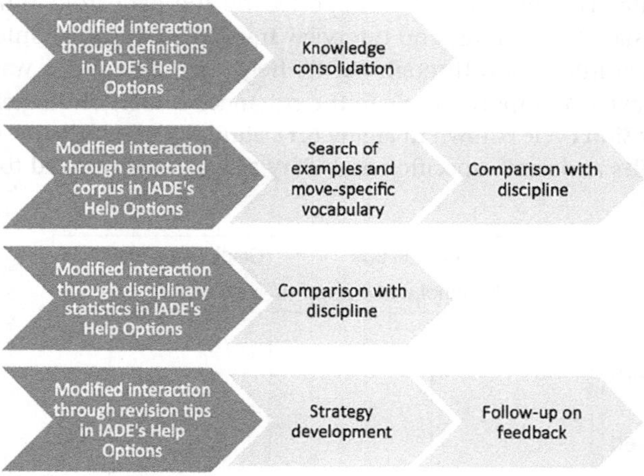

Figure 6.12 Modified interaction effects

Pearson product-moment correlation indices between the total number of clicks on help options and the overall draft improvement scores was not statistically significant (r = –.177, N=105), which does not lend inferential support to the claim that modified interaction with IADE contributes to improvement. However, the small sample size may account for this result. Additionally, after analyzing the data by separating it into individual moves and length modules, it became clear that the patterns were conflicting (Figure 6.13), and the lack of statistical significance is therefore not surprising.

Further exploring whether modified interaction with IADE may contribute to improvement, one-way ANOVA tests with a .05 significance

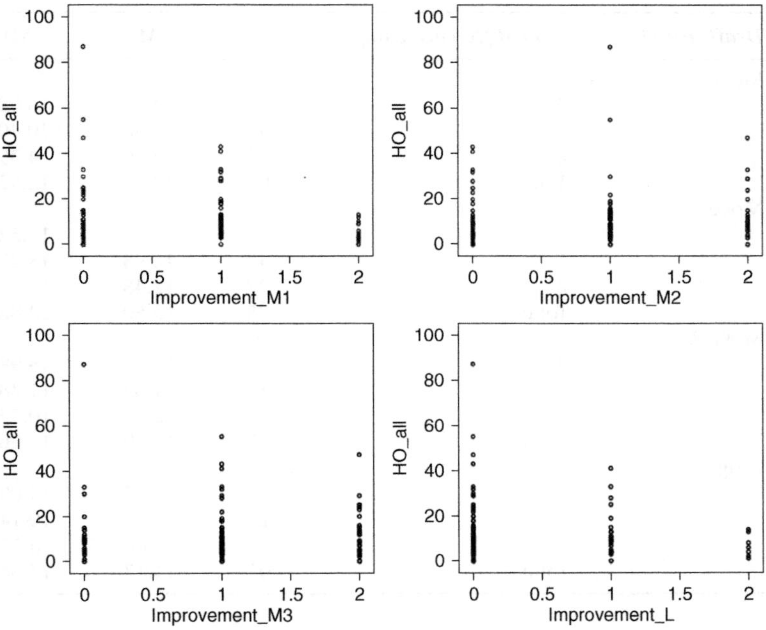

Figure 6.13 Help options and improvement on individual moves and draft length

level were performed to examine the effect of using help options on the improvement of individual moves and draft length. Table 6.19 contains the respective descriptive statistics. Although ANOVA results revealed no statistical differences, it was interesting to see a small exception in the case of Move 1. For this move, weak evidence was found ($F = 2.712$, $p = .071$), which suggests that the group with the highest improvement accessed the help options the least number of times. This may mean that the students who made the highest progress on Move 1 had acquired better declarative knowledge of this move and, thus, did not have much need to consult the supporting resources provided in IADE. Or, perhaps this move was less challenging for them.

6.1.4.3 Summary

This first section of this chapter presented integrated quantitative and qualitative evidence that support four claims about the nature and strengths of IADE's Language Learning Potential:

Table 6.19 Relationship between modified interaction and improvement

Draft aspect	*Score difference group*	*N*	*M*	*SD*
Move 1				
	0	45	14.56	16.026
	1	45	12.58	10.409
	2	14	5.50	4.398
	Total	104	12.48	12.921
Move 2				
	0	38	12.05	11.524
	1	40	12.93	15.234
	2	27	12.48	11.126
	Total	105	12.50	12.860
Move 3				
	0	20	14.80	18.998
	1	55	11.85	11.385
	2	30	12.13	10.520
	Total	105	12.50	12.860
Length				
	0	73	13.22	14.095
	1	25	11.96	10.143
	2	7	6.86	5.113
	Total	105	11.17	12.860

- IADE feedback can stimulate focus on and noticing of discourse form
- Focus on discourse form triggered by IADE feedback can facilitate learning gains
- Focus on discourse form triggered by IADE feedback can facilitate improvement in rhetorical quality
- Practice and modified interaction with IADE may contribute to improvement

Focus on discourse form indeed occurred. It was triggered by both numerical and color-coded feedback as well as by IADE's help options, which helped the learners notice less salient characteristics of rhetorical moves, particularly those that were expressed with move-specific vocabulary. Focus on discourse form was the head of a revision cycle with such subsequent phases as noticing of negative evidence, enhanced understanding, and output modification. These phases were prompted by the automated feedback and occurred causatively and sequentially in every iteration of the cycle.

The second claim also holds because empirical evidence suggests that interaction with IADE contributed to students' learning of Introduction rhetorical moves. After having revised their drafts with the program, the students enhanced their knowledge of moves and steps, and the learning gains were found to be statistically significant. Students' judgments of causes of learning mirrored the introspective evidence regarding the elements of the revision cycle, supporting the value of this phenomenon.

The third claim found support in students' perceptions of how and why improvement occurred as well as in evidence of statistically significant improvement from first to last drafts. Manual analysis of a sample of 32 first and last drafts not only confirmed that the rhetorical quality improved; it also revealed multi-level output modifications to content, structure, vocabulary, grammar, and mechanics.

Fourth, it can be assumed that practice and modified interaction facilitated by IADE played an important role in learning and improvement. Although most of the students thought that improvement was facilitated by both these factors, statistical analysis indicated a relation between practice and overall draft improvement but not between modified interaction and overall improvement. However, multiple qualitative data showed that the students engaged in modified interaction with different types of help options for different purposes such as knowledge consolidation, search of examples, comparison with disciplinary writing, and strategy development. These behaviors facilitated the production and revision of intended discourse elements.

6.2 Meaning Focus

6.2.1 Focus on functional meaning

Based on both perceptual and non-perceptual data, it can be claimed that IADE possesses potential to direct learners' attention to the functional meaning of their discourse. The data sources and the degree of evidence they yielded are summarized in Table 6.20.

6.2.1.1 L2 writers' perceptions

Perception-based evidence for the assumption about focus on functional meaning was sought in the responses to Likert-scale, yes/no, and open-ended survey questions (Table 6.20). According to the Likert-scale results, almost all students believed they paid attention to meaning when they were revising with IADE. Only one student selected *not at all*, while 81 percent indicated that they focused on meaning *a lot*; 15 percent, somewhat; and 3 percent, *a little*. Students' answers to the open-ended survey question were largely positive. Of 83 respondents, 92 percent focused on the functional meaning of the moves. The remaining 8 percent explained

Table 6.20 Overall evidence of Meaning Focus

Data source	*N*	Evidence	No evidence
Likert-scale	88		
Q-n 1 [focus on meaning]		99%	1%
Q-n 2 [miscommunicated meaning]		100%	0%
Yes/No and open-ended	83		
Q-n 1 [focus on meaning]		92%	8%
Q-n 2 [miscommunicated meaning]		100%	0%
Think-aloud protocols/Camtasia	16		
(total 1,227 idea units)		252 idea units	
Semi-structured interviews	16		
(total 233 idea units)		54 idea units	
Observations	16		
(total 460 idea units)		77 idea units (of 460)	

that their main goal was including the *'right content'* and improving their draft rather than thinking about what they meant with the moves. For example, Student 7 wrote *'I don't think every author thinks about moves when he or she starts to write a research article.'* This is in fact a valid remark because the researchers' starting point is indeed the need to present scientific knowledge, and it is only natural for them to primarily think of content substance and scope. It also suggests that, as a novice writer, this student was more concerned with knowledge telling. However, experienced writers, who implicitly acquire the writing conventions of their disciplinary community over time, are able to relate the content and at the same time transform the knowledge completing the rhetorical task. Inexperienced writers are often unaware of the social dimension of research writing and, therefore, need explicit instruction in order to develop genre knowledge as situated cognition embedded in disciplinary communication, as was argued in Chapter 1. Some novices, like Student 7 for instance, may initially perceive the knowledge of moves as nothing but theory. Gradually, they may begin to realize the importance of achieving communicative goals, especially when they interact with peer or professional reviewers, who are very likely to raise questions when the content is not effectively communicated and lacks the power of argumentation.

Explanations of why the students thought they focused on functional meaning fell into several thematic categories. In their positive responses, the majority of the students (68.4 percent) reasoned that they thought of the functions of their sentences when the color-coded feedback displayed a move color differently than expected. For example, *Before I revised I thought I always had the meaning in mind, but I didn't think about function. The meaning of words may be fine, but it's not enough for my message. When I see blue instead of red, I figure I don't have the right function* (*Student 52*); *This was the hard part. Because, I cannot express well what I want to express, sometime the program shows other moves instead of what I want to express. And then I think what I'm saying* (*Student 42*). Other students (11.8 percent) explained that they had to think about the meaning of their moves in order to ensure the effectiveness of the communicative purpose of their discourse – *If I want reader to know that I point to gap, I think about how I should say to point to gap* (*Student 14*); *They won't accept my paper if they don't understand where's centrality, where problem, where purpose for my research, so I am attentive to do this right* (*Student 81*). In addition, 9.2 percent comprehended that only by focusing on the functional meanings of the moves could they better understand what they had been taught in class and therefore make better corrections to their drafts. This theme is exemplified by the following student quotes: *The meaning of moves is in definitions and I looked at that and tried to do what it say, so it makes sense now for me* (*Student 89*); *Actually, to know the moves you have to understand how they work, not only know them from lessons. That's why I thought of move meaning* (*Student 7*). No follow-up explanations were provided by the remaining 10.5 percent.

Another set of survey questions inquired whether there were instances when the students meant one move, but IADE displayed a different move. Here, all the students indicated that this was indeed the case. Almost half of the respondents (44.3 percent) noticed such a mismatch *a lot*; 40.9 percent, *somewhat*; and 13.6 percent, *a little*. Their explanations revealed that the color-coded feedback helped them notice that they had miscommunicated functional meaning because the color in the feedback did not match the move they had in mind. Noticing such a mismatch tended to trigger either a cognitive reaction or an immediate action. As shown in Table 6.21, many students commented on their thoughts (39.8 percent), and some commented on their actions (60.2 percent) at the moment. The thoughts included self-questioning as to what might have caused the mismatch (12.1 percent), self-verification as to whether IADE was wrong and whether they were right in expressing its function (22.9 percent), and self-planning speculations as to what should or should not be done when developing a given move (4.8 percent). Students' actions upon receiving feedback that was in disagreement with their communicative intent consisted of immediate attempts to modify their output (19.3 percent), consulting the help options (13.2 percent), and searching for and using move-specific phraseology (27.7 percent), which then led to output modification.

Table 6.21 Reactions to noticing a meaning mismatch (open-ended survey)

Thoughts	39.8%	
Self-questioning		12.1%
Self-verification		22.9%
Self-planning		4.8%
Actions	60.2%	
Immediate modification of output		19.3%
Consulting IADE's HO		13.2%
Searching for and using move-specific phraseology		27.7%

Consider a few examples:

- Self-questioning: *I think what is the problem with my sentence.* (*Student 65*)
- Self-verification: *I will check the sentence and make sure that if I am right. If I am right, I just leave it alone. Otherwise, I change the sentence.* (*Student 74*)
- Self-planning: *Like when I saw red in the beginning, I think you shouldn't have move 2 to start. You should have move 1 and I thought how move 1 should be. That I need to add why my topic is important first.* (*Student 6*)
- Immediate output modification: *I try to rewrite the sentence to what I really wanted it to be and in the same time balance the color.* (*Student 38*)
- Consulting help options: *I think there is something wrong. I read the papers in the IADE to figure out.* (*Student 76*)
- Searching for and using move-specific phraseology: *I try to find out the differences between the moves and then use right expression on the move.* (*Student 30*)

It also seemed that during their interaction with IADE, the students were discovering a connection between certain vocabulary and the functional meaning of moves and steps, and therefore directing their attention to key words and expressions indicative of such meaning. For instance, Student 8 wrote *I realized that one word could change my thoughts. So, as I want to maintain my ideas of movements, I changed some expression to convert the sentences into other move or step*. Student 12 implied a similar idea saying, *I was trying to change and insert specific words because I realized that my steps depends on the right words*. Student 4 explained, *I was trying to find that if I used the wrong key word so it created the different meaning with what I really wanted to mean*. Twenty-two students named some lexical items that they had clearly connected with functional meaning while revising with IADE; for example, *use modal verbs (could/would/should) to give some justification meaning to the sentence, or suggest things and not assure them* (*Student 8*); *I learned new ways to express centrality without showing explicit the importance of the topic, expression as 'in recent years'* (*Student 71*); *Move 1: interest, importance, emphasize; Move 2: no/little work has been reported on, If this tendency were accounted for, results differ substantially; Move 3: Our experiment focuses on, The purpose of this study is, This paper examines* (*Student 30*). These responses are consistent with the theme about noticing move-specific vocabulary that emerged in the survey data related to Language Learning Potential.

6.2.1.2 Introspections

The Meaning Focus quality was also examined by analyzing the introspective accounts of students' experience with IADE. Of 1,227 idea units identified in the think-aloud/Camtasia data, 252 were coded for Meaning Focus (Table 6.20), which averages 15.7 idea units per participant. The observation transcripts contained 77 Meaning Focus idea units from a total of 460 identified in this source of data, with an average of 4.8 idea units per student. The interview transcripts had 54 Meaning Focus idea units out of 203, with an average of 3.4 per student. All these data sources contained evidence of phenomena that were mentioned by in the survey responses. Judging by the 16 students' utterances and actions reflected in the recordings, IADE's color-coded feedback played an important role in directing their focus to the meaning of their discourse. Moreover, the analysis of the Meaning Focus idea units indicated that the students' focus on functional meaning was manifested in a number of ways. Having seen the colors marking their moves, the students took time to reflect on how effectively or ineffectively they expressed the intended meaning. They also focused on meaning by noticing that in some cases the intended functional meaning was displayed with the color of a different move. In addition, they seemed to realize that the effectiveness of expressing functional meaning was directly related to certain lexical choices; therefore, they modified their output with move-specific phraseology that they found in the help options. Percentages for each of these themes per data source are given in Table 6.22.

Here's how the students verbalized their thoughts when they noticed a mismatch, pondered the functional meaning of their moves, connected it with vocabulary items, and used those to better construct functional meaning.

- Noticing a mismatch between intended and expressed functional meaning: *The last sentence is recognized as m1, but I meant it as m3.* (*Student 27, think-aloud*)

Table 6.22 Evidence of focus on functional meaning (transcripts)

	Think-aloud/ Camtasia	***Observations***	***Interviews***
Noticing a mismatch between intended and expressed functional meaning	29.8%	32.5%	44.5%
Reflection on functional meaning	17.5%	40.3%	22.2%
Connecting functional meaning lexical choice	37.7%	16.9%	33.3%

- Reflection on functional meaning: *Justifies the use of m3 in the middle of the text, explaining what the intended effect is.* (*Student 29, observation*)
- Connecting functional meaning and lexical choice: *I didn't really think you have to write steps with some key words. I figured out when I saw another color and I looked again at examples and then I changed some words. You know, it doesn't work just with words, but ... like ... I changed one sentence with negative, and it showed the problem better. It became red.* (*Student 64, interview*)

The think-aloud/Camtasia and observation transcripts helped with understanding the process of focus on functional meaning. This process is exemplified in Figure 6.14, where Student 40 first saw that his move 3 had the color of move 1. Then he reflected about the functional meanings of a number of rhetorical steps within moves 1, 2, and 3 that he was trying to convey – establishing the field through a preview of previous research, establishing a niche by highlighting a problem, and occupying the niche by describing the model he had developed in his study. After that, viewing examples in the annotated corpus, he realized that researchers refer to their own work with the help of personal pronouns.

The semi-structured interviews provided additional insights. One such insight is that the students did not think of functional meaning when they started revising their draft. They seemed to focus on that more consistently later in the revision process, after having come across discrepancies displayed by the color-coded feedback. When asked why he referred to specific steps more frequently towards the end of the think-aloud, Student 43 said, *'I didn't even think about moves and steps when I first write my introduction. But when I saw no red, it was like something is missing, so I start thinking what. I don't know, so I look at definitions and examples. So I realize it's not so simple. If I don't think about moves or steps, it affects the whole thing.'* Another observation is

Noticing a mismatch between intended and expressed functional meaning
So this part I want it to be m3, but uh it still displays in m1. I don't know why.

Reflection on functional meaning
See here, this part. [highlights a blue part of the text] in my mind I wanted to write about method. So I think I describe the method, but it's m1. I don't know why. So, see... [highlights a blue sentence] this sentence may be review to describe the reason, but in this model ... [highlights a blue sentence] this sentence I think I want to describe the model, how it works. So this, uh, some parameters and ... the method. Actually I don't know which move it will be. I just want to first ... in my mind, I think first I describe the field, uh, the technology in this field. Second, I do some reviews, and later I um ... from the review I find some um ... maybe not perfect in the previous research, so I can do something more. And in this part ... so I describe what I want to do in this paper, and briefly, briefly introduce my method.

Connecting functional meaning and lexical choice
Let me see some examples [opens AC in the HO. looks at green sentences and their steps. highlights some.] Hmmm. Let me find some more examples to describe the model. [opens the AC, scrolls down to the green text in an annotated introduction, checks the steps by clicking, highlights parts of the green text. opens another annotated text and does the same] maybe I can write it as description. [speaks aloud and emphasizes] 'our work', 'of our proposed system'... Let's try this first.

Figure 6.14 Example of focus on functional meaning (think-aloud/Camtasia)

that, initially, noticing a mismatch in the colors was mostly accidental, and, as the revision continued, it became intentional. In other words, the students began to intentionally verify their sentences to see if they were displayed in *'the right color.'* For example, Student 29 explained in the interview, *'I don't even think much about colors at beginning. I looked at percent for my field. When I want to add to my move 2 to make it increase, I saw that one sentence I think is move 2 was blue. Then I start checking every time because if it's wrong color, it does not do what is supposed to do.'*

6.2.2 Construction of functional meaning

As with Language Learning Potential, it was reasonable to anticipate that if the automated feedback could trigger focus on functional meaning, then it could also facilitate construction of functional meaning. This assumption found support in the evidence summarized in Table 6.23.

Table 6.23 Overall evidence of construction of functional meaning

Data source	*N*	Evidence	No evidence
Likert-scale	88		
Q-n 1 [feedback and meaning construction]		100%	0%
Yes/No and open-ended	83		
Q-n 1 [feedback and meaning construction]		75.9%	24.1%
Think-aloud protocols/Camtasia	16		
(total 1,227 idea units)		38 idea units	
Semi-structured interviews	16		
(total 233 idea units)		30 idea units	
Observations	16		
(total 460 idea units)		8 idea units	

6.2.2.1 *L2 writers' perceptions*

In their answers to the Likert-scale, all 88 respondents reported that the feedback helped them express intended meaning to a certain extent: 29.6 percent thought it helped *a lot*, 54.5 percent thought it *somewhat* helped, and 15.9 percent thought it helped *a little*. In the open-ended question, the students reflected on whether the feedback helped them better communicate the meanings of the moves. *Yes* answers were provided by 75.9 percent, *No* by 18.1 percent, and 6 percent were *not sure*. Interestingly, negative answers were accompanied by positive explanations such as *It helped me think about what my move actually is, but it doesn't help much to fix it* (*Student* 57); *If I see blue and not red, I know where I'm wrong, so that really helps* (*Student* 13); *It does not help to better express meaning because it not give suggestion how to express meaning better* (*Student* 64). In other words, the feedback was not entirely helpful to some students in this respect because it only pointed to miscommunicated functional meaning, without providing a specific direction for remediation.

Nevertheless, the color-coded feedback appeared to have helped the majority of respondents in a number of ways. It made 30.2 percent of students aware of having miscommunicated intended functional meaning (*It makes me see whether I have expressed some sentences in a wrong way* (*Student 21*); *I only made good revise when I begin to think what I do and say with my sentence* (*Student 53*)). It made 12.7 percent pay attention to how they were verbalizing their moves (*It helped me to pay more attention to how to say the moves* (*Student 27*); *I learned what sentences did not express my moves correctly because they said not quite what I wanted* (*Student 50*)). IADE also prompted 57.1 percent to attempt to clarify the meaning by more carefully selecting lexical means that they could link to certain step functions (*I figured out which words and how to properly choose the words in each move* (*Student 1*); *The feedback told me the moves sometimes different from what I try to express. It told me whether I have expressed some sentences in a wrong way and I changed the way to express it, especially using certain word to signify them* (*Student 82*)). As was mentioned earlier in this chapter, the annotated corpus played an important role in helping students make this link.

6.2.2.2 Introspections

Evidence of construction of new functional meaning was found in 15.1 percent of the think-aloud/Camtasia data and in 10.4 percent of the idea units in interviews. It points to the cyclical nature of the process of focus on functional meaning described in the previous section. In short, focus on functional meaning originated with the color-coded feedback drawing the students' attention to the mismatch between what they intended to do in their discourse and what they actually did. That triggered their reflection on functional meaning, which often had not even been considered during the writing of the first draft. When trying to find a way to better express what they meant in their moves, the students tended to look up examples in the help options, where they noticed certain lexical items that were clearly indicative of certain functions. These actions, stimulated by focus on meaning, culminated in modifying the original expression of ideas to make them more explicitly communicatively charged. This meaning focus process (Figure 6.15) continued in a similar sequence, as the students moved from sentence to sentence.

While this sequence appeared quite prominently in the transcript data, what seemed to be more consistent was the causative effect of two elements. First, noticing a mismatch between intended and expressed meaning led to reflection on functional meaning (*And here I find another misunderstanding.* → *[reads the sentence] My intent is to justify my … I guess it could be m2 or m3, but not m1* (*Student* 27, think-aloud); *When the color is not right,* → *I think what step I want it in that sentence* (*Student* 58, interview)). Second, making connections between functional meaning and lexical choice led to the construction of new meaning (*Goes to the help options to see move 3. Utters all the key words in the given examples.*

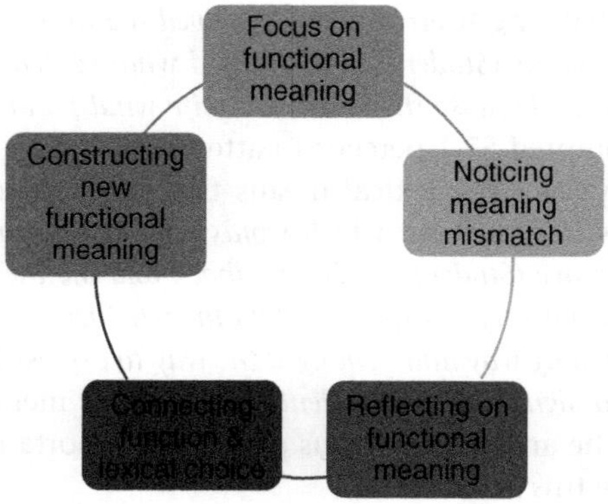

Figure 6.15 Cyclical process generated by focus on functional meaning

Pauses. → *Adds 'in this paper' and re-submits* (*Student* 61, think-aloud/ Camtasia); *Wants to express m2 hypothesis* → *and changes 'can' to 'could'* (*Student* 44, observation)).

The Meaning Focus sequential process intersects with the revision cycle indicative of Language Learning Potential described earlier in Section 6.1. In both cases, IADE feedback initiated focus on discourse form and focus on meaning, which then stimulated specific interactive behaviors on the part of the students. The behaviors triggered by focus on meaning can be attributed to a particular stage of the revision cycle. Specifically, noticing a mismatch between intended and expressed meaning is a form of noticing negative evidence. Reflecting on functional meaning and connecting function with lexical choice are forms of acquiring an enhanced understanding of given rhetorical phenomena. And students' attempts to construct new functional meaning qualify as output modifications made at different levels.

As discussed in the section on improvement in rhetorical quality, the students made a wide variety of changes to their drafts. However, their modifications triggered by focus on meaning differed from those triggered by focus on form in that here they were largely lexical and entirely move-specific. For example, the excerpt from the think-aloud/ Camtasia transcript presented in Figure 30 contains the following entry: *[reads his text, then changes 'In this model, tungsten cones with different sizes are used to enhance the optical field.' To 'In our model, several tungsten cones with different sizes were chosen to enhance the optical field.'* (*[submits]* (*Student 40*)). Having realized that writers in his field commonly use personal pronouns to make it clear that they refer to the reported study, this student uses *our* to ensure that the readers understand that he is describing his model. Interestingly, once the students realized that vocabulary can express functions, they began paying more attention to their own choice of words and expressions. For instance, my observation notes for Student 30 read, *He spots the word 'previous', thinking that it is the reason for why his intended m3 appears as m1. Hypothesizes about what would be a good lexical replacement that would indicate the intended step in m3.* For Student 29 I wrote, *'Thinks that "can" makes m3 Value sound like Hypothesizing. Wants to try "contribution is".'* A similar example comes from a think-aloud/Camtasia transcript, *'I think the last two sentences are m3, but the program marked the sentences as blue. [highlights a blue sentence] this sentence should be m3. hmmm... There's something wrong with my ... uh... language? I think it's because I use "those"... maybe I need "these" to say it's results in this study?'* (*Student 61*).

Generally, employing move-specific vocabulary helped the students construct functional meaning more effectively, and their lexical modifications led to formative feedback that indicated the intended move. However, there may be a potentially negative implication here. At the interview, 9 out of 16 students mentioned that when they realized that certain words could help them build certain moves, they tended to rely increasingly on lexical modifications. Along these lines, Student 64 said, *'I used those words there because they work. Actually, this is good that I know that because after that I changed many words many times.'* Having this awareness is certainly a positive thing; however, replacing some vocabulary items with others as a main strategy may be confining for learning.

6.2.2.3 Summary

The Meaning Focus findings suggest that IADE and its feedback hold strong potential for stimulating learners' focus on functional meaning. Multiple pieces of evidence allow for the conclusion that automated feedback was the main factor that made the students think about the meaning they intended to convey. This occurred mainly when the students noticed a mismatch in move colors and realized that they had expressed an unintended meaning. Consequently, after reflecting about the communicative purpose that had not been achieved, the students sought to improve their rhetorical clarity by making multiple revisions and resubmissions. Gradually, they discovered a connection between the functional meaning and vocabulary indicative of a given move or step, which helped them understand the importance of appropriate lexical realizations of functional meanings and construct new meaning more effectively.

Additionally, causative effects were observed. Noticing a mismatch between intended and expressed meaning led to reflection on functional meaning, and making connections between functional meaning and lexical choice led to construction of new discourse meaning. The latter observation, however, must be interpreted with caution. On the one hand, it is quite encouraging that the students became cognizant of the fact that certain functional meaning can be rendered through certain lexical items; this helped them construct more communicatively effective discourse. On the other hand, it may be a caveat because, once students discover the connection between functional meaning and vocabulary, they may rely on lexical modifications more than necessary, developing this behavior into a major revision strategy.

6.3 Learner Fit

The evidence on modified interaction presented earlier in Section 6.1 showed that the students frequently used IADE's features, which tangentially indicates Learner Fit, or appropriate level of linguistic difficulty. In other words, frequent interaction with IADE features can be attributed to the fact that the writing task was sufficiently difficult and appealing for the students. If they had completed the task making little or no use of the features, the level of linguistic difficulty could have been considered either inappropriately low because it required no help, or inappropriately high because the students were not able to engage. The analysis of survey responses and transcript data yielded more direct evidence of appropriateness for students with the targeted characteristics. Table 6.24 lists the data sources along with the cumulative evidence obtained from each source.

6.3.1 L2 writers' perceptions

The program and its automated feedback were perceived by 90.4 percent of students as appropriate (Table 6.24). Similarly, in a Likert-scale question 27.3% chose *very* appropriate, 59.1% chose *somewhat*, and 13.6% chose *a little*. None of the respondents chose *not at all*. The few students for whom the feedback was not so appropriate explained that it gave *'too little information'* (*Student 38*), that it was *'not very specific'* (*Student 35*), or that it was *'not really helpful because the ratios of different moves vary in different journals'* (*Student 51*). The positive answers were also accompanied by explanations, which mostly pointed to reasons why the students thought the feedback was appropriate. The most common theme, mentioned by 44 percent, was the individual orientation of the

Table 6.24 Overall evidence of Learner Fit

Data source	*N*	Evidence	No evidence
Likert-scale	88		
Q-n 1 [understanding of feedback]		100%	0%
Q-n 2 [helpfulness of feedback characteristics]		95.5%	0.5%
Q-n 3 [appropriateness of feedback]		100%	0%
Q-n 4 [motivation]		100%	0%
Q-n 6 [attitude towards IADE]		100%	0%
Yes/No and open-ended	83		
Q-n 1 [appropriateness of feedback]		90.4%	9.6%
Q-n 2 [motivation]		80.7%	19.3%
Q-n 3 [attitude towards feedback]		100%	0%
Q-n 4 [liked least about feedback]		32.5%	57.8%
Q-n 5 [other potentially helpful feedback features]		37.5%	51.8%
Think-aloud protocols/Camtasia	16		
(total 1,227 idea units)		121 idea units	
Semi-structured interviews	16		
(total 203 idea units)		43 idea units	
Observations	16		
(total 460 idea units)		84 idea units	

feedback; that is, the fact that the feedback was provided individually and that it was based on their academic discipline. For example: *Because I really want to know how MY steps organized in each move* (*Student 27*); *because it told me about my writing and writing in my field* (*Student 83*). Another 28 percent appreciated that both the colors and the percentages helped them see imperfections in their writing – *It was appropriate for me because I have lots of sentences reflecting the wrong color* (*Student 50*); *It's appropriate for me because it shows my problems* (*Student 44*). For 18.67 percent, the feedback was appropriate because it was clear – *There are two different feedbacks based on the moves, and both to the point and both easy for me to understand* (*Student 80*).

A Likert-scale question asked the students to evaluate the helpfulness of nine feedback characteristics. Figure 6.16 shows that the color-coded feedback was rated as most helpful. Another three feedback characteristics rated relatively high were iterativity, focus on student output, and individual specificity. Other characteristics such as intelligent, negative, and metalinguistic were mostly perceived as somewhat helpful. The conciseness and explicitness of the feedback were thought of as being less helpful, and a few students did not think that IADE was intelligent enough to be very helpful. The positive evaluation of the negative, explicit, and individual-specific characteristics of the feedback is consonant with the themes that were identified in survey answers. Lastly, the metalanguage in the feedback was well understood by most of the students.

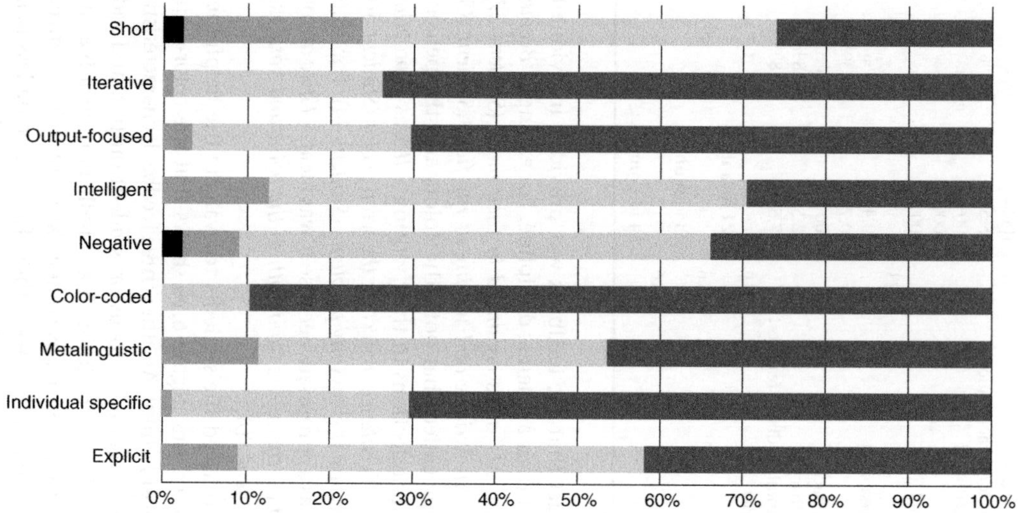

	Explicit	Individual specific	Metalingu-istic	Color-coded	Negative	Intelligent	Output-focused	Iterative	Short
not helpful	0.00%	0.00%	0.00%	0.00%	2.27%	0.00%	0.00%	0.00%	2.27%
of little help	9.09%	1.14%	11.36%	0.00%	6.82%	12.50%	3.41%	1.14%	21.59%
somewhat helpful	48.86%	28.41%	42.05%	10.23%	56.82%	57.95%	26.14%	25.00%	50.00%
very helpful	42.05%	70.45%	46.59%	89.77%	34.09%	29.55%	70.45%	73.86%	26.14%

Figure 6.16 Helpfulness of feedback characteristics

Another survey question asked students whether the fact that the feedback was based on a comparison with their discipline motivated them to revise their draft. Most of the respondents (80.73 percent) answered *yes*, 15.7 percent answered *no*, and 3.6 percent were *not sure*. The motivation of those who answered *yes* can be explained in view of two main reasons: their intrinsic desire to follow disciplinary norms of their academic community and the extrinsic influence of the interaction with the intelligence of the program. In other words, some felt motivated because they wanted to write like the academics in their field – *I think it is the best option to use comparison articles in my own field because I want to write like my field* (*Student 71*); *because as an entrance level researcher, I would like to keep consistent with the norms in my field* (*Student 54*). Others seemed to be motivated because they engaged in an interaction with the computer that approximated interaction with human professionals – *It can instruct me individually, and adapt for me like a reviewer* (*Student 55*); *It's like the professionals give me feedback* (*Student 40*). The *no* responses were accompanied by a clarification of why the comparison with disciplinary norms in the feedback was not a major motivational factor. Some students mentioned that a particular discipline was not represented in IADE (*My field is actually located in between Math and Computer Science. What field do I have to choose? There're so many sub fields inside of Computer Science, those cannot be classified as just computer science. Student 34*)). Other students thought that the comparison couldn't have captured all the peculiarities in different journals (*Not much, because it changes from journal to journal I think we cannot rely on that* (*Student 39*)).

All the students enjoyed interacting with IADE; 73.9 percent liked it *very much* and 26.1 percent *somewhat* liked it. Two open-ended survey questions revealed what they liked and what they disliked about the feedback. As can be seen in Table 6.25, the form in which the feedback was displayed was mentioned the most. The color codes were preferred by 33.7 percent, and the comparison with disciplinary writing given in the numerical feedback was mentioned by 36.1 percent. Another 9.6 percent referred to both these types of feedback. In addition, a few students mentioned liking that the feedback was instant, individualized, intelligent, and clear, and that it helped them see problems in their discourse.

Table 6.25 also lists the qualities of IADE feedback that the students liked the least. The feedback would have been more appropriate if it provided more details on their written performance, judging by the opinion of 19.3 percent who thought that it was not specific enough, and of 30.1 percent who expected to receive feedback at the level of

Table 6.25 Attitude toward feedback (open-ended survey)

Likes		***Dislikes***	
Color-codes	33.7%	Degree of specificity	19.3%
Comparison with discipline	36.1%	Lack of feedback on steps	30.1%
Color-codes and comparison with discipline	9.6%	Accuracy of analysis	8.4%
Negative evidence	6.0%	Nothing	32.5%
Immediacy	3.6%	Not sure	9.6%
Individualization	3.6%		
Intelligence	4.8%		
Clarity	2.4%		

steps, not only at the level of moves. A few students (8.4 percent) questioned the accuracy of automated analysis on which the feedback was based. Some had realized that the program relies on a lexical identification approach and viewed that as a limitation. These comments help better understand why some students evaluated the helpfulness of short, explicit, metalinguistic, and intelligent characteristics of the feedback as either of little help or not helpful (see Figure 6.16). Following are some representative responses.

Likes

- Color-codes: *I liked how the colors showed me what my writing means. (Student 5)*
- Comparison with discipline: *the comparison of my introduction with corpus in my field. (Student 36)*
- Negative evidence: *Tell me my shortcomings. (Student 58)*
- Immediacy: *It's back in a few seconds. (Student 62)*
- Individualization: *It is for one person – me. (Student 51)*
- Intelligence: *I like everything. It's very smart. (Student 30)*
- Clarity: *It's simple and clear. (Student 53)*

Dislikes

- Specificity: *I think it does not give me enough information. (Student 38)*
- Lack of feedback on steps: *I don't know about the steps. (Student 45)*
- Accuracy of analysis: *Sometimes it recognizes the move incorrectly. (Student 35)*
- Nothing: *There is no inappropriate feedback. It's all good for me. (Student 5)*
- Not sure: *I don't know really. (Student 15)*

Some students (32.5 percent) also mentioned that they would have liked to have received feedback on both moves and steps in another survey question. Others (12 percent) suggested that the feedback should also point to language errors such as grammar, word choice, expression, and even spelling. For instance, Student 32 wrote that he would have liked *'Feedback about grammar and words'*; Student 54 wanted the program to *'provide grammar and spelling detection'*, and Student 40 wanted *'to know if some words used are not professional.'* A few students (4.8 percent) thought that a specific remediation direction such as *maybe some tips of revising (Student 59), revising guidelines* (*Student* 63), or *further suggestion about how to improve the ratio of different moves* (*Student 86*) would enhance the degree of feedback helpfulness. It may be that the revision tips in the help options were not very helpful to these students, or they may not have used those hints sufficiently since the records in IADE database show that these particular students only accessed them once or twice. Two other students wished they knew *'how the program determines which move the sentence is'* (*Student 57*) and *'why IADE classify a certain sentence to a move'* (*Student 37*), although it is not clear whether they wanted this information as part of the feedback or whether they were just curious to know more about the program's intelligence. The remaining 37.3 percent were satisfied with the feedback and had nothing to suggest, and 10.8 percent did not know what would make the feedback better or more appropriate for them. Table 6.26 summarizes these findings.

Table 6.26 Desired feedback qualities (open-ended survey)

Feedback on steps	32.5%
Feedback on language errors	12.1%
Specific direction for remediation	4.8%
Explanation of program intelligence	2.4%
None	37.3%
No opinion	10.8%

6.3.2 Introspections

Consistent with the qualitative analyses of IADE's other CALL qualities, evidence of Learner Fit was also sought in the transcripts. The think-aloud/Camtasia protocols contained 121 idea units coded for Learner Fit, averaging 7.6 idea units per student. The observations transcripts had 84 such units, and the interviews had 43, with an average of 5.3 and 2.7 units per student, respectively. The themes that emerged here did not surface in the survey questions and are therefore of special interest.

Table 6.27 Evidence of Learner Fit (transcript)

	Think-aloud/ Camtasia	*Observations*	*Interviews*
Facilitating problem-solving	85.9%	88.1%	20.9%
Expressed difficulty	5.8%	8.3%	
Observed difficulty	80.1%	79.8%	
Learner control	14.1%	11.9%	13.9%
Appropriateness of feedback for task completion			23.3%
Suitability for individual learner characteristics			32.6%
Appropriateness of evaluation method			9.3%

Revising Introduction drafts to better approximate disciplinary conventions was not an easy task for the students, and IADE seemed to reduce the level of difficulty. This inference is based on the analysis of idea units that formed the theme of facilitating problem solving included in Table 6.27. This theme contained two sub-themes: facilitating observed difficulty and facilitating expressed difficulty, both of which marked cases when students were struggling to find a solution for a problem they had identified in their discourse. In the first case, the students explicitly stated whether they were experiencing a difficulty. For example: *Some sentences I cannot find what's the matter because no matter what I write here, maybe the mind is the same. Let's see the corpus* (*Student 40, think-aloud*); *It's not too hard for me now because I had many examples and feedback and definition, so it's ok. It's much harder without help* (*Student 61, interview*). In the second case, their actions indicated that they were trying to solve a certain problem – *[pauses, and then opens the definitions again]* (*Student 44, Camtasia*); *Hypothesizes about what step it could be, but is not sure and checks the definitions again* (*Student 30, observation*). In both cases, accessing help options seemed to facilitate problem-solving.

Further, while the students paid a lot of attention to the feedback, it did not entirely condition their decision-making regarding output modifications, and thus allowed them the necessary degree of learner control (Kraiger & Jerden, 2007). When the feedback returned numbers that did not closely approximate the averages in the field, the students re-read the moves and took time to think about their content, and, if satisfied with the rhetorical structure of their discourse, they chose not to make any changes implied in the feedback. Here are a few quotes from the data: *The problem is that there is just one main objective in this study. Uh ... I don't have maybe enough information to add another objective or description in this case. Because it's jus t... maybe I put a lot of m2 to to present and support the idea. But this is a simple experiment ... One or two different results ... Yes, I think concise is good enough* (*Student 44, think-aloud*); *[Has more than average of Move 1 because of extensive previous research, but decides not to delete anything but rather add more Move 3 content.]* (*Student 62, observation*). Or, in other instances, having noticed a mismatch between the intended meaning and the move color and having carefully reflected about this, the students decided that IADE was not necessarily right – *['hide' sounds like Move 2, but I don't want to change because I want this word. Who reads should understand from the context.]* (*Student 64, think-aloud*); *[Looks very concentrated. Reads the highlighted sentence several times. Explains that by pointing to how problems like this have been solved in his field he is providing background for his study; decides that he is not trying to convey a move 2 function. Decides not to change anything.]* (*Student 40, observation*).

In 9.3 percent of the interview idea units, the students positively appraised IADE's text evaluation method. They explained that it was suitable because it was facilitating rather than assessing, which may be one of the factors that allowed them to make their own final decisions. For example, Student 30 said, *I think it good that the software direct me what to pay attention and not say like you're wrong or something. It show color, and I see if I'm wrong. If color is wrong, I'm ok too because I still think again anyway*. When interviewed, several students commented on such feedback characteristics as individualization, discipline-specificity, and iterativity (23.3 percent) – *The greatest is that is for me personally and about papers of my field* (*Student 58*); *You know what is nice? That you get right away. Doesn't matter if right or wrong. You know right away and when is like that, of course you want go on and go on* (*Student 43*). The feedback was also perceived as suitable for such individual characteristics as personality, learning style, or subject knowledge – all mentioned in 32.6 percent of idea units. For instance, *For me it is good because I can change as much as I want and check myself and don't go ask nobody. I don't like to ask* (*Student 28*); *I always try draw when I learn something. I remember better if I see. So I really like color in feedback even I don't have to remember* (*Student 53*); *With definitions and examples there I don't learn by heart. I hate that. I like to understand not learn like a kid* (*Student 65*). Some students implied in one way or another that they needed time to think, read aloud, verbalize their thoughts, and consult explanatory materials. Since working with IADE did not impose any restrictions, they could adapt revision with it to their usual work strategies (*I like that I take my time, look here, look there, check, go back* (*Student 32*); *It's good to work home or any place, any computer. It's like online dictionary, but for me. [laughs]* (*Student 44*)).

6.3.3 Summary

Cumulative evidence suggests that IADE possesses a relatively strong Learner Fit quality. The students positively evaluated the characteristics of the feedback, placing color-coding and comparison with authentic disciplinary writing at the higher end of their appraisal. Individualization, immediacy, and iterativity of the feedback were also positively rated, contributing to the tool's suitability for L2 writers with targeted learner characteristics. Interacting with a tool intelligent enough to distinguish rhetorical limitations in students' drafts was motivating and rewarding, as the feedback and the help options facilitated problem-solving and created opportunities for learner control. Applying automated analysis of student writing for formative rather than summative assessment was appropriate for the completion of the Introduction writing task and balanced the level of linguistic difficulty inherent to this task. According to the students, the level of appropriateness would increase if the program (1) generated feedback on steps in addition to moves; (2) generated more accurate feedback, (3) was based on a wider spectrum of disciplines to encompass the areas of study that are currently not included in IADE; and (4) had the ability to provide more specific directions for remediation.

6.4 Impact

Considering that IADE was conceptualized and designed with a view to learning and teaching needs, it was hoped that interaction with this tool would exert a positive impact on the students. Although both positive and negative impact effects were identified, positive effects prevailed in all the sources of data. Table 6.28 gives an overview of Impact evidence related to positive experience, motivation, affect, cognition, and pragmatics.

6.4.1 L2 writers' perceptions

The survey provided quantitative evidence of more beneficial rather than negative effects. According to the students' choices in a Likert-scale question, revising with IADE had a certain degree of positive impact on their skill of writing research article Introductions: 54.5 percent perceived the impact as *very* positive, 39.8 percent as *somewhat* positive, and 5.7 percent as *a little* positive. Due to their positive experience, 90.4% of students indicated that they would like to use IADE for future revisions (Table 6.28); some would even use it for conference abstracts, research proposals, and theses. Also, all the students would like to work with a program similar to IADE but developed for all the

Table 6.28 Overall evidence of Impact

Data source	*N*	**Positive evidence**	**Negative evidence**	**No evidence**
Likert-scale	88			
Q-n 1 [motivation]		100%	0%	0%
Q-n 2 [affect]		35.2%	64.8%	0%
Q-n 3 [positive impact]		100%	0%	0%
Q-n 4 [use of IADE for RA]		100%	0%	0%
Yes/No and open-ended	83			
Q-n 1 [motivation]		89.2%	0%	10.8%
Q-n 2 [cognition]		56.6%	0%	43.4%
Q-n 3 [affect]		91.6%	0%	8.4%
Q-n 4 [further use of IADE]		90.4%	0%	9.6%
Q-n 5 [pragmatics]		90.4%	0%	9.6%
Think-aloud protocols/Camtasia	16			
(total 1,227 idea units)		367 idea units	3 idea units	
Semi-structured interviews	16			
(total 203 idea units)		42 idea units	1 idea units	
Observations	16			
(total 460 idea units)		174 idea units	7 idea units	

Table 6.29 Future use of IADE

Incentive for future use of IADE	90.4%	
Helpfulness		51.8%
Appropriate feedback		25.4%
Enhanced motivation		4.8%
Usefulness, effectiveness, or appeal		8.4%
Lack of incentive for future use of IADE	9.6%	
Missing discipline		7.2%
No need to write research articles		2.4%

research article sections, if it were available. Many students would welcome such an opportunity *a lot* (68.2 percent), 26.1 percent would *somewhat* like that, and 5.7 percent would want that *a little*. As shown in Table 6.29, a number of reasons were mentioned: because IADE was helpful; because it provided appropriate feedback; because it enhanced motivation; and because of its usefulness, effectiveness, or appeal. The few students who did not see value in using IADE again (9.6 percent), although they did not say that they had a negative experience with it, explained that it was because their particular discipline was not represented in the program or because they did not expect to be writing research articles in the future.

Consider the following examples:

Incentive for future use of IADE

- Helpfulness: *Sure, when I plan to write a paper I would like to try to use it. Because this is the only program I know to help you to write RA introduction.* (*Student 10*)
- Appropriate feedback: *When I write other introductions of my papers, I would like to use it to analyze my introduction because it actually tells me information very fast and about my paper and my field.* (*Student 86*)
- Enhanced motivation: *I would like to use it for each introduction I need to write, and maybe for other parts of the paper. Why? Because I have seen high improvements in my work and it makes me do better.* (*Student 8*)
- Usefulness: *When I need to write an article again, I will use this program again because of its usefulness.* (*Student 57*)
- Appeal: *Because it is an interesting program.* (*Student 46*)

Lack of incentive for future use of IADE

- Missing discipline: *Not if it doesn't have my area in it.* (*Student 68*)
- No need to write research articles: *Only if I have to, but I don't think so. I want to work in industry and I don't think I write research there.* (*Student 52*)

Motivation was another positive factor. Interaction with IADE was *very* motivational for 46.6 percent, *somewhat* motivational for 42.1 percent, and *a little* motivational for 11.3 percent. The students' open-ended responses helped explain these choices. Table 6.30 summarizes the factors due to which interaction with IADE was perceived as motivational.

It appeared that the feedback was a major motivational factor. It was mentioned by roughly half of the students (40.5 percent) who felt stimulated to improve their drafts when they received positive, negative, or guiding feedback. The positive feedback *really gave some positive power for the every revision* to Student 4; the negative feedback *let [Student 24] know which part to fix,* and the guiding feedback *constantly directed [Student 67] toward improvement.* The disciplinary orientation of IADE was motivating for 28.4 percent *because it compared with other corpus in our discipline* (*Student 33*) and *because it gave a chance to keep consistent with the norms of my field* (*Student 54*). The opportunity for iterative resubmission was mentioned by another 17.6 percent – *IADE motivated me to improve my introduction through resubmitting* (*Student 29*); *it helped*

Table 6.30 Motivational factors

Feedback	40.5%	
Positive		26.7%
Negative		63.3%
Guiding		10.0%
Discipline specificity	28.4%	
Resubmission	17.6%	
No comment	13.5%	

Table 6.31 Causes of positive affect

Feeling of accomplishment	30.3%
Proof of improvement	23.7%
Previous disappointment	9.2%
No explanation	36.8%

me to revise easy and I was motivated to resubmit all the time (*Student 20*). The remaining 13.5 percent did not elaborate on how IADE motivated them, only stating that it did.

The survey data also suggests affective impact (see Table 6.28). Most of the students (91.6 percent) noted that they were excited to see improvement when the feedback on subsequent changes was returned. For instance, Student 38 wrote, *When I saw my improved feedback, I feel good,* and Student 65 remarked that he *did get excited, not like a child;-) but as a happy student.* Table 6.31 lists the factors that were thought to have generated this emotion.

About a third of the students experienced a feeling of accomplishment, which was often not easy to achieve. In other words, having gone through a series of trial and error attempts to improve their drafts, the students felt like their hard work had paid off when they saw a positive change in IADE's feedback. For example: *I had the feeling that I was achieving my target.* (*Student 75*); *I did a lot to make sure program understands me right, so I was excited of course. It means I made it!* (*Student 93*). For 23.7 percent it was the proof of improvement displayed in the feedback that had this effect: *I was excited when I was in the average. I felt happy because I know that I was in a good point of the introduction.* (*Student 47*); *Why? It is just good to see improvement* (*Student 27*). A few students (9.2 percent) experienced disappointment due to multiple unsuccessful output modifications, but the feeling of excitement was stronger after that: *It didn't happen all the time. Sometimes I try too many times and nothing. But I was really excited when I finally got it right* (*Student 68*); *However not always. It upset me if it was the same when I submit again and again. But sometimes after I'm upset I get so happy!* (*Student 73*). As these two last quotes suggest, some students' experience with IADE was not entirely positive. Responding to one of the Likert-scale questions, 25 percent indicated that they were *somewhat* frustrated during the interaction with the program, and 3.4 percent were *very* frustrated. The rest of the students described their experience as either *a little* or *not at all* frustrating (36.4 and 35.2 percent, respectively).

Another effect, which was at the level of pragmatics, became evident when 90.4 percent (see Table 6.28) acknowledged that the feedback influenced their usual revision process and strategies. Students' comments revealed how their revision strategies were indeed altered (Table 6.32).

Some of the students (6.7 percent) pointed out that they did not have any revision strategies to begin with and that it was difficult for them to express an opinion from this perspective: *I didn't have strategies. I don't know, maybe I have a strategy now.* (*Student 55*); *I didn't have a revision process before I use the program.* (*Student 36*). Others (18.7 percent) referred to acquiring new strategies in addition to what they were used to doing. One of those strategies was reliance on the guidance of the feedback. In other words, if the feedback suggested that a move was in the average range compared to their discipline, some students would not work on it anymore, and if there was some negative evidence about a move (especially numerical), they would try to improve on that particular move. Student 70 wrote, *The feedback influenced my revision strategies in most way. I revised like the feedback told me.* A similar strategy, which was articulated by 10.7 percent, was to set a goal – the goal of reaching the standards of the discipline as presented by the average percentages in the feedback. As Student 75 clarified, *I noticed that I would want the desired percentages*. Additionally, focus on discourse form appeared to become a strategic part of revision for some students (9.3 percent) who

Table 6.32 Revision strategies

Reliance on the guidance of feedback	18.7%	
Setting the goal to reach a standard	10.7%	
Focus on discourse form	9.3%	
Focus on functional meaning	26.6%	
(Move-specific vocabulary search and use)		(8.0%)
No previous strategy	6.7%	
No comment	28.0%	

mentioned that they consistently paid attention to the distribution of the color-coded moves: *I started to think clearly how I organized the introduction* (*Student 82*). A larger group (26.6 percent) mentioned having focused on the functional meanings of the moves – *It was very different than usual. I usually just read one time and if I see mistakes I fix them. Now I consider color first and begin to think of what step my moves are,* wrote Student 82. It seems that the students began to develop a consistent sequence of actions by which they intentionally thought of the functional meaning of each of their sentences. For example, Student 89 explained, *I decided to check every sentence and think what step it function, so I checked if the color was right, then good, if not then I know I have to think about what I say and how make it sound like what should be.* It must be mentioned here that for a few students in this group, focus on meaning took the form of *pay[ing] much attention to wording* (*Student 31*) and of move-specific vocabulary search and use (Table 6.32).

While it is encouraging to find this evidence of strategic revision, I should say that using a certain strategy alone may be a limitation. Some students' heavy reliance on the program's feedback, their desire to reach average percentages in their field, and too much attention to move-specific phraseology may be confining. This may interfere with the development of learner autonomy, which would allow students to make writing decisions that will not be facilitated by IADE or any other computer application. Moreover, what is also concerning is that students may divert from self-evaluating their work products. Rather, they may be more likely to take the automated feedback as the only indication of the quality of their writing, trying to only address the salient negative evidence in the feedback and end their revision as soon as the feedback would display percentages close to the average in their discipline. These may, perhaps, have been the reasons why 24.1 percent indicated in their responses to a survey question that they did not think about how to improve their draft while revising it. Student 50 wrote, *Not a lot, only a little. I know what I lack and then to add the lack.* Similarly, Student 33 remarked, *No, just tried to meet the feedback.* Unfortunately, not all the students addressed this question; 15.7 percent provided brief irrelevant responses and 3.6 percent were not sure how to answer, which is why this interpretation is tentative.

Nevertheless, the responses of 56.6 percent who indicated that they did think about how to improve their writing shed some useful light on this issue. Interestingly, their explanations were directly related to the newly acquired revision strategies that included conscious focus on discourse meaning and form. It seems that those students who focused on the discourse form and functional meaning of their draft found themselves thinking more often than they normally would: *I thought a lot, much more to express the meaning more precisely* (*Student 52*). Some of them believed that the more they revised, the more deeply cognitively engaged they became. In Student's 72 words, *Actually not at the beginning, not when I began to revise, but I did more thinking later after I figured my idea didn't match with colors*. Others explained that it was necessary to think a lot on their own *because if I don't think a lot about how to improve, I can't get real feedback about my structure from every revision* (*Student 25*) and *because there is no best, only better* (*Student 27*), possibly meaning that having reached average percentages did not necessarily indicate that the draft was perfect.

6.4.2 Introspections

Additional introspective insights on Impact were gained from the transcripts. In think-aloud/Camtasia data, 143 idea units were coded for Impact, with an average of 8.94 idea units per student. In observations, the number of Impact idea units amounted to 181, with an average of 11.31 idea units per student. The interviews yielded 43 idea units, with an average of 2.69 idea units per student. These data sources substantiated the survey findings with evidence about affective, intrinsic, pragmatic, and cognitive effects, which are summarized in Table 6.33.

The think-aloud/Camtasia recordings and the observation notes (38.6 and 25.4 percent, respectively) captured many instances when the students appeared to be cognitively involved. In the interview (30.2 percent of idea units), the students stated that they spent much more time

Table 6.33 Evidence of Impact (transcripts)

	Think-aloud/ Camtasia	***Observations***	***Interviews***
Cognitive			
Deliberate thinking	38.6%	25.4%	30.2%
Pragmatic			
Strategy development	34.3%	31.5%	11.6%
Change in revision process			9.3%
Affective			
Emotional involvement	7.8%	6.6%	
Positive learning experience	7.8%	12.7%	37.2%
Negative learning experience	0.8%	3.9%	2.3%
Intrinsic			
Motivation	10.5%	19.9%	9.3%

on revision because they had to think more than usual. They engaged in self-reflection, self-analyzed their output, explained their intent, confirmed or rejected self-generated hypotheses, and drew conclusions based on the feedback and on the help options materials: *[highlights the next sentence and reads carefully] I'm wondering why the research papers do not have that. Maybe they just don't include hypothesis in my field? I guess so... we know exactly the problem. Maybe that's why I see a lot highlighting the problem* (*Student 27, think-aloud/Camtasia*). Cognitive involvement was also noticeable in students' actions. They often highlighted and re-read parts of their writing, made long pauses and used interjections, and even their body language and facial expression suggested deep thinking. What is interesting, although not surprising, is that thinking was more called for when the students noticed negative evidence related to intended functional meaning and the rhetorical form of their discourse: *[pauses. whispers quietly] I have no idea why it's... they are classified as move 1. [opens definitions for move 1] it's not the centrality... topic generalization... they are also not the general statement. Obviously, they are not belongs to previous research. [back to the color-coded feedback. reads the sentence again trying to figure out what it's function would be]* (*Student 29, think-aloud/Camtasia*).

In terms of pragmatic influence, the transcripts attested to the students' development of new revision strategies during interaction with IADE. The Impact idea units coded as strategy development were second in frequency after cognitive involvement. The emerging strategies were very similar to the ones mentioned in the survey responses – following the feedback and focusing on discourse form and meaning. To a certain extent, these strategies were determined by the program's features, which offered opportunities for resubmission, immediate feedback of numerical and color-coded types, and access to help options. While making use of these features was common for all the observed students, the sequence and frequency with which they were used changed gradually as the revision process unfolded. Reliance on feedback and resubmission were more frequent at the beginning as opposed to cognitive involvement and consultation of help option materials, which became more prominent later on.

All the students began revising by trying to improve the move that was the farthest from the average in their discipline. For example, Student 30 was thinking aloud, *OK. Because I have average about 55 percent of move 1, I have 61 percent roughly, so it's ok for me. And for move 2, the average is about 14, and I have 14 percent. And for move 3 the average is 30 percent, and I have so little. It's ok. I think I just have to add more move 3*. Later, the students developed a more thoughtful approach and acted more based on their self-reflection, constantly accessing the help options and comparing the definitions and examples of moves and steps with their own draft. Some reached this stage more slowly than others. They appeared to continue focusing mainly on the numerical feedback, taking actions only when it displayed some negative evidence and attending to that by making quick minor modifications, which they resubmitted multiple times. The excerpts in Figure 6.17 show how different the nature of Student's 29 output modifications was initially and subsequently.

Another important observation is that focus on meaning seemed to be a determining factor in the development of new, more effective revision strategies. Figure 6.18 captures the point where Student 61 transitions from sporadic to more thoughtful revision that involved focus on functional meaning, more cognitive involvement, and more effective use of help options. The revision tips particularly facilitated such a transition. Those students who consulted the revision tips began to focus on meaning earlier in the process. However, even those who did not access this kind of help gradually developed strategies that included meaning focus.

Although the students did not finish revising their drafts when being observed and recorded, towards the end of the session some of them reached a stage where their strategy consisted of very detailed self-verification. In short, they began checking the colors in the feedback against the intended functional meaning sentence by sentence, thus obtaining a better sense of how their Introduction unfolded overall and ensuring the quality of their drafts. Figure 6.19 contains such an example from the transcript of Student 30.

To summarize, an interesting pattern became visible in the think-aloud/Camtasia and observation transcripts. As shown in Figure 6.20, it appeared that at the initial revision stage, when the students mostly paid attention to the numerical feedback, their modifications in the form of change of placement, deletions, and word substitutions were sporadic, inconsistent, and not very successful. As a result, they did not seem motivated and experienced frustration. Further, once they began focusing on functional meaning, they tended to reflect more and revise sentence by sentence, or, when they focused more on the form of their discourse, they tended to revise move by move. In both these cases, the revision process became more organized and sequenced, resulting in more successful output modifications, which were accompanied by frequent bursts of positive emotions.

Initial revisions:

Too much move 1. Let's see if I change the position, what will happen.

[goes down to the revision box and highlights part of his m1 text.] *Let's change some of the previous research review into later.* [moves the highlighted part to another place in the text]

OK, I already changed it, changed the location of it.

Hmm... Although I changed the location, it is still regarded as move 1. I'll try to move it to the end of the paragraph. [cuts and pastes that part to the end of the introduction, then submits]

All right, now I know that it is not because of the location. Maybe it's because of the language since I already changed the location of this.

[goes to the annotated corpus and looks at one annotated introduction] *Oh, just a quick comment. I think another way to revise it would be to add some parts like the structure or the summary of the outcomes.*

Now I've decided to add something. Now I'm focused on the last paragraph of my introduction. I'm trying to add something.

Subsequent revisions:

The last sentence is recognized as move 1, but I meant it as move 3. So, I'm looking at it and see what happens. [reads the sentence]. *It doesn't show that.... hmmm. It should be the principle result of the research, but I don't know why the program detected it as move 1.*

[reads and thinks. looks up examples in the annotated corpus. Goes back to the color-coded feedback] *I'm still looking at the last sentence ... and to see if I can make some changes and the program can respond to these changes. Maybe I can try to be specific and say that 'the results of this paper'. Yeah, let's try to do that.* [makes the change 'The results show that ...' → 'The results of this study show that ...' and submits]

Yep! All right! Now it changed to move 3, it's what I mean. So that's good!

Figure 6.17 Initial and subsequent revision strategies (think-aloud/Camtasia)

I can move it right before the last sentence. [cuts the sentence and places it later in the text.] *well... ok, let us see the result again.* [re-submits]

nothing happened! [looks at the color-coded text. thinks] *maybe I can delete this ... this words* [highlights 'overcome its disadvantages first'] *so ... this should help* [deletes the 'overcome its disadvantages.' [resubmits]

oh... average of move 3 is 6.45. [looks back at colors. goes to the revision box and adds: 'First, the double-notch structure device is developed.' re-submits]

[looks at the modified sentence in the color-coded feedback. the color is still blue] *uh ... structure ...* [goes down to the revision box. cursor over the sentence. thinks] *so, I was confused about the program. Uh, I was trying to make every ... every move of average length. But I can't. So, maybe I can add something to move 3.*

Transition:

So, which is in move 3? [looks at the green part of his text. opens step statistics in the help options, then the definitions] *summarizing methods ... outline the structure ... yeah. research questions ... summarizing method ... announcing principle outcomes ... let me see some examples. Yeah.*

[opens the annotated corpus. reads move 3, cursor over green text] *we identify ...* [indistinct, reads in quiet voice, cursor over] *oh!* [opens another annotated text, finds green text, highlights parts of it] *present tense ... yeah ...* [highlights 'is developed' in his text. thinks. reads in half voice. highlights 'was developed'. sighs.]

[clicks on green sentences in annotated texts to see the steps] *let's see more examples.* [opens another annotated text and clicks on green sentences] *definition move 3. outlining structure ... we have organized this paper. here ... this paper ... yeah.* [checks the definitions in the help options] *so, they have a ... they have strong words to indicate that the research results belongs to this paper.*

[reads the sentence he has previously modified and adds 'in this paper' at the end] *let me try again.* [resubmits]

Figure 6.18 Transition from sporadic to more consistent revision (think-aloud/Camtasia)

It's great! And it is still below average in my discipline. Uh, I need to add something else because in move 3 I only outline the structure, but nothing else. So, move 3. [looks at the colored text]

move 3 has other steps. [opens the step statistics] *announcing the purpose ...* [opens definitions with the few examples provided there] *the aim of this study was bla-bla ... the purpose of the present study was ...*

ok. What I wanna do ... [reads his own text meant as move 3] *the special structure ... um ...* [thinks] *what ...* [mumbles] *yeah ...* [deep sigh] *know what ... um ...* [highlights a sentence] *this is the first step. And then ...*

[changes: 'First, the special structure and analytical results of DTMCPS was discussed. Then, the double-notch structure device is developed in this paper.' resubmits]

[blue sentences changed to green] *Yeah, the program becomes smarter. First, then ...* [reads from the blue sentences left meant as move 3] *in fact ... after that ... yeah. That's what I want to say.* [looks at the numerical feedback] *and ... move 1, move 2, move 3. All about average in my discipline. That's great!*

Figure 6.18 Contiuned

So, right now the structure at move level seems to be fine because all my moves are about average. And now I check the moves for the presence and quality of each step. ok.

[opens the move/step definitions and reads. then looks up at the colored text]

The first sentence is move 2 because move 2 aims at showing the reader the existing gaps or problems, and I did mean to criticize the previous work, so I think move 2 is ok because aims at showing the existing gaps or problems, and my work is based on our previous work. So, I first do the introduction of our previous work, refer to the first paper, which works on this problem, and my work is ... [pauses]

I use this solution proposed in the first paper to solve a real problem in our life. So, the second sentence is move 1. Move 1 is establishing a field. In these sentences I introduce this specific field in which our previous

Figure 6.19 Self-verification (think-aloud/Camtasia)

solution can be used. So, I think for these sentences move 1 is ok because for dynamic MRI this method can be used.

And this is also move 2. [checks move 2 in definitions] Yeah, in this sentence I mean to say why our method is helpful for such applications because the MRI image is time-consuming and expensive to take completely samples. So we use this method to reduce the samples we need to take. So I mean to demonstrate that this specific topic, in other words, this method is helpful to this. So, I use move 2 to uh ... highlight a problem or indicate a gap? [checks definitions] *Yeah, this is move 2, step 2, highlighting a problem. And then* [reads and highlights a sentence in the colored text] *yeah, this is some other works which also aim to solve this problem using different methods than us, and this sentence points out this existing method is a batch solution, not sequential, and so that ... that's an advantage of our method. So it's move 2, red one.*

I think it should be [checks the definitions again] ... *also step 2 of move 2, highlighting a problem because it illustrates limitations of existing works. And this one, highlighting a... this one, the red one.*

And after that, this ... 'on the other hand ...' bla bla ... this is ... [highlights a sentence] *this gives some general information of our method, why it is better than existing methods which I introduced above.*

And then after that I give the some general discussion of ... I give some specific work in this paper. [mouse over green text] *For example, I outline the work I do in this paper. We developed a method, then second we use the result of such things to test our algorithm, and it is ... move 3.* [thinks, and then opens the definitions again] *Yes, I think it belongs to summarizing methods and announcing principle outcomes.*

In the last sentence I indicate that the simulation result is given in section 4, in picture 1b. So, it is uhh ... outlining the structure? not outlining the structure of the paper ... it's also m3 announcing principle outcomes. [keeps checking move 3 steps definitions while deciding and confirming the move/step for her sentences]

[goes back to the colored text, highlights part of the green text] *So, I revise here.*

Figure 6.19 Contiuned

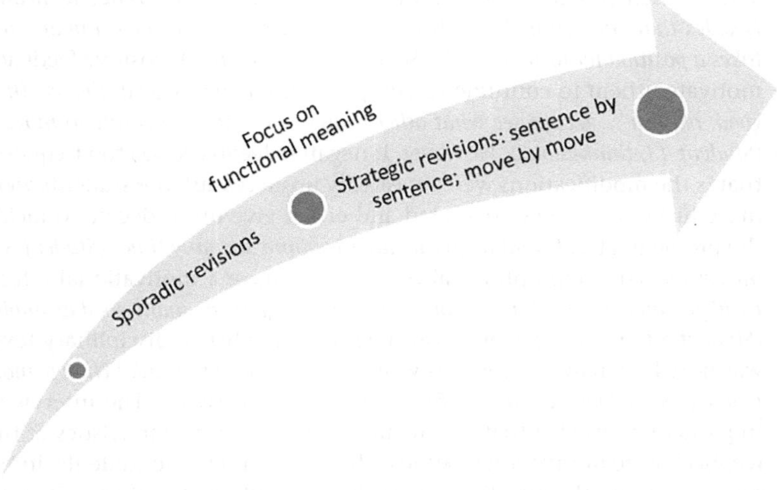

Figure 6.20 Change in the revision process

Affective impact was noted in the recordings of 12 out of 16 observed students, particularly when excitement was verbalized: *Oh, great! that looks nice! A lot of Move 2 appears* (*Student 43, think-aloud*); *Resubmits a few times, and the last sentence is successful. Gets very excited.* (*Student 65, observation*). In many cases, without getting emotionally engaged, the students simply expressed satisfaction when receiving positive feedback upon resubmission or when self-confirming successful output modifications, which spoke of a positive learning experience: *Yes, the part that I add in move 2 shows as move 2 now. ok* (*Student 44, think-aloud*); *To see how colors change and average change is so good for me because I know I did good* (*Student 32, interview*). On the other hand, their dissatisfaction when seeing negative feedback, which was often returned for repeated attempts to modify the same piece of writing, was indicative of a negative learning experience: *She obviously needs guidance. She struggles, is disappointed, doesn't know what else to do* (*Student 30, observation*). Positive experiences appeared to be more frequent compared to negative ones, however (see Table 6.33), possibly because the students realized that improvement does not come easy, that *it's normal that I don't get right the first time* (*Student* 43, interview), and that *Too much needs to be considered in writing!* (*Student* 65, think-aloud).

Next, it appeared that the students gradually developed an intrinsic desire to improve and that their motivation was driven by IADE's both negative and positive feedback. Negative feedback motivated them to address their problems: *She immediately says that it's not what she means. Decides that she definitely needs to revise. Moves closer to the computer and takes a position for focused work. (Student 28, observation)*. Positive feedback motivated them to continue revising: *ok, the number is good, the length is good. ok. hm ... let me see what other things I need to incorporate in move 3 (Student 43, think-aloud)*. However, if negative feedback was too frequent, that is the modifications were repeatedly unsuccessful, the students were more likely to become frustrated and either give up or decide to tackle the problem later: *I want to give up after I submit so many times (Student 32, interview)*. The help options also seemed to have a motivational effect: *I will go home and continue because the software gives me many good examples (Student 53, interview)*. Comparison with the published disciplinary texts was noted by many students as well: *You know, I don't think I change more if not this feedback about my field (Student 61, interview)*. The interviews in particular revealed that the iterative and instant characteristics of the feedback were motivational because they maintained the students' interest in verifying the effectiveness of their output modifications. Student 32 clarified, *It helps because what I change is still fresh and it make sense when I have feedback right away. When I get some back from the teacher, I forget and don't worry about every comment too much*. It also seemed that the more cognitively engaged the students were and the more effective revision strategies they employed, the more motivated they became: *Most of the time when I check if I have right move, especially if I think about steps, I see the good color when submitting. So of course it made me happy and I want to go on because I know what to do to get better. (Student 30, interview)* Given these insights, it can be inferred that the students experienced impact at different levels, and these effects seemed to have been interrelated.

Figure 6.21 depicts the dimensions of impact exerted on the students. The depth of cognitive involvement appeared to condition the use of revision strategies, thus influencing the pragmatic aspect of the revision process. Specifically, when the students almost entirely relied on the numerical automated feedback, the degree of cognitive involvement was low; therefore, they made superficial and ineffective output modifications. Later in the process, when the students started to focus on functional meaning due to the color-coded feedback, the degree of cognitive involvement increased; therefore, they made consistent and more successful changes to their drafts. These pragmatic choices, in turn, had either positive or negative effects at the affective and motivational levels. Although the numerical and color-coded feedback were both perceived as beneficial, they may have had opposite effects on the students' approach to revision. The former may have inhibited the effectiveness

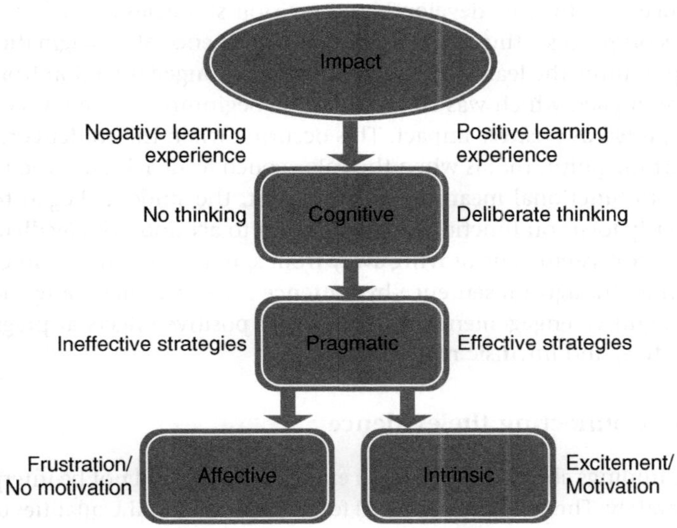

Figure 6.21 Dimensions of impact

of the revision strategies they employed, possibly encouraging revision to approximate percentages. The latter, on the contrary, seemed to enhance this process by facilitating focus on meaning. Considering the observed effect of chosen revision strategies on students' motivation and emotions, it can be presumed that the type of automated feedback is directly related to the type of impact experienced by students.

6.4.3 Summary

The data on student interaction with IADE yielded sufficient evidence in support of the claim that the program can have a beneficial impact on L2 writers' learning experience. Based on their largely positive impressions, most students indicated willingness to use a program with IADE's capabilities for writing other research article sections and other genres. There were various reasons for their interest in using an expanded version of IADE, including perceived helpfulness, usefulness, appropriateness, and appeal of such an AWE program. The feedback played a major role in motivating the students to revise and resubmit their drafts for formative evaluation, which allowed them to see improvement and overcome the feeling of disappointment sometimes caused by unsuccessful attempts to better express intended meaning. In addition to positive affective and intrinsic effects, interaction with IADE helped the students develop better revision strategies and enhance the revision process, thus exerting desirable influence at a pragmatic level. Importantly, the learning experience curve changed direction from negative impact, which was common at the beginning of the revision process, towards positive impact. This occurred when the students reached a turning point, that is when the color-coded feedback drew their attention to functional meaning. At that point, the students began to consciously focus on functional meaning and to act upon the feedback in a more consistent way, moving away from sporadic output modifications to more thoughtful sentence-by-sentence revisions. Increasing the level of cognitive engagement was decisive for positive effects at pragmatic, affective, and intrinsic motivation levels.

6.5 Connecting the evidence

The findings about IADE's overall effectiveness should not be interpreted separately. The evidence obtained for its individual CALL qualities denote interrelated processes. As summarized in Figure 6.22, the Language Learning Potential quality, whose core was a cycle with four iterative elements, appeared to be contingent on the strength of Meaning Focus,

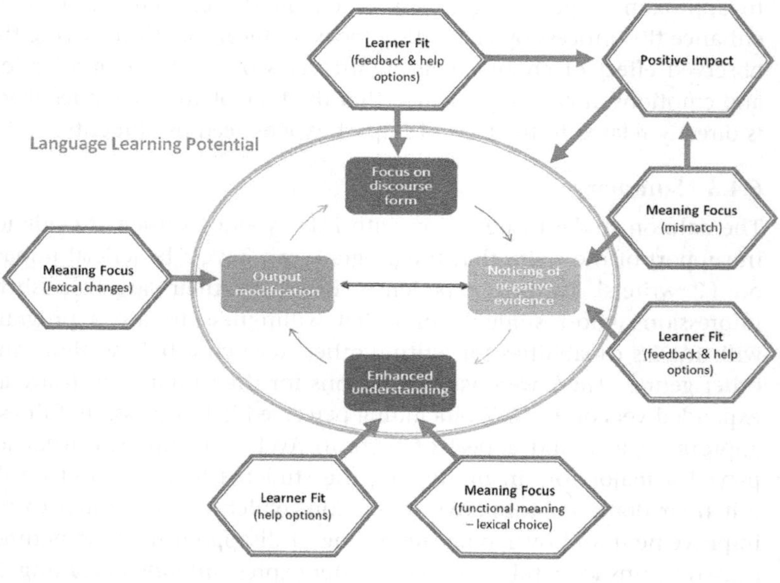

Figure 6.22 CALL qualities interrelated

Learner Fit, and Impact. Meaning Focus seemed to be crucial for positive Impact, which also depended on the degree of Learner Fit.

Notable intersections can be distinguished between Language Learning Potential and Meaning Focus; more specifically, between the students' process of focus on functional meaning and the elements of the revision cycle discovered in the analysis of Language Learning Potential. Noticing of negative evidence was realized in Meaning Focus through students' noticing of the mismatch between intended and expressed meaning. Enhanced understanding occurred when they identified a connection between lexical choice and functional meaning. Lexical changes were a form of output modifications. Consequently, it can be inferred that focus on functional meaning contributed to learning and improvement.

Learner Fit is also related to the revision cycle in Language Learning Potential due to IADE's feedback and help options. The individual-specific and output-focused feedback enhanced the Language Learning Potential quality by making the students focus on discourse form and notice negative evidence in their writing. The help options, especially the annotated corpus, also reinforced focus on form and encouraged modified interaction, which contributed to their understanding of targeted rhetorical conventions.

Finally, positive Impact appeared to spring from Meaning Focus and to eventually influence the Language Learning Potential. Positive Impact began when learners realized the role of functional meaning, which reinforced new iterations of the revision cycle. On the one hand, Meaning Focus caused deeper cognitive involvement, which led to enhanced understanding; on the other hand, it stimulated the development of effective revision strategies that led to effective output modifications. Moreover, positive affect increased students' intrinsic motivation to repeatedly go through the revision cycle and to improve their written discourse. Considering these intersections and the strength of evidence for each individual CALL quality, it can be concluded that IADE is an appropriate AWE application for the targeted L2 research writing instructional context.

It is of utmost importance to emphasize that the implementation context is a key factor that can determine the strength of the CALL qualities, and, therefore, this conclusion may be generalizable for contexts that are similar to the instructional context of this study, for example, at universities in English-medium countries that enroll international graduate students. A similar context would have to share a number of critical aspects that made IADE work the way it did: the corpus-based pedagogy, the teaching of the research article genre, the specific research writing goals of the course targeted to an academically heterogeneous group of students, the characteristics and the level of language ability, the beliefs and practices of the instructors who employed corpora in the teaching of academic writing, and the computer-based classroom environment. IADE, or a similar program, would be less effective if one or more CALL qualities were weakened by context differences such as the degree of integration, instructional goals, pedagogical approaches and strategies, targeted learners, and so on. Undoubtedly, IADE would be of little value for non-academic writing instruction or for undergraduate level composition courses. Also, even though the help options contain instructional materials and annotated corpora, by no means is IADE meant to replace classroom instruction. As demonstrated in this study, it was effective when implemented as a supplemental formative tool used for learning a subset of course objectives.

6.6 Implications for the design of genre-based AWE for L2 research writing

In the first part of this volume, I proposed a conceptual design model for genre-based AWE. The model is anchored in a judgmental evaluation (Chapelle, 2001) of different theoretical and operational perspectives deemed relevant for addressing the learning and teaching needs in a genre-based L2 research writing course. The design decisions that were made judgmentally are substantiated by the empirical evaluation of the IADE prototype.

6.6.1 Utility of theoretical approaches

Considering that SFL is an important pillar for enhancing the focus on language as a systematic resource, IADE brings forth functional meaning in a number of ways. Trained on texts annotated for rhetorical units, the program can recognize and provide feedback on the rhetorical conventions of student discourse. The functionality of its help options also relies on annotated corpora, where each sentence is glossed with its function. Had not IADE drawn students' focus to functional meaning, their final work products would have been less effective. Mere identification of structural components of texts, observed by students in their disciplinary corpora in class, and attempting to replicate model structures would not have been sufficient for them to develop the skill of using appropriate rhetorical and linguistic conventions. The implementation of IADE showed that when the students focused only on the discourse form, they did not produce effective rhetorical moves that would clearly define the targeted genre. The rhetorical quality appeared to improve only when the students realized that texts should be made of functionally organized language, which encodes various meanings. For instance, the introspective insights revealed that it was focus on functional meaning that played a key role in the rhetorical improvement of student drafts. These results support the informative value of SFL for the teaching of L2 genre writing.

The constructs of the interaction approach to SLA as applied to computer-assisted learning also played a central role. Students' modified input, which was provided to them in the form of their own automatically processed output, became a productive source for their linguistic hypotheses. Feedback stimulated computer-learner interaction by confirming or invalidating those hypotheses, prompting revised output. What became particularly prominent in this study was the value of noticing negative evidence. This phenomenon led to intra-personal interaction, during which the students appeared to construct a better understanding of the discourse conventions and to eventually produce better quality output. Input enhancement was also very potent. The color-codes made noticing of negative evidence more salient and therefore stimulated the students to test hypotheses, which they generated with regards to the nature of the miscommunicated message. The main implication is that interactionist models can be more confidently extrapolated to AWE environments, in general, and to AWE for L2 writing, in particular.

Guided by SAT, IADE was meant to account for the procedural, or practice, stage of skill development. It was intended to provide students with practice opportunities by giving them the option of resubmitting their drafts as frequently as needed. Although a relation between practice and improvement was expected and qualitatively observed, that relation was confirmed statistically only for overall draft improvement and not for the improvement of individual moves and length. This finding may imply that multiple re-submission may not have been a sufficient condition for the students to transform their new declarative knowledge into automatic behavior. It is possible that, if IADE was used for practicing the writing of individual moves separately, with more time being given for each move, the relation between practice and improvement might have been stronger. Another possible explanation may be the fact that the students worked on the revision of a single text, and, to be able to reach the production/automatization stage of skill development, they would need to practice writing more texts, applying their knowledge of rhetorical conventions to different topics. Nonetheless, the overall results did suggest that improvement occurred and that practice through resubmission was perceived as fundamental for improvement. Finally, SAT postulates that practice is essential for gradual changes in the cognitive mechanisms activated by learners to carry out a certain task. There was evidence in this study that practicing with IADE triggered cognitive mechanisms, which resulted in enhanced understanding and output modifications that were repeatedly submitted. This too adds substantiation for the applicability of this theory.

6.6.2 Utility of operational principles

IADE was implemented as a formative assessment complement to L2 research writing instruction. Observable evidence drawn from and delivered to individual students helped transform a writing task into a construct-centered learning experience. Different characteristics of IADE feedback made it an appropriate formative means for completing a research writing task in the given context and for enhancing the formative assessment goal of improving student motivation and learning. Specifically, Learner Fit and Impact findings revealed that IADE's feedback was a powerful motivator because it stimulated the students to follow disciplinary academic writing norms and to engage in careful revision, devoting greater efforts to their progress from draft to draft. As for learning, the results on Language Learning Potential demonstrated not only that learning and improvement occurred, but also that the feedback played an important role in the unfolding of these processes. Furthermore, the program's strong Meaning Focus was a key factor that induced cognitive involvement, which is one of the most important qualities of formative feedback. The color-coded feedback triggered students' cognitive mechanisms by making negative evidence salient and thus pointing to gaps between actual and intended discourse meaning. Another essential quality of formative feedback is goal orientation. Students' willingness to work with IADE in order to improve their research writing skills, to pursue the challenging revision task, and to employ new strategies for the completion of that task speaks of the goal orientation learning type, which is most desirable for learning (Fisher & Ford, 1998). The appropriateness of specificity and timing qualities of formative feedback were supported by Learner Fit results, which also suggested that IADE's feedback played directive, informative, advising, and summarizing roles thought of as characteristic of effective formative feedback (Sales, 1993). The only weaker aspect of IADE's feedback was complexity; the informative tutoring aspect of the feedback (see Narciss & Huth, 2004) was not as potent as the learners wished it had been. While the automated feedback was sufficiently verifying, it was not elaborative enough; in other words, it did not provide sufficient direction for remediation.

Since IADE was evaluated as a formative assessment tool, the different claims presented throughout this chapter can be interpreted in terms of warrants to specific inferences of a validity argument for the use of this AWE tool in research writing instruction. While developing a validity argument is beyond the scope of this volume, I'd like to exemplify some aspects of it that can be supported by empirical evidence acquired due to the ECD principles integrated in the design of IADE. First and foremost, the ECD principles allowed for delivering a task that required students to produce texts conforming to the conventions of research article Introductions within their own disciplines – an important inference related to authenticity. This inference can be supported by evidence that the annotated corpus representing disciplinary writing conventions in authentic texts available from the database, or Evidence Composite Library, helped the students complete the writing task. The database also helped gather evidence of improvement in the rhetorical quality of student drafts, which can warrant a possible generalization inference that IADE is beneficial for learning. Another generalization inference can be warranted by the fact that IADE provided consistent feedback across the instances of the same rhetorical move in a particular discipline. This was possible due to the capability of the program's Response Processing, or analysis module, which reliably classifies students' texts and generates move-level feedback. The analysis module capable of re-analyzing multiple submissions also allowed for obtaining evidence that the students used the feedback to modify their rhetorical moves, which may speak to a possible utilization inference that IADE feedback is useful in helping L2 writers make decisions about revisions. Additionally, the Response Processing plays an important role for a number of possible inferences that can be made in view of the ICALL characteristics embodied in IADE feedback. An evaluation inference may warrant that IADE feedback provides students with appropriate information to target relevant areas for revision, improvement, and learning based on evidence indicating that the students used the informative-tutoring feedback types (numerical as verification and color-coded and metalinguistic as elaboration) to produce writing similar to their discipline. An explanation inference can be warranted by the fact that the feedback is pertinent to the quality of individual students' research article Introductions and supported by evidence that the automated feedback was relevant to the improvement of their writing. Finally, the Presentation Process, or web interface facilitated the students' interaction with IADE and thus contributes to making extrapolation inferences based on cumulative evidence of positive impact.

7
From Prototyping to Principled Practical Realization

Justified with theoretical, operational, and empirical rationales, the design model for the IADE prototype was expanded into a full-fledged corpus-based AWE program for L2 research writing pedagogy – the Research Writing Tutor (RWT). This last chapter demonstrates how SLA-driven empirical insights supporting cognitive and socio-disciplinary dimensions of genre writing inform scaling up from IADE to RWT. I will describe RWT in terms of its features and how they are intended to enhance aspects of research writing, connecting various points made throughout the book with specific operational decisions pertinent to RWT design. Prior to that, I will provide a brief overview of RWT architecture for a better understanding of the features incorporated in this program.

7.1 The Research Writing Tutor

Designed as a formative assessment tool, RWT follows the conceptual framework developed for IADE and expands on the affordances of this prototype in two major ways. First, it enlarges the scope of the automated analysis and feedback from only the Introduction section to all the sections of the research article. Second, it extends the feedback and help option capabilities to three separate modules: Analysis, Demonstration, and Learning (Figure 7.1).

The contents of all three modules are based on extensive move analysis of each section of the research article (Cotos et al., 2013a, b, 2014). Following are the cross-disciplinary move/step schemas for Introduction, Methods, Results, and Discussion/Conclusion sections that were used for RWT automated analysis and feedback as well as for the help materials included in the Demonstration and Learning modules. Without going into much descriptive detail, I will note

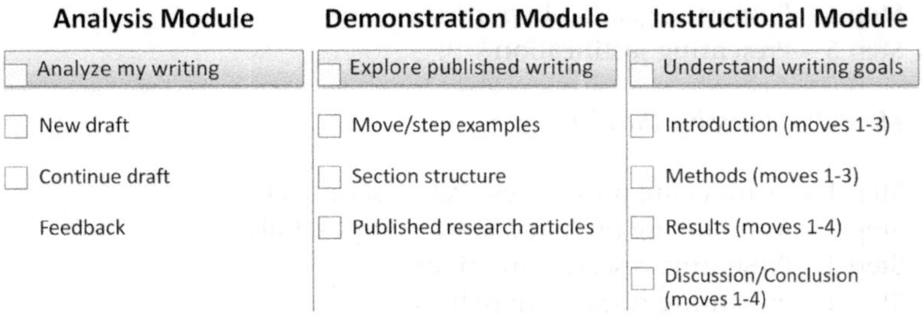

Figure 7.1 RWT modules

that the Introduction moves and steps are based on Swales (1981, 1990) and that the schemas for the other sections were developed in view of previous genre analysis of research articles (Ayers, 2008; Berkenkotter & Huckin, 1995; Brett, 1994; Bruce, 2008b; Cargill & O'Connor, 2009; Chang & Kuo, 2011; Dudley-Evans, 1994; Glasman-Deal, 2010; Holmes, 1997; Kamoksilapatham, 2005, 2007; Lim, 2006, 2010; Martinez, 2001; Nwogu, 1997; Parkinson, 2011; Peacock, 2002; Salager-Meyer, 1990; Swales & Feak, 2004; Weissberg & Buker, 1990; Williams, 1999; Yang & Allison, 2004). The move/step schemas for each section maintain the Swalesian metaphorical colouring and, like the Swales' CARS model, specify rhetorical functions without connoting linearity in the structural development of the discourse. Another note is that the Results and Discussion/Conclusion schemas share some rhetorical units to account for discussions embedded in the presentation of results.

<u>Introduction sections of research articles</u>

Move 1: Establishing the territory

Step 1 – Claiming centrality
Step 2 – Providing general background
Step 3 – Reviewing previous research

Move 2: Identifying a niche

Step 1 – Indicating a gap
Step 2 – Highlighting a problem
Step 3 – Raising general questions

Step 4 – Proposing general hypotheses
Step 5 – Presenting justification

Move 3: Addressing the niche

Step 1 – Introducing present research descriptively
Step 2 – Announcing present research purposefully
Step 3 – Presenting research questions
Step 4 – Presenting research hypotheses
Step 5 – Clarifying definitions
Step 6 – Summarizing methods
Step 7 – Announcing principle outcomes
Step 8 – Stating the value of present research
Step 9 – Outlining the structure of the paper

<u>Methods sections of research articles</u>

Move 1: Contextualizing the study methods

Step 1 – Referencing previous works
Step 2 – Providing general information
Step 3 – Identifying the methodological approach
Step 4 – Describing the setting
Step 5 – Describing the subjects/participants
Step 6 – Rationalizing pre-experiment decisions

Move 2: Describing the study

Step 1 – Acquiring the data
Step 2 – Describing the data
Step 3 – Identifying variables
Step 4 – Delineating experimental/study procedures
Step 5 – Describing tools/instruments/materials/equipment
Step 6 – Rationalizing experiment decisions
Step 7 – Imparting incremental measures/observations

Move 3: Establishing credibility

Step 1 – Describing data processing
Step 2 – Describing data analysis
Step 3 – Rationalizing data processing/analysis

Results sections of research articles

Move 1: Approaching the niche

Step 1 – Providing general orientation
Step 2 – Restating study specifics
Step 3 – Justifying study specifics

Move 2: Occupying the niche

Step 1 – Reporting specific results
Step 2 – Indicating alternative presentation of results

Move 3: Construing the niche

Step 1 – Comparing specific results with literature
Step 2 – Accounting for results
Step 3 – Explicating results
Step 4 – Clarifying expectations
Step 5 – Acknowledging limitations

Move 4: Expanding the niche

Step 1 – Generalizing results
Step 2 – Claiming the value
Step 3 – Noting implications
Step 4 – Proposing directions

Discussion/Conclusion sections of research articles

Move 1: Re-establishing the territory

Step 1 – Drawing on general background
Step 2 – Drawing on study-specific background
Step 3 – Announcing principal findings
Step 4 – Previewing the discussion 'road map'

Move 2: Framing principal findings

Step 1 – Accounting for results
Step 2 – Explicating results
Step 3 – Clarifying expectations
Step 4 – Rationalizing limitations

Move 3: Reshaping the territory

Step 1 – Supporting with evidence from the literature
Step 2 – Countering with evidence from the literature

Move 4: Establishing additional territory

Step 1 – Generalizing results
Step 2 – Claiming the value
Step 3 – Noting implications
Step 4 – Proposing directions

The Analysis Module is an extension of IADE's main interface where the students were provided with the color-coded and numerical feedback. In RWT, an interactive *Analyze My Writing* prompt offers the students two options: to begin a new draft and to continue a draft that was started and saved earlier. The drafts can be created and accessed by research article section. Once a new draft is submitted for analysis, it is stored in the database together with the formative feedback and can be accessed whenever needed.

The Demonstration Module is a scale-up from the annotated corpus and step statistics in IADE's help options and is rendered through the *Explore Published Writing* link in the top menu. It offers the students a function-based concordancer that can be queried for authentic examples of specific steps within the moves of each section. In this module, the students can also see the move and step distribution of section texts in annotated corpora representative of 30 disciplines (30 research articles per discipline) as well as the original publication form of all the articles.

The Learning Module subsumes IADE's help option with move and step definitions. Encouraging the writers to *Understand Writing Goals*, it provides detailed descriptions of the moves explained as communicative goals that are attainable by means of specific functional steps. In addition, there are videos of an instructor who presents short lectures explicating and demonstrating the realization of individual moves with examples. Such lectures are available for each section of the research article. This module also offers so-called Language Focus guidelines, which highlight some lexico-grammatical patterns characteristic of a given research article section.

As a formative assessment tool, RWT is designed to enhance the most essential qualities of formative feedback: cognitive involvement, goal orientation, complexity, specificity, and timing. Moreover, this new program aims to reinforce L2 writers' individual cognitive resources and augment enhanced cognition with social presence and interaction. In other words, interaction with different features of RWT is expected to activate a series of cognitive processes that can re-shape the internal realization of the written text and at the same time engage the writer in a rhetorical behaviour. Additionally, RWT situates the artifact drafted by the writer in the midst of a discipline-specific corpus, bridging the individual-cognitive and socio-disciplinary dimensions. Finally, RWT design also accounts for possible individual preferences, building in flexibility for L2 writers to choose which features to use and how to tailor them into personal revision strategies.

7.2 Enhancing the cognitive dimension

Being a knowledge-transforming activity, L2 research writing entails engaging in highly reflective processes on the part of the writer in order to produce artifacts that effectively present the outcomes of empirical inquiry in a re-constructive synthesis of existing and newly acquired domain knowledge. Reflective processes, especially those that distinguish novice and expert writers, play a central role, particularly when it comes to revision – a task that the IADE prototype was meant to facilitate. Revision of a written text, one of the most complex stages in the writing process, 'involves identifying discrepancies between intended and instantiated text, deciding what could or should be changed in the text and how to make desired changes, and [...] making the desired changes' (Fitzgerald, 1987, p. 484). It is undoubtedly an intense cognitive operation. In some influential cognitive models of writing discussed in Chapter 1, it is conceived as an 'evaluation of both text representation and production' (Chanquoy, 2009, p. 83). In other words, revision involves critical reading of the text in order to detect and diagnose potential problems.

The implementation of IADE with L2 writers provided an understanding of the cognitive activity inherent to revising with this prototype of genre-based AWE. More precisely, the empirical insights obtained with IADE align with the key processes described by cognitive writing models, especially evaluating the written text vis-à-vis the intended text, detecting dissonances, and moving from evaluation to internal and/or external text modifications. The compare, detect, diagnose, and operate processes theorized in highly influential cognitive writing models (Bereiter & Scardamalia, 1983; Hayes et al., 1987) accord with the elements of the revision cycle headed by focus on form (Chapter 6, Figure 6.1), which can be considered one of the strongest aspects of IADE's Language Learning Potential. Therefore, the findings regarding focus on discourse form and meaning, noticing of negative evidence, and problem solving through increased understanding and output modification have informed the design of specific RWT affordances. The affordances are realized by various features aimed at increasing L2 writers' cognitive capacity. Figure 7.2 previews the built-in cognitive enhancements of RWT, which I will further describe in terms of cognitive model processes matched with IADE evaluation findings.

7.2.1 Compare: focus on form and meaning

Learner interaction with IADE involved consistent focus on discourse form, which is a key aspect of the program's Language Learning Potential quality. The understanding of how focusing on form contributes to the interplay of various cognitive abilities during revision with IADE substantiates the need for creating conditions to reinforce this phenomenon. The Analysis and Demonstration modules in RWT are designed to devise multiple opportunities for focus on discourse form in order to help L2 writers detect and diagnose problematic rhetorical patterns. At the same time, scaffolded focus on discourse form may help reduce the cognitive demand imposed on L2 writers so that they can have an easier transition from evaluation to revision changes.

In the Analysis Module, focus on form is enhanced by different types of feedback. Inherited from IADE, the color-codes are applied to the student drafts to display rhetorical structure. This color-coded feedback is provided next to a more complex realization of the numerical feedback, which maintains the metaphorical use of color-codes. One realization of the numerical feedback that allows for goal orientation through comparison with published disciplinary writing takes the form of two pie-charts. The first pie-chart represents the move structure of the student's draft, and the second, the average move structure of the target section in the student's discipline (Figure 7.3a).

Additionally, to make the focus on form more pragmatically meaningful and to increase goal orientation, another realization of numerical feedback is presented as bar graphs. Here, based on the analysis of the draft in view of disciplinary norms, the percentages placed inside a longer bar show ranges of minimum, average, and maximum distributions of a given move. The shorter bar above points to the percent range

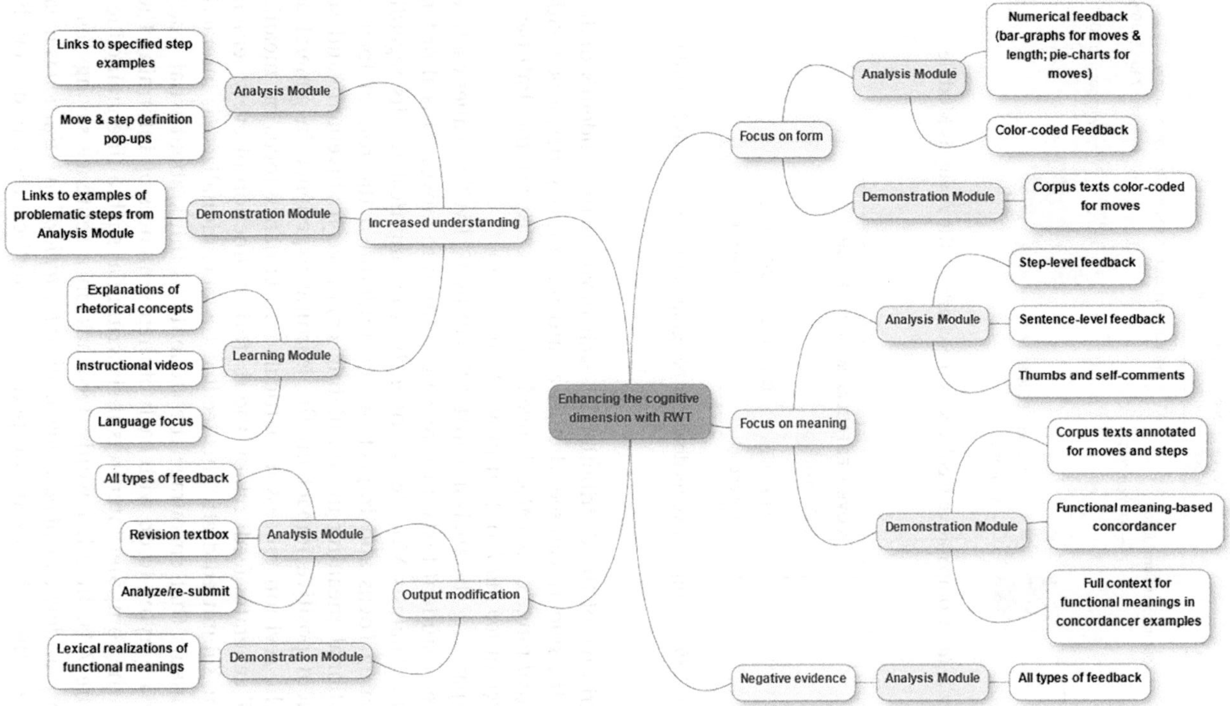

Figure 7.2 Enhancing the cognitive dimension with RWT

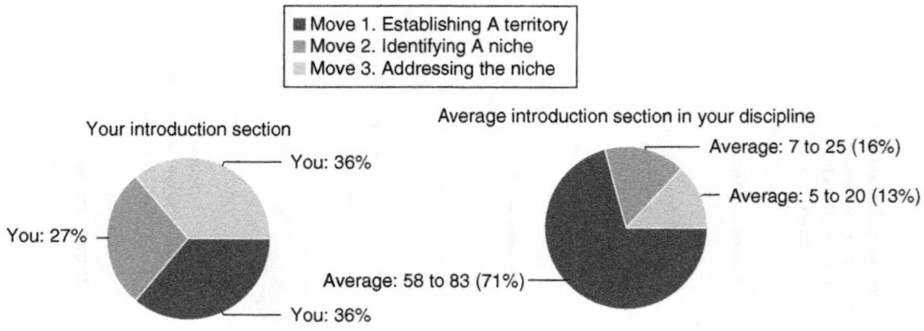

Figure 7.3a Comparative feedback as pie-charts in the Analysis Module

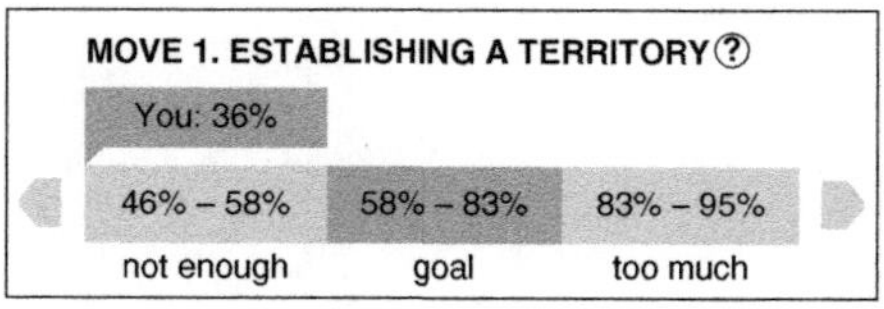

Figure 7.3b Comparative feedback as bar graphs in the Analysis Module

descriptive of the distribution of each move in the student's draft, so that the student can see whether a particular move is developed within the *goal* range or whether it needs more work because the draft has *not enough* or *too much* of that move (Figure 7.3b).

Expanding the analysis capabilities of IADE, RWT classifies each sentence of student texts into steps in addition to moves. This affordance of the Analysis Module is driven by the empirical results regarding Meaning Focus and Impact, which underlined the role of focus on functional meaning in stimulating cognitive involvement and subsequent positive impact on the learning experience in general and on the revision process in particular. To enhance focus on meaning, RWT generates feedback on the rhetorical function of every sentence of the submitted draft. This feedback is operationalized as interactive comments that encourage the students to think about what exactly they are trying to do with each of their sentences by informing them how the computer interprets their writing at such a fine-grained level (Figure 7.4). In other words, feedback on a sentence saying *You are likely providing general background about the topic of investigation* is meant to help the writers form or, perhaps, strengthen their understanding

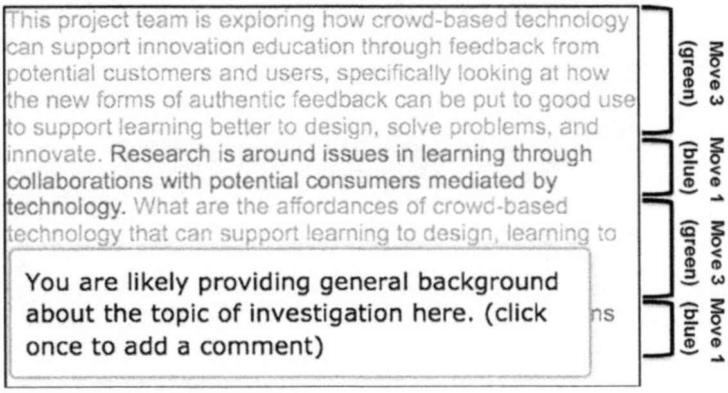

Figure 7.4 Sentence-level feedback in the Analysis Module

of the communicative intent, which is likely to be very weak or even initially lacking. Once this abstract internal representation is self-clarified, the student should be able to compare it better with the actual written representation and decide what, why, and how needs to be changed.

The Demonstration Module also draws attention to discourse form, but in a more qualitative way. Here, the section texts from the corpus appear color-coded for moves in the same way as the draft in the Analysis Module (Figure 7.5a). This presentation visualizes the actual distributional occurrence of the moves in authentic texts and scaffolds the discovery of discipline-specific patterns. For example, a student in Agricultural and Bio-Systems Engineering may discover that the Introduction sections in her field almost always begin with the communicative move of establishing a territory; that the Methods sections are almost exclusively developed with descriptions of the methodology; that the Results sections rarely remind the reader of specifics of the study but rather demonstrate how the study occupies the niche from the very beginning of the section; and that in the Discussion/Conclusion sections authors first re-establish the knowledge territory before arguing that their work re-shapes it.

The discovery of possible patterns at the step level is facilitated by visuals consistent with the Analysis Module. These are pie-charts representing the distribution of steps within a given move placed next to the query in the concordancer (Figure 7.5b).

The Demonstration Module also aims to prompt focus on the macrostructure of research articles in general by illustrating the articles in the corpus in their original published version, where the students can see

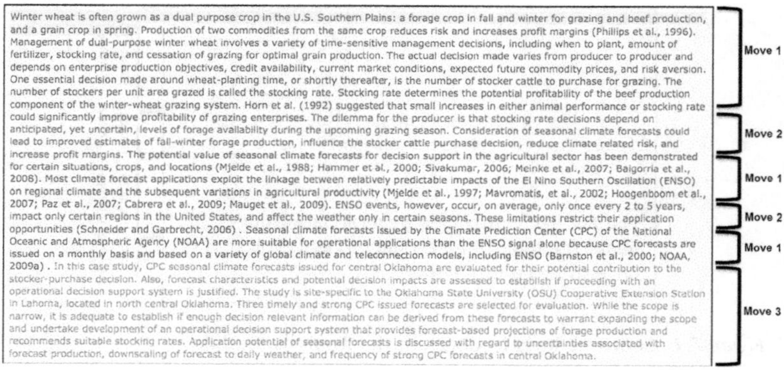

Figure 7.5a Annotated texts in the Demonstration Module

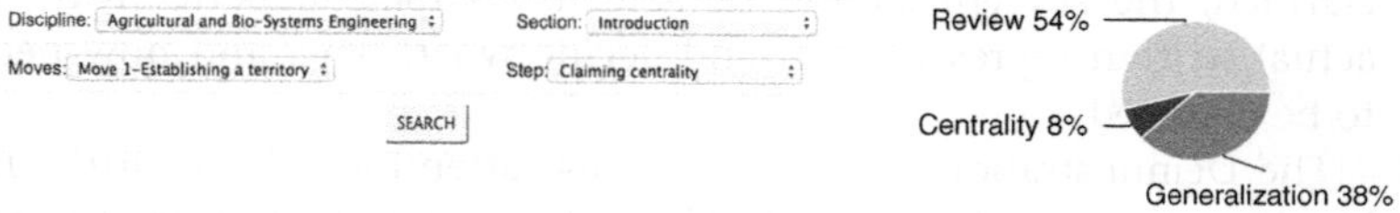

Figure 7.5b Step distribution as a pie-chart in the Demonstration Module

the sequence of the component sections, the titles and subtitles they are marked by, and other organization indicators characteristic of the field or the journal.

7.2.2 Detect: noticing negative evidence

IADE directed L2 writers' attention to aspects of the discourse form and target language through input enhancement, operationalized as color-coded feedback, and through negative evidence, operationalized as numerical feedback. Focusing on the distribution of the moves made areas that needed improvement more salient to the students, who were noticing issues such as faulty logic in the structural arrangement of moves, insufficiently developed content that weakened the communicative intent in certain moves, divergence from disciplinary patterns, inappropriate or unclear expression of rhetorical functions, and so on. Thus, noticing of negative evidence triggered by IADE's feedback is clearly a detection operation of the evaluation process inherent to revision as interpreted by cognitivists (Flower et al., 1986; Hayes & Flower, 1983; Hayes et al., 1987).

To scaffold this phenomenon of identifying discrepancies between intended and instantiated text, RWT equips the feedback with visual and textual details. The move-level feedback displays arrows over the bar graphs showing average distribution percentages for each move (see Figure 7.3b). If a move is insufficiently developed compared to disciplinary practice, the arrow will point to the range marked as *not enough*. If a move appears to be over-developed, the arrow will point to the range marked as *too much*. In both cases, the arrow would also specify exactly how much of the given move RTW identified in the student's text. Another visual depiction of move-level discrepancies appears in the two pie-charts that show the move structure holistically (see Figure 7.3a). A simpler but similar direction is given for the length of the section draft based on the number of words (Figure 7.6).

The same principle for comparison is applied in the step-level feedback, but in this case the feedback is verbal rather than graphic. For each move, an exclamation mark indicates the number of steps that may need more work, and a smiley face commends the writer on good work (Figure 7.7). Further down, for steps that need more work because they are lacking or underused, the feedback is stated as *Not enough focus on [step] compared to [discipline]*. For steps that approximate disciplinary use, the feedback statement motivates the writer with a positive confirmation that the use of a given *[step] is very similar to [discipline]*.

Knowing that focus on functional meaning engendered noticing a mismatch between intended and expressed meaning, that is between internal and external text representation, the sentence-level feedback provided by RWT may contain comments that directly or indirectly prompt noticing of negating evidence. For example, a comment like *Not sure what you are trying to do. Can you be more explicit?* is a signal that

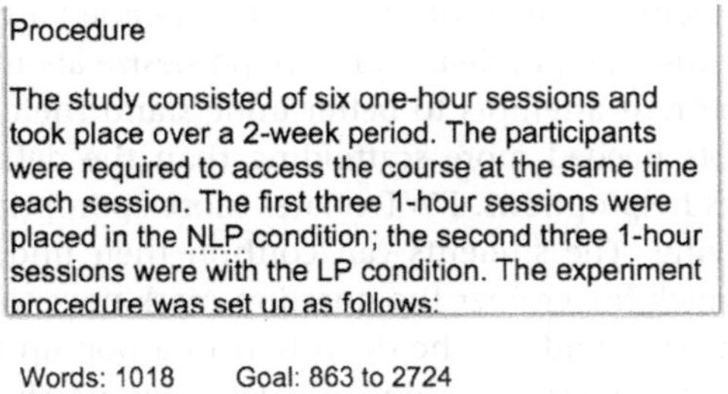

Figure 7.6 Feedback on text length in the Analysis Module

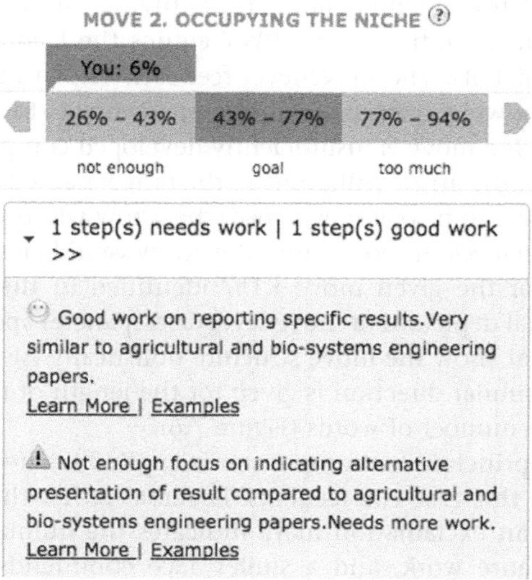

Figure 7.7 Step-level feedback in the Analysis Module

a sentence may not be clear from a rhetorical function standpoint, while *You may be providing general background about the topic of investigation, but you may also be reviewing previous research. Which is your main communicative focus?* can be a more indirect hint at a possible confusion because of how the functional meaning of the sentence is expressed or a tentative confirmation of intended multifunctionality. This type of feedback is likely to engage L2 writers in intra-personal interaction whereby they will begin to understand themselves as writers, which is an important step towards developing metarhetorical awareness.

7.2.3 Diagnose: increased understanding

Detecting ill-defined representations of the intended text induced IADE users to diagnose the problem and to hypothesize about its cause. This involved recurrent attempts to better understand rhetorical functions; these attempts needed more scaffolding than the definitions embedded in IADE's help options. RWT creates more appropriate scaffolds for problem solving. The students can confirm their understanding of a move by a quick hover over the question mark next to the move that seems problematic and see the definition in a pop-up window. When they are trouble-shooting a problem with a step on the Analysis page, they can click on *Learn more* or *See examples* (see Figure 7.7). By clicking on the former, they can consult the materials in the Learning Module and consolidate their declarative knowledge. Alternatively, they can choose to see examples of that step displayed as concordance lines (in lighter shade in Figure 7.8).

Because the larger context is often needed to better understand the rhetorical function of a step, the entire text is available by clicking on an example sentence. The texts are color-coded and glossed with moves and steps for each sentence (Figure 7.9). This is meant to stimulate reflective reading that should enable the students to evaluate their own text production better.

This feature is also important because rhetorical functions overlay scientific content, and therefore rhetorical concepts become concrete rather than abstract. The students may understand very well that the 'framing principal findings' move in the Discussion section involves,

File: VETM_03

Since its emergence in the late 1980s, the porcine reproductive and respiratory syndrome virus (PRRSV) has spread widely throughout pig-producing countries, **imposing a considerable economic burden on the swine industry worldwide (1). Clinical signs associated with the syndrome vary greatly.**

File: VETM_17

The porcine reproductive and respiratory syndrome (PRRS) is widely accepted as being one of the most important infectious disease affecting swine industry worldwide. **The severity of the reproductive form of the disease and the respiratory complications frequently associated with other viral and bacterial infections are major consequences of PRRSV infection.**

File: VETM_18

The immunostimulatory effects of the oligodeoxyribonucleotides containing unmethylated CpG dinucleotides (CpG ODN) in certain base contexts have been extensively studied in human and mice **[1], [2], [3] and [4]. CpG ODN is now recognized as a pathogen-associated molecular pattern that could induce B-cell proliferation, NK cell activation and production of Th1-type cytokines [5] and [6].**

File: VETM_04

Porcine respiratory disease complex (PRDC) remains an important economic problem for swine producers worldwide. **PRDC is characterized by slow growth, decreased feed efficiency, anorexia, fever, cough, and dyspnea in finishing pigs.**

Figure 7.8 Concordancer examples of rhetorical steps in the Demonstration Module

Figure 7.9 Glossed annotated text in the Demonstration Module

for instance, the 'accounting for results' step. However, they may have great difficulty comprehending what 'accounting for results' means content-wise, even though they may understand that the communicative intent is to reason why the results turned out to be the way they are. Being able to see numerous examples with the help of the concordancer, the students may find a way to self-clarify what type of content is generally used to develop this step and to evaluate what ideas may be appropriate in their case. Let's suppose that a student specializes in Biomedical Sciences. Based on examples of accounting for results (some are listed below), s/he may note that authors may refer to: a phenomenon, speculating about what may have caused it (as in 1); a specific result, hypothesizing about what it may be related to (as in 2); a factor, confidently claiming that it explains a specific result (as in 3); or previous research findings that may explain a specific result (as in 4).

(1) Autoimmunity probably results from the formation of many germinal centers that were present in the spleens of the ABIN1[D485N] mice and are responsible for antibody isotype switching and the production of pathogenic antibodies.

(2) The lower OR rate in our study may have been related to the higher-risk profile of this patient population and to response being evaluated by an independent review committee.

*(3) We have identified one such genetic factor, a constellation of SNPs (including the NCR3*3790 SNP) that explains the relative overexpression of the immunosuppressive NKp30c isoform among half of the profile-C individuals.*

(4) Research suggests that disparities in treatment according to race or ethnic group may be due to geographic differences resulting in inadequate access to high-quality care, particularly specialty care [23–25].

Because IADE users found useful and frequently looked up the definitions of moves and steps, RWT transforms this help option into a separate informative module with multi-modal renditions (definitions, explanations, video lectures) of the rhetorical concepts. If the students need a quick reminder about a given step, accessing a brief overview of its function would perhaps suffice. Otherwise, they can watch an instructor explain in more detail all or some steps that are not clear (Figure 7.10).

In addition, RWT offers descriptions of prominent lexico-grammatical patterns, which are particularly useful for L2 writers. For instance, the *Language Focus* for the Results section highlights such patterns as the use of: present tense when referring to a figure or a table in the step of alternative presentation of results, past tense when reporting exact findings, verbs of variation (rise, fall, increase, decrease, remain constant) when explaining observed processes, verbs of correlation (correlate with, associate with, related to) when discussing relationships between variables, modals and tentative verbs (suggest, seem, appear, tend, to be possible, to be likely) when accounting for the nature of specific results, and so on.

7.2.4 Operate: output modification

Better understanding allows writers to define or refine their internal, often fuzzy, representation of the text and set more substantive goals

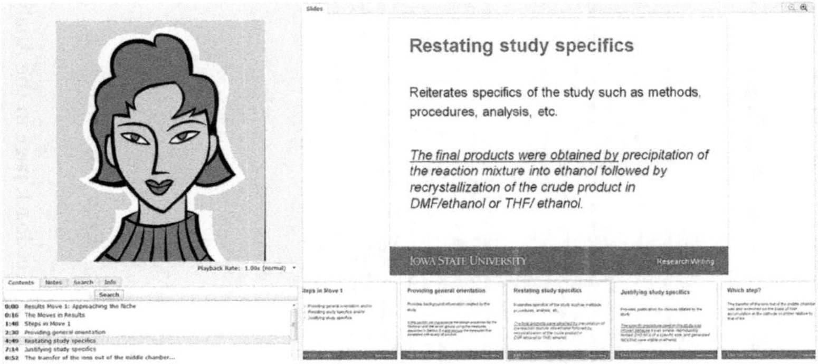

Figure 7.10 Video lecture in the Learning Module

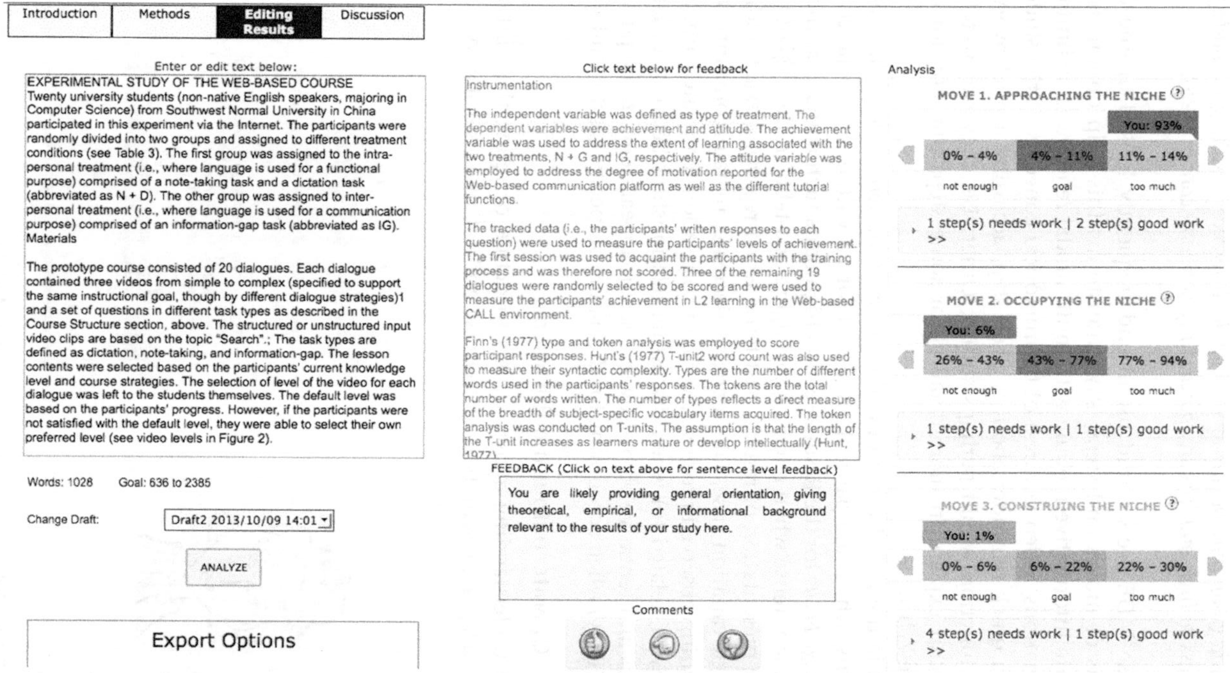

Figure 7.11 Feedback page in the Analysis Module

for how to operate, or what changes to make in order to improve their draft. Receiving feedback on every single change in IADE facilitated setting operative goals and paving the cognitive path for internal evaluation. In addition to the most essential ability to analyze student texts and encouraging re-submission with a salient *Analyze* button, RWT adds features that are likely more conducive to goal-driven output modification. For example, if the feedback indicates that a certain move is underdeveloped, the student can focus on modifying that move in the editing box and be able to do that while monitoring how it was realized in the previous, color-coded draft. Alternatively, the student can comment on the intended step function in response to the feedback on individual sentences, and then refer to those notes to modify problematic sentences one by one. Either way, RWT allows the students to make revision changes and concurrently draw on feedback by placing the editing text box and the different types of feedback side-by-side (Figure 7.11). With that, it creates an environment where the students can detect a particular problem and attempt to fix it as soon as it is diagnosed. This feature is not only meant to reinforce the use of information still accessible in short-term memory, but also eliminates the need for back and forth navigation between the feedback and editing interfaces (as in IADE), which can potentially disrupt the train of thought and increase the cognitive load.

7.3 Enhancing the socio-disciplinary dimension

Cognitive writing models explain writing and revision as highly orchestrated cognitive processing that takes place in view of the task environment, which includes the rhetorical problem pertaining to the social and physical environment. In research writing, the rhetorical problem is rather complex, especially because the task is to present a scientific argument to a highly critical and largely unknown discourse community. This task has to be effectively executed both in terms of conforming to disciplinary conventions expected by the gate-keepers and in terms of clarity in the functional expression of meaning. Considering that appropriate diagnosing during the revision stage allows the writer to move from text evaluation to internal and external modifications of discourse form and meaning, it is important to enhance the social dimension at the detection and diagnosis stages in order to facilitate a clearer translation of the text representation present in the writer's mind to the target audience. While this would be a rather daunting enterprise in traditional environments, it is not as inconceivable for computer-based environments like IADE and consequently RWT.

IADE's color-coded feedback helped the students notice a mismatch at the level of functional meaning, which is an essential aspect of the program's Meaning Focus quality. Often, what they intended to do communicatively was different from their internal representation. In many cases, a meaning-oriented internal representation was lacking, and the students began to gradually develop it piece by piece. Noticing a mismatch in meaning made them think about how their writing would be interpreted by another person or the computer. At that point, they stepped out of the writer-artifact circle into the world of the target audience and began progressing from telling the knowledge as they knew it to communicating the knowledge so that it would be understood and accepted by the disciplinary community. Focus on meaning can thus reinforce the social dimension at the cognitive diagnosis stage of revision and is, therefore, a major finding that underpins the decision to equip RWT with features that can create fostering conditions for co-creation of meaning, which IADE did not have.

Furthermore, a major reason that can account for most novice L2 writers' ill-defined internal representations is the lack of knowledge of the conventionalized forms of the research article genre. Also, while they may be aware of the purposes of the genre as social practice, they are not aware of preferred structural patterns and linguistic means that authors in their field recurrently use to engage in this social practice through writing. Neither do their teachers have knowledge of disciplinary preferences. RWT fully integrates specialized corpora to provide students with opportunities for socio-disciplinary encounter, although indirect, with members of their disciplinary community. At the same time, it aims to scaffold the students' revision process with annotated model papers, visibly marking the features of the genre that are otherwise likely to remain undiscovered. RWT affordances for the enhancement of the socio-disciplinary dimension are depicted in Figure 7.12.

7.3.1 Co-creation of meaning

IADE's ability to discern the moves in student discourse and to generate feedback on communicative effectiveness is in itself a unique affordance that, to my knowledge, has not been materialized in any existing AWE programs. It becomes even more valuable due to the effects it appeared to have on L2 writers' meaning making. Even though an underlying conversation was not enhanced by IADE in any direct way, it created an environment where the student and the analyzer intersected for meaning making, and the students tried to make the program understand what they meant.

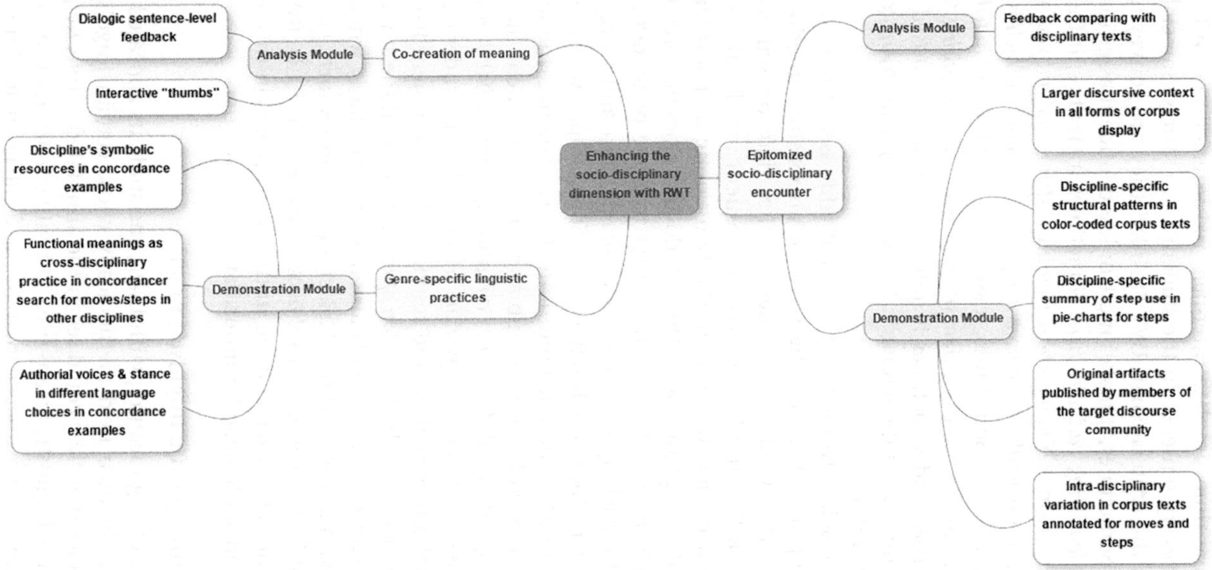

Figure 7.12 Enhancing the socio-disciplinary dimension with RWT

To help writers engage in cognitive, intra-personal interaction and at the same time simulate inter-personal interaction, RWT initiates a dialog for every sentence in the student's text. The sentence-level feedback tells the writers what RWT "thinks" they are conveying in each sentence. Sometimes, it makes more or less confident assertions like *You are likely identifying variables here.* Sometimes it clarifies, if the sentence is multi-functional: *You may be describing instruments, but you may also be describing experimental procedures employed in your study. Which is your main communicative focus?* Sometimes, it asks questions: *It's hard to tell ... Are you describing instruments used in your study, or referring to acquiring the data, or something else?* And sometimes it indicates that it is confused about the intended function of the sentence: *Not sure what you are trying to do ... Can you be more explicit?*

The feedback is worded as a personal address in the hope that this type of appeal will create the sense of an existing interlocutor and, therefore, make writing for someone other than oneself an immediate reality. RWT can play the role of a patient interlocutor who never ceases to encourage the writer to clarify meaning no matter how many attempts at change are made. This interlocutor does not pretend always to be right; in fact, it wants the writer to agree or disagree with the feedback by clicking on a respective *thumb* icon and to reply with a comment explaining the intended step. For example, when RWT recognizes only one function in a multi-functional sentence, the student can click on the *partially agree* thumb and write a comment like *Yes, I am reporting a specific result here, but I am also explaining what it means.* If the feedback says *Not sure what you are trying to do,* the student can clarify the internal representation and respond with a comment like *I want to set the scene for a broader discussion of my results.* Or, if the student thinks that the feedback is not entirely accurate, she can clarify where the mismatch is with a comment like *I am citing previous research, but to propose a hypothesis not to provide general background* (Figure 7.13). RWT retains the computer's feedback and the student's comments in this potentially constructionist dialogue for immediate or delayed use.

7.3.2 Genre-specific linguistic practices

While co-creating meaning with IADE, the students appeared to notice that writers in their field methodically chose certain linguistic units. The examples that they could see in the annotated corpus helped them recognize the linguistic means used to attain specific rhetorical purposes of the genre. The positive changes in the feedback helped them, on the one hand, understand how important it is to be linguistically explicit

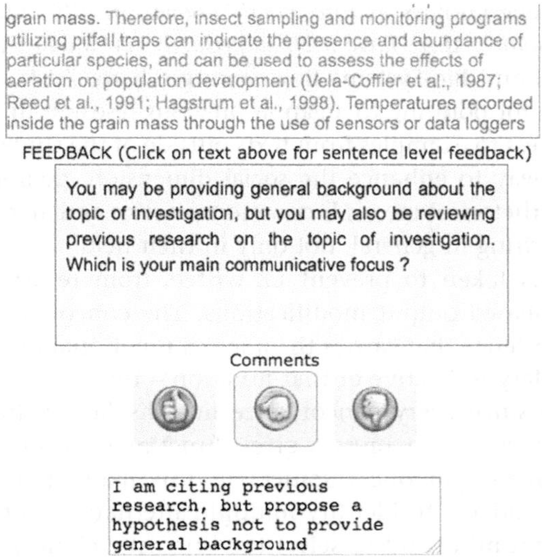

Figure 7.13 Thumb icons and comment option in the Analysis Module

in order to convey well-constructed social meanings and, on the other hand, assimilate the symbolic resources of functional language in order to effectively develop a scientific argument within their discipline. This awareness is essential to L2 writers' development of the formal and rhetorical domains of genre knowledge needed to engage in socio-disciplinary communication.

Building on IADE's demonstrated potential to evoke intricate thinking that leads to connecting communicative purposes with the features of texts, RWT aims to facilitate L2 writers' discovery of this connection and thus enhance their focus on functional meaning. The program intentionally does not draw students' attention to the lexical realizations of steps in the feedback, in order to reduce possible adverse effects of focus on individual lexical items early in the revision process. RWT assigns this affordance to the concordancer in the Demonstration Module, which the students can access to diagnose problems and then address issues in their discourse by realizing specific communicative actions with language choices that are appropriate to the context as well as the expectations of their disciplinary community. Because the linguistic means that realize certain rhetorical functions are not necessarily discipline-specific, the system allows students to select different disciplines in the concordancer and see more examples if they need to.

Such language choices as *rare, poorly known, insufficient, quite limited,* and *unfortunately there have been surprisingly few studies* that appear in Agricultural and Bio-Systems Engineering (Figure 7.14) would be very appropriate for pointing to a gap in previous research in any other discipline. Access to examples from texts outside of the students' discipline is another way to enhance the social dimension, demonstrating that employing rhetorical moves is common practice and an expectation for scientific writing in general, not only in their field.

Caution is taken to prevent L2 writers from resorting to limited vocabulary-based output modifications. The concordance lines highlight the sentence that carries the queried functional meaning and not the vocabulary indicative of that function – that is up to the students to discover since every concordance line displays a different lexico-grammatical way to express a given functional meaning. Presenting the discipline's symbolic resources in this manner, RWT strives to encourage students to identify multiple alternatives with which they can create meaning and to select the linguistic choices that are most

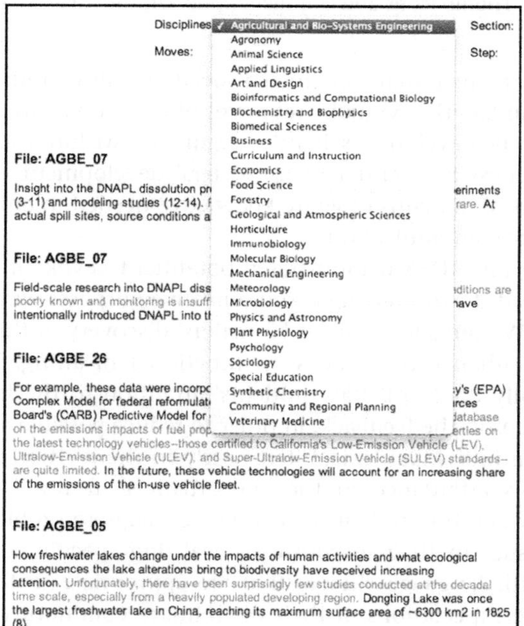

Figure 7.14 Access to examples from different disciplines in the Demonstration Module

appropriate for effective translation of their internal idea representation into external written representation. For instance, reviewing previous research is an extensive step in Move 1 of the Introduction section, and a writer cannot repeatedly say *Author A reported that* or *Authors B and C found that*. Similarly, if the Introduction is developed with repeated Move1/Move2 sequences, the student might need to highlight multiple problems, in which case different ways to realize this function linguistically are needed. In addition, to implicitly emphasize that the step function the students see in the concordance lines is contributing to achieving the goal of a move, a simple click on a sentence places it back in the bigger context of the annotated source text (as in Figure 7.9).

The disciplinary corpora embedded in RWT have the attributes of a stance corpus indicating representative linguistic forms of argumentation in a given field (Chang & Schleppegrell, 2011). In other words, being annotated for moves and steps, these corpora are means of presenting L2 writers with numerous instances of authorial voices, which are sometimes very assertive, sometimes make claims tentatively, and at other times objectively present factual information. All the sentences displayed as a result of querying the corpus for a particular step are examples of how to effectively impart interpersonal meanings when positioning claims within a larger discursive context. This affordance of RWT equips the students with a variety of prosodic choices that they can make to coherently project their authorial stance.

7.3.3 Patterns and variation in epitomized socio-disciplinary encounter

Enculturation of novice L2 scholars into the dynamic and rigid socio-disciplinary discourse is very important, although it is not a course of action that can be entirely carried out in the classroom. Nevertheless, it is essential for research writing pedagogy to create an environment where the students could be exposed to the practices of expert inhabitants of the genre and could begin to perceive themselves as socially situated writers. RWT can assist in doing that by directing the students to specialized corpora, which can be viewed in different modes – as entire articles in published form, as color-coded annotated sections, and as sets of examples sought by communicative function.

While this affordance can be used by students for scaffolding during revision, it could also be useful for more visible and explicit pedagogy (Hyland, 2007). Teachers could design corpus exploration activities similar to those exemplified in Chapter 5 with the Demonstration Module of RWT to help the students consolidate their declarative knowledge. For example, the *Section Structure* component of RWT, where all the texts are color-coded and annotated, demonstrates how authors in the discipline organize their discourse in the rhetorical ways presented in class and, by doing that, establishes an indirect but practical connection to the practices of the target discourse community. Moreover, the salient display of rhetorical structure can help students identify the patterns that are commonly used by published authors in their field. For instance, a student in Animal Science exploring the move distribution in Methods sections could observe that authors in that field employ all the moves and thus construct richer arguments when writing about their methodology. A student in Bioinformatics, on the other hand, would notice that here authors tend to predominantly employ one move, focusing almost exclusively on describing study-specific details. As a result of exploring the annotated corpus, the students in these two fields would be able to develop an awareness of move patterns in Methods sections characteristic of their discipline and create an internal representation of the rhetorical structure for their own text. They could confirm the validity of their own representation by juxtaposing it with visual summaries of move distribution available in the Analysis Module of RWT.

RWT also makes the overall patterns for step use salient through the pie-charts showing the average distribution of steps per move in the Demonstration Module. This is a short-cut that students can use either when planning how to develop a section or when revising a draft. For example, knowing that in Mechanical Engineering Introduction sections the communicative goal of Move 2 is largely realized by highlighting problems, while hypotheses are very rarely proposed, could help a student specializing in that field take an appropriate direction to identifying the niche. A student in Sociology, on the other hand, would know that in her field it is very common for authors to hypothesize as much as highlight a problem, indicate a gap, and justify the need to address those (Figure 7.15).

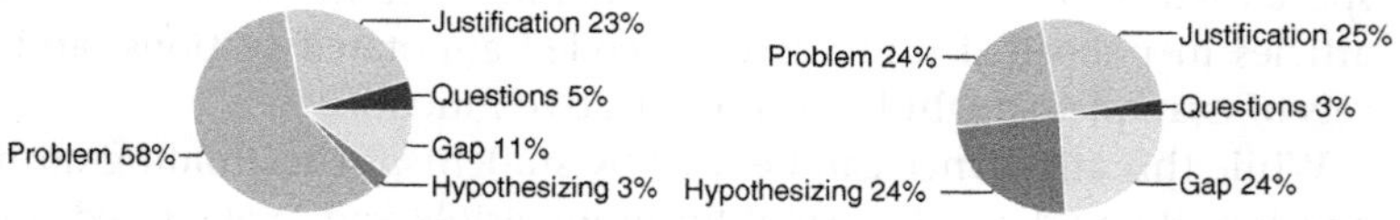

Figure 7.15 Step distribution in Mechanical Engineering (left) and Sociology (right) Introduction Sections

The Demonstration Module of RWT can also be used by teachers to aid the students' discovery of variation ingrained in disciplinary discourse. Assigned to examine the move structure of multiple color-coded texts, the students would come across exemplars that deviate from a particular pattern; for example, Introductions that begin by highlighting the niche instead of establishing a territory where the niche is to be identified. Explorations of the composition of moves glossed with step functions for each sentence can reveal that authors freely operate with different rhetorical steps depending on when and what functional meaning they want to project. The students would learn that they have to highlight a niche because that is a distinct pattern they observed, but they would also learn that it is up to them how to develop that move – which step to use, when, and how. Similarly, the concordancer clearly exhibits linguistic variation in the numerous examples it provides, which not only demonstrate freedom in language choices but could also be indicative of one's identity as an author.

Thus, RWT can complement instruction as a tool with which teachers could emphasize disciplinary practice and foster student engagement with the practices of the discourse community. By integrating RWT's corpus affordances in learning activities aimed at helping the students uncover disciplinary patterns and different levels of variation, teachers could better prepare their students for higher order critical discussions. These discussions could build on the discourse purposes and the significance of rhetorical effectiveness. Drawing on the corpora in RWT, teachers could gear their students towards reasoning about the social culture of the research article genre. Discussions could include conformity to the norms expected by disciplinary communities in view of their beliefs and values, communication constrains, the sociopolitical challenge of being a novice in those communities, and the implications that language choices may have on projecting confidence and stance when engaging in interaction with the gate-keepers that is often power-unequal.

7.4 Enhancing the learning experience

While promoting the cognitive and socio-disciplinary dimensions of research writing, RWT also capitalizes on the evidence of Impact, especially of positive influences, that IADE had on students. To enhance L2 writers' personal learning experience, the individualized feedback of RWT is a built-in determinant of motivation for students to write about their own study. RWT aims to boost instrumental motivation by incorporating connections with the disciplinary community outside the classroom through corpora, embedding the rhetorical concepts within a highly authentic task, and relating it to the students' academic life.

Giving language learners the freedom to choose their own learning path and optimizing learner control is believed to positively impact motivation and learning (Ushioda, 1996). Following the insights about IADE's Learner Fit and Impact qualities, along with the widely accepted axiom that an autonomous learner is one who is intrinsically motivated, RWT feeds intrinsic motivation by providing students with opportunities to develop their own learning strategies, assume the necessary level of control over their revision process, and have sufficient practice to exercise writing autonomously. Creating an environment where the students can personalize and self-regulate (Zimmerman, 2008) their learning experience is likely to give them a sense of improved competency and empowerment. RWT combines affordances to enhance motivation, meta-strategic awareness, and learner control (Figure 7.16)

7.4.1 Motivation

IADE created basic motivational conditions by personalizing the input it provided to students through the analysis of their own writing. Comparison to texts in the students' own discipline made the feedback meaningful and relevant, which heightened their motivation to write like researchers in their field. The availability of the annotated corpus inspired them to apply the patterns they discovered in published texts to their revisions, which were supported by the program's capability to instantaneously analyze their iterative submissions.

RWT takes Learner Fit and personal relevance to the next level. Preserving the characteristics of the feedback that were positively perceived by IADE users, RWT is designed to jumpstart motivation with textual and visualization techniques potentially suitable for different learning styles. Visualization techniques, in particular, bolster clarity and user-friendliness; for example, the move colors are consistently the same in the student's color-coded draft, bar-graphs, pie-charts, concordancer lines, and annotated texts. This way, the colors acquire a meaning of their own and become mnemonics that could engage the students in setting optimal goals. The visuals themselves are designed to be intuitive and are likely to appeal especially to science students for whom numerical information and graphical representation are second nature.

To sustain motivation, RWT feedback is autonomy-supportive in that it is accessible (in some cases available on demand upon a click or a hover), non-prescriptive, and can be both positive and negative.

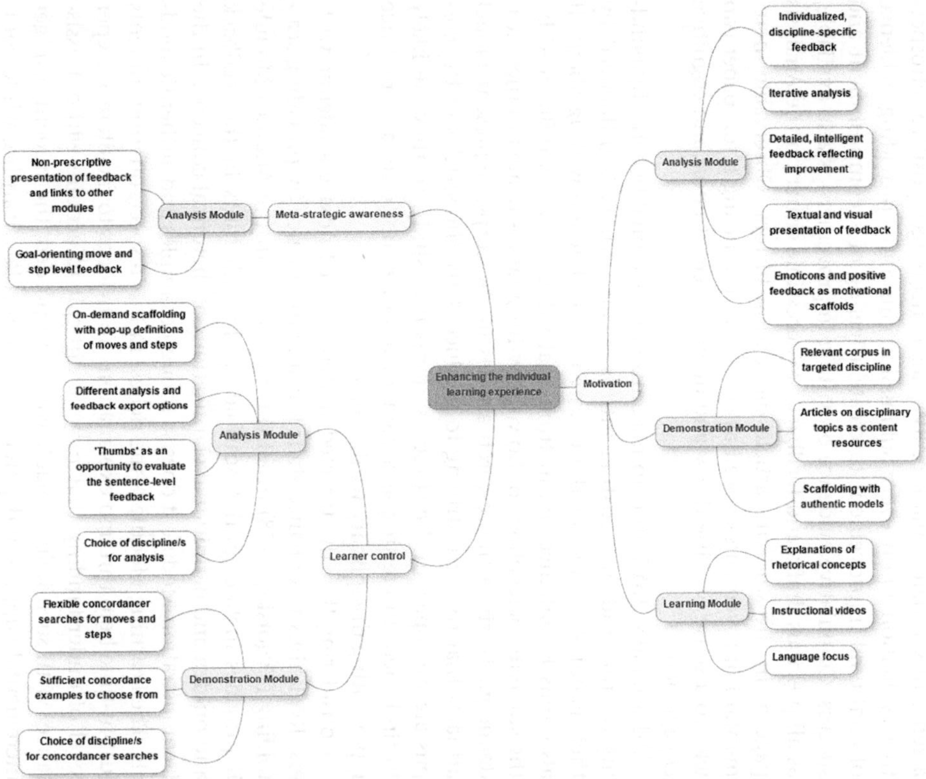

Figure 7.16 Enhancing the learning experience with RWT

The positive step-level feedback, for example, is worded in a friendly tone and accompanied by a smiley face to reinforce a sense of intrinsic enjoyment. The negative feedback is not too critical, but rather suggests that there is not enough focus on some functional meaning to reinforce a sense of self-determination. RWT also encourages positive retrospective evaluation upon every submission, instantly providing evidence of continual improvement to create a feeling of accomplishment and success. Cumulative evidence of writing improvement is also available, as all previous drafts and feedback are accessible either on the Analysis page or in the student's article submission history. Observable incremental improvements as well as success in producing a full paper can lead to a sense of self-efficacy and higher levels of effort and cognitive engagement.

Additionally, RWT aims to maximize motivational benefits by building on the students' existing intrinsic value, which is influenced by their genuine interest in the research topic they are writing about. It also aims to enhance the instrumental value, which is influenced by the students' perceptions of how the writing task is related to their academic goals, since the research articles in the corpus represent model artifacts that they are striving to produce. Plus, the articles in the corpus are on topics in the students' domain of study, so they are likely to find them interesting as a content resource, not only as a resource representing disciplinary writing practices.

Considering that the targeted students are L2 novice academic writers, RWT aims to enhance their learning experience by providing scaffolding (Vygotsky, 1978) in all three modules. In the Analysis Module it provides meta-cognitive scaffolding through hints in the feedback and on-demand definitional clarifications of rhetorical concepts. In the Demonstration Module it does so though examples and authentic models. The Learning Module is the richest in this respect, offering students just-in-time help through explanations and videos to facilitate a deeper level of understanding that may be difficult to acquire without assistance. With such help available whenever needed, the students can get incremental support and potentially self-regulate learning while completing the task. The motivational scaffolds of RWT also involve features designed to maintain encouragement and improve the students' sense of attribution (for example emoticons and feedback comments like *Very similar to [discipline] papers*).

Lastly, individual motivational characteristics are also likely to be enhanced due to all the features that meet the appropriateness, or Learner Fit criterion. RWT provides more specific directions for remediation by increasing the level of detail with additional feedback on steps and enriched feedback on moves. The issue of accuracy, which is tangent with trust, is addressed through different levels of tentativeness in the sentence-level feedback statements. These statements reflect the analyzer's confidence of classification depending on probability thresholds. For example, if a sentence is classified as a particular step with a probability of 90 percent and above, the feedback indicates only that step. If the probability value is within a range below 90 percent, the feedback suggests two step functions whose probabilities fall within that range. For lower thresholds, the feedback may solicit a clarification about two possible steps or ask for more explicitness.

7.4.2 Meta-strategic awareness

The cognitive activities triggered during revision with IADE had pragmatic outcomes in that the students seemed to develop specific strategies resultant from their interaction with the program's feedback. Their revision changes evolved from sporadic to consistent and intentional, and focus on functional meaning was a key landmark in this transition. Equally important is the fact that the students were becoming aware of their personal preferences, understanding that meaning-focused revision strategies were more successful.

Consequently, RWT forefronts functional meaning through multiple features in order to create an environment where L2 writers could develop effective strategic paths leading to successful revisions. Such meta-strategic awareness is needed to become an expert writer (Horning & Robertson, 2006). As it is theoretically plausible to anticipate that some students may be initially stimulated by negative evidence about discourse form (as was the case with IADE), the step and sentence-level feedback of RWT may draw their attention to discourse meaning early in the revision process, thus fostering their progression towards employing more operative strategies and making audience-oriented output modifications. Alternatively, it is reasonable to hypothesize that for other students the strategies may originate from negative evidence about functional meaning, which is purposefully fostered by RWT through visual saliency and textual reiteration. Irrespective of the starting point, whether form-focused or meaning-focused, RWT can potentially gear students towards meaning-driven revision strategies.

While not yet empirically supported, this hypothesis is derived from pilot data collected in the process of iterative refinement of RWT. A few L2 graduate students who used RWT were asked to demonstrate and explain how they used the tool. The first narrative below is a representative example of a possible revision path that begins with focus on discourse form driven by move-level feedback. The second is an example of a possible revision path that begins with focus on functional meaning driven by sentence-level feedback. In both cases, the students' attention to meaning is clearly pronounced, especially in the underlined utterances. (Unlike the student quotes in Chapter 6, these two excerpts were edited; the edits were confirmed with each student.)

Strategy development driven by focus on discourse form:

> *I first submit my draft for analysis and feedback. I look at the pie-charts for overall evaluation, and then at the bar-graphs to see how the development of each of my moves compares to the texts in my field. Next I determine where I want to start – the weakest move, the opening move, or the move that is biggest in my discipline. I try to clarify to myself if I understand the communicative goal of that move. If not or not completely, I read the definition next to the name of the move, or I go to 'Understand writing goals' to learn more. Once I determine which move to work on and understand it better, I compare the distribution of this move in my draft and in the color-coded texts in my discipline. I go to Section Structure for that. I try to see patterns, I read carefully and think about the content and the overall communicative goal of the move I'm working on. Am I missing anything, or is something unclear or misplaced? To better find the problems in my draft, I pay attention to the colors in it. Do the colors always match the move I have in mind? If not, I think – why might RWT misunderstand me? To clarify to myself what I mean, I click on the sentences with a color mismatch one by one and see the feedback at the bottom. What does RWT think? Do I agree? If I do, I give it a 'thumbs-up.' If not, I make a comment and click on 'thumbs-down.' My comments help me remember where I need to make changes. I prefer to finish verifying the entire move and then make changes, but you can do that right away, sentence by sentence, as soon as you find the problem. I decide what other move I need to work on and begin to revise it in the same way. When I finish revising my moves, I like to submit to see if the draft improved. When I get the feedback this time, I focus on the steps of my moves. What steps does the program show as needing more work? I usually double-check if I understand those steps. If not or not completely, I try to read about and understand them better. Sometimes I need to learn more about a step that is not enough, so I click on 'Learn more' and 'See examples.' Then I go back to the analysis page and find the sentences that I think belong to that step in the color-coded text. Are they colored as a different move than what I have in mind? Why*

might RWT misunderstand me? Asking these questions helps me think what I am trying to say and compare that to the feedback on each sentence. I also comment, basically making notes for myself, and then try to phrase my meaning more clearly. I find it helpful to repeat this procedure for all the weak steps one by one, and then I submit for analysis. Another thing I sometimes do with my color-coded draft is also try to find the sentences with the steps for which RWT thinks I did a 'Good job.' Does RWT actually understand it correctly or not? Are they good enough, or maybe I need to fix something? If I decide to improve some more, I go to the 'Explore published writing' tab to see more examples of how some steps that I have are expressed by other writers in my field. Then I submit my new draft for analysis and new feedback and analyze it again. Sometimes the feedback shows changes not only in the move that I revised, but also in other moves. Sometimes after I improve a move, RWT can put it in the 'too much' area. This may be because I didn't work on other moves yet, so I never delete any content from that move just because the feedback is too much. ('Bob')

Strategy development driven by focus on functional meaning:

I submit the text and get the feedback. I begin analyzing my draft based on the sentence feedback. For that, I click on a sentence, see what RWT thinks it does, then comment and click on the appropriate thumb. If I'm not sure what the step in the feedback means, I go to 'Understand writing goals' to read more about that step. If I disagree with the feedback on a sentence or if RWT is confused, I try to change that sentence to better express what I mean. I also often search for more examples of that step under 'Explore published writing' tab to see many ways in which it can be expressed. I analyze and revise sentence by sentence, then I submit my new draft for new feedback. When I get the feedback again, I look at the sentences that I changed and at what RWT thinks they are doing. Sometimes I need to make more changes where I think the meaning is not clear enough. And I can look for more examples again. I analyze like this until I'm happy with how clear my draft is. Next, I look at the pie-charts and the bar-graphs to see where I am with each move compared to my field. I think I can work on moves when my writing is clear. ('Jack')

7.4.3 Learner control

IADE feedback and help options facilitated rhetorical problem-solving and created opportunities for the students to modify their output depending on need and level of difficulty. They independently chose what, when, where, and how to revise. RWT intends to heighten the opportunities for L2 writers to control their goal-setting, pacing, and sequence of actions in order to enhance learner autonomy, which involves independent action in addition to critical reflection and decision-making (Benson, 2001; Little, 1991, p. 4).

RWT offers L2 writers control over the computer-based learning environment, enabling them to interact with it in their own way. There is no pre-determined sequence of actions characteristic of intelligent tutoring systems. To engage students in greater levels of interaction and enhance the degree of learner control, RWT enables non-linear navigation within and between the Analysis, Demonstration, and Learning modules. For instance, if students diagnose a problem and set the procedural goal to begin the text with a particular move, then they can navigate between tabs to view the section structure of other texts and potentially confirm the hypothesis that writers in their discipline indeed begin a given section in that way. Or, if the feedback specifies a certain step that needs work, the students may set a more substantive goal to better convey the functional meaning of that step. In that case, easy access to the Demonstration Module to see concordancer examples or to the Learning Module to see an explanation without having to completely leave the analysis page is likely to facilitate translation of consolidated knowledge into output modifications. Plus, students can afford to address more than one diagnosed issue at a time if that's a strategy they choose to enact.

A more covert expected effect of this approach to accessing RWT features is increased control over internal cognition, which may result from the development of personal strategies. The previous section exemplifies two revision paths generalized as being based on focus on discourse form or being meaning-focused. While potentially having one of these two foci as a starting point, L2 writers' revision process is going to be much more complicated. For example, irrespective of what the students primarily focus on when they receive feedback from RWT, they will reach a point where they will diagnose a problem with a move or a step and will decide to make changes to improve it. At that point, the revision cycle will likely involve going through a repeated loop of noticing negative evidence and enhanced understanding. However, this loop can take numerous forms and sequences (learn more then see examples; see examples then learn more; see move definition then move distribution; see step definition then step examples; and so on) depending on individual preferences, learning style, level of linguistic difficulty, or specific learner characteristics. RWT is flexible in that it allows the students to disentangle their own customized interaction pathway, which may be conducive to subsequent self-regulation.

Independent action needed to become an autonomous learner also applies to the social dimension. The students can be more confident in undertaking their new role as novices when working with RWT, being able to explore in a non-threatening way the practices of a power-unequal socio-disciplinary context exhibited in the Demonstration Module. They can experiment with different rhetorical models they identify in the corpus, adopt a model they see as more fit for their purposes, and learn from authors who they recognize as having made a significant impact in their field, since RWT provides them with complete citations and original articles. Being corpus-based, RWT also provides discovery-oriented learning opportunities; that is, it encourages students to undertake a researcher role, engaging them in active and autonomous learning as they analyze corpora (Boulton, 2009; Braun, 2007) and learn from published authors.

Lastly, RWT offers writers the option to export their own notes for later use, either as a whole or as categorized selections based on the sentences where they agree or disagree with the feedback, which are captured through their choice of *thumb* icons. This interactive feature can be used by students as a goal-setting tool for a revision plan and further modifications, especially when the feedback points to negative evidence. In other words, the students can export the comments they write in response to a mismatch in intended and expressed meaning marked by *thumbs-down* and make the changes necessary to clarify the functional meaning in sentences where it may be less clear. This affordance is another means to support students' individual revision trajectories, which can contribute to increasing learner control.

Conclusion: Glimpse into the Future

RWT was designed to enhance L2 research writing pedagogy with formative AWE affordances for engaging students in intra- and inter-personal communicative activity aimed at creating exemplars of genre writing, while customizing their own revision process. As I have demonstrated throughout the book, RWT development has undergone rigorous judgmental and empirical evaluations, which support the suitability of this tool for use with L2 novices to scholarly writing. Ellis (2004) argues that '[w]hen genre-based literacy pedagogy is supported by technology, the potential for student control over learning increases. While the technology increases the potential for control, it is not the technology per se that motivates its design' (p. 231). I concur, and I would also add that it is not the technology that drives implementation. Therefore, the work described in this volume is only the first step towards conceptualizing an AWE-augmented approach to L2 genre and corpus-based writing instruction.

Skilled research writing is a complex socio-cognitive activity that involves problem solving and the deployment of strategies to achieve communicative goals. L2 genre-based literacy pedagogy supported by RWT can potentially facilitate productive writing processes and strategic problem solving. A comprehensive understanding of how various socio-cognitive abilities interact, especially of the role that evaluation skills play during revision with RWT, will help determine effective instruction techniques. Consequently, I envision that the next step towards providing specific recommendations for RWT implementation is to conduct design-based research (DBR), which integrates empirical educational research with the theory-driven design of learning environments to obtain an understanding of how, when, and why educational innovations are effective in practice (Design-Based Research Collective, 2003).

The purpose of future DBR work involving RWT will be to formulate a practical theory of writing with this AWE formative assessment tool intended to assist the development of research writing competence. The practical objective with pedagogical implications will be to study the effects of RWT in iterative cycles of classroom implementation in order to improve it with new affordances, especially features that would expose students to the intricacies of both individual cognitive and social dimensions (for example peer feedback, teacher feedback, disciplinary expert feedback, peer blogs, integration of student-compiled corpora, individual planning options and idea logs, strategy tutorials) by creating a remote collaboration environment supported by communities of practice (Johnson, 2001). This will result in engineering a conceptual corridor that would contain successful 'trajectories' to be traversed by novice L2 writers for better learning of research genre writing. On the larger scale of theory, this future work will inform the formulation of a socio-cognitive model of the revision process supported by interactive intelligent learning technologies, which is a vital and long-awaited perspective in the increasingly ubiquitous computer-assisted academic writing environment.

Notes

1 Learning and Teaching Challenges of Research Writing

1. Differentiating between novice and expert writers, Bereiter and Scardamalia (1987) maintain that the former write for knowledge-telling, presenting their knowledge about a topic and moving from one idea to the next. Expert writers, on the other hand, write for knowledge-transformation, approaching the writing task as a problem-solving task. In transforming knowledge, problem solving involves analysis of both topical and rhetorical aspects and developing elaborate content and rhetorical goals.
2. L2 writing instruction evolved in view of the L1 composition theory and praxis. A comprehensive survey of its evolution as a discipline going through traditional, current-traditional, and process-based models can be found in Ferris and Hedgcock (2012).
3. Another approach widely embraced in the United States is Writing in the Disciplines (WiD), which views writing as being indispensable from the learning of a discipline and propagates the integration of writing development in subject curricula, recognizing that disciplines employ distinctive rhetorical and language conventions (Russell et al., 2009). This approach, however, has been adopted at undergraduate level without a focus on research writing.

2 Automated Writing Evaluation

1. These additions were explored with a number of tests to find whether they could indicate distinctions among levels of writing proficiency.
2. A corpus-based approach is different from a theoretical approach in which features are hypothesized based on characteristics expected to be found in the corpus data sample.
3. AES developers acknowledge, however, that the scoring engines can measure only a subset of the writing construct because they cannot understand the meaning conveyed through writing. For a substantial discussion see Shermis and Burstein (2013).
4. This dualism and tensions remind of the apprehensions regarding the teaching of genre writing that have emerged from non-linguistic and linguistic philosophical views in Rhetoric and Composition/Writing studies and in Applied Linguistics, respectively, discussed in Chapter 1.
5. AWE systems have also been used for the purposes of placement, diagnostic, and achievement testing. Validation evidence for Criterion^{SM} in particular is increasingly being accumulated (see Elliot & Klobucar, 2013; Ramineni, 2013).

3 Conceptualizing Genre-Based AWE for L2 Research Writing

1. Cognitive performance was accepted as skilled behavior in the 1960s. Prior to the cognitive revolution of that period, the definition of skilled performance was restricted to psychomotor behaviors.

Bibliography

Ackerman, P. L. (1988). Determinants of individual differences during skill acquisition: Cognitive abilities and information processing. *Journal of Experimental Psychology: General, 117*, 288–318.

Ade-Ibijola, A. O., Wakama, I., & Amadi, J. C. (2012). An expert system for Automated Essay Scoring (AES) in computing using shallow NLP techniques for inferencing. *International Journal of Computer Applications, 51*(10), 37–45.

Ädel, A. (2010). Using corpora to teach academic writing: Challenges for the direct approach. In M. C. Campoy-Cubillo, B. Belles-Fortuño, & L. Gea-Valor (eds), *Corpus-based approaches to ELT*. London: Continuum.

Aijmer, K. (ed.). (2009). *Corpora and language teaching*. Amsterdam, Netherlands: John Benjamins.

Aitchson, C. & Lee, A. (2006). Research writing: Problems and pedagogies. *Teaching in Higher Education, 11*(3), 265–278.

Almond, R. G., Steinberg, L. S., & Mislevy, R. J. (2002). A four-process architecture for assessment delivery, with connections to assessment design. *Journal of Technology, Learning, and Assessment, 1*(5), 1–63.

Alter, C. & Adkins, C. (2006). Assessing student writing proficiency in graduate schools of social work. *Journal of Social Work Education, 42*(2), 337–354.

Ammon, U. (2000). Towards more fairness in international English: Linguistic rights of non-native speakers. In R. Phillipson (ed.), *Rights to language, equity, power, and education* (pp. 111–116). Mahwah, NJ: Lawrence Erlbaum.

Ammon, U. (ed.) (2001). *The dominance of English as a language of science*. Berlin, New York: Mouton de Gruyter.

Anderson, J. R. (1983). *The architecture of cognition*. Cambridge, MA: Harvard University Press.

Anderson, J. R. (1987). Skill acquisition: Compilation of weak-method problem solutions. *Psychological Review, 94*, 192–210.

Anderson, J. R. (1995). Developing expertise. In J.R. Anderson (ed.), *Cognitive psychology and its implications*, Fourth Edition (pp. 272–304). New York: W.H. Freeman and Company.

Anthony, L. (1999). Writing research article introductions in software engineering: How accurate is the standard model? *IEEE Transactions of Professional Communication, 42*, 38–46.

Anthony, L. & Lashkia, G. (2003). Mover: A machine learning tool to assist in the reading and writing of technical papers. *IEEE Transactions on Professional Communication, 46*(3), 185–193.

Aston, G. 2002. The learner as corpus designer. In B. K Ettemann & G. Marko (eds), *Teaching and learning by doing corpus analysis* (pp. 9–25). Amsterdam: Rodopi.

Attali, Y. (2004). Exploring the feedback and revision features of the criterion service. Paper presented at the *National Council on Measurement in Education Annual Meeting*, San Diego, CA. Retrieved on November 12, 2007 at http://www.ets.org/Media/Research/pdf/erater_NCME_2004_Attali_B.pdf.

Attali, Y. (2013). Probable cause: Validity and reliability of automated scoring. In M. D. Shermis & J. Burstein (eds), *Handbook of automated essay evaluation: Current applications and new directions* (pp.181–198). New York: Routledge.

Attali, Y. & Burstein, J. (2006). Automated essay scoring with e-rater® V.2. *Journal of Technology, Learning, and Assessment, 4*(3). Available from http://ejournals.bc.edu/ojs/index.php/jtla.

Attali, Y., Lewis, W., & Steier, M. (2013). Scoring with the computer: Alternative procedures for improving the reliability of holistic essay scoring. *Language Testing, 30*, 125–141.

Attali, Y. & Powers, D. (2008). Effect of immediate feedback and revision on psychometric properties of open-ended GRE Subject Test items. *GRE Board Research Report No GRE-04-05*. Princeton, NJ: ETS.

Ayers, G. (2008). The evolutionary nature of genre: An investigation of the short texts accompanying research articles in the scientific journal *Nature*. *Journal of English for Academic Purposes, 27*, 22–41.

Bachman, L. F. (1990). *Fundamental considerations in language testing*. New York: Oxford University Press.

Badley, G. (2009a). Academic writing as shaping and re-shaping. *Teaching in Higher Education 14*(2), 209–219.

Badley, G. (2009b). Academic writing: contested knowledge in the making? *Quality Assurance in Education, 17*(2), 104–117.

Bakhtin, M. M. (1981). *The dialogic imagination: Four essays by M.M. Bakhtin*. Austin: University of Texas Press.

Barnett, R. (2005) (ed.) *Reshaping the university: New relationships between research, scholarship and teaching*. Maidenhead, UK: SRHE and Open University Press.

Bates, L., Lane, J., & Lange, E. (1993). *Writing clearly: Responding to ESL compositions*. Boston: Heinle & Heinle.

Bawarshi, A. (2003). *Genre and the invention of the writer: Reconsidering the place of invention in composition*. Logan, Utah: Utah State University Press.

Bawarshi, A. & Reiff, M. (2010). *Genre: An introduction to history, theory, research, and pedagogy*. West Lafayette, IN: Parlor Press.

Bay-Borelli, M., Rozunick, C., Way, D., & Weisman, E. (2010). Considerations for developing test specifications for common core assessments: Adopting curriculum standards – only the first step (White paper from Pearson). San Antonio, TX; Iowa City, IA; & Austin, TX: Pearson.

Bazerman, C. (1988). *Shaping written knowledge: The genre and activity of the experimental article in science*. Madison, WI: The University of Wisconsin Press.

Belcher, D. (1994). The apprenticeship model to advanced academic literacy: Graduate students and their mentors. *English for Specific Purposes, 13*(1), 23–34.

Belcher, D. & Braine, G. (1995). Introduction. In D. Belcher & G. Braine (eds), *Academic writing in a second language* (pp. xiii–xxxiv). Portsmouth, NH: Boynton/Cook.

Bereiter, C. & Scardamalia, M. (1987). *The psychology of written composition*. Hillsdale, NJ: Lawrence Erlbaum Associates.

Benson, P. (2001). *Teaching and researching autonomy in language learning*. London: Longman.

Bereiter, C. & Scardamalia, M. (1983). Schooling and the growth of intentional cognition: Helping children take charge of their own minds. In Z. Lamm (ed.), *New trends in education* (pp. 73–100). Tel-Aviv: Yachdev United Publishing Co.

Berkenkotter, C. & Huckin, T. N. (1995). *Genre knowledge in disciplinary communication: cognition/culture/power*. Lawrence Erlbaum Associates.

Berkenkotter, D., Huckin, T. N., & Ackerman, J. (1991). Social context and socially constructed texts: The initiation of a graduate student into a writing research community. In C. Bazerman & J. Paradis (eds), *Textual dynamics of the professions: Historical and contemporary studies of writing in professional communities* (pp. 191–215). Madison: University of Wisconsin Press.

Bernardini, S. (2004). Corpora in the classroom: An overview and some reflections on future developments. In J. M. Sinclair (ed.), *How to use corpora in language teaching* (pp. 15–36). Amsterdam, Netherlands: John Benjamins.

Bhatia, V. K. (1993). *Analyzing genre – Language use in professional settings*. London: Longman, Applied Linguistics and Language Studies Series.

Bhatia, V. K. (2002). Professional discourse: Towards a multi-dimensional approach and shared practice. In C. C. Candlin (ed.), *Research and practice in professional discourse* (pp. 39–60). Hong Kong: City University of Hong Kong Press.

Bhatia, V. K. (2004). *Worlds of written discourse*. London: Continuum.

Bianchi, F. & Pazzaglia, R. (2007). Student writing of research articles in a foreign language: Metacognition and corpora. In R. Fachinetti (ed.), *Corpus linguistics 25 years on* (pp. 259–287). Amsterdam: Rodopi.

Biber, D., Johansson, S., Conrad, S. & Finegan, E. (1999). *Longman grammar of spoken and written English*. Harlow: Longman.

Bishop, R. L. (1975). The JOURNALISM programs: Help for the weary writer. *The Best of Creative Computing, 1*(2), 28–30.

Bishop, W. & Ostrom, H. (eds) (1997). *Genre and writing: Issues, arguments, alternatives*. Portsmouth, NH: Boynton/Cook.

Bitchener, J. & Basturkmen, H. (2006). Perceptions of the difficulties of postgraduate L2 thesis students writing the discussion section. *Journal of English for Academic Purposes, 5*, 4–18.

Bitchener, J. & Ferris, D. (2012). *Written corrective feedback in second language acquisition and writing*. New York: Routledge.

Bitchener, J. & Basturkmen, H. (2006). Perceptions of the difficulties of postgraduate L2 thesis students writing the discussion section. *Journal of English for Academic Purposes, 5*, 4–18.

Bjork, L., Brauer, G., Rienecker, L., & Jorgensen, P. (2003). Teaching academic writing in European higher education: An Introduction. In G. Rijlaarsdam (ed.), *Studies in writing*, Volume 12 (pp. 1–15). Amsterdam, The Netherlands: Kluwer.

Blackburn, R., Behymer, C., & Hall, D. (1978). Correlates of faculty publications. *Sociology of Education, 51*, 132–141.

Blakeslee, A. M. (1997). Activity, context, interaction, and authority: Learning to write scientific papers in situ. *Journal of Business and Technical Communication, 11*(2), 125–169.

Black, P. & Wiliam, D. (1998). Inside the black box: Raising standards through classroom assessment. *Phi Delta Kappan, 80*, 139–148.

Block, D. (2003). *The social turn in second language acquisition*. Edinburgh: Edinburgh University Press.

Bloom, B. S. (1984). The 2 Sigma problem: The search for methods of group instruction as effective as one-to-one tutoring. *Educational Researcher, 13*(6), 4–16.

Boice, R. (1992). *Professors as writers. A self-help guide to productive writing.* Stillwater, OK: New Forums Press.

Boote, D. N. & Beile, P. (2005). Scholars before researchers: On the centrality of the dissertation literature review in research preparation. *Educational Researcher, 34*(6), 3–15.

Borg, E. (2000). Citation practices in academic writing. In P. Thompson (ed.), *Patterns and perspectives: Insights for EAP writing practice* (pp. 14–25). Reading, UK: CALS, The University of Reading.

Boulton, A. (2009). Testing the limits of data-driven learning: Language proficiency and training. *ReCALL, 21*(1), 37–54.

Boulton, A. (2010). Data-driven learning: Taking the computer out of the equation. *Language Learning, 60*(3), 534–572.

Bradley, G. (2009). Academic writing: Contested knowledge in the making? *Quality Assurance in Education, 17*(2), 104–117.

Bransford, J. D., Brown, A. L., & Cocking, R. R. (2000). *How people learn: Brain, mind, experience, and school.* Expanded Edition. Washington, DC: National Academies Press.

Braun, S. (2007) Integrating corpus work into secondary education: From data-driven learning to needs-driven corpora. *ReCALL, 19*(3), 307–328.

Brett, P. (1994). A genre analysis of the results sections of sociology articles. *English for Specific Purposes, 13*, 47–59.

Bridgeman, B. (2013). Human ratings and automated essay evaluation. In M. D. Shermis & J. Burstein (eds), *Handbook of automated essay evaluation: Current applications and new directions* (pp. 221–232). New York: Routledge.

Brown, S. & Knight, P. (1994). *Assessing learners in higher education.* London: Kogan Page.

Bruce, I. (2008a). *Academic writing and genre.* London: Continuum.

Bruce, I. (2008b). Cognitive genre structures in METHODS section sections of research articles: A corpus study. *Journal of English for Academic Purposes, 7*, 38–54.

Burstein, J. (2003). The E-rater scoring engine: Automated essay scoring with natural language processing. In M. D. Shermis and J. C. Burstein (eds), *Automated essay scoring: A cross-disciplinary perspective.* Mahwah, NJ: Lawrence Erlbaum Associates.

Burstein, J. (2012). Fostering best practices in writing instruction and assessment with E-rater®. In N. Elliott and L. Perelman (eds), *Writing assessment in the 21st century – Essays in honor of Edward M. White* (pp. 203–217). Creskill, NJ: Hampton Press.

Burstein, J., Chodorow, M., & Leacock, C. (2004). Automated essay evaluation: The criterion online writing service. *AI Magazine, 25*(3), 27–36.

Burstein, J., Kukich, K., Wolff, S., Lu, C., & Chodorow, M. (1998). Enriching Automated Scoring Using Discourse Marking. In the *Proceedings of the Workshop on Discourse Relations & Discourse Marking,* Annual Meeting of the Association of Computational Linguistics. Montreal, Canada.

Button, S. B., Mathieu, J. E., & Zajac, D. M. (1996). Goal orientation in organizational research: A conceptual and empirical foundation. *Organizational Behavior and Human Decision Processes, 67*, 26–48.

Byrne, D. (1986). *Teaching Oral English,* Second Edition. Harlow, UK: Longman.

Byrnes, H. (2005). Review of task-based language learning and teaching. *The Modern Language Journal, 89*, 297–298.

Cadman, K. (1997). Thesis writing for international students: A question of identity? *English for Specific Purposes, 16*, 3–14.

Caffarella, R. S. & Barnett, B. G. (2000). Teaching doctoral students to become scholarly writers: The importance of giving and receiving critiques. *Studies in Higher Education, 25*(1), 39–52.

Canagarajah, A. S. (2002). *Critical academic writing and multilingual students*. Ann Arbor, MI: University of Michigan Press.

Canagarajah, A. S. (2003). A somewhat legitimate and very peripheral participation. In C. P. Casanave & S. Vandrick (eds), *Writing for scholarly publication: Behind the scenes in language education* (pp. 197–210). Mahwah, NJ: Lawrence Erlbaum.

Canale, M. (1983). On some dimensions of language proficiency. In J. W. Oller, Jr. (ed.), *Issues in language testing research* (pp. 333–342). Rowley, Massachusetts: Newbury House.

Canale, M. & Swain, M. (1980). Theoretical bases of communicative approaches to second language teaching and testing. *Applied Lingusitics, 1*, 1–47.

Cargill, M., Cadman, K., & McGowan, U. (2001). Postgraduate writing: Using intersecting genres in a collaborative, content-based program. In I. Leki (ed.), *Academic writing programs* (pp. 85–96). Alexandria, VA: TESOL.

Cargill, M. & O'Connor, P. (2009). *Writing scientific research articles: Strategies and steps*. Hoboken, NJ: Wiley-Blackwell.

Carroll, S. (1999). Putting "input" in its proper place. *Second Language Research, 15*, 337–388.

Carroll, S. (2001). *Input and evidence: The raw material of second language acquisition*. Amsterdam: Benjamins.

Carroll, S. & Swain, M. (1993). Explicit and implicit negative feedback: An empirical study of the learning of linguistic generalizations. *Studies in Second Language Acquisition, 15*, 357–366.

Carter, N. (2012). Action research: Improving graduate-level writing. *Educational Action Research, 20*(3), 407–421.

Casanave, C. P. (2002). *Writing games: Multicultural case studies of academic literacy practices in higher education*. Mahwah, NJ: Lawrence Erlbaum.

Casanave, C. P. & Hubbard, P. (1992). The writing assignments and writing problems of doctoral students: Faculty perceptions, pedagogical issues, and needed research. *English for Specific Purposes, 11*(1), 33–49.

Celce-Murcia, M., Dörnyei, Z., & Thurrell, S. (1995). Communicative competence: A pedagogically motivated model with content specifications. *Issues in Applied Linguistics 6*(2), 5–35.

Chang, C.-F. & Kuo, C.-H. (2011). A corpus-based approach to online materials development for writing research articles. *English for Specific Purposes, 30*, 222–234.

Chang, P. & Schleppegrell, M. (2011). Taking an effective authorial stance in academic writing: Making the linguistic resources explicit for L2 writers in the social sciences. *Journal of English for academic purposes, 10*(3), 140–151.

Chanquoy, L. (2009) Revisions processes. In R. Beard, D. Myhill, J. Riley & M. Nystrand (eds), *The sage handbook of writing development* (pp. 80–97). London: Sage.

Chapelle, C. A. (1998). Multimedia CALL: Lessons to be learned from research on instructed SLA. *Language Learning & Technology, 2*(1), 22–34.

Chapelle, C. A. (2001). *Computer applications in second language acquisition*. Cambridge: Cambridge University Press.

Chapelle, C. A. (2007). Technology and second language acquisition. *Annual Review of Applied Linguistics, 27*, 98–114.
Chapelle, C. A. & Chung, Y.-R. (2010). The promise of NLP and speech processing technologies in language assessment. *Language Testing, 27*(3), 301–315.
Chapelle, C. A., Cotos, E., & Lee, J. (2013). Diagnostic assessment with automated writing evaluation: A look at validity arguments for new classroom assessments. Paper presented at the *35th Language Testing Research Colloquium, 'Future of diagnostic language assessment: Moving beyond where we are' Symposium*. Seoul, Korea.
Chapelle, C. A., Enright, M. K., & Jamieson, J. (2010). Does an argument-based approach to validity make a difference? *Educational Measurement Issues and practice, 29*, 3–13.
Chapman, M. (2013). Review of the book writing assessment in the 21st century: Essays in honor of Edward M. White by N. Elliot & L. Perelman. *Assessing Writing, 18*, 182–185.
Charles, M. (2006). Phraseological patterns in reporting clauses in citation: A corpus-based study of theses in two disciplines. *English for Specific Purposes, 25*(4), 310–331.
Charles, M. (2007). Reconciling top-down and bottom-up approaches to graduate writing: Using a corpus to teach rhetorical functions. *Journal of English for Academic Purposes, 6*(4), 289–302.
Chen, C. F & Cheng, W. Y. (2008). Beyond the design of automated writing evaluation: Pedagogical practices and perceived learning effectiveness in EFL writing classes. *Language Learning and Technology, 12*(2), 94–112.
Chen, L. & Tokuda, N. (2003). A new template-template-enhanced ICALL system for a second language composition course. *CALICO Journal, 20*(3), 561–578.
Chen, L., Tokuda, N., & Xiao, D. (2002). A POST parser-based learner model for template-based ICALL for Japanese-English writing skills. *Computer Assisted Language Learning, 15*(4), 357–372.
Cheng, A. (2008). Analyzing genre exemplars in preparation for writing: The case of an L2 graduate student in the ESP genre-based instructional framework of academic literacy. *Applied Linguistics, 29*, 50–71.
Cheng, W. (2012). *Exploring corpus linguistics: Language in action*. London: Routledge.
Cheng, W., Warren, M. & Xu, X. (2003). The language learner as language researcher: Putting Corpus linguistics on the timetable. *System, 31*(2), 173–186.
Chenoweth, A. & Hayes, J. (2001). Fluency in writing: Generating text in L1 and L2. *Written Communication, 18*, 80–98.
Christie, F. (1993). The 'received tradition' of literacy teaching: The decline of rhetoric and corruption of grammar. In B. Green (ed.), *The insistence of the letter: Literacy studies and curriculum theorizing* (pp. 75–106). London: Falmer Press.
Cho, S. (2004). Challenges of entering discourse communities through publishing in English: Perspectives of nonnative-speaking doctoral students in the United States of America. *Journal of Language, Identity, and Education, 3*(1), 47–72.
Cheville, J. (2004). Automated scoring technologies and the rising influence of error. *English Journal, 93*(4), 47–52.
Chung, G. & Baker, E. (2003). Issues in the reliability and validity of automated scoring of constructed responses. In M. D. Shermis & J. C. Burstein (eds), *Automated essay scoring: A cross-disciplinary perspective* (pp. 23–40). Mahwah, NJ: Lawrence Associates.

Cilliers, C. B. (2012). Student perception of academic writing skills activities in a traditional programming course. *Computers & Education, 58*, 1028–1041.

Coates, R., Sturgeon, B., Bohannan, J., & Pasini, E. (2002). Language and publication in cardiovascular research articles (Editorial). *Cardiovascular Research, 53*, 279–285.

Coe, R. M. (2002). The new rhetoric of genre: Writing political briefs. In A. M. Johns (ed.), *Genre in the classroom: Multiple perspectives* (pp. 197–210). Mahwah, NJ: Lawrence Erlbaum.

Coffin, C. & Donohue, J. P. (2012). Academic Literacies and systemic functional linguistics: How do they relate? *Journal of English for Academic Purposes, 11*, 64–75.

Condon, W. (2013). Large-scale assessment, locally-developed measures, and automated scoring of essays: Fishing for red herrings? *Assessing Writing, 18*, 100–108.

Conference on College Composition and Communication (CCCC) (2006). *Writing assessment: A position statement.* Retrieved October 10, 2008, from http://www.ncte.org/cccc/resources/positions/123784.htm.

Connor, U. (2004). Intercultural rhetoric research: Beyond texts. *Journal of English for Academic Purposes. Special Issue on Contrastive Rhetoric in EAP, 3*(4), 291–304.

Cook, V. J. (1991). *Second language learning and language teaching*. London: Edward Arnold.

Cooley, L. & Lewkowicz, J. (1995). The writing needs of graduate students at the University of Hong Kong: A project report. *Hong Kong Papers in Linguistics and Language Teaching, 18*, 121–123.

Cooley, L. & Lewkowicz, J. (1997). Developing awareness of the rhetorical and linguistic conventions of writing a thesis in English: Addressing the needs of ESL/EFL postgraduate students. In A. Duszak (ed.), *Culture and styles of academic discourse* (pp. 113–140). Berlin: Mouton de Gruyter.

Cope, B. & Kalantzis, M. (1986). *The powers of literacy: A genre approach to teaching writing*. Philadelphia, PA: University of Pittsburgh Press.

Cope, B., & Kalantzis, M. (1993). *The powers of literacy: A genre approach to teaching writing*. Pittsburgh, PA: University of Pittsburgh Press.

Corbett, A. T. & Anderson, J. R. (2001). Locus of feedback control in computer-based tutoring: Impact on learning rate, achievement and attitudes. In *Proceedings of ACM CHI 2001 conference on human factors in computing systems* (pp. 245–252). New York: ACM Press.

Cortes, V. (2007). Genre and corpora in the English for academic writing class. *ORTESOL Journa1, 25*, 9–16.

Cortes, V. (2013). The purpose of this study is to: Connecting lexical bundles and moves in research article introductions. *Journal of English for Academic Purposes, 12*, 33–43.

Cotterall, S. (2011). Doctoral students writing: Where's the pedagogy? *Teaching in Higher Education, 16*(4), 413–425.

Cotos, E. (2012). Towards effective integration and positive impact of automated writing evaluation in L2 Writing. In G. Kessler, A. Oskoz & I. Elola (eds). *Technology across writing contexts and tasks, CALICO Monograph Series* (Vol. 10, pp. 81–112). CALICO: San Marcos, TX.

Cotos, E., Huffman, S., Link, S., & Paben, T. (2013a). Methods, Methodology, Procedures: Devising a Swalesian Move/Step Schema for Research Article

Methods Sections. *64th Annual Convention, Conference on College Composition and Communication.* Las Vegas, USA.

Cotos, E., Huffman, S., Link, S., & Paben, T. (2013b). Discerning Moves and Steps in Cross-Disciplinary Results Discourse. *American Association for Applied Linguistics Conference.* Dallas, USA.

Cotos, E., Huffman, S., Link, S., & Paben, T. (2014). A Cross-disciplinary Move Schema for Research Article Discussion/Conclusion Sections. *American Association for Applied Linguistics Conference.* Portland, Oregon, USA.

Cowie, B. & Bell, B. (1999). A model of formative assessment in science education. *Assessment in Education: Principles, Policy and Practice, 6*(1), 32–42.

Creswell, J. W. (2003). *Research design: Qualitative, quantitative, and mixed methods approaches.* London: SAGE Publishers.

Cresswell, A. (2007). Getting to 'know' connectors? Evaluating data-driven learning in a writing skills course. In E. Hidalgo, L. Quereda, & S. Juan (eds), *Corpora in the foreign language classroom* (pp. 267–287). Amsterdam, Netherlands: Rodopi.

Cuthbert, D. & Spark, C. (2008). Getting a GRiP: Examining the outcomes of a pilot program to support graduate research students in writing for publication. *Studies in Higher Education, 33*(1), 77–88.

Dansdill, T. T., Hoffman, M. E., & Herscovici, D. S. (2008). Exposing gaps, exploring legacies: Paradoxes of writing use in computing education. *Journal of Computing Sciences in Colleges, 23*(5), 24–33.

Deane, P. (2013a). On the relation between automated essay scoring and modern views of the writing construct. *Assessing Writing, 18*, 7–24.

Deane, P. (2013b). Covering the construct: An approach to automated essay scoring motivated by a socio-cognitive framework for defining literacy skills. In M. D. Shermis & J. Burstein (eds), *Handbook of automated essay evaluation: Current applications and new directions* (pp. 298–312). New York: Routledge.

de Bot, K. (1996). The psycholinguistics of the output hypothesis. *Language Learning, 46*, 529–555.

de Jong, N. (2005). Can second language grammar be learned through listening? An experimental study. *Studies in Second Language acquisition, 27*, 205–234.

DeKeyser, R. M. (1997). Beyond explicit rule learning: Automatizing second language morphosyntax, *Studies in Second Language acquisition, 19*, 195–221.

DeKeyser, R. M. (2007a). *Practice in a second language: Perspectives from applied linguistics and cognitive psychology.* Cambridge: Cambridge University Press.

DeKeyser, R. M. (2007b). Skill acquisition theory. In B. VanPatten & J. Williams (eds), *Theories in second language acquisition* (pp. 97–113). Mahwa, New Jersey: Laurence Erlbaum Associates, Publishers.

DeKeyser, R. M. & Sokalski, K. (2001). The differential role of comprehension and production practice. In R. Ellis (ed.), *Focus on form in classroom second language acquisition* (pp. 197–261). New York: Cambridge University Press.

del Saz Rubio, M. M. (2011). A pragmatic approach to the macro-structure and metadiscoursal features of research article introductions in the field of Agricultural Sciences. *English for Specific Purposes, 30*, 258–271.

Dempsey, J. V., Discoll, M. P., & Swindell L. K. (1993). Text-based feedback. In J. V. Dempsey & G. C. Sales (eds), *Interactive instruction and feedback* (pp. 21–53). Englewood Cliffs, N.J.: Educational Technology Publications.

Design-Based Research Collective. (2003). Design-based research: An emerging paradigm for educational inquiry. *Educational Researcher*, 32(1), 5–8.

Dessus, P., Lemaire, B., & Vernier, A. (2000). Free text assessment in a virtual campus. In *Proceedings of the 3rd International Conference on Human System Learning (CAPS'2000)*, 61–75, Paris, France.

Devitt, A. (2004). *Writing genres*. Carbondale, IL: Southern Illinois University Press.

Devitt, A., Reiff, M. J., & Bawarshi, A. (2004). *Scenes of writing: Strategies for composing genres*. New York: Longman/Pearson.

Dewey, J. (1991). *How We Think*. Amherst, NY: Prometheus.

Dikli, S. (2006). An overview of automates scoring of essays. *The Journal of Technology, Learning, and Assessment*, *5*(1), 4–35.

Dong, Y. (1998). Non-native graduate students' thesis/dissertation writing in science: Self-reports by students and their advisors from two US institutions. *English for Specific Purposes, 17*, 369–390.

Donohue, J. P. (2012). Using systemic functional linguistics in academic writing development: An example from film studies. *Journal of English for Academic Purposes, 11*, 4–16.

Drury, H. (2004). Teaching academic writing on screen: A search for best practice. In L. Ravelli & R. Ellis (eds), *Analysing academic writing* (pp. 233–253). London: Continuum.

Dudley-Evans, T. (1994). Genre analysis: An approach to text analysis for ESP. In M. Coultard (ed.), *Advances in written text analysis* (pp. 219–228). London: Routledge, 219–228.

Dudley-Evans, T. (2004). Thoughts on the past and the future of EAP. In L. Sheldon (ed.), *Directions for the future: Issues in English for academic purposes* (pp. 23–30). Oxford: Peter Lang.

Dunlosky, J. & Metcalfe, J. (2009). *Metacognition*. Thousand Oaks, CA: Sage.

Dweck, C. S. (1986). Motivational processes affecting learning. *American Psychologist, 41*, 1040–1048.

Dweck, C. S. & Leggett, E. L. (1988). *A social-cognitive approach to motivation and personality. Psychological Review, 95*(2), 256–273.

Ebel, R. L. & Frisbie, D. A. (1991). *Essentials of educational measurement*, Fifth Edition. Englewood Cliffs, N.J.: Prentice Hall, Inc.

Eckstein, G., Chariton, J., & McCollum, R. M., (2011). Multi-draft composing: An iterative model for academic argument writing. *Journal of English for Academic Purposes, 10*, 162–172.

Ellis, R. (1999). *Learning a second language through interaction*. Amsterdam: John Benjamins.

Ellis, R. (2004). Supporting genre-based literacy pedagogy with technology – the implications for the framing and classification of the pedagogy. In L. Ravelli & R. Ellis (eds), *Analysing academic writing* (pp. 210–232). London: Continuum.

Elliot, N. (2013). Assessing writing special issue: Assessing writing with automated scoring systems. *Assessing Writing, 18*, 1–6.

Elliot, N. & Klobucar, A. (2013). Automated Essay Evaluation and the teaching of writing. In M. D. Shermis & J. Burstein (eds), *Handbook of Automated Essay Evaluation: Current applications and new directions* (pp. 16–35). New York: Routledge.

Elliot, S. (2003). IntelliMetric: From here to validity. In M.D. Shermis and J.C. Burstein (eds) *Automated essay scoring: A cross-disciplinary perspective*. Mahwah, NJ: Lawrence Erlbaum Associates.

Elliot, S. & Mikulas, C. (2004). The impact of MY Access!™ use on student writing performance: A technology overview and four studies. Paper presented at the *Annual Meeting of the American Educational Research Association*. San Diego, CA.

Elton, L. (2010). Academic writing and tacit knowledge. *Teaching in Higher Education, 15*(2), 151–160.

Ericsson, K. A., & Simon, H. A. (1987). Verbal reports on thinking. In C. Faerch. & G. Kasper (eds), *Introspection in second language research* (pp. 25–53). Philadelphia: Multilingual Matters.

Ericsson, P. (2006). The meaning of meaning: Is a paragraph more than an equation? In P. F. Ericsson & R. Haswell (eds), *Machine scoring of student essays: Truth and consequences* (pp. 28–37). Logan, UT: Utah State University Press.

Ericsson, P. F. & Haswell, R. H. (eds). (2006). *Machine scoring of student essays: Truth and consequences*. Logan, UT: Utah State University Press.

Eyres, S. J., Hatch, D. H., Turner, S. B., & West, M. (2001). Doctoral students' responses to writing critique: Messages for teachers. *Journal of Nursing Education, 40*(4), 149–155.

Fairclough, N. (1995). *Critical discourse analysis: the critical study of language*. London: Longman.

Fang, Y. (2010). Perceptions of the Computer-Assisted Writing Program among EFL College Learners. *Educational Technology & Society, 13*(3), 246–256.

Farr, J. L., Hofmann, D. A., & Ringenbach, K. L. (1993). Goal orientation and action control theory: Implications for industrial and organizational psychology. In C. L. Cooper & I. T. Robertson (eds), *International review of industrial and organizational psychology* (pp. 193–232). New York: Wiley.

Feez, S. (1998). *Text-based syllabus design*. Sydney: National Centre for English Language Teaching and Research.

Fergie, G., Beeke, S., McKenna, C, & Creme, P. (2011). "It's a Lonely Walk": Supporting postgraduate researchers through writing. *International Journal of Teaching and Learning in Higher Education, 23*(2), 236–245.

Ferris, D. (1995). Student reactions to teacher response in multiple-draft composition classrooms. *TESOL Quarterly, 29*, 33–53.

Ferris, D. (2003). *Response to student writing: Implications for second language students*. Mahwah, NJ: Lawrence Erlbaum.

Ferris, D. (2006). Does error feedback help student writers? New evidence on the short- and long-term effects of written error correction. In K. Hyland & F. Hyland (eds), *Feedback in second language writing: Contexts and issues* (pp. 81–104). Cambridge: Cambridge University Press.

Ferris, D. R. & Hedgcock J. S. (2012). *Teaching ESL composition: Purpose, process, and practice*, Third Edition. New York/London: Routledge, Taylor and Francis Group.

Fisher, S. L. & Ford, J. K. (1998). Differential effects of learner effort and goal orientation on two learning outcomes. *Personnel Psychology, 51*, 397–420.

Fitts, P. M. & Posner, M. I. (1967). *Human performance*. Belmont, CA: Brooks/Cole.

Fitzgerald. J. (1987). Research on revision in writing. *Review of Educational Research, 57*(4), 481–506.

Flavell, J. H. (1976). Metacognitive aspects of problem solving. In L. B. Resnick (ed.), *The nature of intelligence* (pp. 231–236). Hillsdale, NJ: Erlbaum.

Flower, L. & Hayes, J. R. (1981). A cognitive process theory of writing. *College Composition and Communication, 32*(4), 365–387.

Flower, L., Hayes, J. R., Carey, L., Schriver, K., & Stratman, J. (1986). Detection, diagnosis, and the strategies of revision. *College Composition and Communication, 37*, 16–55.

Flowerdew, J. (1999). Problems in writing for scholarly publication in English: The case of Hong Kong. *Journal of Second Language Writing, 8*, 243–264.

Flowerdew, J. (2000). Discourse community, legitimate peripheral participation, and the nonnative-Englishspeaking scholars. *TESOL Quarterly, 34*, 127–150.

Flowerdew, J. (2001). Attitudes of journal editors to nonnative speaker contributions. *TESOL Quarterly, 35*, 121–150.

Flowerdew, J. (2002). Genre in the classroom: A linguistic approach. In A. M. Johns (ed.), *Genre in the classroom: Multiple perspectives* (pp. 91–104). Mahwah, NJ: Lawrence Erlbaum.

Flowerdew, J. (2011). Reconciling contrasting approaches to genre analysis: The whole can equal more than the sum of the parts. In D. Belcher, A. M. Johns & B. Paltridge (eds), *New directions in research for English for specific purposes* (pp. 119–144). Ann Arbor, MI: University of Michigan Press.

Flowerdew, J. & Li, Y. (2007). Language re-use among Chinese apprentice scientists writing for publication. *Applied Linguistics, 28*(3), 440–465.

Foltz, P., Laham, D., & Landauer, T. (1999). The intelligent essay assessor: Applications to educational technology. *Interactive Multimedia Electronic Journal of Computer-Enhanced Leaning, 1*(2). Retrieved on December 8, 2008 at http://imej.wfu.edu/articles/1999/2/04/index.asp.

Ford, J. K., Smith, E. M., Weissbein, D. A., Gully, S. M., & Salas, E. (1998). Relationships of goal orientation, metacognitive activity, and practice strategies with learning outcomes and transfer. *Journal of Applied Psychology, 83*, 218–233.

Frase, L. T, Macdonald, N. H, Gingrich, P. S., Keenan, S. A., & Collymore, J. L. (1981). Computer aids for text assessment and writing instruction. *Performance & Instruction, 20*(9), 21–24.

Freedman, A. (1999). Beyond the text: Towards understanding the teaching and learning of genres. *TESOL Quarterly, 33*, 764–767.

Freedman, A. & Medway, P. (1994). *Genre and the new rhetoric*. Bristol, PA: Taylor & Francis.

Frost, A. (1999). Supervision of NESB postgraduate students in science-based disciplines. In Y. Ryan & O. Zuber-Skerritt (eds), *Supervising postgraduates from non-speaking backgrounds* (pp. 101–109). Birmingham, UK: Open University Press.

Gardner, S. (2012). Genres and registers of student report writing: An SFL perspective on texts and practices. *Journal of English for Academic Purposes 11*(1), 52–63.

Garner, M. & Borg, E. (2005). An ecological perspective on content-based instruction. *Journal of English for Academic Purposes, 4*, 119–134.

Garrett, N. (1987). A psycholinguistic perspective on grammar and CALL. In W. F. Smith (ed.), *Modern media in foreign language education: Theory and implementation* (pp. 169–196). Lincolnwood, IL: National Textbook.

Gaskell, D. & Cobb, T. (2004). Can learners use concordance feedback for writing errors? *System, 32*, 301–319.

Gass, S. (1997). *Input, interaction, and the second language learner*. Mahwah, NJ: Lawrence Erlbaum Associates.

Gass, S. & Mackey, A. (2006). Input, interaction and output: An overview. *AILA Review, 19*, 3–17.

Gass, S. M., & Mackey, A. (2007). Input, interaction, and output in second language acquisition. In B. VanPatten & J. Williams (eds), *Theories in second language acquisition: An introduction* (pp. 175–199). Mahwah, NJ: Lawrence Erlbaum.

Gass, S., Mackey, A., & Ross-Feldman, L. (2005). Task-based interactions in classroom and laboratory settings. *Language Learning, 55*, 575–611.

Geisler, C. (1994). Literacy and expertise in the academy. *Language and Learning across the Disciplines, 1*(1), 35–57.

Ghadessy, M., Henry, A., & Roseberry, R. (eds) (2001). *Small corpus studies and ELT Theory and practice*. Amsterdam: Benjamins.

Gentil, G. (2011). A biliteracy agenda for genre research. *Journal of Second Language Writing, 20*(1), 6–23.

Giddens, A. (1979). *Central problems in social theory*. Berkeley, CA: University of California Press.

Giles, H. & Johnson, P. (1987). Ethnolinguistic identity theory: A social psychological approach to language maintenance. *International Journal of the Sociology of Language, 68*, 69–99.

Gilquin, G., Granger, S., & Paquot, M. (2007). Lerner corpora: The missing link in EAP pedagogy. *Journal of English for Academic Purposes, 6*(4), 319–335.

Gladon, R., Graves, W., & Kelly, M. (2011). *Getting published in the life sciences*. Hoboken, NJ: Wiley-Blackwell.

Glasman-Deal, H. (2010). *Sciences research writing for non-native speakers of English*. Danvers, MA: Imperial College Press.

Gledhill, C. (2000). The discourse functions of collocation in research article introductions. *English for Specific Purposes, 19*(2), 115–135.

Gor, K. & Long, M. H. (2009). Input and second language processing. In W. C. Ritchie & T. J.Bhatia (eds), *Handbook of second language acquisition* (pp. 445–472). New York: Academic Press.

Granger, S. (2009). The contribution of learner corpora to second language acquisition and foreign language teaching: A critical evaluation. In K. Aijmer (ed.), *Corpora and language teaching* (pp. 13–32). Amsterdam, Netherlands: John Benjamins.

Granath, S. (2009). Who benefits from learning how to use corpora? In K. Aijmer (ed.), *Corpora and language teaching* (pp. 47–65). Amsterdam, Netherlands: John Benjamins.

Grimes, D. & Warschauer, M. (2008). Learning with laptops: A multi-method case study. *Journal of Educational Computing Research, 38*(3), 305–332.

Grimes, D. & Warschauer, M. (2010). Utility in a Fallible Tool: A Multi-Site Case Study of Automated Writing Evaluation. *Journal of Technology, Learning, and Assessment, 8*(6). Retrieved November, 2011 from http://www.jtla.org.

Groom, N. (2000) 'A workable balance': Self and sources in argumentative writing. In S. Mitchell and R. Andrews (eds), *Learning to argue in higher education* (pp. 65–73). Portsmouth, NH: Boynton/Cook Heinemann.

Hacker, D. J., Keener, M. C., & Kircher, J. C. (2009). Writing is applied metacognition. In D. J. Hacker, J. Dunlosky, A.-C. Graesser (eds), *Handbook of metacognition in education* (pp. 154–172). New York: Routledge.

Halliday, M. A. K. (1971). Language in a social perspective. *The context of language: educational review, 23*(3), 165–188.

Halliday, M. A. K. (1978). *Language as a social semiotic: The social interpretation of language and meaning*. London: Edward Arnold.

Halliday, M. A. K. (1985). *An introduction to functional grammar*. London: Edward Arnold.

Halliday M. A. K. (1989a). Register variation. In M. A. K. Halliday & R. Hasan, *Language, context, and text* (pp. 29–43). Oxford, UK: Oxford University Press.

Halliday M. A. K. (1989b). Functions of language. In M. A. K. Halliday & R. Hasan, *Language, context, and text* (pp. 15–26). Oxford, UK: Oxford University Press.

Halliday, M.A.K. & Hasan, R. (1976). *Cohesion in English*. Longman, London.

Halliday, M. A. K. & Hasan, R. (1989). *Language, context, and text: Aspects of language in a social-semiotic perspective*. Oxford, UK: Oxford University Press.

Halliday, M. A. K. (1994). *An introduction to functional grammar*, Second Edition. London: Edward Arnold.

Halliday, M. A. K. (2007). *Language and education*. London: Continuum.

Halliday, M. A. K. & Martin, J. R. (1993). *Writing science: Literacy and discursive power*. London: Falmer.

Halliday, M. A. K. & Webster, J. (2003). *On language and linguistics*. Collected Works of MAK Halliday, Vol. 3. Continuum, New York.

Hamp-Lyons, L. (ed.) (1991). *Assessing second language writing in academic contexts*. Norwood, NJ: Ablex Publishing.

Hammond, J. & Macken-Horarik, M. (1999). Critical literacy: Challenges and questions for ESL classrooms. *TESOL Quarterly, 33*, 528–544.

Hanauer, D. (1998). The effect of three literary educational methods on the development of genre knowledge. *Journal of Literary Semantics, 27*, 43–57.

Hasan, R. (1978). Text in the systemic-functional model. In W. U. Dressler (ed.), *Current trends in text linguistics* (pp. 228–246). Berlin & New York: duGruyter.

Hasan, R. (1989). The structure of a text. In M. A. K. Halliday & R. Hasan (eds), *Language, context, and text* (pp. 52–68). Oxford, UK: Oxford University Press.

Harasim, L. (2012). *Learning theory and online technologies*. New York: Routledge.

Hayes, J. R. & Flower, L. (1983). A cognitive model of the writing process in adults. *National Institute of Education* (ED). Washington, DC.

Hayes, J. R., Flower, L., Schriver, K. A., Stratman, J. F., & Carey, L. (1987). Cognitive processes in revision. In S. Rosenberg (ed.), *Advances in applied psycholinguistics* (Vol. 2, pp. 176–241). New York, NY: Cambridge University Press.

Hegelheimer, V., Dursun, A., Li, Z., Saricaoglu, A., & Yang, H. (2011). The use of Criterion® as formative assessment tool in second language writing classrooms. Paper Presented at the conference of *Midwest Association of Language Testers*, Ames, IA.

Heidorn, G. E., Jensen, K., Miller, L. A., Byrd, J. R., & Chodorow, M. S. (1982). The EPISTLE text-critiquing system. *IBM System Journal, 21*(3), 305–326.

Heift, T. (2001). Error-specific and individualized feedback in a web-based language tutoring system: Do they read It? *ReCALL, 13*(2), 129–142.

Heift, T. (2002). Learner control and error correction in ICALL: Browsers, peekers and adamants. *CALICO Journal, 19*(3), 295–313.

Heift, T. (2003) Multiple learner errors and meaningful feedback: A challenge for ICALL systems. *CALICO Journal, 20*(3), 533–548.

Heift, T. (2004). Corrective feedback and learner uptake in CALL. *ReCALL, 16*(2), 416–431.

Heift, T. (2005) Corrective feedback and learner uptake in CALL. *ReCALL, 17*(1), 32–46.

Heift, T. (2008). Corrective feedback in CALL: A longitudinal study of learner uptake. Paper presented at the *AAAL 2008 Conference*, Washington DC.

Heift, T. & Nicholson, D. (2001). Web delivery of adaptive and interactive language tutoring. *International Journal of Artificial Intelligence in Education, 12*(4), 310–325.

Heift, T. & Rimrott, A. (2008). Learner responses to corrective feedback for spelling errors in CALL. *System, 36*(2), 1–18.

Heift, T., Toole, J., McFetridge, P., Popwich, & Tsiplakou, S. F. (2000). Learning Greek with an intelligent and adaptive hypermedia system. *IMEJ of Computer-Enhanced Learning, 2*(2), October 2000 (http://imej.wfu.edu).

Henry A. (2007). Evaluating language learners' response to web-based, data-driven, genre teaching materials. *English for Specific Purposes, 26*, 462–484.

Henry, A. & Roseberry, R. (1998). An evaluation of a genre-based approach to the teaching of EAP/ESP writing. *TESOL Quarterly, 32*, 147–156.

Herrington, A. & Moran, C. (2001). What happens when machines read our students' writing? *College English, 63*, 480–499.

Herrington, A. & Moran, C. (2012). Writing to a machine is not writing at all. In N. Elliot & L. Perelman (eds), *Writing assessment in the 21st century: Essays in honor of Edward M. White* (pp. 219–232). New York, NY: Hampton Press.

Hewings, M. (2006). English language standards in academic articles: Attitudes of peer reviewers. *Revista Canaria de Estudios Ingleses, 53*, 47–62.

Hirvela, A. & Belcher, D. (2001). Coming back to voice: The multiple voices and identities of mature multilingual writers. *Journal of Second Language Writing, 10*, 83–106.

Holland, M., Maisano, R., Alderks, C., & Martin, J. (1993). Parsers in tutors: What are they good for? *CALICO Journal, 11*(1), 28–46.

Holmes, R. (1997). Genre analysis and the social sciences: An investigation of the structure of research article discussion sections in three disciplines. *English for Specific Purposes, 16*(4), 321–337.

Horning, A. (2002). *Revision Revisited.* Cresskill, NJ: Hampton Press.

Horning, A. & Robertson, J. (2006). Basic writers and revision. In A. Horning & A. Becker (eds), *Reference guide to revision history, theory, and practice* (pp. 50–62). Colorado: Parlor Press and the WAC Clearinghouse.

Howarth, P. (1996). *Phraseology in English academic writing.* Tubingen, Germany: Max Niemeyer Verlag.

Huot, B. (1996). Toward a new theory of writing assessment. *College Composition and Communication, 47*(4), 549–566.

Hyland, F. (1998). The impact of teacher written feedback on individual writers. *Journal of Second Language Writing, 7*(3), 255–286.

Hyland, K. (1999). Disciplinary discourses: writer stance in research articles. In C. N. Candlin & K. Hyland (eds), *Writing: texts, processes and practices*. London: Longman.

Hyland, K. (2000). *Disciplinary discourses: Social interactions in academic writing.* London: Longman.

Hyland, K. (2002). *Teaching and Researching Writing*. Longman, London.

Hyland, K. (2003a). Genre-based pedagogies: A social response to process. *Journal of Second Language Writing, 12*, 17–29.

Hyland, K. (2003b). *Second language writing.* Cambridge, UK: Cambridge University Press.

Hyland, K. (2004a). *Disciplinary discourses: Social interactions in academic writing.* Harlow, England: Longman.

Hyland, K. (2004b). *Genre and second language writing.* Ann Arbor, MI: University of Michigan Press.

Hyland, K. (2007). Genre pedagogy: Language, literacy and L2 writing instruction. *Journal of Second Language Writing, 16,* 148–164.

Hyland, K. & Hamp-Lyons, L. (2002). EAP: Issues and directions. *Journal of English for Academic Purposes, 1,* 1–12.

Hyland, K. & Hyland, F. (eds) (2006). *Feedback in second language writing: Contexts and issues.* New York: Cambridge University Press.

Hyon, S. (1996). Genre in three traditions: Implications for ESL. *TESOL Quarterly, 30,* 693–722.

Ingleton, C. & Cadman, K. (2002). Silent issues for international postgraduate research students: Emotion and agency in academic success. *Higher Education,* 17(2), 93–113.

James, K. (1984). The writing of theses by speakers of English as a foreign language: A case study. In R. Williams, J. Swales, & J. Kirkman (eds), *Common ground: Shared interests in ESP and communication studies, ELT documents* (pp. 99–113). Oxford: Pergamon Press.

Jenkins, S., Jordan, M., & Weiland, P. (1993). The role of writing in graduate engineering education: A survey of faculty beliefs and practices. *English for Specific Purposes, 12,* 51–67.

Johns, T. (1988). Whence and whither classroom concordancing? In T. Bongarerts, P. de Haan, S. Lobbe, & Wekker, H. (eds), *Computer applications in language learning.* Dordrecht, Holland: Foris.

Johns, T. (1991). Should you be persuaded – two samples of data driven learning materials. *English Language Research Journal, 4,* 1–13.

Johns, A. M. (1995). Genre and pedagogical purposes. *Journal of Second Language Writing, 4*(2), 181–190.

Johns, A. M. (1997). *Text, role, and context: Developing academic literacies.* New York: NY: Cambridge University Press.

Johns, A. M. (2002). *Genre in the classroom: Multiple perspectives.* Mahwah, NJ: Lawrence Erlbaum.

Johns, A. M. (2003). Genre and ESL/EFL composition instruction. In B. Kroll (ed.), *Exploring the dynamics of second language writing* (pp. 195–217). Cambridge, UK: Cambridge University Press.

Johns, A. M. (2008). Genre awareness and the novice student: An ongoing quest. *Language Teaching, 41,* 239–254.

Johns, A. M. (2011). The future of genre in L2 writing: Fundamental, but contested, instructional decisions. *Journal of Second Language Writing, 20,* 56–68.

Johns, A. M, Bawarshi, A., Coe, R. M., Hyland, K., Paltridge, B., Reiff, M. J., & Tardy, C. (2006). Crossing the boundaries of genre studies: Commentaries by experts. *Journal of Second Language Writing, 15,* 234–249.

Johnson, C.M. (2001). A survey of current research on online communities of practice. *Internet and Higher Education, 4,* 45–60.

Johnson, L., Lee, A., & Green, B. (2000). The PhD and the autonomous self: Gender, rationality and postgraduate pedagogy. *Studies in Higher Education, 25,* 135–147.

Jolliffe, D. A. & Brier, E. M. (1988). Studying writers' knowledge in academic disciplines. In D. A. Jolliffe (ed.), *Advances in writing research: Vol. 2. Writing in academic disciplines* (pp. 35–77). Norwood, NJ: Ablex Publishing Company.

Jones, E. (2006). ACCUPLACER'S essay-scoring technology: When reliability does not equal validity. In P. F. Ericsson & R. H. Haswell (eds), *Machine scoring of student essays: Truth and consequences* (pp. 93–113). Logan, UT: Utah State University Press.

Juozulynas, V. (1994). Errors in the compositions of second-year German students: An empirical study for Parse-based ICALI. *CALICO Journal, 12*(1), 5–17.

Kamler, B. 2008. Rethinking doctoral publication practices: Writing from and beyond the thesis. *Studies in Higher Education, 33*(3), 283–294.

Kamler, B. & Thomson, P. (2008). The failure of dissertation advice books: Toward alternative pedagogies for doctoral writing. *Educational Researcher, 37*(8), 507–514.

Kane, M. (2006). Validation. In R. Brennen (ed.), *Educational measurement*, Fourth Edition (pp. 17–64). Westport, CT: Greenwood.

Kane, M. (2013). Validating the Interpretations and Uses of Test Scores. *Journal of Educational Measurement, 50*(1), 1–73.

Kamoksilapatham, B. (2005). Rhetorical structure of biochemistry RAs. *English for Specific Purposes, 24*, 269–292.

Kanoksilapatham, B. (2007). Rhetorical moves in biochemistry research articles. In D. Biber, U. Connor, & T. Upton (eds), *Discourse on the move: Using corpus analysis to describe discourse structure* (pp. 73–119). Amsterdam/Philadelphia: John Benjamins.

Kaplan, R. (1968). Contrastive rhetoric: Teaching composition to the Chinese students. *Journal of English as a Second Language, 3*, 1–13.

Keith, T. Z. (2003). Validity and automated essay scoring systems. In M. D. Shermis & J. C. Burstein (eds), *Automated essay scoring: A cross-disciplinary perspective*. (pp. 147–167). Mahwah, NJ: Lawrence Erlbaum.

Kennedy, C. & Miceli, T. (2001). An evaluation of intermediate students' approaches to corpus investigation. *Language Learning & Technology, 5*(3), 77–90.

Kettemann, B. & Marko, G. (eds) (2006). *Planning, gluing and painting corpora: Inside the applied corpus linguist's workshop*. Frankfurt: Peter Lang.

Kiley, M. (2009). Identifying threshold concepts and proposing strategies to support doctoral candidates. *Innovations in Education and Teaching International, 46*(3), 293–304.

Kmcaid, J. P, Aagard, J. A., O'Hara, J. W., & Cottrell, L. K. (1981). Computer readability editing system. *IEEE Transactions on Professional Communication*, 1, 38–41.

Knight, N. (1999). Responsibilities and limits in the supervision of NESB research students in the social sciences and humanities. In Y. Ryan & O. Zuber-Skerritt (eds), *Supervising postgraduates from non-English speaking backgrounds* (pp. 93–100). Buckingham, UK: Open University Press.

Koschmann, T. (1996). Paradigm shifts and instructional technology: An introduction. In T. Koschmann (ed.), *CSCL: Theory and practice*. Mahwah, NJ: Lawrence Erlbaum Associates.

Koutsantoni, D. (2006). Rhetorical strategies in engineering research articles and research theses: Advanced academic literacy and relations of power. *Journal of English for Academic Purposes, 5*, 19–36.

Kraiger, K., & Jerden, E. (2007). A meta-analytic investigation of learner control: Old findings and new directions. In S. M. Fiore, & E. Salas (eds), *Toward a science of distributed learning*. (pp. 65-90). Washington, DC, US: American Psychological Association.

Krashen, S. (1984). *Writing: Research, theory, and application*. Oxford: Pergamon Press.

Krashen S. (1985). *The input hypothesis: Issues and implications*, London: Longman.

Kress, G. (1996). Representational resources and the production of subjectivity. Questions for the theoretical development of critical discourse analysis in a multicultural society. In C. R. Coulthard and M. Coulthard (eds), *Texts and Practices*. London/New York: Routledge.

Kroll, B. (1977). Combing ideas in written and spoken English: A look at subordination and coordination. In E. Keenan and T. Bennett (eds), *Discourse Across Time and Space*. SCOPIL (Southern California Occasional Papers in Linguistics) *No* 5. Los Angeles: University of Southern California Press.

Kulhavy, R. W. & Stock, W. (1989). Feedback in written instruction: The place of response certitude. *Educational Psychology Review, 1*(4), 279–308.

Kulik, J. A. & Kulik, C. -L. C. (1988). Timing of feedback and verbal learning. *Review of Educational Research, 58*(1), 79–97.

Kushner, S. (1997). Tackling the needs of foreign academic writers: A case study. *IEEE Transactions on Professional Communication, 40*(1), pp. 20–25.

Labrie, G. & Singh, L. (1991). Parsing, error diagnostics, and instruction in a French tutor. *CALICO Journal, 9*(1), 9–25.

Lai, I. -h. (2010). Which do students prefer to evaluate their essays: Peers or computer program. *British Journal of Educational Technology, 41*, 432–454.

Lalande, J. F. (1982). Reducing composition errors: An experiment. *The Modern Language Journal, 66*, 140–149.

Landauer, T., Laham, D., & Foltz, P. (2003). Automated scoring and annotation of essays with the intelligent essay assessor. In M. D. Shermis and J. C. Burstein (eds), *Automated essay scoring: A cross-disciplinary perspective*. Mahwah, NJ: Lawrence Erlbaum Associates.

Lankshear, C. & Knoble, M. (2003). *New literacies: Changing knowledge and classroom learning*. Buckingham: Open University Press.

Latour, B. & Woolgar, S. (1986). *Laboratory life: The construction of scientific facts*, Second Edition. Princeton, NJ: Princeton University Press.

Lave, J. & Wenger, E. (1991). *Situated learning: Legitimate peripheral participation*. Cambridge: Cambridge University Press.

Lavelle, E. & Bushrow, K. (2007). Writing approaches of graduate students. *Educational Psychology, 27*(6), 807–822.

Lax, J. (2002). Academic writing for international graduate students. *Proceedings in 32nd ASEE/IEEE Frontiers in Education Conference*. Boston, MA.

Lea, M. (2004). Academic literacies: A pedagogy for course design. *Studies in Higher Education, 29*(6), 739–756.

Lea, M. R. & Street, B. V. (1998). Student writing in higher education: An academic literacies approach. *Studies in Higher Education, 23*(2), 157–172.

Lea, M. & Street, B. (2006). The 'Academic Literacies' model: Theory and applications. *Theory into Practice, 45*(4), 368–377.

Leah Rock, J. (2007). The impact of short-term use of *CriterionSM* on writing skills in ninth grade. Research report. Educational Testing Service, Princeton, NJ.

Retrieved on December 8, 2008 from http://www.ets.org/Media/Research/pdf/RR-07-07.pdf.

Lee, D. & Swales, J. M. (2006). A corpus-based course for NNS doctoral students: Moving from available specialized corpora to self-compiled corpora. *English for Specific Purposes, 25*(1), 56–75.

Lepper, M., Woolverton, M., Mumme, D., & Gurtner, J. (1993). Motivational techniques of expert human tutors: Lessons for the design of computer-based tutors. In S. Lajoie & S. Derry (eds), *Computers as cognitive tools*. Hillsdale, NJ: Lawrence Erlbaum Associates.

Levin, L., Evans, D., & Gates, D. (1991). The ALICE system: A workbench for learning and using language. *CALICO, Journal 9*(1), 27–56.

Levis, J. & Muller-Levis, G. (2003). A project-based approach to teaching research writing to nonnative writers. *IEEE Transactions on Professional Communication, 46*(3), 210–220.

Li, Y. (2006). A doctoral student of physics writing for publication: A sociopolitically-oriented case study. *English for Specific Purposes, 25*, 456–478.

Li, Y. Y. & Flowerdew, J. (2007). Shaping Chinese novice scientists' manuscripts for publication. *Journal of Second Language Writing, 16*(2), 100–117.

Lightbown, P. M. & Spada, N. (1997). *How languages are learned*. Oxford: Oxford University Press.

Lillis, T. M. (2006). Moving towards an 'academic literacies' pedagogy: Dialogues of participation. In L. Ganobcsik-Williams (ed.), *Teaching academic writing in UK higher education* (pp. 30–45). Basingstoke: Palgrave Macmillan.

Lillis, T. & Scott, M. (2007). Defining academic literacies research: Issues of epistemology, ideology and strategy. *Journal of Applied Linguistics, 4*(1), 5–32.

Lillis, T. & Turner, J. (2001). Student writing in higher education: Contemporary confusion, traditional concerns. *Teaching in Higher Education, 6*(1), 57–68.

Lim, J. M-H. (2006). Method sections of management research articles: A pedagogically motivated qualitative study. *English for Specific Purposes, 25*, 282–309.

Lim, J. M-H. (2010). Commenting on research results in applied linguistics and education: A comparative genre-based study. *Journal of English for Academic Purposes, 9*, 280–294.

Lim, J. M-H. (2012). How do writers establish research niches? A genre-based investigation into management researchers' rhetorical steps and linguistic mechanisms. *Journal of English for Academic Purposes, 11*, 229–245.

Liou, H. C. (1991). Development of an English grammar checker: A progress report. *CALICO Journal, 9*(1), 57–70.

Little, D. (1991). *Learner autonomy 1: Definitions, issues and problems*. Dublin: Authentik.

Long, M. (1983). Does second language instruction make a difference? A review of the research. *TESOL Quarterly, 17*, 359–382.

Long, M. (1996). The role of the linguistic environment in second language acquisition. In W. Ritchie & T. K. Bhatia (eds), *Handbook of language acquisition: Vol. 2. Second language acquisition* (pp. 413–468). San Diego, CA: Academic Press.

Long, M. H. (2007). *Problems in SLA*. Mahwah, New Jersey: Erlbaum.

Loi, C. K. (2010). Research article introductions in Chinese and English: A comparative genre-based study. *Journal of English for Academic Purposes, 9*, 267–279.

Looney, J. (ed.) (2005). *Formative assessment: Improving learning in secondary classrooms*. Paris: Organization for Economic Cooperation and Development.

Loritz, D. (1992). Generalized transition network parsing for language study: The GPARS system for English, Russian, Japanese, and Chinese. *CALICO Journal, 10*(1), 5–22.

Lyster, R. (1998). Negotiation of form, recasts, and explicit correction in relation to error types and learner repair in immersion classrooms. *Language Learning, 48*, 183–218.

Macaro, E. (2003). *Teaching and learning a second language. A guide to recent research and its applications*. London/New York: Continuum.

Macdonald, N. H. (1983). The UNIX™ writer's workbench software: Rationale and design. *The BELL System Technical Journal, 62*(6), 1891–1908.

Macdonald, N. H., Frase, L. T., Gingrich, P. S., & Keenan, S. A. (1982). Writer's workbench: Computer aid for text analysis. *IEEE Transactions on Communications, Special Issue on Communication in the Automated Office, 30*(1), 105–110.

Mackey, A. (2006). Feedback, noticing and instructed second language learning. *Applied Linguistics, 27*(3), 405–430.

Mackey, A., Gass, S., & McDonough, K. (2000). How do learners perceive interactional feedback? *Studies in Second Language Acquisition, 22*(4), 471–497.

Mason, B. J. & Bruning, R. (2001). Providing feedback in computer-based instruction: What the research tells us. Retrieved December, 2, 2008, from http://dwb4.unl.edu/dwb/Research/MB/MasonBruning.html.

Ming, P. Y., Mikhailov, A. A., & Kuan, T. L. (2000). Intelligent essay marking system. In C. Cheers (ed.), *Learners Together, Feb. 2000*, NgeeANN Polytechnic, Singapore. http://ipdweb.np.edu.sg/lt/feb00/intelligent_essay_marking.pdf.

Macken-Horarik, M. (2002). Something to shoot for: A systemic functional approach to teaching genre in secondary school science. In A. M. Johns (ed.), *Genre in the classroom: Multiple perspectives* (pp. 14–42). Mahwah, NJ: Lawrence Erlbaum.

Martin, J. R. (1985). Process and text. In J. D. Benson & W.S. Greaves (eds), *Systemic perspectives on discourse* (Vol. 1, pp. 248–274). Norwood, NJ: Ablex Publishing.

Martin, J. R. (1992). *English text: System and structure*. Amsterdam: Benjamins.

Martin, J. R. (1993). A contextual theory of language. In B. Cope & M. Kalantzis (eds), *The powers of literacy. A genre approach to teaching writing*. London: The Falmer Press.

Martin, J. R. (1999). Mentoring semogenesis: 'Genre-based' literacy pedagogy. In F. Christie (ed.), *Pedagogy and the shaping of consciousness: Linguistic and social processes* (pp. 123–155). London: Cassell (Open Linguistics Series).

Martin, J. R. (2002). A universe of meaning – How many practices? In A. M. Johns (ed.), *Genre in the classroom: Multiple perspectives*. Marwah, NJ: Lawrence Erlbaum Associates.

Martinez, I. (2001). Impersonality in the research article as revealed by analysis of the transitivity structure. *English for Specific Purposes, 20*, 227–247.

Mason, O. & Grove-Stephenson, I. (2002). Automated free text marking with paperless school. In *Proceedings of the 6th International Computer Assisted Assessment Conference*.

Masson, M. E. J. (1990). Cognitive theories of skill acquisition. *Human Movement Science, 9*, 221–239.

Mauranen, A. (1993). Cultural differences in academic discourse-problems of a linguistic and cultural minority. In L. Lofman, L. Kurki-Suonio, S. Pellinen,

& J. Lehtonen (eds), *The competent intercultural communicaror* (pp. 157–174). Jyvaskyla, Finland: Association Finlandaise de Linguistique Appliquee.

Mayfield, E. & Penstein Rosé, C. (2013). LightSIDE: Open source machine learning for test. In M. D. Shermis & J. Burstein (eds), *Handbook of automated essay evaluation: Current applications and new directions* (pp. 124–135). New York: Routledge.

McCune, V. & Hounsell, D. (2005). The development of students' ways of thinking and practising in three final-year biology courses. *Higher Education, 49*, 255–289.

McGee, T. (2006). Taking a spin on the intelligent essay assessor. In: P. F. Ericsson & R. H. Haswell (eds), *Machine scoring of student essays: Truth and consequences* (pp. 79–92). Logan, UT: Utah State University Press.

McKenna, C. (2003). From skills to subjects; the reconceptualisation of writing development in higher education. In C. Rust (ed.), *Improving student learning: Theory and practice* (pp. 67–74). Oxford: Oxford Centre for Staff and Learning Development.

McNabb, R. (2001). Making the gesture: Graduate student submissions and the expectations of journal referees. *Composition Studies, 29*, 9–26.

Messick, S. (1989). *Validity*. Macmillan: American Council on Education.

Messick, S. (1996). Validity and washback in language testing. *Language Testing 13*(3), 241–256.

Miller, C. (1984). Genre as social action. *Quarterly Journal of Speech, 70*, 151–167.

Mislevy, R. J. & Gitomer, D. H. (1996). The role of probability-based inference in an intelligent tutoring system. *User-Modeling and User-Adapted Interaction, 5*, 253–282.

Mislevy, R. J. & Haertel, G. D. (2006). Implications of evidence-centered design for educational testing. *Educational Measurement: Issues and Practice, 25*(4), 6–20.

Mislevy, R. J., Steinberg, L. S., & Almond, R. A. (2002). Design and analysis in task-based language assessment. *Language Assessment, 19*, 477–496.

Mislevy, R. J., Steinberg, L. S., & Almond, R. A. (2003). On the structure of educational assessments. *Measurement: Interdisciplinary Research and Perspectives, 1*, 3–67.

Mitchell, T. M. (1997). *Machine Learning*. New York: McGraw-Hill.

Mitchell, R. & Myles, F. (1998). *Second Language Learning Theories*. London: Edward Arnold.

Mohan, B. A. & Lo, A. W. (1985). Academic writing and Chinese students: Transfer and developmental factors. *TESOL Quarterly, 19*, 515–534.

Mory, E. H. (2004). Feedback research review. In D. Jonassen (ed.), *Handbook of research on educational communications and technology* (pp. 745–783). Mahwah, NJ: Erlbaum Associates.

Mullen, C. (2001). The need for a curricular writing model for graduate students. *Journal of Further and Higher Education, 25*(1), 117–125.

Nagata, N. (1993). Intelligent computer feedback for second language instruction, *The Modern Language Journal, 77*(3), 330–339.

Nagata, N. (1995). An effective application of natural language processing in second language Instruction. *CALICO Journal, 13*(1), 47–67.

Nagata, N. (2009). Robo-Sensei's NLP-based error detection and feedback generation. *CALICO Journal*, 26 (3), 562–579.

Napolitano, D. M & Stent, A. (2009). TechWriter: An evolving system for writing assistance for advanced learners of English. *CALICO Journal, 26*(3), 611–625.

Narciss, S. & Huth, K. (2004). How to design informative tutoring feedback for multimedia learning. In H. M. Niegemann, D. Leutner, & R. Brunken (ed.), *Instructional design for multimedia learning* (pp. 181–195). Munster, NY: Waxmann.

Neal, M. R. (2011). *Writing assessment and the revolution in digital technologies*. New York: Teachers College Press.

Negretti, R. & Kuteeva, M. (2011). Fostering metacognitive genre awareness in L2 academic reading and writing: A case study of pre-service English teachers. *Journal of Second Language Writing, 20*, 95–110.

Newell, A. & Rosenbloom, P. (1981). Mechanisms of skill acquisition and the law of practice. In J. R. Anderson (ed.), *Cognitive skills and their acquisition* (pp. 1–55). Hillsdale, NJ: Lawrence Erlbaum Associates.

Nightingale, P. (1986). *Improving student writing. Green Guide No 4*. Adelaide, Australia: Higher Education Research and Development Society of Australasia.

Norris, J. M. & Ortega, L. (2003). Defining and measuring L2 acquisition. In C. Doughty and M.H. Long (eds), *Handbook of second language acquisition* (pp. 717–761). New York: Blackwell.

Nwogu, K. N. (1990). *Discourse variation in medical texts: Schema, theme and cohesion in professional and journalistic accounts*. University of Nottingham: Monographs in Systemic Linguistics, 2.

Nwogu, K. N. (1997). The medical research paper: Structure and functions. *English for Specific Purposes, 16*(2), 119–138.

Oliver, R. & Mackey, A. (2003). Interactional context and feedback in child ESL classrooms. *Modern Language Journal, 87*(4), 519–543.

O'Sullivan, I. & Chambers, A. (2006). Learners' writing skills in French: Corpus consultation and learner evaluation. *Journal of Second Language Writing, 15*(1), 49–68.

Ozturk, I. (2007). The textual organisation of research article introductions in applied linguistics: Variability within a single discipline. *English for Specific Purposes, 26*, 25–38.

Page, E. B. (1994). New computer grading of student prose, using modern concepts and software. *Journal of Experimental Education, 62*(2), 127–142.

Page, E. (2003). Project essay grade. In M.D. Shermis and J.C. Burstein (eds), *Automated essay scoring: A cross-disciplinary perspective*. Mahwah, NJ: Lawrence Erlbaum Associates.

Page, E. B., Keith, T., & Lavoie, M. J. (1995). Construct validity in the computer grading of essays. Paper presented at the *Annual Meeting of the American Psychological Association*. New York, NY.

Page, E. B. & Petersen, N. S. (1995). The computer moves into essay grading: Updating the ancient test. *Phi Delta Kappan, 76*(7), 561–565.

Paltridge, B. (1997). Thesis and dissertation writing: Preparing ESL students for research. *English for Specific Purposes, 16*, 61–70.

Paltridge, B. (2002). Thesis and dissertation writing: An examination of published advice and actual practice. *English for Specific Purposes, 21*, 125–143.

Pang, T. T. (2002). Textual analysis and contextual awareness building: A comparison of two approaches to teaching genre. In A. M. Johns (ed.), *Genre in the classroom: Multiple perspectives* (pp. 145–161). Mahwah, NJ: Lawrence Erlbaum.

Parkinson, J. (2011). The Discussion section as argument: The language used to prove knowledge claims. *English for Specific Purposes, 30*, 164–175.

Parry, S. (1998). Disciplinary discourse in doctoral education. *Higher Education, 36*, 273–299.

Pavlenko, A. & Lantolf, J. (2000). Second language learning as participation and the (re)construction of selves. In J. Lantolf (ed.), *Sociocultural theory and second language learning* (pp. 155–177). Oxford: Oxford University Press.

Paxton, M. (2011). How do we play the genre game in preparing students at the advanced undergraduate level for research writing? *Teaching in Higher Education, 16*(1), 53–64.

Peacock, M. (2002) Communicative moves in the discussion section of research articles. *System, 30*(4), 479–497.

Pendar, N. & Cotos, E. (2008). Automatic identification of discourse moves in scientific article introductions. In *The Proceedings of The 3rd workshop on innovative Use of NLP for Building Educational Applications* (pp. 62–70). Columbus, Ohio.

Perelman, L. (2012a). Construct validity, length, score, and time in holistically graded writing assessments: The case against automated essay scoring (AES). In: C. Bazerman, C. Dean, J. Early, K. Lunsford, S. Null, P. Rogers, & A. Stansell (eds), *International advances in writing research: Cultures, places, measures* (pp. 121–131). Fort Collins, Colorado: WAC Clearinghouse/Anderson.

Perelman, L. (2012b). Mass-market writing assessments as bullshit. In: N. Elliot & L. Perelman (eds), *Writing assessment in the 21st century: Essays in honor of Edward M. White* (pp. 425–437). New York, NY: Hampton Press.

Pearson Education, Inc. (2007). General overview of WriteToLearn™ and its components. Retrieved on December 8, 2008, http://www.knowledge-technologies.com/papers/WTLOverview-101507.pdf.

Pérez Marín, D. R. (2007). *Adaptive Computer Assisted Assessment of free-text students' Answers: An Approach to Automatically Generate Students' Conceptual Models*. Unpublished dissertation, Universidad Autonoma de Madrid.

Polio, C. & Williams, J. (2011). Teaching and testing writing. In M.H. Long & C.J. Doughty (eds), *Handbook of language teaching* (pp. 486–517). Malden, MA: Blackwell.

Posteguillo, S. (1999). The schematic structure of computer science research articles. *English for Specific Purposes, 18*(2), 139–160.

Pratt, M.L. (1991). Arts of the contact zone. *Profession, 91*, 33–40.

Pridemore, D. R. & Klein, J. D. (1995). Control of practice and level of feedback in computer-based instruction. *Contemporary Educational Psychology, 20*, 444–450.

Prior, P. (2007). From Voloshinov and Bakhtin to mediated multimodal genre systems. In A. Bonini, D. de Carvalho Figueriedo and F. J. Rauen (eds), In *Proceedings of the 4th International Symposium on Genre Studies* (pp. 270–286). Santa Catarina, Brazil: University of Southern Santa Catarina.

Pufahl, R. M. (1984). Response to Richard M. Collier. *College Composition and Communication, 35*, 91–93.

Pylyshyn, Z. (1989). Computing in cognitive science. In M. Posner (ed.), *Foundations of cognitive science*. Cambridge, MA: MIT Press.

Ramanathan, V. & Kaplan, R. B. (2000). Genres, authors, discourse communities: theory and application for (L1 and) L2 writing instructors. *Journal of Second Language Writing, 9*(2), 171–191.

Ramineni, C. (2013). Validating automated essay scoring for online writing placement. *Assessing Writing, 18*, 40–61.

Ramineni, C. & Williamson, D. M. (2013). Automated essay scoring: Psychometric guidelines and practices. *Assessing Writing, 18*, 25–39.

Ramirez, A. (2005). Review of the social turn in second language acquisition. *The Modern Language Journal, 45*, 292–293.

Ranta, L. & Lyster, R. (2006). A cognitive approach to improving immersion students' oral production abilities: The awareness, practice, and feedback sequence. In R. DeKeyser (ed.), *Practicing in a second language: Perspectives from applied linguistics and cognitive psychology.* New York: Cambridge University Press.

Reuer, V. (2003). Error recognition and feedback with Lexical Functional Grammar. *CALICO Journal, 20*(3), 497–512.

Riazi, A. (1997). Acquiring disciplinary literacy: A social-cognitive analysis of text production and learning among Iranian graduate students of education. *Journal of Second Language Writing, 6*, 105–137.

Rich, C. S., Harrington, H., Kim, J., & West, B. (2008). Automated Essay Scoring in state formative and summative assessment. Paper Presented at the *American Educational Research Association.* New York, NY, March.

Rich, C. S, Schneider, M. C, & D'Brot, J. M. (2013). Applications of automated essay evaluation in West Virginia. In M. D. Shermis & J. Burstein (eds), *Handbook of automated essay evaluation: current applications and new directions* (pp. 99–123). New York: Routledge.

Richardson, L. (1998). Writing: A method of inquiry. In N. Denzin and Y. Lincoln (ed.), *Handbook of qualitative research* (pp. 345–371). London: Sage.

Ricento, T. (2002). Considerations of identity in L2 learning. In E. Hinkel (ed.), *Handbook of research in second language teaching and learning* (pp. 895–910). New York: Routledge.

Riedel, E., Dexter, S. L., Scharber, C., & Doering, A. (2003). Experimental evidence on the effectiveness of automated essay scoring in teacher education cases. Paper presented at the *86th Annual Meeting of the American Educational Research Association*, Montreal, CA.

Robinson, P. (1997). Generalizability and automaticity of second language learning under implicit, incidental, enhanced, and instructed conditions. *Studies in Second Language Acquisition, 19*, 223–247.

Römer, Ute. (2010). Using general and specialized corpora in English language teaching: Past, present and future. In: M. C. Campoy-Cubillo, B. Belles-Fortuño, & L. Gea-Valor (eds), *Corpus-based approaches to English language teaching* (pp. 18–35). London: Continuum.

Rosa, E. & Leow, R. (2004). Awareness, different learning conditions, and second language development. *Applied Psycholinguistics, 25*, 269–292.

Rudner, L. M., Garcia, V., & Welch, C. (2006). An Evaluation of the IntelliMetric Essay Scoring System. *Journal of Technology, Learning, and Assessment, 4*(4). Retrieved from http://www.jtla.org.

Russell, D., Lea, M., Parker, J., Street, B., & Donahue, T. (2009). Exploring notions of genre in 'academic literacies' and 'writing across the curriculum': Approaches across countries and contexts. In C. Bazerman, A. Bonini, & D. Figueiredo (eds), *Genre in a changing world* (pp. 395–423). Fort Collins, Colorado: The WAC Clearinghouse and Parlor Press.

Ryan, Y. & Zuber-Skerritt, O. (eds) (1999). *Supervising postgraduates from non-English speaking backgrounds.* Buckingham: The Society for Research into Higher Education and Open University Press.

Sadler, D. R. (1989). Formative assessment and the design of instructional systems. *Instructional Science, 18,* 119–144.
Salager-Meyer, F. (1990). Discoursal flaws in medical English abstracts: A genre analysis per research-and text type. *Text, 10*(4), 365–384.
Sales, G. C. (1993). Adapted and adaptive feedback in technology-based instruction. In V. Dempsey & G. C. Sales (eds), *Interactive instruction and feedback* (pp. 159–175). Englewood Cliffs, NJ: Educational Technology Publications.
Samraj, B. (2002). Introductions in research articles: Variations across disciplines. *English for Specific Purposes, 21*(1), 1–17.
San Miguel, C. & Nelson, C. (2007). Key writing challenges of practice-based doctorates. *Journal of English for Academic Purposes, 6,* 71–86.
Sanders, R. (1991). Error Analysis in Purely Syntactic Parsing of Free Input: The Example of German. *CALICO Journal, 9*(1), 72–89.
Schmidt, R. W. (1994). Deconstructing consciousness in search of useful definitions for applied linguistics. *AILA Review*, 11, 11–26.
Schraw, G. & Dennison, R. S. (1994). Assessing metacognitive awareness. Contemporary Educational Psychology, 19, 460–475.
Schroeder, J., Grohe, B., & Pogue, R. (2008). The impact of Criterion writing evaluation technology on criminal justice student writing skills. *The Journal of Criminal Justice Education, 19*(3), 432–445.
Shaalan, K. (2005). An intelligent computer assisted language learning system for Arabic learners. *Computer Assisted Language Learning, 18*(1–2), 81–108.
Shepard, L. A. (2008). Formative assessment: Caveat emptor. In C. A. Dwyer (ed.), *The future of assessment: Shaping teaching and learning* (pp. 279–303). Mahwah, NJ: Erlbaum.
Shermis, M. D. & Burstein, J. C. (2003). *Automated essay scoring: A cross-disciplinary perspective*. Mahwah, NJ: Lawrence Erlbaum Associates.
Shermis, M. D. & Burstein, J. C. (2013) (eds). *Handbook of automated essay evaluation: Current applications and new directions*. New York: Routledge.
Shermis, M. D., Burstein, J., & Bliss, L. (2004). The impact of automated essay scoring on high stakes writing assessments. Paper presented at the *Annual Meetings of the National Council on Measurement in Education*. San Diego, CA.
Shermis, M. D., Burstein, J., Higgins, D., & Zechner, K. (2010). Automated essay scoring: Writing assessment and instruction. In E. Baker, B. McGaw and N. S. Petersen (eds), *International Encyclopedia of Education* (Vol. 4, pp. 20–26). Oxford, UK: Elsevier.
Shermis, M. D. & Hammer, B. (2012). Contrasting state-of-the-art automated scoring of essays: Analysis. Paper presented at the *Annual Meeting of the National Council of Measurement in Education*. Vancouver, BC, Canada.
Shermis, M. D., Burstein, J., & Apel Bursky, S. (2013). Introduction to automated essay evaluation. In M. D. Shermis & J. Burstein (eds), *Handbook of automated essay evaluation: Current applications and new directions* (pp. 1–15). New York: Routledge.
Shohamy, E., Donitsa-Schmidt, S., & Ferman, I. (1996). Test impact revisited: Washback effect over time. *Language Testing, 13*(3), 298–317.
Silva, T. (1993). Toward and understanding of the distinct nature of L2 writing: The ESL research and its implications. *TESOL Quaterly, 27*(4), 657–677.
Sinclair, J. 1997. Corpus evidence in language description. In A. Wichmann, S. Fligelstone, T. McEnery, and G. Knowles (eds), *Teaching and language corpora* (pp. 27–39). Harlow: Addison Wesley Longman.

Sinclair, J. (2005). Corpus and text - Basic principles. In M. Wynne (ed.), *Developing linguistic corpora: A guide to good practice*. Oxford: Oxbow Books. Retrieved from http://www.ahds.ac.uk/creating/guides/linguistic-corpora/chapter1.htm.

Schmidt, R. & Frota, S. (1986). Developing basic conversational ability in a second language: A case study of an adult learner of Portuguese. In R. Day (ed.), *Talking to learn: Conversation in second language acquisition* (pp. 237–326). Rowley, MA: Newbury House.

Si-Quing, C. & Luomai, X. (1990). Grammar-debugger: A parser for Chinese learners. *CALICO Journal, 8*(2), 63–75.

Shute, V. (2008). Focus on formative feedback. *Review of Educational Research, 78*(1), 153–189.

Sleeman, D. & Brown, J. S. (1982). Introduction: Intelligent tutoring systems. In D. Sleeman & J. S. Brown (eds), *Intelligent Tutoring Systems* (pp. 1–11). New York: Academic Press.

Soler-Monreal, C. & Gil-Salom, L. (2011). A cross-language study on citation practice in PhD theses. *International Journal of English Studies, 11*(2), 53–75.

Spack, R. (1997). The acquisition of academic literacy in a second language: A longitudinal study. *Written Communication, 14*, 3–62.

Straub, R. (1997). Students' reactions to teacher comments: An exploratory study. *Research in the Teaching of English, 31*, 91–119.

Surratt, C. K. (2006). Creation of a graduate oral/written communication skills course. *American Journal of Pharmaceutical Education, 70*(1), Article 5.

Sutton, R. (1995). *Assessment for learning*. Salford, England: RS Publications.

Swain, M. (1985). Communicative competence: Some roles of comprehensible input and comprehensible output in its development. In S. Gass & C. Madden (eds), *Input in second language acquisition* (pp. 235–253). Rowley, MA: Newbury House.

Swain, M. (1995). Three functions of output in second language learning. In G. Cook & B. Seidlhofer (eds), *Principle and practice in applied linguistics* (pp. 125–144). Oxford: Oxford University press.

Swales, J. M. (1981). Aspects of articles introductions (*Aston ESP Reports, No. 1*). The Language Studies Unit: The University of Aston in Birmingham.

Swales, J. M. (1990). *Genre analysis: English in academic and research settings*. Cambridge: Cambridge University Press.

Swales, J. M. (1998). *Other floors, other voices: A textography of a small university building*. Mahwah, NJ: Lawrence Erlbaum.

Swales, J. (2004). *Research genres*. Cambridge: Cambridge University Press.

Swales, J. M. & Feak, C. B. (2000). *English in today's research world: A writing guide*. Ann Arbor, MI: University of Michigan Press.

Swales, J. & Feak, C. (2004). *Academic writing for graduate students: Essential tasks and skills*, Second Edition. Ann Arbor: University of Michigan Press.

Tang, J., & Rich, C. (2011). *Online technology-enhanced English language writing assessment in the Chinese classroom*. Paper presented at the annual meeting of the American Educational Research Association, New Orleans, LA.

Tardy, C. M. (2005). 'It's like a story': Rhetorical knowledge development in advanced academic literacy. *Journal of English for Academic Purposes, 4*, 325–338.

Tardy, C. M. (2009). *Building genre knowledge*. West Lafayette, IN: Parlor Press.

Thompson, P. (1999). Exploring the contexts of writing: Interviews with Ph D supervisors. In P. Thompson (ed.), *Issues in EAP writing research and instruction* (pp. 37–54). Reading, PA: Centre for Applied Language Studies, University of Reading.

Thompson, P. & Tribble, C. (2001). Looking at citations: Using corpora in English for academic purposes. *Language Learning & Technology, 5*(3), 91–105.

Thurstun, J. & Candlin, C. N. (1998). Concordancing and the teaching of the vocabulary of academic English. *English for Specific Purposes, 17*, 267–280.

Tokuda, N. & Chen, L. (2001). An online tutoring system for language translation. *IEEE Multimedia, 8*(3), 46–55.

Tokuda, N. & Chen, L. (2004). A new KE-free online ICALL system featuring error contingent feedback. *Computer Assisted Language Learning, 17*(2), 177–201.

Toole, J. & Heift, T. (2002). The tutor assistant: An authoring system for a Web-based intelligent language tutor. *Computer Assisted Language Learning, 15*(4), 373–386.

Torrance, H. & Pryor, J. (1998). *Investigating formative assessment: Teaching, learning and assessment in the classroom*. Buckingham: Open University Press.

Torrance, M. S. & Thomas, G. V. (1994). The development of writing skills in doctoral research students. In R. G. Burgess (ed.), *Postgraduate education and training in the social sciences* (pp. 105–123). London: Jessica Kingsley Publishers.

Torrance, M. S., Thomas, G. V., & Robinson, E. J. (1992). The writing experiences of social-science research students. *Studies in Higher Education, 17*(2), 155–167.

Torrance, M. S., Thomas, G. V., & Robinson, E. J. (1994). The writing strategies of graduate research students in the social sciences. *Higher Education, 27*, 379–392.

Towell, R., Hawkins, R., & Bazergui, N. (1996). The development of fluency in advanced learners of French. *Applied Linguistics, 17*, 84–119.

Tsou, W. (2008). The effect of a web-based writing program in college English writing classes. *IEEE Computer Society*, Washington, DC, USA. Retrieved on October 20, 2009 from: http://portal.acm.org/citation.cfm?id=1381740.

Turner, J. (2012). Academic literacies: Providing a space for the socio-political dynamics. *Journal of English for Academic Purposes, 11*, 17–25.

Ushioda, E. (1996). *Learner autonomy 5: The role of motivation*. Dublin: Authentik.

Valenti, S., Nitko, A., & Cucchiarelli, A. (2003). An overview of current research on automated essay grading. *Journal of Information Technology Education (Information Technology for Assessing Student Learning Special Issue), 2*, 319–329.

van der Linden, E. (1993). Does feedback enhance computer-assisted language learning. *Computers & Education, 21*(1–2), 61–65.

van Dijk, T. A. (1996). Discourse, power and access. In C. Caldas-Coulthard & M. Coulthard (eds), *Texts and practices: Readings in critical discourse analysis* (pp. 84–106). London: Routledge.

Vann, R. & Myers, C. (2001). Academic ESL options in a large research university. In I. Leki (ed.), *In academic writing programs* (pp. 73–84). Alexandria, VA: TESOL.

VanPatten, B. and Williams, J. (2007). Introduction: The nature of theories. In B. VanPatten and J. Williams (eds), *Theories in second language acquisition: An introduction* (pp. 1–16). Mahwah, NJ: Lawrence Erlbaum.

Vantage Learning. (2007). *MY Access!* Efficacy Report. Newtown, PA: Vantage Learning. Retrieved on December 6, 2008, from http://www.vantagelearning.com/school/research/myaccess.html.

Ventola, E. (1982). *Contrasting schematic structures in service encounters*. University of Sydney: Mimeo.

Viete, R. & Ha, P. L. (2007). The growth of voice: Expanding possibilities for representing self in research writing. *English Teaching: Practice and Critique, 6*(2), pp. 39–57.

Vojak, C., Kline, S., Cope, B., McCarthey, S., & Kalantzis, M. (2011). New spaces and old places: An analysis of writing assessment software. *Computers and Composition, 28*(2), 97–111.

Vygotsky, L. S. (1978). Interaction between learning and development. In M. Cole, V. John-Steiner, S. Scribner, & E. Souberman (eds), *Mind in society: The development of higher psychological processes* (pp. 79-91). Cambridge, MA: Harvard University Press.

Wardle, E. & Roozen, K. (2012). Addressing the complexity of writing development: Toward and ecological model of assessment. *Assessing Writing, 17*(2), 106–119.

Warschauer, M. & Grimes, G. (2008). Automated writing assessment in the classroom. *Pedagogies: An International Journal, 3*, 22–36.

Warschauer, M. & Ware, P. (2006). Automated writing evaluation: Defining the classroom research agenda. *Language Teaching Research, 10*(2), 1–24.

Weigle, S. C. (2010). Validation of automated scores of TOEFL iBT tasks against non-test indicators of writing ability. *Language Testing, 27*(3), 335–353.

Weigle, S. C. (2013a). English as a second language writing and Automated Essay Evaluation. In M. D. Shermis & J. Burstein (eds), *Handbook of automated essay evaluation: Current applications and new directions* (pp. 36–54). New York: Routledge.

Weigle, S. C. (2013b). English language learners and automated scoring of essays: Critical considerations. *Assessing Writing, 18*, 85–99.

Weissberg, R. & Buker, S. (1990). *Writing up research: Experimental research report writing for students of English*. Englewood Cliffs, NJ: Prentice Hall.

Welford, A.T. (1968). *Fundamentals of skill*. London: Methuen.

Wharton, S. (2012). Epistemological and interpersonal stance in a data description task: Findings from a discipline-specific learner corpus. *English for Specific Purposes, 31*, 261–270.

White, L. J., Hixson, N., & Rhudy, V. (2010). WESTEST 2 online writing scoring comparability study. *Research Brief*. Charleston, WV: West Virginia Department of Education.

White, L. J., Hixson, N., & Whisman, S. A. (2011). *Writing Roadmap usage and additional predictors of WESTEST 2 online writing scores*. Charleston, WV: West Virginia Department of Education, Division of Curriculum and Instructional Services, Office of Research.

Whitehead, D. (2002). The academic writing experiences of a group of student nurses: a phenomenological study. *Journal of Advanced Nursing, 38*(5), 498–506.

Whithaus, C. (2006). Always already: Automated essay scoring and grammar checkers in college writing courses. In P. E. Ericsson & R. Haswell (eds), *Machine scoring of student essays: Truth and consequences* (pp. 166–176). Logan, UT: Utah State University Press.

Wiemer-Hastings, P., Allbritton, D., & Arnott, E. (2004). RMT: A dialog-based research methods tutor with or without a head. In *Proceedings of the ITS2004 Seventh International Conference*. Berlin, Springer.

Wiliam, D. (2011). *Embedded formative assessment.* Bloomington, IN: Solution Tree Press.

Wiliam, D. & Black, P. (1996). Meanings and consequences: A basis for distinguishing formative and summative functions of assessment? *British Educational Research Journal, 22,* 537–548.

Williams, R. (1999). Results section of medical research articles: An analysis of rhetorical categories for pedagogical purpose. *English for Specific Purposes, 18*(4), 347–366.

Williams, R. & Dreher, H. (2004). Automatically grading essays with Markit. In *Proceedings of Informing Science Conference.* Rockhampton, Queensland, Australia.

Williamson, D. M. (2013). Probable cause: Developing warrants for automated scoring. In M. D. Shermis & J. Burstein (eds), *Handbook of automated essay evaluation: Current applications and new directions* (pp. 153–180). New York: Routledge.

Williamson, D. M., Xi, X., & Breyer, F. J. (2012). A framework for evaluation and use of automated scoring. *Educational Measurement: Issues and Practice, 31*(1), 2–13.

Wingate, U. (2012). Using Academic Literacies and genre-based models for academic writing instruction: A 'literacy' journey. *Journal of English for Academic Purposes, 11,* 26–37.

Woltz, D. J. (1988). An investigation of the role of working memory in procedural skill acquisition. *Journal of Experimental Psychology: General, 117,* 319–331.

Xi, X. (2010). Automated scoring and feedback systems: Where are we and where are we heading? *Language Testing, 27*(3), 291–300.

Yang, N. (2004). Using MY Access!® in EFL Writing. Paper presented at the International *Conference and Workshop on TEFL & Applied Linguistics.* Compiled by the Department of Applied English, Ming Chuan University.

Yang, J. C., & Akahori, K. (1998). Error analysis in Japanese writing and its implementation in a computer assisted language learning system on the world wide web. *CALICO Journal, 15*(1–3), 47–66.

Yang, R. & Allison, R. (2004). Research articles in applied linguistics: Structures from a functional perspective. *English for Specific Purposes, 23,* 264–279.

Yasuda, S. (2011). Genre-based tasks in foreign language writing: Developing writers' genre awareness, linguistic knowledge, and writing competence. *Journal of Second Language Writing 20,* 111–133.

Yazdani, M. (1991). The LINGER project: An artificial intelligence approach to second-language tutoring. *Computer Assisted Language Learning, 4*(2), 107–116.

Yeh, Y., Liou, H. C., & Yu, Y. T. (2007). The influence of automatic essay evaluation and bilingual concordancing on ESL students' writing. *English Teaching and Learning, 31,* 117–160.

Yoon, C. (2011). Concordancing in L2 writing class: An overview of research and issues. *Journal of English for Academic Purposes, 10,* 130–139.

Yoon, H. & Hirvela, A. (2004). ESL student attitudes toward corpus use in L2 writing. *Journal of Second Language Writing, 13,* 257–283.

Zimmerman, B. J. (2008). Investigating self-regulation and motivation: historical background, methodological developments, and future prospects. *American Educational Research Journal, 45,* 166–183.

Index

9781137333360